Tourism Marketing

Tourism and Hospitality Management Series

Series Editors:

Professor Roy C. Wood
The Scottish Hotel School, University of Strathclyde, UK

Stephen J. Page
Massey University, New Zealand

Series Consultant:

Professor C. L. Jenkins
The Scottish Hotel School, University of Strathclyde, UK

Textbooks in this series:

Books in this series are available on free inspection for lecturers considering the texts for course adoption. Details of these and any other International Thomson Business Press titles are available by writing to the publishers (Berkshire House, 168–173 High Holborn, London WC1V 7AA) or by telephoning the Promotions Department on 0171 497 1422.

Tourism Marketing

Les Lumsdon

INTERNATIONAL THOMSON BUSINESS PRESS
IⓉP® An International Thomson Publishing Company

London • Bonn • Boston • Johannesburg • Madrid • Melbourne • Mexico City • New York • Paris
Singapore • Tokyo • Toronto • Albany, NY • Belmont, CA • Cincinnati, OH • Detroit, MI

Tourism Marketing

Copyright © 1997 International Thomson Business Press

First published by International Thomson Business Press

I**T**P ®   A division of International Thomson Publishing Inc.
The ITP logo is a trademark under licence

British Library Cataloguing-in-Publication Data
A catalogue record for this book is available from the British Library

First edition 1997
Reprinted 1999

Typeset by Columns Design Ltd, Reading
Printed and bound by Antony Rowe Ltd, Eastbourne

ISBN 1-86152-045-X

International Thomson Business Press
Berkshire House
168–173 High Holborn
London WC1V 7AA
UK

http:// www.itbp.com

Dedicated to Leila, Gina, Alex and Chloe

Contents

Series editors' foreword

The International Thomson Business Press series in Tourism and Hospitality Management is dedicated to the publication of high quality textbooks and other volumes that will be of benefit to those engaged in tourism, hotel and hospitality education, especially at degree and postgraduate level. The series is based on core textbooks on key areas of the curriculum and is complimented by highly focused and shorter texts on particular themes and issues. All the authors in the series are experts in their own fields, actively engaged in teaching, research and consultancy in tourism and hospitality. Each book comprises an authoritative blend of subject-relevant theoretical considerations and practical applications. Furthermore, a unique quality of the series is that it is student oriented, offering accessible texts that take account of the realities of administration, management and operations in tourism and hospitality contexts, being constructively critical without losing sight of the overall goal of providing clear accounts of essential concepts, issues and techniques.

The series is committed to quality, accessibility, relevance and originality in its approach. Quality is ensured as a result of a vigorous referencing process, unusual in the publication of textbooks. Accessibility is achieved through the use of innovative textual design techniques, and the use of discussion points, case studies and exercises within books, all geared to encouraging a comprehensive understanding of the material contained therein. Relevance and originality together result from the experience of authors as key authorities in their fields.

The tourism and hospitality industries are diverse and dynamic industries and it is the intention of the editors to reflect this diversity and dynamism by publishing quality texts that enhance topical subjects without losing sight of enduring themes. The Series Editors and Consultant are grateful to Steven Reed of International Thomson Business Press for his commitment, expertise and support of this philosophy.

Series Editors

Dr Stephen J. Page
Massey University – Albany
Auckland
New Zealand

Professor Roy C. Wood
The Scottish Hotel School
University of Strathclyde
United Kingdom

Series Consultant

Professor C. L. Jenkins
The Scottish Hotel School
University of Strathclyde
United Kingdom

Preface

In recent years there has been a considerable increase in the number of tourism text-books on the library shelves. This is to be applauded for the paucity of material available prior to this has not helped tourism to establish itself within academic circles. Now, tourism as a subject of study at undergraduate and masters level is in ascendancy. There appears to be much more research being undertaken than hitherto, and tourism courses are still well subscribed despite the rapid increase in provision which some argued would lead to an oversupply.

Tourism management is also gaining recognition and it is important to establish a serious interest in this specialism given the increasing demands of the market. The tourism business is different from other sectors. This is especially the case when referring to the management of destinations. The overall principles might be the same but applications are somewhat different.

Tourism marketing deserves particular attention. The role of the marketer is an important one in every organization. If the customer is the lifeblood of the company then the marketer manages the interface. This book seeks to introduce the core principles of tourism marketing and apply them to current applications within the business.

I am particularly indebted to authors of previous tourism marketing texts for they have provided a framework of study for many students during the past decade. However, I have been aware for some time that writers in the area have not paid sufficient attention to the growing literature in the field of services marketing. Furthermore, I have been conscious of the developments regarding internal and relationship marketing which are very apposite in the business of tourism. Therefore, I have been prompted to offer this work; I hope it adds to the valuable collection of material that we now have.

Les Lumsdon

Acknowledgements

Many thanks are due. Firstly, I am indebted, as ever, to Pat Lumsdon for providing excellent research support and a constructive initial edit of the draft text. Thanks also go to Deborah Radburn for writing a welcome chapter on organizational buyer behaviour, an area worthy of more research. I also extend thanks to several colleagues in the Marketing Division, Business School of Staffordshire University for their support during the crucial months of writing. Above all else, I am grateful to the students I have taught during my years at Staffordshire University, many of whom are now managers in the tourism and leisure business.

Of course, any errors or omissions which you might find are solely attributable to the author.

LIST OF PERMISSION ACKNOWLEDGEMENTS

Figures

1.1 © Massey University, Auckland, New Zealand; 1.2 © World Tourism Organization, Madrid; 1.4, 10.1 © Prentice Hall, Upper Saddle River, NJ; 1.5, 3.4, 13.2, 14.2 © Addison Wesley Longman Ltd; 1.8 © Cumbria Tourist Board; 2.1 © *Journal of Marketing*, American Marketing Asssociation; 3.2 © Canadian Tourism Commission; 4.1 © Allyn & Bacon, Boston, MA; 5.2 and 6.3 © The Free Press, New York; 6.1 © HarperCollins, London; 6.2, 13.3 © John Wiley & Sons, Chichester; 6.5, 10.2, 20.2 © Elsevier Science Ltd, Kidlington, Oxon; 6.7 © McGraw-Hill International; 6.8 Arthur D. Little Inc, Cambridge, MA; 8.1 © Butterworth-Heinemann, Oxford; 9.2 © Select Service Partner Airport Restaurants Ltd.; 12.4 © Admap/NTC Publications Ltd, Henley-on-Thames, Oxon; 12.5, 15.1 © The Dryden Press, Harcourt Brace & Company, London; 12.6 © *Insights*, BTA/ETB; 13.2 © Pitman, London; 16.1 © South African Tourist Board; 17.3 © Business Education Publishers Ltd, Tyne and Wear; 17.4 © Methuen & Co, New York; 18.2 © Wales Tourist Board; 20.1 © CAB International, Wallingford, Oxon.

Tables

1.3, 17.3 © World Travel and Tourism Commission, London; 1.4, 1.5, 1.6, 7.1, 17.2 © World Tourism Organization, Madrid; 1.7, 16.7, 16.8 © Mintel International Group Limited; 1.8, 6.1 and Example 8.3 © *Insights*/ETB/BTA; 1.9 © CRN; 5.4 © Gallup-Media Finland/United Magazines Ltd; 9.4 © Macmillan Press Ltd, Basingstoke; 9.5

© South African Tourist Board; 11.1 © Business Education Publishers Ltd, Tyne and Wear; 11.2 © Elsevier Science Ltd, Kidlington, Oxon; 15.2, 15.3 © Admap/NTC Publications Ltd, Henley-on-Thames, Oxon; 16.1 © Travel & Tourism Intelligence 1996; 16.2 © The Economist Intelligence Unit Limited 1994; 16.7 © CAA/Mintel; 16.8 © IPS/Mintel; 18.1 © Wales Tourist Board; 19.1 © John Wiley & Sons, Chichester; 19.2, 19.3 © Multilingual Matters Ltd, Clevedon.

The tourism marketing environment 1

OBJECTIVES

This chapter explains:

- the definitions of tourism, and the relationship between tourism, leisure and recreation;
- the core principles underlying tourism;
- the different perspectives of tourism;
- tourism as a system;
- the main global, regional and national tourism trends.

1.1 INTRODUCTION

Tourism is primarily about human activity which involves travel from an originating area to a destination for pleasure or business purposes. The concept embraces cultural, economic and social exchange processes. These elements are inextricably bound together in a mesh of activity which we refer to as travel and tourism. Furthermore, writers often refer to tourism within the context of an origin–destination matrix. Pearce, for example, in referring to Thurot's multiple origin–destination model comments:

> Tourism is thus a multi-faceted activity and a geographically complex one as different services are sought and supplied at different stages from the origin to destination. Moreover, in any country or region there is likely to be a number of origins and destinations, with most places having both generating (origin) and receiving (destination) functions.
>
> *(Pearce, 1989, p. 2)*

Few have offered a holistic explanation of the phenomenon. Krippendorf (1987), in his seminal work *The Holidaymakers*, explores a multiplicity of factors which might explain why tourism, as an activity in society, is increasing. He investigates changing values which favour travel, such as the desire of people to escape the surroundings of urban areas. He also examines the pull factors which encourage visitors to travel to places. Invariably, most studies set out to explain the symbiotic relationship between originating areas and destinations. This is the essence of tourism marketing: the attraction of a potential visitor from a generating area to a receiving destination. Every area has some tourism potential, if only for welcoming friends and relatives or as a consequence of trading or social activities. Some areas, however, have significant appeal which makes them primary destinations for a number of generating areas. One classic example is the Canary Islands which have an all year appeal to colder, urban generating areas of northern Europe. The transit route in this instance happens to be a four to five hour flight. Leiper first developed a model in 1979 (which he then updated in 1990) to explain the relationship between the generating and destination areas by way of a transit route or region. Figure 1.1 adopts a similar approach to Leiper but stresses both internal and two way flows between regions as characterized by such a tourism system. The expression of these internal or localized markets is important in terms of volume if not value. Uruguay's tourism base is a prime example. It is dominated by short stay visitors from neighbouring Argentina, accounting for as much as 85 per cent of all trips. More affluent residents of Buenos Aires fly or take the boat for the short trip (four to five hours) to the beautiful beaches at Punta del Este by way of Montevideo.

1.1.1 Tourism definitions

The issue of definition is an interesting one. It has taken several decades to achieve agreement between governments as to which categories of travellers or visitors should be included in the definition of tourism. There is also still a question of the validity of statistical comparisons, because governments do not collect statistics for the same reasons, nor in a similar manner. The World Tourism Organization has, however, presented a definition which is both workable and which has gained acceptance on a global basis. It is outlined in Figure 1.2.

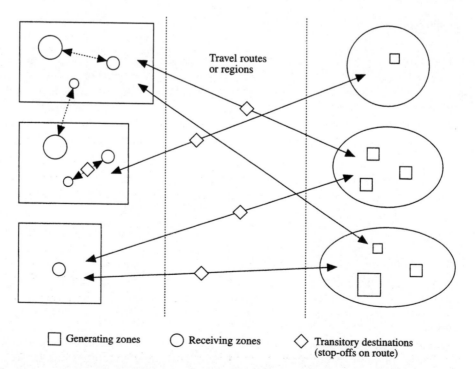

Figure 1.1 Tourism flows. *Source*: Adapted from Leiper (1990).

In recent years the day excursionist or day visitor has been included in the statistics. Day visits clearly make up an important sector of the tourism business in many economies. But here too there are definitional issues. Practitioners have attempted to standardize the definition of the day excursionist (or day visitor) to afford comparison but there are, however, variations. For example, a day visit in Canada is classified as a trip of over 50 miles in each direction. In the UK, in comparison, a day visit is one which is of a duration of over three hours or more but not involving an overnight stay.

Of all of the working definitions of tourism proffered, such as Burkhart and Medlik (1989: 42), or Middleton (1994: 8–9), the one presented by Mill and Morrison (1992:

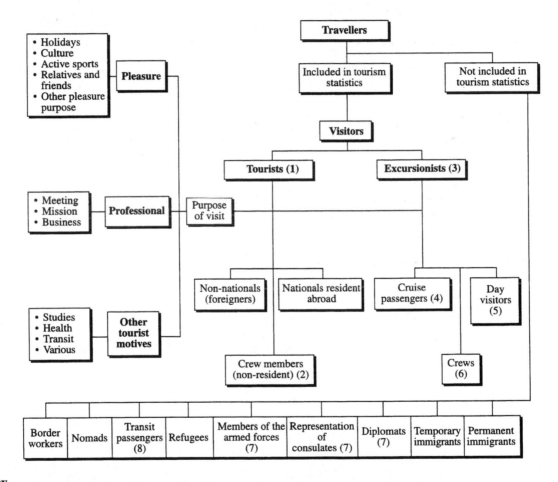

Key
1. Visitors who spend at least one night in the country visited.
2. Foreign air or ship crews docked or in lay over and who use the accommodation establishments of the country visited.
3. Visitors who do not spend the night in the country visited although they may visit the country during one day or more and return to their ship or train to sleep.
4. Normally included in excursionists. Separate classification of these visitors is nevertheless recommended.
5. Visitors who come and leave the same day.
6. Crews who are not residents of the country visited.
7. When they travel from their country of origin to the duty station and vice-versa (including household servants and dependants accompanying or joining them.)
8. Who do not leave the transit area of the airport or the port. In certain countries, transit may involve a stay of one day or more. In this case, they should be included in the visitors statistics.

Figure 1.2 Classification of travellers. *Source*: World Tourism Organization (1993).

9) is perhaps more comprehensive. It recognizes the importance of pre- and post-trip activity as well as that which takes place at the destination. The implications for the tourism marketer in understanding the entire process, rather than simply concentrating on the travel journey and destination, are fundamental:

> Tourism is the term given to the activity that occurs when tourists travel. This encompasses everything from the planning of the trip, the travel to the place, the stay itself, the return, and the reminiscences about it afterwards. It includes the activities the traveller undertakes as part of the trip, the purchases made and the interactions that occur between host and guest. In sum, it is all of the activities and impacts that occur when a visitor travels.
>
> *(Mill and Morrison, 1992: 9)*

This definition encompasses four overlapping phases of consumer activity:

- pre-purchase activity such as finding information, discussing the prospect with friends and family, booking the holiday or travel arrangements for a day visit, and preparation before travel;
- the journey to and from the destination, possibly including an overnight stop en route;
- the activities undertaken at the destination, which might be uniform in nature or characterized by a very wide range of activities;
- post-consumptive behaviour such as processing photographs, and talking about experiences.

These overlapping phases provide a useful starting point for the analysis of the tourism business. They provide an insight into why and how travel is purchased, the elements of a holiday which people really value and how a destination can secure repeat business.

1.1.2 Principles of tourism

Whilst definitions vary according to discipline, perspective, or purpose, there tends to be a common thread throughout the literature. Therefore, you will find that many analyses of tourism refer to a number of defining principles which have been summarized by Burkhart and Medlik (1989: 39–40):

- Tourism is an amalgam of phenomena and relationships.
- Two elements, the journey to the destination (dynamic element) and the stay (static element), are fundamental.
- This type of activity takes place away from the normal place of residence and work and is therefore different to those enjoyed by residents in the areas through which the visitor travels or stays.
- Movement is short term and is intended to be of a temporary nature.
- Visits to destinations take place for a number of reasons, but exclude taking up permanent residence or employment, which is remunerated.

Add to these three additional characteristics:

- Tourism includes the activities of day visitors or excursionists (Middleton, 1994: 8–9).
- It concerns primarily the consumption of a wide range of products and services, provided by public and private organizations (Jefferson and Lickorish, 1988: 1; Middleton, 1994: 11; Morgan, 1996: 8–9).

- It is not an entirely neutral process but can involve considerable benefits and dis-benefits to society (Burns and Holden, 1995: 14–21).

The combined eight general principles underlie the core definition, but there are also a number of technical descriptions which enhance understanding of both the scope of tourism and the components which make up the overall structure of the system. These will be illustrated later in the chapter. First, there is a need to distinguish between the terms leisure, recreation and tourism.

1.1.3 Tourism, recreation and leisure

How does tourism relate to the concept of leisure? Most commentators agree that tourism falls within the conceptual framework of leisure as defined by Cooper *et al.* (1993: 5):

> in essence leisure can be thought of as a combined measure of time and attitude of mind to create periods of time when other obligations are at a minimum.

Recreation is defined as a legitimate pursuit or activity undertaken during such leisure time, which tends to be mainly home or locally based. Tourism sits at the other end of the spectrum in terms of the level of organization, distance travelled and often spending undertaken in the pursuit of a variety of pastimes. It relates specifically to trips away from home where recreational activities form part of the overall experience. Morgan (1996: 9) suggests that tourism and leisure, in terms of the nature of activities undertaken during leisure time, are almost indistinguishable except for location. He argues that as the definition of tourism now encompasses day visits, 'the dividing line between leisure and tourism becomes very difficult to see'.

This argument does not hold true on two counts. Morgan concedes that the major distinguishing feature is location. Leisure and recreation form part of a lifestyle which is mainly home or neighbourhood based. Tourism, on the contrary, is about leisure and recreational activities adopted as part of a different lifestyle to that carried out at home; this is the very reason for a travel break.

More importantly, it invariably involves different patterns of behaviour at a destination, including consumption patterns. Consider, for example, the difference between purchasing a video for home consumption and a three week holiday abroad. The former constitutes almost routine expenditure requiring little forethought, the latter would involve a more complicated risk-laden process. Leisure, recreation and tourism are clearly distinguishable on these grounds.

1.1.4 Technical terms

These are particularly salient, for example, when attempting to analyse quantified data on a comparative scale, possibly between supply sectors or across countries. Therefore, terms such as day excursion, short break, and distinctions between domestic and international travel, inbound and outbound, make up a necessary vocabulary used in the analysis of the tourism system. There is little dispute about the terms themselves or what they mean. The discussion tends to focus on the lack of consistency in the collection of tourism data between countries, the validity of the statistics collected and the difficulties of comparative analysis (Cooper *et al.*, 1993: 46–7; Smith, 1995: 9–10). Table 1.1 provides a summary of the key technical definitions.

Table 1.1 Technical definitions: tourism

Traveller, visitor or tourist	Terms used to describe a person travelling to and staying in a place away from their usual environment for more than one night but less than one year, for leisure, business and other purposes.
International tourism	Travel between countries by various modes of travel for the purpose of tourism. This can be subdivided as follows:
Long haul	Travel which involves long distances (say over 1000 miles) for example, between continents.
Short haul	Travel between countries which involves shorter distances or travel time (say 250–1000 miles).
Inbound	Visits to a country by non-residents (importation of overseas currency).
Outbound	Visits by residents of one country to another country (exporting currency to other countries).
Internal tourism	Travel by residents in their own country.
Domestic tourism	Internal travel and inbound tourism in total.
National tourism	Internal travel and outbound tourism.
Excursionist or same day visitors	Visitors who begin and end their visit from the same base (home or holiday base) within the same 24 hour period.

1.1.5 Different perspectives

This book is written from a marketing management perspective. It focuses primarily on an understanding of the consumer of travel and tourism. It considers how the consumer might be (more than) satisfied by suppliers who make up the tourism business sector. The emphasis is placed on how organizations satisfy such wants commercially.

However, the tourism marketer needs to be able to manage the interaction between supply and demand within appropriate social and environmental constraints, and in a manner which is commensurate with the principles of sustainability. This requires an understanding of tourism from a variety of disciplinary approaches. McIntosh, Goeldner and Ritchie (1995: 17–21) provide a useful outline which is summarized below:

- **Institutional approach:** This focuses on the functional aspects of travel intermediaries, technically classified as a subset of the management approach.
- **Product approach:** The study of tourism products and how they are marketed.
- **Historical approach:** Emphasis on the evolution of tourism, including the innovation, rise and decline of tourism in past times.
- **Managerial approach:** Exploration of the management of tourism enterprises to meet changing patterns of demand in society.
- **Economic approach:** An economic perspective relating to aspects of supply and demand, employment and balance of payments but also development and economic gain.
- **Sociological approach:** The study of tourism behaviour, patterns of participation and its impact on society.
- **Geographical approach:** Specializing in the spatial and development aspects of tourism but very wide ranging in approach.
- **Interdisciplinary approaches:** Reference to other disciplines such as anthropology, psychology and political science in the understanding of culture and other societal dimensions of tourism.

● **Systems approach:** The authors suggest a preference for this approach which emphasizes systems. A system is defined as a 'set of interrelated groups co-ordinated to form a unified whole and organized to accomplish a set of goals'. The approach can be applied either in a micro or macro context.

Much of the tourism management literature to date has concentrated on the functional aspects of the tourism business sector. It has suffered from being descriptive rather than analytical in approach. There is clearly a danger in narrowing the scope of analysis, certainly within the early stages of such an investigation of tourism, and when attempting to unravel complicated social and economic phenomena. Marketing management therefore needs to be both rigorous and eclectic in style if it is to embrace the changing patterns of social and economic values across many cultures.

1.1.6 Tourism models

There are a number of models which seek to explain tourism within a conceptual framework. For example, one of the fundamental areas of discussion at present is the nature of tourism development in developing countries. Models which are often quoted, such as that by Mathieson and Wall (1982: 15–16) and Lea (1988: 17) suggest that an elementary stage of tourism development inevitably leads to the next. This approach is illustrated in Figure 1.3. In reality, this type of approach might be appropriate, but it is not necessarily so. Development might not occur at a scale or scope envisaged in the model. The factor of growth, for example, would depend on the participant stakeholders (developers, marketers, planners, local community representatives) involved, the degree of complementarity with other sectors of the economy, and the nature and accountability of primary markets.

In this context there is perhaps a case for refinement of the generic explanatory models of tourism to reflect the complexity of the social, cultural and economic forces interacting on development and how tourism managers can attempt to shape these forces, in order to stimulate longer term, sustainable offerings and markets. A more detailed discussion is presented in Chapter 19.

It has been argued that such different approaches to the study of tourism mentioned above have brought about a degree of fragmentation in research:

> Tourism often lacks credibility in the eyes of policy analysts and decision-makers because the field is poorly defined and because the data used to substantiate many of the claims concerning the size and importance of the industry are inadequate.
>
> *(Smith, 1995: 9)*

This might be the case but it is not simply a problem confined to tourism. The global communications market presents another wide ranging sector with similar definitional problems. Some markets are inherently complex and do not lend themselves to simplistic diagnosis. Equally, there are benefits which are associated with the rich diversity of approach. This should not be underestimated. They have given rise to differing frameworks of analysis and prescriptions for future development which are certainly thought provoking.

1.2 A SYSTEMS APPROACH

In reviewing a number of perspectives, outlined above, the systems approach is in many respects most appropriate for tourism marketing management. Above all else it

Stage	Characteristics	Degree of planning/regulation
Early stage	• Low level of visitor arrivals • Mixed local economy • Undiscovered • Lacking international image • Limited interest by entrepreneurs • Limited investment in visitor facilities • Few hotels of any size, small scale accommodation	• Limited planning for tourism • Not a priority • Minimal danger of regulation
Impact stage	• Awakening of the market • Increased arrivals bringing overcrowding of existing accommodation base • Increased purchasing of second homes • Reconnaissance by hotel chains and tour operators • Awareness level of government increased	• Need to assess rate of development and plan accordingly
Growth stage	• Promotion to market by tour operators, destinations and government agencies • Partnership deals between local and multi-national hotel chains to build large scale hotels • Improvement of visitor facilities including rise in restaurants, bars, as well as public amenities • Change in nature of mixed economy • Environmental, social and economic impacts affect existing balance of community, bringing a measurable degree of tension and negatives	• Planning policies adapted as a reaction to rapid development
Longevity stage	• Continued, but more selective promotion of the destination • Efforts to modify and enhance tourism offering – new attractions and facilities • Maintenance of visitor facilities becomes more pressing • Economy dominated by tourism • More vocal opposition to mass tourism development	• More sophisticated planning techniques and regulations applied to the tourism sector

Figure 1.3 Model of tourism development.

introduces to the discussion linkages between consumers, suppliers and destinations. The core of the tourism system lies within the exchange mechanism of the market which brings consumers from generating areas to receiving destinations. However, to understand the system the tourism marketer needs to be aware of other perspectives which help to explain consumer motivation, political structures, societal commitment and ecological implications, etc. for they all impact on the business of tourism.

1.2.1 The tourism system

Several authors argue that it is appropriate to analyse tourism as a system (a set of inter-related parts which form a cohesive whole) rather than as an industry or a market.

Those that adopt a **supply sector approach** tend to concentrate on defining the parameters of each element of supply activities. The five key sectors – accommodation and catering, transport, visitor attractions, travel distribution, and selling and marketing organizations – have been the subject of detailed analysis and a summary is provided in Chapter 16. This type of framework suggests that tourism suppliers form the linchpin of the tourism system between the consumer and the destination. It is a useful form of analysis but there is an additional point to note. The linkages between supply sectors provide a degree of overlap. Tour operators own travel agencies, transport providers own accommodation, and major groups own entertainment, restaurants and accommodation. Nevertheless, the sectoral approach has its merits in terms of understanding economic processes which function within the system as expressed in terms of suppliers.

The market approach is more comprehensive in that it highlights the exchange processes occurring between consumers and suppliers, i.e. it emphasizes the consumption process, which is what tourism is essentially about. As a framework of analysis, it tends to take less into account factors in the macro environment, which can have a major impact on the tourism system, such as the realignment of political structures, natural disasters or economic downturns . Examples include the breakup of the Soviet Bloc, political unrest in African states, or the continued depletion of resources across the world. They all have an impact on the tourism system and patterns of demand in the long run, if not in the short term.

In this respect it is apposite to view tourism as a system with the market process at its core. Mill and Morrison (1992: 9–10), for example, draw attention to four integrated parts of the tourism system, which they describe as follows:

- **The market.** This section of the model emphasizes the need to understand consumer behaviour which occurs within social and cultural constraints. This obviously leads to the purchase of travel in a wide variety of forms.
- **Travel.** This part refers to travel segments, the flows of visitors, their characteristics, existing trends and forecasts for the future. These factors shape travel demand to different destinations.
- **Destination.** This refers to the mix of facilities and attractions desired by different segments of visitors, as well as policy formulation and marketing planning to address these wants. The destination stimulates the selling of travel.
- **Marketing.** This involves destination marketing to existing and potential visitors through a variety of intermediaries, following a market plan and using marketing management tools accordingly.

The four parts of the tourism system are represented in Figure 1.4.

Poon (1993), on the other hand, describes tourism in terms of a 'tourism production system' which links consumers to facilitators (finance and insurance services), distributors (tour operators and travel agents), and producers (airlines, hoteliers, etc.). This is similar to the approach adopted by Mathieson and Wall (1982: 8–15) and illustrated in Figure 1.5.

The model delineates the following elements:

- **dynamic element**, which refers to demand and the forms of tourism;
- **static element**, which relates the characteristics of tourists to those of the destination;
- **consequential element**, which highlights economic, physical and social impacts and impact control.

The model draws a network of links within each element and between elements thus forming a system which incorporates feedback. It builds on earlier work by introducing elements which are more influential in tourism development than hitherto, such as the travel media and the rapid change in communications systems.

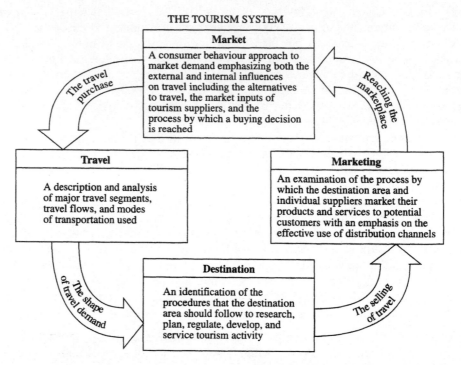

Figure 1.4 The tourism system. *Source*: Mill and Morrison (1992).

Secondly, it builds into the system the driving forces of the macro environment, such as population change and urbanization in newly generating countries, emergence of new tourism destinations, etc. These factors affect all sectors of the tourism system, some more than others. It also incorporates micro level impacts, those which are more controllable by companies and destinations, but which nevertheless affect the system. Such micro factors include the level of competition in national or regional markets, for example, or the effects of pollution at a destination, etc.

Finally, the model recognizes the interdependence and hence two way flows at all levels; for instance, between regions and countries or between suppliers in alliance at a global or destination level. It accepts that there is a link between consumers, host communities and suppliers, and the constantly changing impacts and relationships between these parts of the system, which in many respects is the 'hothouse' of the chain as well as its weakest link.

1.2.2 The tourism industry

Can tourism be described as an industry or not? The literature brings a mixed response in this respect; it is not easily defined. Jefferson and Lickorish (1988: 1) refer to it as 'a movement of people, a demand force and not a single industry'. Smith (1995: 9–10) argues that it is more accurate to describe it as 'a group of several related industries'.

The discussion revolves around the point that the tourism related supply sectors are not solely engaged in the business of tourism. The transport sector, for example,

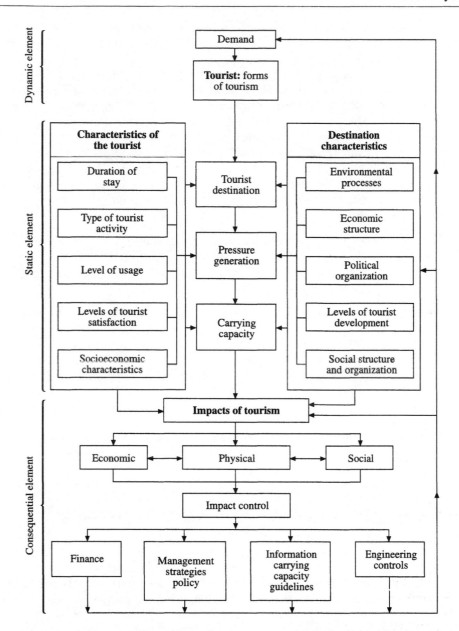

Figure 1.5 A conceptual framework of tourism. *Source*: Mathieson and Wall (1982). Reprinted by permission of Addison Wesley Longman Ltd.

provides freight and commuter services. In many places, the catering business sector services local residents or businesses and visitors simply add to profitability during the main season. Thus, while such organizations recognize the contribution of tourism to their business, it is not the prime driving force for their existence. Tourism is therefore often described as an amalgam of supply factors, some sectors which are entirely driven by it and others less so. More than one writer has indicated that it might be feasible to estimate the revenue contribution from local people, business trade and visitors in order to classify the primary consumer base. If the latter happens to be dominant, it would only then be possible to classify the business as being part of the tourism sector.

There is also another important dimension to the discussion. Destinations readily consume natural resources such as landscapes, historic sites, and local culture, more often than not to differentiate from competing places. They also use, to a greater or lesser extent, the infrastructure which exists for residents and visitors alike, such as road and sewerage systems. In this respect the use of 'public goods' in tourism is a crucial factor. Throughout the world, and regardless of political regimes, tourism development relies heavily on a partnership between government and the private sector. The importance of government as an agent of tourism development makes it less easy to describe tourism as an industry in a traditional sense. Jenkins (1994: 3) is unequivocal about the point:

> The multi-faceted nature of tourism does not permit it to be described as an industry in a technical sense; it has no single production characteristic, or defined operational parameters. Its economic dimension cannot occur without inputs of a social, cultural and environmental nature.

Nevertheless, there is a growing recognition amongst tourists, the travel media, and between supply sectors, that they are using or providing services within an increasingly integrated group of business sectors, which have come about in the past decade as part of the process of global convergence.

Some predict that given the increasing importance of strategic alliances between airlines, hotels and tour operators (which is referred to as diagonal integration) and the continuing degree of vertical integration (seeking ownership at more than one level of the supply chain) and horizontal integration (buying out competitors at the same level of the supply chain), tourism supply sectors will become even more unified than at present. On first consideration, this argument seems very convincing, in that there is firm empirical evidence, especially in the airline and hospitality sector, of business integration and convergence of strategies (Go and Pine, 1995: 5–10; Seaton and Bennett, 1995: 382).

The counter argument is that despite the growth of multinationals in the international tourism market, the tourism system is still dominated by local and national markets serviced mainly by a world of small and fiercely independent enterprises. Furthermore, with predicted impacts such as continued privatization and competitiveness sweeping developing countries (Jenkins, 1994: 1–9) and government policies which stress the retention of tourism spend in local economies, the tourism system is likely to remain fragmented.

There is no definitive response to the question, but there is incremental evidence to suggest that consumers are coming to view tourism as an industry. The major supply sectors which make up the tourism sector are outlined in Figure 1.6. They comprise what we might tentatively refer to as the tourism industry, but perhaps more accurately, as tourism business sectors.

Figure 1.6 outlines the main supply sectors. Note that this includes consumer and interest groups as well as the media, which help to shape opinions and possibly values. This framework also incorporates the notion of the local community, in both an unpaid and paid capacity, forming part of the overall supply sector.

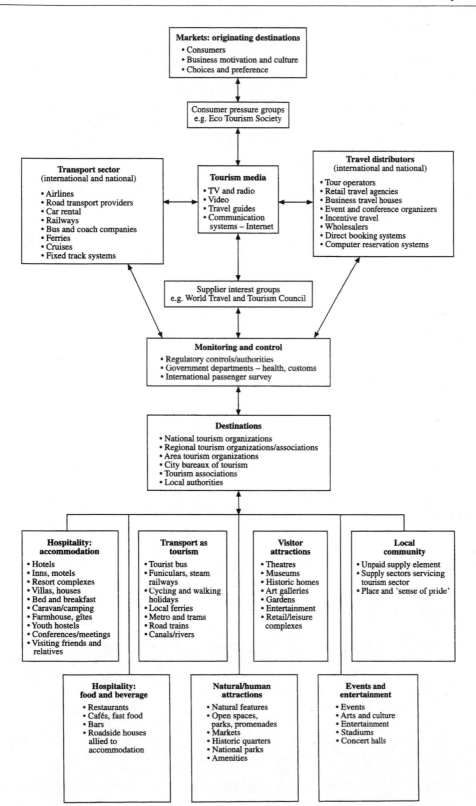

Figure 1.6 Tourism supply sectors.

1.3 THE MARKETING ENVIRONMENT

The marketing environment has been defined as the 'actors and forces that affect a company's capability to operate effectively in providing products and services to its customers' (Jobber, 1995: 120).

This can be subdivided into the micro environment and the macro environment. The **micro environment** includes those factors which prevail in the immediate environment. The company has a certain degree of influence over them, such as its relationship with other suppliers or with distributors. For example, tour operators form close relationships with hotels and airlines to provide packages.

The **macro environment**, however, relates to a much broader set of forces which affect all tourism businesses to some degree. They are cultural, political, economic, social and technological in nature. They bring opportunities, such as a rise in travel expectations in Eastern European countries, but also threats, such as continued political unrest in the Middle East. Table 1.2 lists the key micro and macro environment factors which marketers need to take into consideration.

It is essential for the marketer to bring all of the forces which impact on the marketing decision making process into a structural framework to assist the marketing planning process. Figure 1.7 brings the conceptual elements together, accepting the importance of both micro and macro factors, which affect the tourism flows between generating areas and receiving destinations. Understanding this framework is crucial to understanding how the tourism system functions.

For the marketer to be able to plan ahead it is essential to be conversant with key trends in the marketplace. In general terms, analysis is conducted at four levels – global, regional, country and resort or destination level. Most analysts predict that growth trends are set to continue in the twenty-first century. Baum (1995: A117) argues that 'this growth can partially be explained in terms of a number of key factors:

- economic prosperity in the developed world as well as in the rapidly developing countries of Asia;
- lifestyle and work related changes, giving greater free time for travel and leisure;
- technological change (especially in aviation and communications);
- changes in demographic structure of most affluent societies, especially improved health among those retired;
- reduced international tensions and the elimination of much of the bureaucracy of travel to and from many countries; and
- a growing awareness of an interest in other cultures and ways of living, a sense of belonging to "one world".'

Baum points out that these driving forces offer only a part explanation of the trends as overall there are a multiplicity of causal factors, some of which are more important than others. They do, however, provide a useful outline of the issues which marketers should consider when evaluating existing and potential markets. The next section of the chapter attempts to present an overview of trends at global, regional, country and destination levels. It provides an indication of the scale and scope of the tourism system.

As a generalized overview, it is obviously subject to the criticism that each market sector has its own specific defining qualities, a point which is salient when investigating a particular marketing environment. For example, the trends which are illustrated in the mature markets of Western Europe will not be appropriate to those of Eastern

Table 1.2 The external marketing environment

Factor	Examples
1. Political environment	• Government interest in free trade and exchange of visitors • Government and intergovernmental involvement in rules and regulations (international airline routes, etc.) • Environmental awareness and legislation • Growth of interest (lobbying on behalf of commercial sectors) and pressure group influence
2. Economic environment	• Affluence of 'North' and debt laden 'South' • Growth in economies, such as Asia • Differential rates of personal discretionary income available for tourist expenditure • Changing consumer patterns of expenditure, leisure and tourism are now more important • Privatization and lesser role of government in tourism provision
3. Social/cultural environment	• Changing patterns of cultural values • Fragmentation of societies into subcultural groupings • Changing patterns of life cycle and life styles such as more single households • Environmental and social consciousness • Growth of 'skilled customers' i.e. more knowledgeable
4. Technological environment	• Accelerating pace of technological change • Accessibility and rapid diffusion of technology in western countries • Technological enhancements in the home, including 'virtual reality' holidays in near future • Positive regulation of technical change
5. Ecological environment	• Increasing consumer and governmental awareness of ecological issues especially pollution and depletion of resources • Continued questioning of short termism by increasingly articulate groups • Consumer choice based on environmentally friendly tourism offerings
6. Demographics	• Population growth in developing countries • Slowdown in birth rate in western economies • Ageism in western economies • Geographical shifts of population • Migration to cities in developing countries and the opposite in advanced economies • Change in family structures and fragmentation of life styles

Europe or Asia. Nevertheless, the review below offers a series of guideposts which could direct organizational effort.

1.3.1 Global trends

Where to go in 1997? Just about everywhere is the answer, as the boom in pleasure travel continues unabated, and no part of the globe is free from tourism's touch. Long haul, once the preserve of the monied elite or the peripatetic, backpack laden poor, is the true growth area as the exotic becomes almost commonplace, and locations you once had to search for in atlases turn up in brochures.

(Elms, 1997)

This is how one correspondent described the arrival of the main 1997 season. It is a remarkably accurate portrayal of the tourism trends of the 1990s. Estimates of predicted growth in the global market differ but most commentators agree that there has

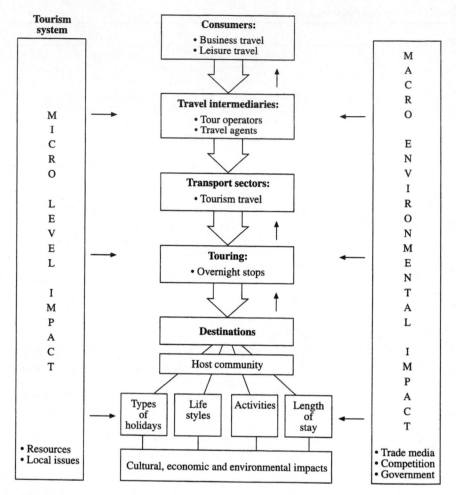

Figure 1.7 The marketing environment: structural framework and trends in the market.

been and will continue to be a sustained increase in tourism flows. These are summarized in Table 1.3.

In terms of economic spend, international visitors are very important to receiving countries, especially those which depend mainly on tourism. Wheatcroft (1994: 1) estimates that travel and tourism accounts for 12 per cent of world consumer spending. International visitors are particularly important: they tend to be high spending tourists either on business trips, or on main holidays. Despite setbacks in the mid-1970s (following increases in oil prices) and the effects of the Gulf War in the early 1990s, international tourism has remained one of the most resilient of business sectors. Table 1.4 outlines the pattern of growth in the top 20 global destinations.

1.3.2 Regional trends

This data, however, does not indicate the spread of global tourism. Table 1.5 indicates the growth of tourism in different regions.

Table 1.3 Comparison of global travel forecasts

	Measure of demand	Period	Annual growth (%)
WTTC	Expenditures	1996–2006	3.8
WTO	Arrivals	1990–2010	4.1
Boeing	RPK	1995–2014	5.1
MDC	RPK	1994–2013	5.7
Airbus	RPK	1995–2014	5.1

Source: WTTC Growth Forecasts 1996.

Table 1.4 Tourism arrivals: the world's top 20 tourism destinations, 1985 and 1994–95 (millions of arrivals)

	1985		1994		1995[a]	
	No.	Rank	No.	Rank	No.	Rank
France	36.7	1	61.3	1	60.0	1
Spain	27.5	2	43.2	3	44.9	2
USA	25.4	3	45.5	2	43.5	3
Italy	25.0	4	27.5	4	30.0	4
UK	14.4	6	21.0	7	23.7	5
China	7.1	13	21.1	6	23.4	6
Hungary	9.7	11	21.4	5	20.7	7
Mexico	11.9	9	17.2	10	20.2	8
Poland	2.7	23	18.8	8	19.2	9
Austria	15.2	5	17.9	9	17.2	10
Canada	13.2	7	16.0	12	16.9	11
Czech Republic	4.9[b]	16	17.0	11	15.5	12
Germany	12.7[c]	8	14.5	13	14.8	13
Switzerland	11.9	10	12.2	14	11.5	14
Hong Kong	3.7	19	9.3	16	10.2	15
Greece	6.6	14	10.7	15	10.1	16
Portugal	5.0	15	9.1	17	9.7	17
Malaysia	3.1	22	7.2	18	7.5	18
Thailand	2.4	26	6.2	21	7.0	19
Netherlands	3.3	21	6.2	20	6.6	20

Source: World Tourism Organization.
Notes
[a] Provisional figures.
[b] Former Czechoslovakia.
[c] Former West Germany only.

Europe still dominates in terms of international arrivals and it is predicted to maintain this position in the foreseeable future. However, in relative terms, tourism in Europe is static, for example, with respect to overnight stays. Other data show an increasing average spend but, when considering longer term trends, Europe's ascendancy is slowly slipping away to other regions of the world. All other markets, except North America, are expected to grow substantially, especially Latin America, the Far East and South East Asia.

If one considers originating destinations, however, much of the travel is intraregional rather than interregional. International tourism primarily concerns travel between neighbouring countries. In this context it is also useful to make a distinction

Table 1.5 Regional growth in tourist arrivals, 1985–95 (thousands of arrivals)

	1985	1995	% change 1995ᵃ/85	Share of world arrivals (%)	Percentage originating in region
Europe	213 795	333 299	55.9	59.4	85.4
Central/East	28 978	72 608	150.6	–	–
West	184 817	260 691	41.1	–	–
Americas	66 432	110 612	66.5	19.7	75.9
North America	50 477	80 551	59.6	–	–
Central and South America	7 979ᵇ	15 901	99.3	–	–
Caribbean	7 976	14 160	77.5	–	–
Asia and Pacific	33 361	87 302	161.7	14.8	79.1
East Asia	27 918	74 911	168.3	–	–
South Asia	2 540	4 270	68.1	0.8	16.1
Pacific	2 903	8 121	179.7	–	–
Africa	9 710	18 707	92.7	3.3	44.3
Northern	5 202	7 240	39.2	–	–
Rest of Africa	4 508	11 467	154.4	–	–
Middle East	6 240	11 107	78.0	2.0	47.0
World	329 538	561 027	70.2	100.0	–

Source: World Tourism Organization.
ᵃ Provisional figures.
ᵇ Includes former East Germany.

Table 1.6 Tourist arrivals from long haul markets

Destination	Tourist arrivals from long haul markets		Average growth rate (%) 95/85	Market share (% of total arrivals)	
	1985	1995		1985	1995
Africa	4 893	8 694	5.9	60.7	46.4
Americas	9 293	26 643	11.1	14.2	23.8
East Asia/Pacific	8 426	18 066	7.9	28.7	21.0
Europe	34 568	41 481	1.8	17.5	12.5
Middle East	3 893	5 887	4.2	45.7	53.3
South Asia	1 509	3 652	9.2	59.9	83.5

Source: World Tourism Organization.

between short haul and long haul arrivals. For example, Table 1.6 illustrates the breakdown of the long haul market across regions.

Table 1.7 illustrates the make up of the long and short haul market (outward bound) from the UK. The long haul market increased by 39 per cent between 1990 and 1995, amounting to 39 million trips in 1995. While there is certainly a degree of volatility between markets, the overall pattern is one of growth. For example, following incidents of violence and terrorism in Florida and Kenya, tourists switched to Asia. Despite such hiccups, short haul travel is losing share to long haul.

1.3.3 Country trends

It is often forgotten that, in terms of volume, most tourism is internal, i.e. people taking holidays in their own country, especially if day visits are included in the analysis.

The marketing environment

Table 1.7 UK market share of overseas short/long breaks, 1990–95

	Short haul			Long haul			Total	
	Number (millions)	Index	%	Number (millions)	Index	%	Number (millions)	Index
1990	18.5	100	87	2.8	100	13	21.3	100
1991	17.9	97	86	2.9	104	14	20.8	98
1992	20.0	108	86	3.2	114	14	23.2	109
1993	19.5	105	85	3.4	121	15	22.9	108
1994	19.6	106	85	3.5	125	15	23.1	109
1995 (est)	20.8	112	84	3.9	139	16	24.7	116

Source: ETB/BTA/IPS/Mintel.

There are considerably different rates of people taking main holidays in their own countries. If one takes a general overview of holiday taking in Europe, based on analysis of commercial reports, such as Euromonitor, and EU briefing documents, it becomes apparent that the level of holiday taking patterns (domestic and foreign) is split between north and south. For example, 70% of adults in Switzerland and Sweden take at least one holiday, in comparison to 39% in Spain, and 46% in Italy. The pattern is somewhat different when considering domestic holidays, with France and Sweden leading, with approximately 50% of adults taking a domestic holiday, whereas Germany, Ireland and Belgium are lowest, with less than 25% of the adult population taking a holiday in their home country.

Within the pattern of holiday taking the market is usually sub-divided into short breaks (1–3 nights) and long stay (4 plus nights) holidays. The decline of long holidays in Britain is illustrated in Table 1.8.

Within any given country it is also important to consider the day visitor or excursion markets, which can be considerable in terms of volume if not value. In the UK, for example, the United Kingdom Day Visits Survey indicates the breakdown of visits shown in Table 1.9.

This suggests that in Britain nearly 5500 million day visits were made by adults during 1994. The overwhelming majority of these are for leisure purposes, emphasizing the importance of day excursions within the tourism market.

1.3.4 Destination or resort

The fourth level of data relates to trends within a resort or destination area. This is vital information for the local tourism business sector so that performance can be

Table 1.8 Estimated number of 4+ night holidays taken by the British (adults and accompanying children)

Year	Britain (millions)	Abroad (millions)	Total (millions)
1984	34.00	15.50	49.50
1992	32.00	21.75	53.75
1993	32.50	23.50	56.00
1994	31.50	26.25	58.00

Source: UK Statistics, *Insights*, ETB/BTA, July 1995.

Table 1.9 Number and purpose of day visits in Great Britain, 1994

	England %	England Number (millions)	Wales %	Wales Number (millions)	Scotland %	Scotland Number (millions)	Great Britain %	Great Britain Number (millions)
Leisure day visits from home	95	4503.2	94	250.2	94	424.0	95	5177.3
Day visits from holiday bases	4	177.3	5	14.4	5	20.7	4	217.7
One-off business trips from home	1	61.5	1	2.8	1	4.4	1	68.8
All day visits	–	4742.0	–	267.4	–	449.1	–	5463.8
Base number: leisure day visits		11416		6542		5966		23924
holiday visits		685		134		224		1043
business visits		189		79		68		336

Source: UK Day Visits Survey 1994, published by CRN (1996).
Base: All day visits, Quarters 1, 2, 3 and 4.
Notes
1. Figures are rounded to the nearest 100 000 visits.
2. Where percentages do not sum to one hundred, this is due to the figures being rounded up.

evaluated and the fortunes of the destination compared to others. For example, the graphs in Figure 1.8 show the changing volume and value of tourism in one of the UK's major tourism destination areas, Cumbria.

While it is important for the tourism marketer to be aware of the scope of tourism throughout the world, for many practitioners the premier market will be local or national. Understanding the volume, value and trends in the market is the foundation on which the marketer builds an analysis of the marketing environment.

1.4 SUMMARY The tourism marketer needs to be in a position to define and appreciate the dynamics of the tourism system. In analysing tourism as a commercial activity there is also a need to understand the functional necessities of managing demand in a complex market. The marketer also has to be cognisant of environmental and societal processes which impact on the system.

It is important for the tourism marketer to be aware of the scope of tourism throughout the world. For many practitioners the premier market will be local or national, but for others long haul international travel will be the key. Understanding the volume, value and trends in the market allows the marketer to build an analysis of the marketing environment.

Tourism marketers should therefore embrace conceptual frameworks offered by other disciplines, as a way of sharpening the skills required to craft sophisticated strategic frameworks, or to develop markets and tourism offerings.

The process begins by understanding the driving forces of the tourism system and tourism flows which exist at present at a global and local scale.

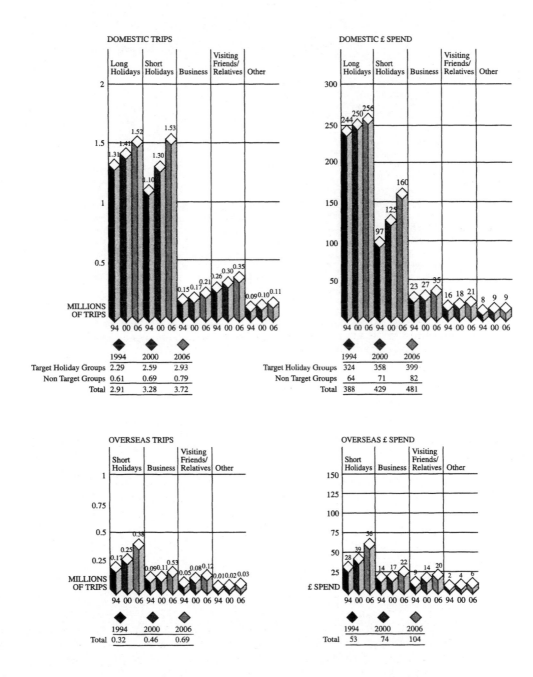

Figure 1.8 Target changes in volume and value of tourism in Cumbria to the years 2000 and 2006. *Source*: Cumbria Tourist Board.

REFERENCES

Baum, T. (1995) Trends in International Tourism. *Insights*, **6** (Mar), A117–20.

Burkhart, A.J. and Medlik, S. (1989) *Tourism: past, present and future,* 2nd edition, Heinemann, Oxford.

Burns, P.M. and Holden, A. (1995) *Tourism: A New Perspective*, Prentice Hall, Hemel Hempstead.

Cooper, C. (1994) The destination life cycle: an update. In *Tourism: The State of the Art* (eds A.V. Seaton *et al.*), Wiley, Chichester.

Cooper, C., Fletcher, J., Gilbert, D. and Wanhill, S. (1993) *Tourism: Principles and Practice,* Pitman, London.

Cumbria Tourist Board (1996) *The Future of Tourism in Cumbria.*

Elms, R. (1997) How Far Do You Want To Go This Year? *The Sunday Times,* January 19.

Go, F.M. and Pine, R. (1995) *Globalization Strategy in the Hotel Industry,* Routledge, London.

Jefferson, A. and Lickorish, L. (1988) *Marketing Tourism,* Longman, Harlow.

Jenkins, C.L. (1994) Tourism in developing countries: the privatisation issue. In *Tourism: the State of the Art* (eds A.V. Seaton *et al.*), Wiley, Chichester.

Jobber, D. (1995) *Principles and Practice of Marketing*, McGraw-Hill, Maidenhead.

Krippendorf, J. (1987) *The Holidaymakers: Understanding the Impact of Leisure and Travel*, Butterworth-Heinemann, Oxford.

Lea, J. (1988) *Tourism and Development in The Third World,* Routledge, London.

Mathieson, A. and Wall, G. (1982) *Tourism: economic, physical and social impacts,* Longman, Harlow.

McIntosh R.W., Goeldner, C.R. and Ritchie, J.R.B. (1995) *Tourism, Principles, Practices, Philosophies*, Wiley, Toronto.

Middleton, V. (1994) *Marketing in Travel and Tourism,* 2nd edition, Butterworth-Heinemann, Oxford.

Mill, R.C. and Morrison A.M. (1992) *The Tourism System,* 2nd edition, Prentice Hall International, London.

Morgan, M. (1996) *Marketing for Leisure and Tourism,* Prentice Hall, Hemel Hempstead.

Pearce, D. (1989) *Tourist Development,* 2nd edition, Longman, Harlow.

Poon, A. (1993) *Tourism, Technology and Competitive Strategies*, CAB International, Wallingford.

Seaton, A. and Bennett, M. (1995) *Marketing the Tourism Product*, Thomson Business Press, London.

Smith, S.J. (1995) *Tourism Analysis,* 2nd edition, Longman, Harlow.

Wheatcroft, S. (1994) *Aviation and Tourism Policies, Balancing The Benefits*, Routledge, London.

Tourism marketing management $\boxed{2}$

OBJECTIVES

This chapter explains:

● the definitions of marketing and suggests a revised definition for tourism marketing;
● marketing as a philosophy, a set of guiding principles or as an orientation;
● the underlying principles of service marketing as applied to tourism;
● the factors which make tourism marketing different;
● tourism marketing as a function.

2.1 THE EXCHANGE PROCESS

Marketing in its widest sense refers to an exchange process and classic definitions invariably focus on this prime tenet of exposition. Consider three different approaches to shaping a definition:

> It is the process by which sellers are brought together with buyers to exchange their goods and services for something of value.
>
> *(Buell, 1985: 19)*

The writings of well known management theorists such as Drucker (1954: 91) and Levitt (1986) have been influential. They, amongst others, have emphasized the importance of consumer orientation. For example, Kotler *et al.* (1996: 23) assert that:

> Marketing is a social and managerial process by which individuals and groups obtain what they need and want through creating and exchanging products and value with others.

In contrast, a number of writers stress the supplier or management system rather than the consumer:

> Marketing consists of individual organizational activities that facilitate and expedite satisfying exchange relationships in the dynamic environment through the creation, distribution, promotion and pricing of goods, services and ideas.
>
> *(Dibb* et al., *1991: 5)*

2.1.1 A definition of tourism marketing

Current definitions of marketing provide a useful set of guidelines for analysis. By emphasizing consumer–supplier interaction and the dynamic nature of the environment, they offer some insight, but tend to be too general for the tourism marketer. There is a need to consider four additional and salient factors which signal what Poon (1993) has described as the 'new tourism' (a more volatile, fragmented and sophisticated market) which she contrasts with the 'old tourism' (mainly mass packaged tourism) of previous decades. Taking into account Poon's analysis, tourism marketing perhaps needs to embrace the following:

(a) Anticipation of market changes

Tourism marketing is about the anticipation of the changing desires (needs and wants) of the existing tourist. **Visitor retention** is a core concept in this respect; but visitors now want extra value and new experiences. This is more important for a tourism company or destination to address in comparison to the identification of new visitors. The supposition is based on empirical evidence (Reichheld and Sasser, 1990: 105–11) which suggests that it is far more expensive to attract a new customer than to retain an existing one. This process is referred to by Middleton (1995: A1–8) as the 'leaky bucket syndrome', where destinations consider that all they need to do is to source new customers each year regardless of those they have lost through lack of attention to the existing marketplace.

(b) The highly competitive market

There is a greater need to understand the **highly competitive structure** of the market. Achieving customer satisfaction at a profit can only occur if the tourism offering is superior to the many close substitutes available. This second factor directs attention to the rapid growth of competing destinations and tourism offerings throughout the world. In some regions there is almost certainly excess supply. Furthermore, the trend towards standardized offerings in mature markets erodes the degree of differentiation, which is a hallmark of tourism in its evolutionary stage.

(c) Social and environmental considerations

Tourism marketing needs to absorb underlying social and environmental considerations at a faster pace than hitherto. The traditional emphasis placed on satisfying the consumer is giving way to a revised principle which states that consumer satisfaction can only be achieved within a framework of societal and environmental responsibilities (Mill, 1996).

(d) Consumer power

Markets have become more knowledgeable and sophisticated as education and information are more readily available (Drucker, 1992: 263). Furthermore, there is a continuing fragmentation in the market; it exhibits patterns of change. A number of underlying consumer trends point to the increasing concern about the environment (Carson and Moulden, 1991) and the effects of tourism on host communities (Prosser,

1994: 31–5). Even if suppliers are slow to readjust, consumers are likely to become increasingly influential in a market which they know more about than ever before and where substitutes are the order of the day. The way in which the customer is treated by the company has become crucial to tourism marketing and **interactive marketing** is gaining ascendancy (Barnes, 1989: 11–21; Mayo, 1990: 33–41). These essential ingredients have been incorporated into a revised definition of tourism marketing as follows:

> Tourism marketing is the managerial process of anticipating and satisfying existing and potential visitor wants more effectively than competitive suppliers or destinations. The management of exchange is driven by profit, community gain, or both; either way long term success depends on a satisfactory interaction between customer and supplier. It also means securing environmental and societal needs as well as core consumer satisfaction. They can no longer be regarded as mutually exclusive.
>
> *(Lumsdon, 1997)*

2.2 PHILOSOPHY OR FUNCTION?

The definition offered by the author describes tourism marketing as a 'managerial process'. A review of marketing literature, however, highlights a distinction which is often made between marketing as a management philosophy, and marketing as a process or functional attribute of an organization. This distinction is worthy of exploration as there is sometimes confusion about the use of the term.

2.2.1 Guiding principles

Throughout the literature you will find references to marketing as a philosophy (Baker, 1985; Kotler *et al.*, 1996: 23). Marketing in this context is explained as a way of thinking, or as a set of guiding principles which should, it is argued, pervade an organization. These principles revolve around the concepts of consumer satisfaction and profit maximization. They have even been presented as principles which might also guide the tourism marketer in a personal capacity:

> Whether you want to be a restaurant manager, executive housekeeper, or any other career choice, marketing will directly affect your personal and professional life. This book will start you on a journey that will cause your customers to embrace you and make marketing your management philosophy.
>
> *(Kotler* et al.*, 1996: 23)*

This approach has been subject to criticism. Brownlie and Saren (1992: 34–47), for example, question the value of theorists presenting marketing as an ideology or body of instruction without recourse to other values or organizational principles relevant to a company's success. They argue that marketing is not an article of faith. It is one of several strands of management theory which combine to drive an organization towards its corporate goals. Marketing might be a primary strand but it is not absolute.

2.2.2 Marketing orientation

It is perhaps better to regard tourism marketing as an orientation or a perspective, albeit an essential one, rather than an overarching management philosophy. The case for such an approach is based on three related points:

- Marketing is essentially a collection of strategic and tactical management tools which are circumscribed by a set of guiding principles. This does not constitute a management philosophy *per se*.
- Tourism management by necessity requires an interdisciplinary approach. Airlines and theme parks are as much about the application of operational management principles as about those of marketing. Both are necessary for the exchange process to work satisfactorily.
- Tourism development is concerned with markets, but it is also very much about the built environment, design, culture, and socioeconomic impacts, many of which are beyond the scope of marketing.

Marketing orientation might also be contrasted to four other perspectives, drawn together by Kotler (1983: 14–21) in one of his earlier classic works. The orientations are summarized below:

- **Production or operation:** Consumers prefer products that are readily available and affordable, therefore companies should stress efficient operation and distribution.
- **Product:** The quality, performance and appealing features of the product are the main determinants of success. The product is all.
- **Selling:** The only way to perform well in the market is through aggressive selling.
- **Societal marketing:** This orientation stresses the importance of preserving or enhancing society's well-being as well as satisfying needs and wants of individual customers.

These contrast with marketing orientation which is described by Kotler *et al.* (1996: 23) as follows:

> The marketing concept holds that the key to achieving organizational goals consists in determining the needs and wants of target markets and delivering the desired satisfactions more effectively and efficiently than competitors.

It has subsequently been argued that these respective management orientations have dominated commercial thinking at different times. Based on an extensive literature review of the subject, Gilbert and Bailey (1990: 6–13) suggest that tourism management has passed through three broad stages in chronological order:

- the production era
- the sales era
- the marketing era.

This generalized theory of marketing development is of some interest to the tourism marketer as it is possible to discern a number of parallels in the tourism life cycle, a model which suggests that tourism develops from infancy to maturity. Tourism marketing might now have reached a new era, the 'societal and environmental' stage, which is perhaps beginning to replace the marketing era.

It is important, however, to recognize that these are generalizations. Most organizations exhibit dimensions of all of these orientations. It is unrealistic to assume otherwise. Companies and organizations have varying mission statements and objectives which reflect management values and therefore differing degrees of commitment to marketing. Many organizations exhibit the outward signs of marketing orientation, but when a detailed analysis of resource commitment is made, operational, selling or financial perspectives are evident. This is particularly the case when small to medium size enterprises are analysed, where owners and managers view their hotel or visitor attraction as a lifestyle business, for example.

The same applies to destinations. Some generating markets are mature, such as the USA and most countries in northern Europe. They are beginning to exhibit similar signs of maturity such as fragmentation, the desire for less packaging, increased interest in the impacts of tourism, and pressure for increased quality without commensurate price increases. In these countries societal marketing is gaining ascendancy, but others, such as India and Indonesia, clearly exhibit the signs of a market in infancy, both in terms of generating demand and receiving large numbers of visitors. How will they progress?

Furthermore, many destinations, while partially embracing the concept of marketing, still exhibit a sales perspective, i.e. the major resource commitment is given over to promotional material, attendance at exhibitions or selling rather than devoting attention to the entire menu of marketing, which includes planning, monitoring and control.

The characteristics which marketing orientated organizations in tourism might exhibit are detailed in Table 2.1.

It is appropriate to return to the concept of societal marketing as formulated by Kotler (1983: 14–21). In his discussions, Kotler points out that consumer markets exhibit a much greater interest in societal and environmental issues than previously. It is argued that the concept of societal marketing is also being absorbed into the corporate cultures of companies and organizations, as well as governments. The explanation is straightforward. Like many other business sectors, tourism suppliers have become sensitive to societal and environmental issues because their customers are demanding change. The process might well be incremental, but in those societies which are generating the major flows of international tourism, consumer interest in sustainability, cultural and environmental, is growing. Vandermerwe (1993: 213) predicts that companies must:

Table 2.1 Marketing orientation

An organization would exhibit some or all of the following characteristics:
- A clearly defined approach to existing, potential and long term markets
- Policies and actions which reflect concern for consumer wants in relation to societal and environmental requirements
- Implementation which involves internal marketing (own staff), consumer orientation and consideration of stakeholders including host communities
- Market environmental scanning which includes short and long term scenarios
- Marketing planning process which is part of the culture of the organization and includes genuine reappraisal of internal resources
- A structure and culture which leads to long term vision

learn to deal not only with new customer values but also with new societal values, and to extend their thinking and activities to encompass managing for the world as a whole.

This includes local and national governments and their approach to tourism development. These bodies recognize the need to act in this sphere, if only to satisfy pressing demands from consumer groups. The relationship between marketing and sustainability in tourism is explored in Chapter 19.

2.3 TOURISM MARKETING: THE UNDERLYING PRINCIPLES

Tourism is usually classified as part of the service sector of an economy. It ranks alongside finance, retailing, commercial and professional services. During the past two decades, there has been a growing body of literature dedicated to the marketing of services, initially primed by a number of influential articles (Bateson, 1977: 77–115; Grönroos, 1978: 588–61; Shostack, 1977: 34–43) and by a succession of comprehensive texts such as Bateson (1991), Cowell (1984) and Palmer (1994).

Most writers refer to a set of five underlying principles which make the marketing of services different to the marketing of industrial or fast moving consumer goods. They are **intangibility**, **perishability**, **heterogeneity**, **inseparability** and **lack of ownership**. Table 2.2 defines and explains these principles and their implications for tourism marketers.

The debate is not entirely settled, however, as to whether the differences are substantive or whether services should simply fall beneath the generic banner of marketing. There appears to be some degree of consensus that there is a conceptual continuum between goods and services, as projected by Grönroos (1978: 588–601), where either tangibles or intangibles are dominant (see Figure 2.1). Beyond this, the recognition of services marketing as an emerging area of scholarly activity is relatively low in the discussion of tourism marketing.

In the case of tourism, intangible benefits dominate with respect to virtually all tourism offerings, so it makes little sense to refer to them as goods or products, even though a tourism offering will include some tangibles such as food, beverages or souvenirs. It is essentially about offering intangible benefits such as relaxation, education and entertainment, or feeling superior, etc.

There are two further points which strengthen the argument. The first relates to the extent to which the concept of intangibility dominates all parts of the tourism system. Pre-consumption involves the selling of dreams prior to a visit. Pictorial references, word of mouth recommendation, etc., feature intangible benefits. The stay itself is mainly about consuming intangible benefits such as relaxation and hopefully pleasant experiences. These in turn should lead to happy memories which might be held years after consumption (post-consumption dreaming). Therefore, the length of the tourism consumption process has an important impact on the marketing task. Furthermore, the marketer has to assure continuity and consistency throughout a person's stay, which is often an almost impossible task given the complexity of the external environment of a destination. There is nowhere like the degree of control associated with the provision of tangible products.

The second point relates to what has been described as the service encounter (Shostack, 1985: 34–43) where provision and consumption of the service offering are

Table 2.2 The underlying principles of services marketing

Principle	Explanation	Implications
Intangibility	Unlike products, services are mainly intangible by nature. It is impossible for the consumer to touch, smell, feel or hear the service offering in the same way as they can test a product	Tourism marketers tend to 'tangibilize' the tourism offering in brochures and videos – visual displays of the real thing
Perishability	It is not possible to store services. An unoccupied seat on a train or bed in a guest house is lost forever unlike a product which can be stockpiled until demand rises once more	The management task emphasizes managing demand and capacity to a degree of fine tuning. For example, airlines offer standby fares to those willing to fill unexpected empty seats at short notice
Heterogeneity	It is difficult for service marketers to standardize service provision given the close contact between staff and consumers. Performance varies regardless of processes designed to minimize this factor	Tourism marketers design processes to minimize differences in service encounters and provision between different outlets or between different shifts at a hotel, for example. Provision of uniforms and of similar physical surroundings illustrates evidence of standardization
Inseparability	The service provision and consumption occur at the same time and both provider and consumer interact in the process of delivery. This obviously is why standardization of service is so difficult as consumer involvement is high	Marketers attempt to devise delivery systems which ease interaction and invest in campaigns to educate staff and consumers as to how to get the best from the interaction. Training in hotels emphasizes how staff can manage the interaction
Lack of ownership	The consumer does not take title of goods as in product marketing. They bring back memories and feelings from a holiday	The marketer emphasizes pictorial reference and souvenirs to reinforce image of holiday experience

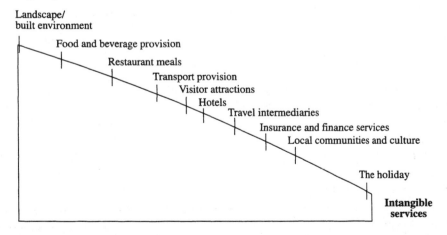

Figure 2.1 Goods–services continuum in tourism. *Source*: redrawn from Shostack (1977).

simultaneous. The process is invariably about staff and consumers sharing an experience. It is a performance in which the consumer participates and in its ultimate form is almost a ritual. This is the most critical element in tourism which requires far more attention than the marketing of goods where production and consumption can and do readily occur at different times and places.

2.3.1 Is tourism marketing different?

There is little or no dispute that the principles of marketing as a discipline can be applied universally across all business sectors. What is fundamental to the argument, however, is that the application of these principles and the emphasis placed on specific marketing management tools are different in tourism. This is particularly true in the crucial dimension of attracting customers to the service offering and the service encounter itself. Furthermore, the marketing of destinations, and to some extent accommodation, visitor attractions and transport networks, is different on the following counts:

● Seasonality (the effect of climate or culture on patterns of demand) is a far more significant factor than for other business sectors, but equally important for many tourism businesses is the cyclical nature of demand during the week.
● The destination is an amalgam of service offerings where a wide range of suppliers are involved. This makes service development or modification more complicated, and in some cases uncontrollable.
● The destination offers a relatively fixed supply of facilities which can only be changed slowly or on an incremental scale, in comparison to patterns of consumer demand which shift rapidly.
● The destination is sold many times over to a multitude of market segments simultaneously. It can therefore be bought in a similar manner, and throughout the world, in some instances.
● It is usually promoted in a similar fashion to all segments; they consume its offerings in a variety of ways, some enjoying the historic or shopping quarters, others the beaches or restaurants.
● There is a lack of control over the 'brand' in the sense that it is associated with the imagery of a country or region, or the suppliers which make up a destination or visitor attraction.

2.3.2 Marketing as a management process

Marketing orientation involves the entire organization working towards the satisfaction of the customer. In tourism this is absolutely critical, for as mentioned previously, the provision and consumption of the service offering usually occurs simultaneously.

Marketing management is undertaken, in line with other functions and external agencies, as a series of key tasks which are referred to as the marketing management process or, by some writers, as a system. Kotler (1983: 623–6) describes it as:

> analysing market opportunities, researching and selecting target markets, developing marketing strategies, planning marketing tactics, and implementing and controlling the marketing effort.

Within the framework of a corporate strategy (which sets out the vision and direction of the organization), the marketing management process involves the following key areas:

(a) The provision of a marketing information system

Establishing an information system which includes marketing research:

- about customers;
- about competitors;
- about the organization's capability and effectiveness.

(b) Marketing planning

This involves the development of a broad marketing strategy based on:

- analysis of the marketing environment;
- evaluation of strategic options regarding service offerings *vis à vis* resources;
- obtaining a best fit between the company's resources and existing and potential markets;
- reappraising mission statements and objectives;
- segmenting and re-positioning.

(c) Planning tactical campaigns

The marketing strategy leads to the design of short term (annual) plans:

- detailed planning of the marketing mix (or marketing tools) in line with strategy;
- campaign objectives, budgets and scheduling.

(d) Marketing operations

This involves implementing the tactical marketing plans on the following basis:

- co-ordinating internal and external marketing activities;
- fine tuning campaigns as they unfold (adjustment of the marketing mix according to localized market trends);
- undertaking programmes of work agreed at the planning stage, i.e. regarding marketing communications, distribution through intermediaries, etc.

(e) Monitoring and control

This is a continuous process which relates to:

- evaluation of sales data and financial performance;
- customer feedback (as part of the marketing research programme);
- staff feedback about campaigns and competitor activities.

The tasks listed above form a systematic process which marketing orientated companies adopt in some form. It would be unrealistic to step into a tourism organization and find it neatly structured as in the textbook; there is a rich variety of marketing cultures and structures. Many tour operators and retail travel agencies, for example, exemplify technologically driven marketing where consumer databases and technological systems are the cornerstone of the process. Visitor attractions are often different in their approach, emphasizing the need to manage flows on site, to offer memorable interpretation and entertainment.

Nor is it realistic to assume that the tasks or phases undertaken are entirely separate. The distinction between strategy and tactics, for example, is less discrete in reality than presented in the book. Short term tactical campaigns which succeed above all expectations often become tomorrow's strategy. In a similar vein, customer reaction or feedback can render longer term marketing strategies dead within weeks. The celebrated example of the promotion of travel incentives to customers of Hoover appliances provides a sharp reminder. Demand was so overwhelming that the agency acting on behalf of the Hoover Company in the 1990s could not meet it. The consequent negative public relations meant that Hoover had to redraw its strategy.

Another major point is that some tourism organizations do not adopt marketing at all, neither as an orientation nor as a management process. Many small to medium size enterprises undertake little or no research, spend most of their time reacting to circumstances and expect guests or visitors to arrive at their doorstep, simply because they exist. They tread a path of survival from season to season and not surprisingly many perform on the margin of profitability.

While such companies exist, there is evidence to suggest that organizations adhering to marketing both in terms of orientation and management processes, perform better than their competitors (Buzzell and Gale, 1987). There is, however, considerable room for improvement in tourism.

2.4 SUMMARY

Marketing is essentially the management of the exchange process between the supplier and customer. In this respect it is important for the marketer to adopt an anticipatory approach to the marketplace as the past, or what has been described as the old tourism, may no longer hold the answers to capturing the new tourism market. Consumer behaviour, patterns of demand and levels of competition are changing constantly.

There is a need to distinguish between tourism marketing as a set of guiding principles which offers direction and marketing as a function which occurs within organizations. The company needs to understand both its orientation and how it conducts marketing in order to become more effective. In the past many tourism organizations exhibited a product or sales orientation. This has given way to marketing orientation and in some markets societal marketing orientation, whereby in order to succeed in the marketplace organizations will have to place greater emphasis on satisfying wider societal aspirations as well as the more focused wants of each respective customer.

REFERENCES

Baker, M.J. (1985) *Marketing Strategy and Management,* Macmillan, Basingstoke.

Barnes, J.G. (1989) The Role of Internal Marketing: If the Staff Won't Buy It, Why Should the Customer? *Irish Marketing Review,* **4**(2), 11–21.

Bateson, J.E.G. (1977) Do We Need Service Marketing? In *Marketing Consumer Services: New Insights,* Marketing Science Institute, Boston.

Bateson, J.E.G. (1991) *Managing Services Marketing,* 2nd edition, Dryden Press, Fort Worth.

Berry, L.L. (1980) Services Marketing is Different. *Business,* **30**(3), 24–9.

Brownlie, D. and Saren, M. (1992) The Four Ps of the Marketing Concept: Prescriptive, Polemical, Permanent and Problematical. *European Journal of Marketing,* **26**(4), 34–47.

Buell, V.P. (1985) *Marketing Management, A Strategic Management Approach,* McGraw-Hill, London.

Buzzell, R.D. and Gale, B.T. (1987) *The PIMS Principles: Linking Performance to Strategy,* Free Press, New York.

Carson, P. and Moulden, J. (1991) *Green is Gold: Business Talking to Business About the Environmental Revolution,* Harper Business, Toronto.

Cowell, D. (1984) *The Marketing of Services,* Heinemann, London.

Dibb, S., Simkin, L., Pride, W.M. and Ferrell, O.C. (1991) *Marketing, Basic Concepts and Decisions*, 8th edition, Houghton-Mifflin, Boston.

Drucker, P.F. (1964) *Managing For Results,* Harper and Row, New York.

Drucker, P.F. (1992) *Managing For the Future,* Butterworth-Heinemann, Oxford.

Gilbert, D.C. and Bailey, N. (1990) The development of marketing: a compendium of historical approaches. *Quarterly Review of Marketing,* **15**(2), 6–13.

Grönroos, C. (1978) A Service Orientated Approach to the Marketing of Services. *European Journal of Marketing,* **12**(8), 588–601.

Kotler, P. (1983) *Principles of Marketing,* 2nd edition, Prentice Hall, Englewood Cliffs, New Jersey.

Kotler, P., Bowen, J. and Makens, J. (1996) *Marketing for Hospitality and Tourism,* Prentice Hall, Englewood Cliffs, New Jersey.

Levitt, T. (1986) *The Marketing Imagination,* Free Press, New York.

Lumsdon, L.M. (1997) Rethinking the Concept of the Tourism Product. Working paper, Business School, Staffordshire University.

Mayo, M.C. (1990) The Services Marketing Literature: A Review and Critique. *Canadian Journal of Marketing Research,* **9**, 33–41.

Middleton, V.T.C. (1995) Leaky Bucket Syndrome. *Insights*, English Tourist Board, July, pp. A1–A8.

Mill, R.C. (1996) Societal marketing – implications for tourism destinations. *Journal of Vacation Marketing*, **2**(3), 215–22.

Palmer, A. (1994) *Principles of Service Marketing,* McGraw-Hill, Maidenhead.

Poon, A. (1993) *Tourism, Technology and Competitive Strategies,* CAB International, Wallingford.

Prosser, R. (1994) Societal Change and the Growth in Alternative Tourism. In *Ecotourism, A Sustainable Option* (eds E. Cater and G. Lowman), Wiley, Chichester.

Reichheld, F. and Sasser, W. (1990) Zero Defections: Quality Comes to Service. *Harvard Business Review,* September–October, 105–11.

Shostack, G.L. (1977) Breaking Free From Product Marketing. *Journal of Marketing,* **41**(2), April 1977, 77.

Shostack, G.L. (1985) Planning the Service Encounter. In *The Service Encounter* (eds J.A. Czepiel, M.R. Solomon and C.F. Suprenant), Lexington Books, Lexington.

Vandermerwe, S. (1993) *From Tin Soldiers to Russian Dolls,* Butterworth-Heinemann, Oxford.

3 Consumer behaviour

OBJECTIVES

This chapter explains:

- the factors which determine visitor buyer behaviour;
  - (i) internal influencing factors
  - (ii) external influencing factors
- tourism typologies;
- the buying behaviour process;
- the integral models of consumer behaviour as applied to the tourism business.

3.1 INTRODUCTION

The cornerstone of classical marketing theory is the satisfaction of the consumer, or in terms of the business of tourism, the passenger or visitor. Therefore, the marketer needs to understand three related aspects of consumer behaviour: consumer motivation, consumer typologies and the consumer purchasing process.

In reality, most organizations in tourism have an imperfect picture of their customers (Swarbrooke, 1996: A67). They might gather intelligence about macro factors shaping customer motivation, such as social and economic values in the market. They might also understand to some extent the buying processes which their customers or visitors pursue. Few organizations, however, monitor patterns of consumer behaviour at a level of detail you might expect, given that the business is all about satisfying customers. There are four possible explanatory reasons for this gap:

- Many organizations consider that they are sufficiently close to their visitors and therefore do not commit resources to more formal consumer studies. Such organizations tend to be small scale and operationally orientated. Small hoteliers and visitor attractions fall readily into this category.
- Researching consumer motivation and buying processes can be a time consuming and difficult exercise. For example, how does an organization find out what customers think about holidays? Will the potential customer really share with a researcher the real reasons behind a proposed trip rather than providing superficial responses? In terms of attitudinal and motivational studies market researchers are required to unlock attitudinal responses in order to obtain meaningful data. This requires specialist skills.

- Many small companies and destinations fail to commit resources to research any aspect of a market because of limited marketing budgets. Promotion is often ranked as a priority above all else. Other marketing functions arc therefore minimized until such times as a crisis emerges, for example, when there is a marked decline in visitor numbers. When tourism organizations have low marketing budgets the commitment of £20 000 for a full scale study would usually be prohibitive. Investment in consumer market research, it is argued, will not bring more visitors in next season.

- Most organizations rely almost entirely on the scanning of secondary consumer data. This is combined with management observation and judgement. However, as the marketing environment is changing rapidly, data drawn from secondary sources loses its currency easily. Consumer patterns recorded in 1998, for example, will most likely have changed by the year 2003 but many companies might still be using this type of information as a benchmark study.

3.2 FRAMEWORK OF ANALYSIS

Despite the pragmatic reasoning for not undertaking consumer studies, the case for an improved understanding of customer motivation is compelling. It is one of the most effective ways of generating competitive differential advantage. Understanding the key triggers which lead to the purchase of a tourism offering, such as a visit or holiday, will be increasingly recognized as one of the key success factors by competitive organizations. The questions a marketer needs to answer are summarized as follows:

- Who buys tourism offerings?
- How does the buying process work?
- What are the main factors affecting choice of an offering?
- Where do people buy tourism services?
- When do they buy them or when are the critical stages in the buying process?

Most consumer studies in tourism fall into one of the following three approaches:

- **Tourism motivational studies.** This involves an examination of why people participate in tourism, and to a lesser extent why certain groups in any given society do not travel at all. They seek to explain psychological and socio-psychological factors such as attitudes, beliefs and perceptions, culture and life styles and their effect on purchasing behaviour. Such studies include consumer typologies.
- **The buying process.** This involves an evaluation of how such factors interrelate in the sequential buying process. These include factors internal to the person, such as personality, as well as external factors such as peer groups and media influence. They focus on the stages of the buying process.
- **Integral models.** These seek to explain the way in which internal and external variables combine to stimulate purchasing behaviour. The models are often portrayed in a diagrammatic form and tend to be deterministic, i.e. they imply that one step follows another in a sequential manner.

No one model or approach presents an all embracing theoretical construct. On the contrary, there are a variety of frameworks drawn from economics, psychology and sociology which offer insight into the influences which shape patterns of buyer behaviour and buying processes. Collectively, they provide a range of tools which can be applied to specific situations in tourism where salient characteristics affecting purchasing can be determined and thus can be of use to suppliers marketing their offerings (Chisnall, 1985).

3.3 TOURISM MOTIVATIONAL STUDIES

Factors influencing motivation and purchase can be grouped into three overlapping dimensions, each of which comprises a number of variables:

- Internal driving forces;
- External influencing factors;
- The nature of the buying situations.

3.3.1 Internal driving forces

A number of internal driving forces, described as a combination of attributes, experience and skills, have been identified in tourism-related research. Many stem from the field of social psychology and others have been constructed as a result of multidisciplinary consumer studies. The key factors are motivation, perception, learning, beliefs and attitudes, personality. There is a brief description of each one below.

(a) Motivation

Motivation relates to the inner desire for satisfaction, which is manifested in a number of ways, and is subject to scholarly debate in the field of psychology. Accepted basic universal needs are those which are not learned, such as the need to satisfy thirst and hunger. Those needs which are learned by humans, such as wanting to belong to a community or to seek social esteem, are more complicated.

There are several schools of thought which are referred to by Pearce (1993:113–34). Some theories of psychology suggest that motivation stems from inner states of tension which must be satisfied. It is postulated that humans strive to maintain a state of equilibrium and that an individual is invariably involved in the process of seeking solutions to relieve such states of tension.

Another explanation is based on Freudian analysis which suggests that there are deep underlying forces which stimulate our behaviour, forces which are mainly unconscious and hence not readily discernible in overt behaviour. This approach suggests that our patterns of behaviour are not entirely predictable. For example, at a superficial level a person might indicate that they are taking a holiday to relax, but their inner state recognizes that they are escaping routine behaviour at home (Krippendorf, 1987: 24).

In contrast, behaviourists assume that patterns of behaviour are more transparent and ordered. A prime example of this approach, widely adopted by marketers, is Maslow's theory of motivation (Maslow, 1954: 80–106). The theory charts a formalized pattern of behaviour based on a hierarchy of needs. Fundamental needs are referred to as physiological needs, i.e. the basics in life such as the provision of security and relief from hunger, etc. Once these are satisfied a person will move to satisfy the next, the higher order needs, such as social esteem and self-actualization.

Figure 3.1 Hierarchy of needs. After Maslow (1954).

The hierarchy of needs which Maslow first outlined has been widely adopted (McIntosh, Goeldner and Ritchie, 1995: 175–6) to explain motivation, presumably because of its appealing simplicity and applicability to different sectors. It has also been used to explain consumer behaviour in tourism.

The theory has, however, a number of limitations. First, it is difficult to justify five discrete levels of need. These are not constructed on the basis of extensive empirical research. Furthermore, the levels of need, as the title implies, infers that humans rise from basic levels to higher order needs. Mill and Morrison (1992: 19–21) question this assumed relationship between the physical, psychological and intellectual needs both in terms of the discreteness of each level and the order. They consider that it is more realistic to accept a degree of interdependence between the levels. Those seeking higher order needs at the same time require equally the satisfaction of lower order needs. Mill and Morrison argue that Maslow's diagrammatic representation of the hierarchy would be better illustrated as a series of 'nested triangles' rather than a pyramid formation. Furthermore, they refer to two additional higher dimensions: first, knowledge and understanding, and, second, aesthetic appreciation. These concepts are appropriate to tourism behaviour, but could possibly be subsumed as an integral part of self-actualization.

Others refer to key inhibitors which act as barriers to travel, such as a lack of discretionary income, peer group pressure and psychological constraints such as risk, or a fear of lack of human security. The classic example would be the fear of flying.

(b) Learning

The concept of learning refers to the way in which visitors receive and interpret a variety of stimuli. People gain experience through taking holidays, by listening to others and through a variety of other sources. The process of absorbing such information might involve a visitor referring to earlier experiences at the same destination or learning from visits to a number of alternative destinations. It might also refer to different accommodation bases, or visitor attractions, for example. As part of the process the visitor develops a mental inventory of expectations about places, a catalogue of good and bad holiday experiences. These form the basis of learned criteria which will be recalled when selecting future holidays and destinations.

(c) Beliefs and attitudes

Beliefs refer to the thoughts which people have about most aspects of their life. In the commercial domain consumers have beliefs about companies, products and services including tourism offerings and destinations. Such thoughts can be positive, such as a trust or confidence in a hotel, or negative, such as a feeling about lack of security on public transport late at night.

Attitudes can be defined as ingrained feelings about a range of subjects. They fit an overall framework of thinking about the world, so therefore involve a set of inter-related thoughts. In this respect, they are difficult to change. A child who has experienced a number of relatively uninspired family holidays at a destination, for example, will find it difficult to accept that the place is worth visiting as an adult.

(d) Perception

Perception is the fourth related concept. It refers to the way in which people filter information which they receive to fit into an overall mind picture of the world. Thus, perception is inextricably bound to the concepts of bias and distortion. People choose to interpret different stimuli in different ways, ignoring some factors while enhancing others. This is known as selective retention.

People often perceive tourism offerings in a way which complements their self image. In this way products or tourism offerings are viewed as a 'bundle of benefits' which are personal to the customer. It is, however, the technical factors (which are termed significative stimuli), through which the marketer can seek to change perception.

There are a number of image shaping forces which Mill and Morrison (1992: 46–8) discuss. They make the marketer's task more complex:

- **Stability of perception.** Impressions gained in the past tend to be retained for a long time. For example, visitors associate Eastern European countries with communist regimes despite the break up of the Soviet Bloc in the late 1980s and early 1990s.
- **Habitual behaviour.** People act in a habitual way and therefore it is difficult to break a pattern of behaviour.
- **Confident or cautious.** Confident visitors take in new messages more speedily than those who are cautious in their travel habits and particularly when there is a complicated buying process involved. Thus, it is easier to promote a new long haul destination to a confident traveller than one who is more conservative in outlook.
- **Limited span of attention.** There is a limit to the number of stimuli a person can take in at any one time. Therefore, there is a need not to overcomplicate messages about tourism services or destinations.
- **Expectations.** People very often have preconceptions about a tourism offering and expect reality to confirm such expectations. It is difficult to break down such preconceptions.

3.3.2 Perceptual mapping

With regard to the last point marketers sometimes use a technique known as perceptual mapping to identify the relationship between the level of perceived importance on the part of the visitor and the actual performance on the part of the supplier. Figure 3.2 illustrates the use of the technique in relation to the Hong Kong travel market with respect to Canada as a destination. On the perceptual map. for example, the market considers that inexpensive restaurants are important but that such restaurants are not well presented in Canada.

Personality

Personality refers to a set of distinctive psychological characteristics which characterize the type of behaviour of an individual. These defining characteristics make each person different from the next, although authors sometimes discuss personality types exhibiting different social characteristics (Kassarjian, 1982: 160–80).

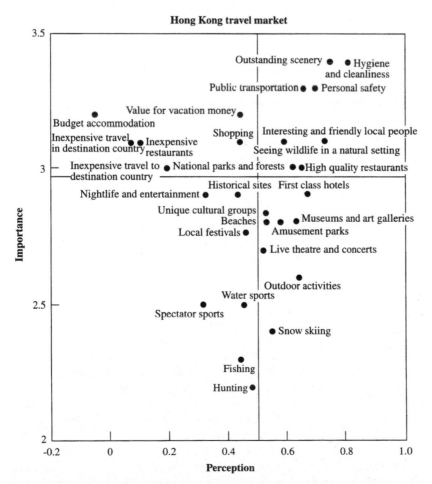

Figure 3.2 Perceptual mapping: attribute importance versus perception – Canada.
Source: Reproduced with permission from *Pleasure Travel Markets to North America*, The Canadian Tourism Commission (1989).

An associated concept is self image, which refers to how consumers like to see themselves rather than an objective assessment of their personality. Travel behaviour, it is argued, often fits self image, such as masculine, self-confident types choosing golfing or yachting holidays. However, there is a question mark over the relationship between personality types and pattern of holiday: the evidence for such an association is weak (Mill and Morrison, 1992: 87–8).

3.3.3 Tourism typologies

The analysis thus far has been about the nature of variables which make up internal motivation. In some studies these variables have been analysed with a view to developing typologies of tourists who carry out tourism roles. Much of the work was undertaken in the 1970s and early 1980s (Cohen, 1972; Dalen, 1989), some of which are reviewed by Lowyck, Van Langenhove and Bollaert (1992: 1–22).

In particular, they discuss the work of the Gallup Organization, commissioned by the American Express Travel Related Services Company in 1989. The aim of the study was to develop a traveller classification. It involved the initial interviewing of 6500 potential respondents in the USA, West Germany, United Kingdom and Japan, the world's four major generating economies. Of the 6500 respondents, 4000 were classified as travellers. In total they were estimated to have generated approximately 13 000 trips during the previous 12 months.

The study identified five distinctive types of people who experience travel in different ways regardless of origin or destination. The consumer profiles were recorded as follows:

- **Adventurers.** Adventurers are independent and confident. They like to try new activities, meet new people and experience different cultures. Generally, they are better educated and more affluent than the members of other groups. For the adventurers travel plays a central role in their lives. Beside, the adventurers are predominantly male and they tend to be younger than other travellers, with 44 per cent of the group being between the ages of 18 and 34.
- **Worriers.** Worriers experience considerable anxiety from the perceived stresses of travel, have little confidence in their ability to make travel decisions and are generally afraid to fly. Overall, worriers tend to be less educated and less affluent than other travellers in their country. Moreover, this category travels the least of the five groups and when they do, they are more likely to travel domestically. Worriers are predominantly female and rather older than other travellers, nearly half over the age of 50.
- **Dreamers.** Dreamers are intrigued with the idea of travel and attach great importance to the meaning it can bring to their lives. Despite reading and talking a lot about new destinations, they have travel experiences that are usually less remarkable than their ideas, and more often oriented toward relaxation than adventure. The dreamers belong to the modest income and education categories and they are usually women aged 50 and over. Most dreamers rely on maps and guidebooks when they travel to new places.
- **Economizers.** Travel provides economizers with a routine outlet for relaxation and is not perceived as an experience that adds meaning to their lives. The economizers seek value in travel and they do not think it is worth paying extra for specialist amenities and services, even if they can afford them. Economizers are more likely

to be men than women and they are slightly older than their travelling counterparts. These people have an average income level and are slightly less educated. They take an average of two trips per year.

- **Indulgers.** Indulgers are generally wealthier than other travellers and they are willing to pay for additional comfort and better service when they travel. The indulgers are more likely than other travellers to stay in large hotels because they like to be pampered. This group of travellers are second only to adventurers in the amount they travel and they are equally divided between men and women.

By categorizing different segments in this way it is possible to determine likely travel patterns and potential destinations.

3.3.4 Plog's typology

The construction of a typology is invaluable in that it enables the marketer to segment according to behavioural aspects, especially if the studies include analysis by lifestyle. The work of Plog (1987) is especially interesting as it links different typologies to psychographic analysis. In the earlier work he relates typologies to the life cycle theory of a destination, a point which is discussed below. Plog initially categorized travellers into eight segments as follows:

- **Venturesomeness.** The seeker and explorer. In terms of destinations, this person is the early explorer.
- **Pleasure seeking.** The traveller who seeks comfort and luxury in travel.
- **Impassivity.** The traveller makes his or her trip decisions speedily, at the last moment and without planning.
- **Self-confidence.** The traveller is interested in unique and unusual experiences.
- **Planfulness.** They think about a trip and plan it well in advance, looking more towards packaged tours.
- **Masculinity.** Action oriented males seeking outdoor activities. Partners reluctantly participate or stay at home.
- **Intellectualism.** The traveller is driven by an interest in history and culture.
- **People orientation.** The traveller seeks to get closer to people through travel and experiencing the cultures of the world.

However Plog (1974: 55–8) is best known for his broader categorization of travellers into three typologies:

- **Allocentrics:** explorer type of person who seeks undeveloped and unspoilt destinations.
- **Pyschocentrics:** not at all adventuresome, seeking the familiar rather than the unusual.
- **Midcentrics:** those who lie somewhere in the middle of the spectrum.

He argues that an undiscovered destination will appeal primarily to allocentrics, i.e. those seeking more of an adventurer-explorer type of holiday, whereas when a resort reaches maturity it attracts predominately pscyhocentrics. It is an appealing theoretical construct, one which gained favour in the 1980s but has since been the subject of criticism on methodological grounds. Smith (1990: 40–3) focuses on the inapplicability of the results to countries other than the USA. In response Plog (1991: 43–5) has argued that Smith did not replicate the original methodology used and therefore refutes the basic criticisms of the initial research. Plog's research, originally undertaken for an American airline, has undoubtedly been influential in the literature and is likely to remain as such until the model is updated by state of the art research.

3.3.5 External influencing factors

The link between internal and external driving forces provides an insight as to how visitors learn about, and more importantly perceive, tourism offerings in the marketplace. Therefore, marketers need to recognize the impact of external influences. Prime external factors include culture, age and gender, social class, lifestyle, life cycle and reference groups.

(a) Culture

Culture may be defined as 'a set of beliefs, values, attitudes, habits and forms of behavior that are shared by a society and are transmitted from generation to generation' (Bennett and Kassarjian, 1972: 123).

In terms of self image and the satisfaction of underlying tensions, most people seek to satisfy their desires in a way which fits into societal norms. For example, it is acceptable to be a green consumer in tourism, but sex tourism is viewed disparagingly. Awareness of cultural shifts is equally important. For example, smokers are increasingly being prohibited from smoking in social places, especially by transport carriers and in restaurants.

Other aspects of culture which are appropriate to motivational studies are:

- **Institutions, such as the church, the media and educational systems which affect cultural patterns.** The church, for example, seeks to retain a special day for worship and hence is reluctant to sanction secularization of this day, often in opposition to the promoters of tourism.
- **Language.** The transmission of culture is primarily through the spoken and written word, but also includes symbolic gestures, including the way in which people are expected to be greeted, degrees of formality, etc. The use of the formal as opposed to informal language in tourism transactions is very important in many cultures.
- **Societal practices.** This includes how we divide the day, our attitudes towards opening hours of facilities, driving laws, etc. For example, it is accepted practice for public houses to close at 11pm or midnight in the UK, whereas in many Mediterranean countries it is common for bars and cafes to remain open until at least 3am in the morning.
- **Subcultures.** Most societies comprise a number of subcultures which exhibit variations of behaviour as a result of ethnicity or regional differentiation.

(b) Age and gender

One traditional way of segmenting markets has been by age. As people reach different ages they tend to exhibit different values and requirements than younger groups. For example, participation in activity holidays drops dramatically among the 55 plus age group, in contrast to passive coaching holidays.

In some societies gender can be important in terms of societal expectations of the roles men and women should play. Research undertaken by Hofstede (1985) divides societies into those which are primarily masculine and those which are mainly feminine in domains. In the former, men are expected to be assertive and individualistic in comparison to women in performing caring roles. In the latter, the division of feminine roles is less clear; sharing and quality of life are the main factors. Thus, Hofstede suggests that countries such as Austria, Germany and Japan feature masculinity, whereas Nordic countries tend to fall more in line with femininity domains. Generalized cultural frameworks can be misleading, but this does provide an interesting analytical pursuit, especially when devising international marketing campaigns.

(c) Social class

As a rule, the higher the level of disposable income a person has the more likely they are to travel. Premium income earners tend to be those people who have studied at a higher educational level. These two factors are encapsulated in the concept of social class defined by Kotler *et al.* (1996: 183) as 'relatively permanent and ordered divisions in a society whose members share similar values, interests, and behaviors'. Social class is still considered to be one of the most important external factors, assessed primarily by occupation and level of income. Whilst the concept has been subject to criticism for being too narrow an indicator of consumption, it still remains one of the fundamental categorizations of socioeconomic grouping. To improve accuracy, it tends to be assessed in relation to the concept of lifestyle.

(d) Lifestyle

This area of study is known as psychographic analysis, which attempts to measure activities, interests and opinions. By profiling groups of people by the way they live it is possible to predict their travel motivations and purchases. One of the best known categorizations in this area has been the Values and Life Styles (VALS) typology framework developed by SRI International. This American study divided the population into nine lifestyle groups defined according to factors such as self image, aspirations, values and products used. Farnsworth-Riche (1989: 25–31) describes the eight lifestyles as follows:

- **Fulfilleds:** These are affluent, home based people from a well educated background. They have a good understanding of society, are receptive to change and exhibit a conscious desire for value for money. They are principle orientated.
- **Believers:** They too are principle orientated but less wealthy than the fulfilleds. They are more rigid in their purchasing patterns, favour American goods and prefer established brands. They are pro-establishment and this is reflected in their interest in the family, church and local community.
- **Achievers:** Work orientation is important within this group but not to the exclusion of the family. They tend to be conservative in outlook and favour existing political structures, established brands and like to show off their ascendancy in society, i.e. they are status orientated.
- **Strivers:** They too are status orientated. They are akin to achievers but do not have a similar resource base or income. They aim to emulate those who have more.
- **Experiencers:** They are younger, proactive types who are very social and like physical exercise. They like to influence their environment. They are inveterate

consumers of fashion items and convenience goods. They are action orientated and try new products and services.

- **Makers:** They are more self-sufficient than experiencers but still seek to influence their environments, although attention is focused on the family, work and locality. Unlike, experiencers they are not much influenced by fashion; they seek primarily functional goods and services.
- **Actualizers:** This group comprises very high income earners who therefore have freedom to explore. Image is of paramount importance in the expression of taste and style. They are receptive to new ideas and products but these will more often than not reflect the esoteric dimensions of life.
- **Strugglers:** They are opposite to actualizers in that they have a poor resource base. They have low incomes and stick to tried and tested brands. Without resource they are not explorers in the marketplace.

This type of analysis is similar to the Acorn classification used in the UK which is used extensively in exercises undertaken by tourism marketers.

(e) Life cycle

The concept of the family life cycle is based on the premise that when people live together their way of life changes. If they subsequently have children their lifestyle changes more radically, as does their level of financial and other commitments. The life cycle model is outlined below in Table 3.1.

Table 3.1 The family life cycle (European/North American Model)

Stage	Characteristics	Tourism behaviour
1. Early childhood	Entirely dependent on parent or guardian. Classic sea and sand holidays	Seeking seaside or inland resorts with entertainment facilities for children
2. Early teenager	More influence on decision making process but still dependent on parent	Resort based holidays with nightlife. Also youth hostels and semi-independent activity holidays. Group based holidays
3. Young person	Young, singles not living at home	Holiday taking dependent on time and resources, therefore wide ranging – 'sunlust' to activities. High on adventure, backpacking and experiences
4. Partnership stage	Couples living together and busier lifestyles. Time is a major barrier to travel	Wide ranging, more short breaks to fit in with dual careers
5. Family stage – early	Includes single parent or separated partners. Financial and school constraints are key factors. Seeking family centred holidays	Key interest in main holidays, or visiting VFR at other times
6. Family stage – late	Still major constraints regarding education. Holiday taking patterns breaking up	Mix of holidays and children seeking semi-independence
7. Empty nest	Children leave home and parent or parents have increased freedom and spending power	Wide ranging but higher prosperity to take more expensive explorer holidays and second breaks
8. Retired	One person or partners retired; income fixed but time available	Continued search for quality. As age increases seeking more passive holidays. Old age no longer a barrier to travel

Notes

This generalized model does not include the increasing number of people who remain single or do not have a family. It does however recognize different family structures, particularly single parent families.

This type of model works well when investigating what might be referred to as the traditional nuclear family featuring two parents and one or more children. It does not, however, purport to represent the increasing proportion of households which do not fall into this pattern, such as single parent families, extended family networks, and those who remain single throughout their life (Bojanic, 1992: 61–79; Lawson, 1991: 12–18).

Oppermann (1995: 535–52) and Pearce (1993: 121) introduce a concept which is described as the travel life cycle or travel career, i.e. the hypothesis that travel patterns and destinations vary as people move through their life cycle. Oppermann also explores the pattern of change between different generations.

(f) Reference groups

Learning also takes place through sharing values and expectations with others in a variety of social groups, including the family, college, workplace, or church. This brings exposure to a normative set of values, i.e. those which set a moralistic tone as to how we should behave in society.

Thus, it is argued that such a combination of internal and external forces leads to a process of buyer behaviour in tourism. They are best regarded as push factors but there are also pull factors which include both the buying situation and the marketing efforts of competing tourism services and destinations.

3.3.6 The buying situations

Theorists have also pointed to the variability of buying situations which will have some degree of influence on the buying process. There are two dimensions to discuss.

(a) The nature of the purchase

The first relates to the nature of the purchase. According to Howard-Sheth (1969) there are three levels of commitment depending on the nature of the purchase:

- **Extended problem solving.** The situation depends on the nature and risk involved in the purchase. For example, there is a considerable difference in terms of level of expenditure and risk in buying a same day excursion and a long haul holiday. The latter will involve a deep level of commitment, a detailed search for information, and an extensive comparison of the alternatives.
- **Limited problem solving.** In this situation the visitor will have some degree of knowledge or experience already, but many factors will be taken for granted and the information search will be far more limited. A second holiday at a favourite Mediterranean destination will be purchased in this way.
- **Habitual problem solving.** This is a repeat purchase of a tried and tested short break or day excursion which requires little or no evaluation. The purchase is made primarily on the basis of a previous satisfactory experience and a good understanding of the destination or brand name of the tourism offering.

(b) Role adoption

The second dimension relates to the relative importance of roles adopted by families and friends as outlined in the model by Engel, Blackwell and Miniard (1990: 174).

This model recognizes five roles:

- **Initiator:** the person who starts the purchasing process and who gathers information, i.e. the person in the group who sees the need to satisfy a desire to travel.
- **Influencer:** a person or persons who express preferences in choice, selection of information, etc. This can be a group of friends, relatives or a partner. Spiro (1983: 393–402) specifies different types of influence from low involvement to emotional influences.
- **Decider:** the person who has the financial control, and possibly the authority within a group of people to make the purchase, for example, the mother in a family.
- **Buyer:** the person who actually makes the purchase, visits the travel agent, and sorts the details.
- **User:** the person or persons who consume the service, i.e. those who actually go on the holiday.

Individuals rarely make travel decisions in isolation to others. Family and friends become involved in the process and complicate what looks in essence to be a simple sequence. Furthermore, the stages leading to purchase and adoption are not discrete. They tend to overlap and the roles adopted by people vary between stages. For example, attitudes towards a destination are most likely formed or re-confirmed at the same time as evaluation of the purchase is taking place. Furthermore, the attitudes of the influencer might be very different from the decider. The children in a family (influencers) might prefer a busy seaside resort where there are discotheques and entertainment while the mother, the decider, prefers a nearby resort where there is some degree of tranquillity. The literature regarding this aspect of buyer behaviour is limited; there is a case for more detailed empirical research to test the theoretical perspective.

3.4 THE CONSUMER BUYING PROCESS

The consumer buying process is often regarded as being similar in tourism to the purchase of other products and services. The assumption is that a consumer moves through a number of stages leading up to purchase as outlined in Figure 3.3.

The stages in the model can be explained as follows:

Stage I: Awareness

Before a tourism offering can be considered, underlying motivations have to be aroused, or to surface as a desire to solve a problem or state of tension. There will also be at the same time a number of inhibitors, such as concerns about buying a different type of holiday, or lack of time availability. These can lead to a period of passivity or possibly terminate the search process. At this stage the process involves vague images or at most a limited degree of knowledge about a destination or service.

Stage II: Search and comprehension

This second stage involves the buyer obtaining more information (Ryan, 1991). This constitutes an attempt to assess the benefits a service or a destination might offer. It

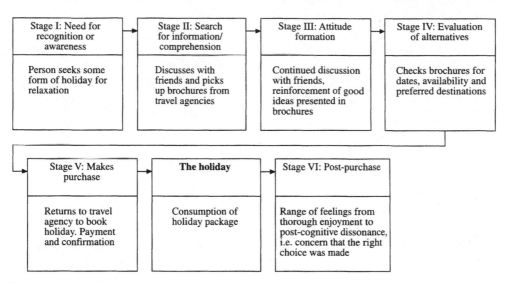

Figure 3.3 Generic consumer buyer behaviour process.

could well involve the assessment of a number of brands or destinations which might meet the requirements of the visitor.

Stage III: Attitude development

This depends on the nature of stimuli received in the previous stage. It also depends on whether the purchase is high involvement (expensive and risk laden) or low involvement (routine and not risky). Consulting others, checking out information, drawing on previous experiences will either reinforce an existing attitude or bring a change on the part of the buyer.

Stage IV: Evaluation

The potential customer will make more detailed comparisons between competing offerings and will move to a preference. A consumer will determine a set of choice criteria such as price, recommendation, convenience, convention, etc. during this stage. Only then will a consumer be in a position to match the benefits offered to their needs. If the match is suitable she or he will proceed to purchase if convinced about the potential benefits.

Stage V: Purchase

The consumer will buy the tourism offering subject to time and financial constraints. The latter two factors could still precipitate a withdrawal from purchase at this late stage.

Stage VI: Adoption and post-purchase behaviour

If the experience is satisfactory the visitor will be well disposed to purchase the type of holiday again. It is possible that a consumer will have misgivings about the purchase or after the holiday trip because actuality did not meet expectations or because the alternatives to such a holiday appear very attractive in comparison. In such circumstances the feeling of concern or anxiety held by the visitor is referred to as cognitive dissonance.

In this form, the model assumes an economic rationality which is not necessarily a mirror of actuality. It nevertheless forms the basis of many of the integral models outlined below.

3.5 INTEGRAL MODELS OF CONSUMER BEHAVIOUR

A number of comprehensive consumer behaviour models have been applied to tourism such as Wahab (1976), Schmoll (1977) and Mathieson and Wall (1982: 27). They draw primarily from the earlier consumer behaviour studies of the 1960s and 1970s, and in particular the work of Engel *et al.* (1968), Howard and Sheth (1969), or the Nicosia model (1966). They could well be classified as behaviourist in approach in that the implicit assumption of all of the models is that the consumer progresses through a series of stages, and proceeds in a rational way, to purchase a product or service (or alternatively to eventually reject the idea). One of the most comprehensive models is that of Mathieson and Wall (1982: 27) which is illustrated in Figure 3.4.

The early consumer models of the 1960s, however, have been subject to criticism by a number of authors (Roberston, 1974: 271–95; Foxall, 1991: 195–206). In applying

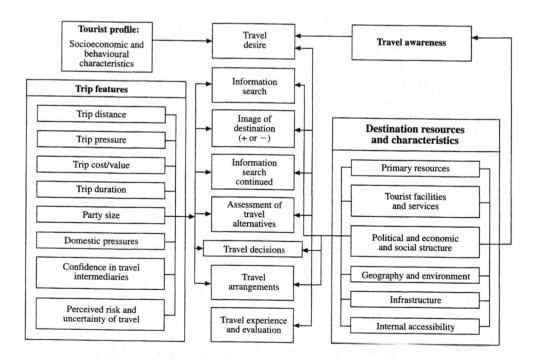

Figure 3.4 The tourist decision-making process. *Source*: Mathieson and Wall (1982). Reprinted by permission of Addison Wesley Longman Ltd.

similar criticisms to the adaption of the models to tourism, Cooper *et al.* (1993: 20–31) provide a useful critique, highlighting a number of commonalities which perhaps require further investigation:

- the models conceptualize consumer behaviour as a decision-making process;
- they focus on the individual rather than incorporating the role of deciders, influencers and gatekeepers played by family and friends;
- they suggest that the consumer is involved in a rational process involving search and evaluation of information sources in a systematic way;
- they imply that buyer behaviour is purposive, i.e. the consumer drives the process along in a deterministic manner;
- they infer that consumers move from limited awareness to a point where they establish specific choice criteria;
- the models feature some form of feedback which relate to future purchases.

Other criticisms of the models are that they do not attribute degrees of importance to causal factors in the buying process *vis à vis* filters or barriers. Nor do they incorporate degrees of involvement which vary according to each particular buying situation.

The models are useful in understanding the factors which underpin consumer buying behaviour in tourism but it would appear that they represent no more than that. They certainly could not be used to explain buyer behaviour in a universal sense; they are too arbitrary to meet such an exactment. There is, therefore, a case for reappraising the way in which we approach the area of study. As Foxall (1991: 128–50) notes:

> ... consumer researchers should recognize more readily the variety inherent in consumer decision making and explore the domains of applicability of the comprehensive and other models of choice. This requires not so much a radical conceptual departure as a re-emphasis on the establishment of a plurality of frames of reference based on the situational determinants of choice.

Thus, while existing models are integral, in terms of offering an explanation of causality, they require reappraisal.

Some of the most successful studies relate to the practicalities of the marketplace. A good example is Ehrenberg's Dirichlet model (1995) which suggests that despite the complexity of markets different brands in any market enjoy a similar degree of loyalty. The variation between brands tends to move in line with market share. Furthermore, while consumers buy more than one brand, they have a propensity to favour one above others (Duckworth, 1996: 30). This work enables the tourism marketer to begin to understand the intricacies of consumer behaviour and brand development management.

3.5.1 Other aspects of consumer behaviour

On-site observation

One area of consumer behaviour that is often overlooked is how people behave at tourism facilities such as at a major theme park or at an event. Observational and pyschological studies have assisted tourism operational staff to design systems and processes which maximize satisfaction or minimize irritation. In an interesting study on the psychology of waiting Maister (1984: 2–3) suggests that visitors perceive unexplained waits to be longer than explained waits. He discovered that pre-process waits feel longer than in-process waits, and that solo waits are longer than group waits. This is why major theme parks, such as Alton Towers in the UK, have designed queuing systems which inform visitors as to how long they will have to wait, seek to entertain them en route and encourage people to talk to each other while standing in a queue. It makes waiting for the ride all the more bearable.

Such practical applications point to the increasing importance of understanding in detail aspects of consumer behaviour which can help to shape processes and elements of physical evidence in the marketing mix.

3.6 SUMMARY The marketer has to be aware of the wide ranging number of internal motivational factors, external influences and the formative stages in the buying process associated with tourism offerings. It is impossible to take into account every permutation that might occur in the buying process but the general framework provides guidance. It has, however, major limitations.

The factors which influence buying behaviour in tourism are those drawn from wider consumer marketing studies. Most authors suggest that the buying process is affected by internal driving forces such as perception and attitude formation and external influences such as social class and lifestyle. Whilst general principles have been applied to the tourism market, there is a need for more research to identify ways in which tourism might differ from other business sectors.

Perhaps of increasing importance to the marketer are the more particularistic studies which seek to identify why people do or do not purchase specific types of holidays or destinations. Such studies tend to focus on an evaluation of criteria for choice and how well a destination might meet these (Witt and Wright, 1990: 1–16).

Thus, the marketer needs to consider how his or her offering might meet the specific motivations of groups of existing and potential visitors. Ryan (1994) indicates that there is also a need to research levels of holiday satisfactions to ascertain what might be acceptable to holidaymakers.

REFERENCES

Bennett, P.D. and Kassarjian H.J. (1972) *Consumer Behavior,* Prentice Hall, Englewood Cliffs, New Jersey.

Bojanic, D.C. (1992) A Look at a Modernized Family Life Cycle and Overseas Travel. *Journal of Travel and Tourism Marketing,* **1**(1), 61–79.

Canadian Tourism Commission (1989) *Pleasure Travel Markets to North America.* Canadian Tourism Commission.

Chisnall, P.M. (1985) *Marketing: a behavioural analysis,* 2nd edition, McGraw-Hill, London.

Cohen, E. (1972) Toward a sociology of international tourism. *Social Research,* **39**, 164–82.

Cooper, C., Fletcher, J., Gilbert, D. and Wanhill, S. (1993) *Tourism, Principles and Practice,* Pitman, London.

Dalen, E. (1989) Research into values and consumer trends in Norway. *Tourism Management,* Sept. 183–6.

Duckworth, S. (1996) Market Modelling: Any Common Threads? *Admap,* December, 30.

Ehrenberg (1995) *Dirichlet-type markets: a review (parts I and II),* South Bank Business School, London.

Engel, J.F., Blackwell, R.D. and Miniard, P.W. (1990) *Consumer Behavior,* Dryden, Orlando.

Engel, J.F., Kollat, D.T. and Blackwell, R.D. (1968) *Consumer Behaviour,* Holt, Rinehart and Winston, New York.

Farnsworth-Riche, M. (1989) Psychographics for the 1990s. *American Demographics,* July, 25–31.

Foxall, G.R. (1980) Marketing Models of Buyer Behaviour: A Critical Review. *European Research,* **8**, 195–206.

Foxall, G.R. (1991) Consumer Behaviour. In *The Marketing Book* (ed. M.J. Baker), Macmillan.

Hofstede, G. (1985) The Cultural Process. In *People and Organizations Interacting* (ed. A. Brakel), John Wiley, New York.

Holman, R. (1984) A Values and Life Styles Perspective on Human Behaviour. In *Personal Values and Consumer Psychology* (eds R.E. Pitts and A.G. Woodside), Lexington Books, Lexington.

Howard, J.A. and Sheth, J.N. (1969) *The Theory of Buyer Behaviour,* Wiley, New York.

Kahle, L.R, Beatty, S.E. and Homer, P. (1986) Alternative Measurement Approaches to Consumer Values: The List of Values and Values and Life Styles (VALS). *Journal of Consumer Research,* **13**, 405–9.

Kassarjian, H.H. and Sheffet, M.J. (1982) Personality and Consumer Behaviour – An Update. In *Perspectives in Consumer Behaviour* (eds H.H. Kassarjian and T.S. Robertson), Scott Foresman & Co.

Kotler, P., Bowen, J. and Makens, J.(1996) *Marketing for Hospitality and Tourism,* Prentice Hall, Upper Saddle River.

Krippendorf, J. (1987) *The Holiday-makers: understanding the impact of travel and tourism,* Butterworth-Heinemann, Oxford.

Lawson, R. (1991) Patterns of Tourist Expenditure and Types of Vacation Across the Family Life Cycle. *Journal of Travel Research,* **29**(4), 12–18.

Lowyck, E., Van Longenhove, L. and Bollaert, L. (1990) Typologies of Tourist Roles. A paper presented to Tourism in the 1990s. Durham, September, pp. 20–6.

Maister, D.H. (1984) The Psychology of Waiting in Lines. In *Harvard Business School Note 9–684–064,* May, 2–3.

Maslow, A.H. (1954) *Motivation and Personality,* Harper and Row, New York.

Mathieson, A. and Wall, G. (1982) *Tourism, Economic, Physical and Social Impacts,* Longman, Harlow.

McIntosh, R.W., Goeldner, C.R. and Ritchie, J.R. (1995) *Tourism, Principles, Practices and Philosophies,* 7th edition, Wiley, New York.

Mill, R.C. and Morrison, A.M. (1992) *The Tourism System,* Prentice Hall, Englewood Cliffs, New Jersey.

Nicosia, F.M. (1966) *Consumer Decision Process,* Prentice Hall, Englewood Cliffs, New Jersey.

Oppermann, M. (1995) Travel Life Cycle. *Annals of Tourism Research,* **22**(3), 535–52.

Pearce, P.L. (1993) Fundamentals of tourist motivation. In *Tourism and Research: critiques and challenges* (eds D. Pearce and W. Butler), Routledge, London.

Plog, S.C. (1974) Why destination areas rise and fall in popularity. *Cornell Hotel and Restaurant Quarterly,* **14**(4), 55–8.

Plog, S.C. (1987) Understanding Psychographics in Tourism Research. In *Travel, Tourism and Hospitality Research, A Handbook for Managers and Researchers* (eds J.R.B. Ritchie and C.R. Goeldner), John Wiley & Sons, New York.

Plog, S.C. (1990) A carpenter's tools: an answer to Stephen L.J. Smith's review of psychocentricism/allocentricism. *Journal of Travel Research,* **28**(4), 43–5.

Robertson, T.S. (1974) A Critical Examination Adaption Process Models of Consumer Behaviour. In *Models of Buyer Behaviour* (ed. J.N. Sheth), Harper and Row, New York.

Ryan, C. (1991) *Recreational Tourism, A Social Science Perspective,* Routledge, London.

Ryan, C. (1994) *Researching Tourism Satisfaction – Issues, Concepts, Problems,* Routledge, London.

Schmoll, G.A. (1977) *Tourism Promotion,* Tourism International Press, London.

Smith, S.L.J. (1990) A test of Plog's allocentric/psychocentric model: evidence from seven nations. *Journal of Travel Research,* **28**(4), 40–3.

Spiro, R.L. (1983) Persuasion in Family Decision-Making. *Journal of Consumer Research,* **9** (March), 393–402.

Swarbrooke, J. (1996) Understanding The Tourist – Some Thoughts on Consumer Behaviour in Tourism. *Insights,* **8** (November), A67–76.

Wahab, S., Crampton, L.J. and Rothfield, L.M. (1976) *Tourism Marketing,* Tourism International Press, London.

Witt, C. and Wright, P. (1990) Tourism Motivation, Life After Maslow, a paper presented to Tourism into the 1990s, Durham, September pp. 1–16.

4 Organizational buyer behaviour

Deborah Radburn MSc, BA

OBJECTIVES

This chapter explains:

- the underlying principles of organizational behaviour;
- the differences between consumer, group and organizational buyer behaviour;
- the buyer behaviour process;
- the appropriateness of the models of organizational buyer behaviour in the rapidly changing tourism marketing environment.

4.1 INTRODUCTION

Tourism marketers need to understand both the decision criteria used, and the process of the decision making undergone by groups and organizations in buying tourism services. It is not a particularly easy area to define. In the UK the business to business, or business to group market is often referred to as the travel trade. It is an imprecise term which includes a collection of businesses which package meetings, tours and conventions for consumers, groups and organizations. The travel trade therefore includes a host of intermediaries such as tour operators, coaching companies, group tour organizers, as well as incentive and conference intermediaries which are discussed below.

The chapter refers primarily to the buying of hospitality services, which includes small scale meetings to much larger conferences and congresses. The most important host locations for conventions and conferences are in the USA, followed by France and the UK (Davidson, 1994: A115–22). It is difficult to indicate with precision the scale of business. Rouse (1996: 3), in reviewing a report commissioned by the European Union in 1995, estimates that the business trips, conventions, meetings, exhibitions and incentive travel market in EU countries is worth 162 billion ECUS. It is segmented in terms of value as follows:

Individual trips	71 per cent
Conventions	3 per cent
Meetings	13 per cent
Exhibitions	11 per cent
Incentive travel	2 per cent

Therefore, whilst the business travel market dominates, nearly 30 per cent of the business to business market can be attributed to group bookings. It is therefore an important sector in tourism and one which has yet to be researched in detail as compared to other areas.

4.2 THE PRINCIPLES OF ORGANIZATIONAL BUYER BEHAVIOUR

Like consumers, organizations ranging from schools to association meetings, need to satisfy wants. The marketing of venues for meetings and conventions is often complex and involves high risk in terms of expenditure, prestige and other factors. For example, consider the risk associated with the following event:

> Galileo, the travel and leisure computerized booking company, called in the Page and Moy Marketing group to organize a worldwide conference in Madrid last year. About 600 travel agency delegates attended the carefully choreographed event, which culminated in a sit-down meal for all delegates at the 18th century Palacio del Negralejo. In extravagant style, the West End cast of Buddy was flown in for one night to entertain guests.
>
> *(Witthaus, 1997: 36)*

The underlying principles are that:

- organizational buying behaviour is a rich and complex decision making process;
- the degree of involvement and risk depends on the nature of the buying process;
- the intensity of the negotiation process requires considerable professional skills on behalf of buyers and sellers;
- increasing technology and global opportunities are altering the process of purchasing.

4.3 DIFFERENCES IN CONSUMER AND ORGANIZATIONAL BUYER BEHAVIOUR

It has been argued that 'it is divisive to make a distinction between consumer and industrial marketing' (Baker, 1985: 115), but most authors differ from this point of view. They argue that unlike the individual consumer, a group or business has a more complex method of choosing a tourism service, and has to accommodate a wide variety of motivational influences before a decision can be reached.

What are the key differences between individual consumer and group decision making behaviour? Davis (1989) suggests that the essence of business marketing is specific segmentation. In comparison to individual consumer markets, it is often far easier to segment groups that will be interested in a product or service. Within such groups, which are often smaller than consumer segments, it is then possible to target, with some degree of accuracy, potential customers.

O'Reilly and Gibas (1995) suggest that group purchases involve a more complex sales-purchasing process. The group or business may have, for example, a professional buying department whose members tend to be well trained, knowledgeable and more demanding in their requirements than an average consumer. Often a purchase may entail large expenditure outlays and require a review of far more technical detail. For both the buyer and seller, therefore, risk assessment criteria is far more important than in a consumer environment. The key differences are summarized in Table 4.1.

Table 4.1 Consumer and organizational buyer behaviour: key differences

Consumer buyer behaviour	Organizational buyer behaviour
One or two people involved in buying process	Several people involved
Relatively simple process but	Depending on nature of purchase, can be complicated
Informal	Formalized
No set formula to buying behaviour	Systematic sequence
Learned behaviour	Professional skill and training
Independent relationship between buyer and seller	Interdependent relationship between buyer and seller

4.4 THE CORE COMPONENTS OF BUYER BEHAVIOUR

4.4.1 Buyphases

Several marketers, many of whom have drawn on the work of Robinson, Faris and Wind (1967), have argued that groups proceed through a number of stages before reaching a final purchase decision. The conference market, for example, follows such a pattern of group decision making. The stages in the decision making process of conference organizers (often known as the 'buyphase'), can be described as follows:

- **Problem recognition.** May occur for internal reasons such as a training or sales meeting organizer requiring a conference venue.
- **General need description.** A corporate meeting planner may discuss with the human resource department the length of the training session, the need for food and beverage, accommodation provision, etc.
- **Product specification.** This may include specifications for certain sizes of meeting rooms or audio visual facilities.
- **Supplier search.** At this stage the conference organizer researches, by using trade directories, conference bureaux, or direct contact, venues which might be suitable to solve a problem, and provide a required specification.
- **Proposal solution.** Venues may offer a budgeted proposal to the enquiring company.
- **Supplier selection.** This may involve several of the key decision makers. A venue will be evaluated according to their decision criteria and negotiation of rates may occur.
- **Order routine specification.** A buyer will initiate the final order with the chosen venue; in turn the venue will inform the buyer of cut off dates for confirmation and guarantees for numbers at food and beverage functions.
- **Performance review.** This involves post purchase evaluation of the conference offering, and can affect whether the buyer will be prepared to buy from the company again.

These buyphases sometimes take a long period of time, depending on the size of the conference or complexity of arrangements, often with lead times of two or three years in some instances and longer in terms of mega events such as the Olympic Games.

4.4.2 Buyclasses: the nature of purchase

The process is also affected by the nature of the purchase, which in the Robinson *et al.* model is defined as buyclasses:

- **New task.** A high degree of risk involved as the client is buying a facility or service for the first time.
- **Modified rebuy.** The client has bought a service offering before, perhaps at another hotel or conference centre within the group, but now seeks to modify the purchase. This might mean a new venue or new specifications for service levels.
- **Straight rebuy.** This is less risk-laden as it involves, for example, re-ordering of a service at the same venue.

In the Robinson model the buyphases and buyclasses are brought together into a grid, illustrated in Figure 4.1, indicating how some phases would be ignored or would not be applicable in certain circumstances. For example, a rebuy of a conference facility which has been used several times previously would not involve a progression through the entire range of buyphase tasks.

4.4.3 The decision making unit

As in industrial buying behaviour, buying is also affected by various members of the firm's decision making unit (DMU). The concept of the decision making unit was introduced by Webster and Wind (1972: 33–67) who described it as 'all those individuals and groups who participate in the decision making process who share common goals and the risks arising from the decisions'.

Kotler, Bowen and Makens (1996: 218–19) have adapted the model to the conference market:

- **Users.** These are the delegates who actually attend and experience the conference. Their satisfaction with a venue may directly affect whether it is chosen again.

		Types of buying situation (buy classes)		
		Repeat routine buy	Modified rebuying	New purchase
Stages of buying (buy phases)	1 Identification of need, or modified need	No	Very often	Yes
	2 Specification of required product or service	No	Very often	Yes
	3 Search for potential suppliers	Sometimes	Sometimes	Yes
	4 Evaluation and selection of suppliers	Sometimes	Sometimes	Yes
	5 Review of performance and relationship building	Yes	Yes	Yes
	6 Sustained relationship	Yes	Possibly	Possibly

Figure 4.1 The buygrid model. *Source*: adapted from Robinson *et al.* (1967). Copyright Allyn and Bacon. Reprinted by permission.

- **Influencers.** They may help to define specifications for the venues and provide information to help evaluate alternatives. Influencers could be past presidents of associations, executive secretaries, spouses or regional managers.
- **Deciders.** They select conference or meeting requirements and suppliers. A company sales manager may select a hotel in one region and negotiate arrangements if a regional sales meeting is held in their area.
- **Buyers.** They have formal authority for selecting suppliers and arranging terms of purchase. This may, for example, be the accounts department.
- **Approvers.** They authorize the proposed actions of deciders and buyers. Therefore, although the sales manager may arrange bookings, contracts may need to be submitted to someone with greater authority for approval.
- **Gatekeepers.** There are a number of people who might adopt this role such as secretaries or receptionists. They can prevent or enable a member of a conference venue sales team from reaching the buying centre.

In order to close a sale within a business to business market it has been argued that the supplier has to identify and satisfy all six stakeholders in the decision making unit and treat each accordingly, although for small conferences certain people may hold more than one role. In the USA the 'deciders' and group leaders who have the most influence over the purchase are often referred to as the 'pied pipers', a rather appropriate phrase.

4.5 DECISION MAKING CRITERIA

Yeshin (1995) suggests that one major difference between consumer and business purchasing is the element of 'rationality' involved. He argues that business people have to spend in a way that delivers a sound return on investment or at least is perceived as doing this. Consumer purchases may often be rational to the buyer but are not so clearly accountable to other individuals as in a business purchasing environment. Bearing this in mind the supplier has to stress the logical, rational aspects of the purchase while also working on emotive aspects to influence the sale. This is especially important within a business service environment such as conference marketing when a destination or key conference event needs to be sold on the strength of its facilities and attractions as well as its value for money and image.

Having identified the key decision makers, and phases in the purchase process, the marketer then has to establish which criteria the decision makers use to differentiate between suppliers. These obviously change constantly according to buy classes and as business travel demands become more exacting. It is essential therefore that there is a continuous process of revaluation of market trends by the supplier. This becomes increasingly important when the group market is targeted. The dynamics of each segment need to be identified in order that the supplier can market profitably to them.

4.5.1 Influential factors

Webster and Wind (1972: 33–7) suggest that there are four main factors which influence the decision making criteria of group/organizational buyers.

- **Environmental.** Buyers are influenced by external factors such as current and expected economic environments. For example, in a recession, hospitality budgets may be cut by 30 per cent.

- **Organizational.** Each company has its own management structure, policies and procedures. Therefore, it is necessary for the sales team to be acquainted with these possible barriers. In particular, they need to know the company's policies or procedural constraints and how they impact on the buyers. They also need to be conversant with members of the DMU and the evaluation criteria which they perceive to be appropriate.
- **Interpersonal.** The buying centre usually involves several participants who have differing levels of interest and authority. In hospitality markets it may be difficult to ascertain group dynamics but sales people can learn about the nature of the personalities that shape the group culture. Is one or more of the team dominant?
- **Individual.** Each person in the buying decision process has personal motivations, perceptions, preferences and attitudes towards risk. Empathy at a personal level may help the buying-selling process.

4.6 THE SCHOOL GROUP MARKET

If these variables are applied, for example, to the school group market in the UK, environmental factors may refer to the allowance in the school/county budget for school trips. The organizational element could be represented by the need for school visits to be linked to the National Curriculum in order to justify expenditure to governing bodies. The interpersonal element would be manifested by the hierarchy of decision makers in a school. Even though the head or deputy head may not participate in the trip, they will probably have the final decision on budget allocation. Finally, the individual would be represented by the class teacher and pupils. Their specific needs and preferences must be met by the service providers in order to fulfil the participants' expectations.

As an example, Legoland at Windsor in the UK opened in 1996. It identified the four criteria mentioned above and developed group packages accordingly. A Legoland brochure was designed specifically to target the educational visit market. It is anticipated that there will be a need for financial incentives, providing discounted rates for group bookings as well as for the individual teacher travelling with the group as a major incentive. The service offering is based heavily on the National Curriculum, satisfying Key Stages 1–3, thereby enabling influencers in the decision making process to justify expenditure on the trip. Finally, the quality and variety of visit options on offer serves to motivate the individual participants to visit Legoland. For example, the educational packages include workshops, a 'miniland' and shows. Legoland also provides school lunch options and 'Windsor Goodie Bags'.

4.7 THE CONFERENCE MARKET

The conference and business travel market can be highly profitable for venue suppliers. There are a variety of terms used to segment the market, such as conference, convention, congress and colloqiums, but in reality the major differences are a function of the level and number attending an organized meeting or event. The logistics and risk, for example, are much higher when a purpose built conference centre in association with a group of hotels is handling 5000 delegates, than when a hotel is servicing a one day workshop for 80.

In both cases, however, the benefits can be considerable. An off peak conference booking at a hotel can serve to revitalize occupancy rates, increase expenditure by business visitors and their partners and raise the image of the venue. The market in the UK is dominated by one day non-residential conferences. One conference market survey (Richards, 1995: B69) indicates that 59.6 per cent of all conferences are for one day only. They attracted the highest number of delegates: 563 270 compared to only 161 541 staying in residential accommodation. Another survey, Conference and Incentive Travel (1995: 18), noted that hoteliers had recognized a sustained trend toward day only meetings. Nevertheless, residential delegates still generate more revenue per head than the day delegates. The 23 per cent of residential delegates in the conference market survey generated 64 per cent of the gross revenue to the host venue, with the average spend for a residential delegate being £164 as opposed to £26.50 for a non-resident.

Therefore, the tourism marketer has the primary task of encouraging group and corporate clients to purchase residential trips. In order to do this successfully, it has been argued that conference venues have to learn how to identify the members of the DMU, identify their key decision making criteria and target their marketing activities accordingly.

4.7.1 Innovative marketing

There is a need for innovative marketing to target the conference market. Richards and Richards (1994) note:

> Maximizing the economic return from conference and exhibition requires a clear understanding of the structure and needs of these markets. Conference and exhibition business is often treated as one segment by hotels, but the variability of markets within this basic category can be considerable.

Hartley and Witt (1994: 275) have also pointed to the lack of fine tuning in marketing to businesses and organizations by conference venues. Their research exercise indicates that responses to enquiries about booking conferences were generally impersonal and non-customized. Furthermore, the majority of key people responsible for conferences had not been trained in convention management and telesales. Most were not employed solely to organize conferences, therefore offered less expertise when dealing with the members of the prospective clients' DMU. This lack of attention to core service training has meant that venues have failed to impress and target key players in the DMU in the first crucial 'buyphase' of search and selection.

Purchase of business travel services such as conference facilities is therefore a more exacting task than many commentators have previously suggested. A conference can represent a significant financial risk for a company or association and is often also a matter of prestige. Depending on the size or length of the conference, the procedure of service specification, supplier search and selection is undertaken with precision, and forward planning. As segments in the conference market are so fragmented it is difficult to generalize about the decision criteria used to choose a venue. In general terms, the market is divided into corporate (businesses) and association (professional, political, societal) clients. However, within these two categories are several sub-segments, each of which have their own particular specifications and needs.

4.7.2 Criteria for the choice of a conference venue

The key tangible and intangible aspects of a conference venue that a conference organizer may look for when making the purchase decision are listed below but not necessarily in order of priority (Radburn, 1996):

- time of year – whether the destination is attractive in this season;
- accessibility – air, road, rail;
- facilities – audiovisual, IT, secretarial;
- recreation and sporting facilities;
- high quality accommodation and facilities in bedrooms;
- variety of meeting and break out rooms;
- catering and banqueting rooms;
- location;
- parking;
- exhibition facilities;
- fast, simple, efficient booking service;
- value for money;
- priority check in and check out facilities;
- efficient and polite staff;
- reputation of site management and staff;
- security;
- image of destination;
- attraction facilities of local area;
- previous destination of conference;
- facilities for partners;
- good acoustics and lighting in meeting rooms;
- availability of technical equipment or the ease of use of such, therefore even the location of electricity sockets;
- proximity to main hall of telephones, toilets, cloakrooms and catering.

The Meetings Industry Association (1996: 60) undertook a survey which sought to investigate the key criteria used for choosing a venue. The results showed that quality of meeting facilities, availability and a good standard of service were rated as important. Poor service and a disappointing staff attitude were singled out as the areas of greatest dissatisfaction. The training and reward of staff who serve delegates should be high on the agenda.

Another interesting study in the USA (Oppermann, 1996: 175–82) investigated the importance of certain convention destination attributes to association meeting planners, evaluating 30 North American convention destinations. The author compares results from his survey with three other current studies. Factors such as hotel service, quality of services, facilities, access and availability figure prominently in the research findings, although respondents indicated a multiplicity of reasons for choosing particular venues.

The results of Oppermann's survey are illuminating. It reveals significant differences between the planning of small and large scale conventions in terms of criteria used. Second, it highlights the importance of previous experience with a destination. Most of all, it indicates variability in terms of destination appeal.

What this and other studies appear to illustrate is that there is no standard benchmark that marketers of conferences and conventions can use to accurately identify decision making criteria.

4.7.3 Role of intermediaries

There is one further consideration which tourism marketers need to take into account, and that is the role and influence of the intermediary in the market. On some occasions intermediaries are engaged on behalf of the end user to be involved throughout the decision making process. These intermediaries have specialized skills, know the market well enough to gain considerable purchasing power over suppliers, and can dedicate a greater amount of time to supplier search and selection. The use of intermediaries in the purchase process demands a more sophisticated marketing strategy by service providers as they can act as a barrier between the potential client and the supplier.

The following are examples of independent intermediaries whose services are employed by group/organizational parties.

(a) Conference organizers

Organizing a conference involves many external as well as internal customers such as caterers, security personnel, technical assistants, interpreters and entertainment providers. Both corporate and association sectors are beginning to realize that to co-ordinate all activities at once is very time consuming. This has prompted the growth in service agencies, specializing in conference organization and marketing. Whether they are called conference placement agencies, conference brokers, venue brokers or finders their functions vary depending on the needs of the customer. Independent conference organizers such as these may solely concentrate on organizing accommodation, transport, catering and entertainment or may be involved with the whole package seeking out suitable speakers and marketing the conference to delegates.

(b) International hotel services

Accommodation providers themselves have realized the potential problems that exist for conference organizers, i.e. end users seeking a venue. They have attempted to reduce the time taken in the decision making process by providing more detailed information at the enquiry stage to enable them to move towards selection. Emphasis has been placed on the informative and often glossy brochure which aims to provide all the information a company or association may need.

Major multinational hotel chains such as Marriott, for example, are gaining a competitive edge over other intermediaries in this respect by offering a conference organization package based at any given hotel in its range; this is branded as Meeting 2000. By moving into conference organization as well as accommodation and catering provision, hotels are attempting to cut out the intermediary, as mentioned above. This enables them to deal directly with the people who have direct purchasing power and form relationships with them.

(c) Conference bureaux

In addition to independent conference organizers is the national or local conference bureau. This bureau may act as the first place for initial enquiries about conference bookings. As cities continue to develop their conference business within the local economy, an increasing number of local authorities and private consortia are establishing conference desks, such as 'Marketing Manchester'. They have a responsibility to promote the region's facilities and again make the process of information search easier for the decision makers. A study conducted by the Scottish Tourist Board and the Scottish Development Agency estimated the value of conference visits to the country to be in the region of £250–300 million. This represents a large proportion of Scotland's £2 billion tourism industry (Baird, 1996: 24). In the 1995 Conference Market Survey undertaken by Richards (1995: B67), hotels were found to benefit most from bureau bookings. This suggests that collective marketing could well prove to be an appropriate line of direction for future strategy development.

(d) Travel managers

Increasingly business travellers are using their own company travel manager to negotiate rates on conference packages. This position can involve many of the roles within the DMU depending on how much responsibility is designated to his/her function within a corporation. For example, in a survey in the USA (Seaton and Bennett, 1992: 321), the corporate travel manager was found to be responsible for 33 per cent of all conference reservations. The advantages in terms of cost reductions and time saving may in these cases justify the salary of the employee.

(e) Expert systems

With the increase in the development of information technology, expert systems are now being developed to make or suggest decisions on corporate travel arrangements. These systems comprise a knowledge base of observations and research, which provide benchmarks relating to a number of factors, such as quality, cost and service procedures. This is then translated into a scoring system so that every alternative can be evaluated. The Thomas Cook Travel Management Centre has recently undertaken research into developing a system which will offer a comprehensive counselling package for prospective clients. The aim is to integrate data on transport and destinations, and, with the use of multimedia technology, make the end service more user friendly (Sussmann, 1995).

(f) Hospitality and destination managers

These are similar to conference organizers, as the service offered is essentially a comprehensive group booking management service. Increasingly, such companies offer a one telephone call group reservations service. Such custom designed packages are targeted to special interest group tours, incentive programmes, meeting and convention organizers. They aim to gain competitive advantage by emphasizing that their staff have specialist destination knowledge, established relationships and purchasing ability to secure suitable venues and packages. These companies are moving to a position where they offer to share some of the responsibility for the success of the group or organizational trip, thereby decreasing the risk factor for the client.

4.8 REAPPRAISAL OF COMMERCIAL BUYER BEHAVIOUR

The challenge to marketers of service provision to group and organizational travel is therefore increasing, as the buying process becomes more fragmented, and as decision makers more often use intermediaries and impersonal technological sources during key buyphases. The question remains as to how robust the traditional transactional models are, given this type of marketing environment. Unlike industrial markets which are becoming more concentrated, tourism markets continue to grow territorially, despite vertical and horizontal integration of the hospitality sector.

A new and continually evolving purchasing environment perhaps requires a modified approach which places less emphasis on management rationality and transactional analysis and takes into account the increasing interaction of the buyer and seller in the buying process. The interactionist approach has been discussed by Häkansson (1982). He stresses that industrial buyer behaviour is primarily about motivations and interactions both between buyers and between buyers and sellers. Kotler *et al.* (1996: 217–18) also makes reference to the consultative nature of organizational buying in tourism. Recently, this approach has been referred to as relationship marketing where 'the emphasis is not on bringing about exchange processes, but on building relationships' (Woodruffe, 1995: 95). The concept is discussed in detail in Chapter 15.

There are two other key considerations for the tourism marketer in the conference and hospitality sector which relate to buyer behaviour. The first is globalization, the second the growing sophistication of information technology in the sector.

4.8.1 Globalization of travel management

Large corporations increasingly seek to go global and to use this as a source of competitive advantage. In terms of the effect on business travel, globalization of travel management companies would mean that intermediaries who are employed to replace key players in the buyphases and the DMU, would gain considerable purchasing power over tourism service suppliers and would seek to curtail suppliers efforts to create relationships with the users in the DMU.

Obviously, the end user still has financial power over the employed intermediaries. However, their key role in the search and selection process will mean that suppliers will have to court the end user more eagerly. Global travel agreements may also necessitate that suppliers conform to a certain quality service level, although service encounters could never be one hundred per cent duplicated. There is evidence of customer pressure for globalization. An increasing number of multinational companies want a uniform service across the globe (*Travel Trade Gazette*, 1996: 21).

4.8.2 Effects of information technology

For suppliers, the new technological advances offer another medium by which they can promote their services and communicate with their customers. Several convention and visitors bureaux, for example, have taken advantage of the World Wide Web, by having a site which includes a meeting industry portion with a convention calendar, convention centre layouts and services and theme function venues. For those purchasing group travel products, the speed of accessibility to information may decrease lead times in booking venues and will also enable far greater choice, without having to pass through the complicated and time consuming 'buy phase' of supplier search and selection. Furthermore, expert systems are likely to become more accessible to the group travel organizer. They will not only provide information but also qualitative opinions on which decisions to make given a set of specifications. This may mean that such systems also become one of the key influencers of the buying decision process.

Central reservation systems will also enable faster response rates than at present. The additional services they are offering to tourism suppliers will assist them to source client requests against availability information more easily. This will enable a booking procedure to be more efficient and personalized.

These current and future innovations will undoubtedly have an effect on the entire process. Even if it is not immediate both the traditional concepts of the DMU and buyphases will need to be modified to reflect a revised pattern of purchasing corporate tourism services.

4.9 SUMMARY
Organizational buying behaviour of services is complex compared to consumer buying processes in that more people are usually involved in a formal procedure. In order for marketers to attain and sustain their customer base it is necessary that they understand the essential make up of the group or organization making the purchase. Furthermore, they need to identify which are the most important decision making criteria in any given situation.

It is likely that in the future the role of intermediaries in organizational decision making processes will increase in importance. It will therefore be necessary for suppliers to be aware of this change and focus on such key influencers or gatekeepers in the decision making process. Globalization and a sophistication of information technology will be to the advantage of those tourism marketers who currently understand how their existing and potential commercial and group customers make decisions. The existing models do not take account of these fast moving trends and perhaps require revision to incorporate changing patterns of organizational buyer behaviour.

REFERENCES

American Society of Association Executives (ASAE) (1992) *Association Meeting Trends*, ASAE, Washington.

Baird, A. (1996) Conferring. *Business and Finance*, February, 24.

Baker, M.J. (1985) *Marketing Strategy and Management*, Macmillan, Basingstoke.

Davidson, R. (1994) The Conference Market in France. *Insights*, English Tourist Board, A115–122.

Davis, M.P. (1989) *Business to Business Marketing and Promotion*, Business Books Ltd.

Edelstein, L.G. and Benini, C. (1994) Meetings market report. *Meetings and Conventions*, August, 60–82.

Fortin, P.A., Ritchie, J.R.B. and Arsenault, J.A. (1976) *A study of the decision making process of North American associations concerning choice of a convention site*, Lavel University, Quebec City.

Häkansson, H. (1982) *International Marketing and Purchasing of Industrial Goods*. John Wiley, New York.

Hartley, J. and Witt, S. (1994) Increasing The Conversion Rate of Conference and Function Enquiries into Sales. *International Journal of Hospitality Management*, **13**(5), 275.

Kotler, P., Bowen, J. and Makens, J. (1996) *Marketing for Hospitality and Tourism*, Prentice Hall, Englewood Cliffs, New Jersey.

Meetings Industry Association (1996) *Meetings and Incentive Travel*, May, p. 60.

Oppermann, M. (1996) Convention destination images: analysis of association meeting planners' perceptions. In *Tourism Management,* **17**(3), 175–82.

Radburn, D. (1996) Relationship Marketing in the Conference Market, unpublished masters dissertation, Staffordshire University.

O'Reilly, D.O. and Gibas, J. (1995) *Building Buyer Relationships,* Pitman, London.

Richards, B. (1995) The Conference Market in the UK, *Insights,* English Tourist Board, March, B67–69.

Richards, B. and Richards, G. (1994) Developing Corporate Business For Hotels Through Conferences and Exhibitions. *Journal of Vacation Marketing,* **1**(1), November.

Robinson, P., Faris, C. and Wind, Y. (1967) *Industrial Buying and Creative Marketing,* Allyn and Bacon, Boston.

Rouse, P. (1996) Euro Optimism? In *Conference and Exhibition Fact Finder*, May, p. 3.

Seaton, A.V. and Bennett, M.M. (1996) *Marketing Tourism Products*, Thomson Business Press, London.

Sussmann, S. (1995) Business Travel Counselling, *Annals of Tourism Research,* **22**(3).

Webster, F. and Wind, Y. (1972) *Organizational Buyer Behaviour,* Prentice Hall, Englewood Cliffs, New Jersey.

Woodruffe, H. (1995) *Services Marketing,* Pitman, London.

Yeshin, T. (1995) Marketing Communications Strategy, *Chartered Institute of Marketing Handbook,* Marlow.

Segmentation, positioning and the marketing mix $\boxed{\textbf{5}}$

OBJECTIVES

This chapter explains:

● the concepts of segmentation, targeting and positioning;
● why and how companies segment visitor and organizational markets;
● the usefulness of the concepts for the formulation of marketing strategy;
● the term 'marketing mix'.

5.1 INTRODUCTION

The theoretical basis of segmentation, targeting and positioning have been the subject of much research in marketing (Frank, Massey and Wind, 1982; Ries and Trout, 1982; Piercy and Morgan, 1993: 123–40). Kotler *et al.* (1996: 244) refers to them as three interrelated steps. Segmentation is essentially the first necessary step, a sub-division of the total market into discrete and identifiable segments in accordance with a number of clearly defined characteristics. Step two relates to the way in which a company then assesses the attractiveness of each segment which subsequently might warrant targeting and application of resources. Step three involves an organization in positioning itself to meet the expectations of its customers, or potential customers, better than its competitors. Figure 5.1 illustrates the relationship between the three steps.

The reasoning behind the three step process lies in the number of advantages to be gained by companies when pursuing such an approach:

● to design company offerings which suit more closely customer expectations;
● new market opportunities;
● a competitive edge;
● measurable markets.

5.2 SEGMENTATION

Segmentation refers to the way in which companies and organizations identify and categorize customers into clearly defined groups with similar characteristics, and similar needs or desires (McDonald and Dunbar, 1995). Each group should comprise

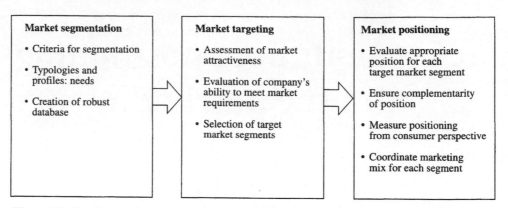

Figure 5.1 The relationship between segmentation, targeting and positioning.

customers who exhibit similar characteristics, for example, young activity holiday takers or high-spending, middle-aged 'empty nesters'. Equally, in the realm of business to business marketing a form of organizational segmentation occurs and this should not be overlooked in the tourism business sectors.

The concept of segmentation is widely adopted in tourism marketing for there are few companies which attempt to appeal to an entire market. It is only in the fast food restaurant sector that segmentation is least in evidence. Companies such as Pizza Hut and McDonald's, for example, have developed strategies where a standardized service is offered to residents and visitors alike across the globe. In effect, they appeal to a total market.

5.2.1 The principles of segmentation

The principles of segmentation are based on the premise that a market can be readily divided into segments for the commercial purpose of targeting offerings. The fundamental point is that buyers differ in their wants or desires, purchasing habits, frequency of purchase and other criteria – but to what extent? There are six defining characteristics. A segment has to be:

● **Identifiable.** The segment has to comprise people who seek identifiably similar benefits from a tourism offering. This is the acid test for if a group of customers seek similar benefits (rather than having differing needs) then they can be targeted with accuracy at a later stage.
● **Cohesive.** A segment has to be clearly identifiable and separate from other segments for measurement purposes, i.e. it has to be discrete. There is a case for segmenting a market according to a number of variables but the fundamental basis for positioning is that a company can target its brand or brands to a specific group of people who present a cohesive whole. The classic example is the 'empty nester' group who have discretionary income and a high level of interest in travel.
● **Measurable.** The marketer should be able to estimate the size and potential spend associated with the segment. The criteria for measurement also has to be socially and commercially appropriate. For example, a company might be interested in customers who have an interest in watersports. This could be a possible criterion; in reality there might not be a suitable database available.

- **Accessible.** The identified segment is only viable if it can be accessed by way of the marketing effort. Unless a segment can be reached effectively it is not possible to target it with any degree of confidence. It is difficult to reach by traditional communication channels the increasing number of people who take holidays in developing countries.
- **Substantial.** Segments have to be sufficiently large, or if small have a high enough spend to be worthwhile pursuing for commercial gain. For a tour operator, it is difficult, for example, to segment all types of activity holiday takers. Therefore, such companies package breaks mainly for those who enjoy walking, cycling and sightseeing in one brochure and those who seek underwater exploration or watersports in another. By grouping people together in this way the tour operator constructs viable segments which are sufficiently substantial to be worthwhile accessing. It would not be possible, however, to segment to smaller groups such as those who enjoy archery or climbing.
- **Actionable.** There needs to be a match between resource level, commitment and achievability in terms of penetrating the defined market segment(s). This relates to the practical limitations encountered in reaching specific segments. It might be possible to segment all those who have blue eyes but is such segmentation worthwhile in any commercial sense? A company needs to be able to action a database or other source of intelligence to ensure effective positioning.

5.2.2 Segmenting customers

Consumer segmentation involves an analysis of a wide ranging number of variables, especially those which have meaning as predictive tools in terms of levels of consumption. Smith (1995) indicates that there are effectively two broad approaches of analysis: segmentation by trip descriptors, such as short haul, long haul, visiting friends and relatives (VFR), etc., and segmentation by tourist descriptors such as 'grey panthers' (early retired and interested in travel), or 'adventurer-explorers' (those seeking unusual and new destinations).

Marketers increasingly use sophisticated multivariate segmentation processes which include behavioural and psychographic variables to build segment profiles with increased degrees of accuracy. The criteria which are most commonly used are discussed in Table 5.1. and the main approaches are discussed below.

(a) Benefit segmentation

Visitors seek different benefits from a holiday. Some prefer more education than entertainment, others status through pursuit of a pastime, and other visitors the convenience of a hotel by the beach. They also place different emphasis on different aspects of provision, which is analysed by a technique known as conjoint analysis, where customers weight different features of a service and these are evaluated to form the basis of benefits analysis. In many respects this is the first stage. From this type of segmentation consumer profiles are often derived, such as those indicated in Table 5.2.

(b) Demographic segmentation

The primary variables age, gender, family life cycle and ethnicity are used to segment markets in tourism. A number of classic examples are listed in Table 5.3.

Table 5.1 Criteria for consumer segmentation

Criteria	Example
Benefit	'Sunlust' holidays – seeking relaxation
Demographic	Activity holidays for children such as Camp Beaumont Summer Camps
Geographic	North European market
Geodemographics	Segmentation by clustered location such as ACORN
Psychographic segmentation	Lifestyle holidays such as Explorer; small group exploratory holidays
Buyer behaviour	Long haul interests such as Exodus, 'Journey Latin America'
Perception	Those who have a predilection for a country-based holiday such as 'The Magic of Spain'
Personality	Club 18–30 appealing to extroverts
Usage	Repeat visitors to a particular resort
Multivariate segmentation	Active senior citizen market following gentle pursuits, walking or bowling
Multilevel segmentation	Expatriate with an interest in history or culture

Table 5.2 Benefit segmentation in tourism

- Relaxation
- Health
- Fun and freedom
- Adventure and challenge ('soft' and 'hard')
- Eroticism/sexual gratification
- Education ('Culture Vulture')
- Sun seeking
- Companionship
- Discovery

(c) Geographic segmentation

The division of markets according to geographical boundaries is a common form of segmentation in tourism. A company might segment its domestic market into a number of territorial regions, each with a different propensity to generate customers, for example.

(d) Geodemographics

This technique enhances geographic segmentation in that it classifies potential market segments according to the residential neighbourhoods in which they live. The market leader in the UK is a system known as ACORN which stands for 'A Classification of Residential Neighbourhoods'. Developed by the CACI Market Analysis Group, it assesses segmentation areas according to 40 variables combined from analysis of the census and other commercial market intelligence which is then collated.

Similar databases are available in a number of countries, either derived from census data on households, or based on telephone ownership. Companies use such

Table 5.3 Demographic segmentation

Category	Profile	Examples
Young children (4–11)	Parents influenced by desires of small children	Legoland, Denmark The World of Disney, Florida
Young people (11–18)	Adventure holidays but with parental approval, guidance	PGL Activity Holidays Youth Hostels Association
Young couples/ groups/solos (18–30)	Good fun, flexible, fast paced holidays, including adventure	Club 18–30 Inter Rail
Family holidays (25–50 with younger children)	Children are the key to the holiday; activities and relaxation	Butlins and Pontins CenterParcs Disney World
Empty nester holidays (45–60)	Active ex parents – discovering new tourism destinations, pastimes without children	Cruise market such as P&O Cruises or Celebrity Cruises
Senior citizens (55+)	Older people, singles and couples, seeking holidays which include culture, but not paced itineraries	Saga Holidays, UK Elderhostel, USA

systems to target likely customers. For example, wealthy achievers in suburban areas will be prospected by timeshare companies.

(e) Psychographic segmentation

Many markets have been categorized according to generalized lifestyle profiles, socioeconomic and personality profiles. It is not exactly the same as geodemographics because people within the same neighbourhood might have similar standards of income and aspirations but completely different approaches to the lifestyle which they wish to enjoy. The classic example is the VALS system adopted in the USA which is referred to in Chapter 2.

(f) Buyer behaviour segmentation

Another approach is to segment the market according to type of buying behaviour exhibited by different groups of people. The level of commitment and degree of purchase by groups to a particular destination or attraction is considered to be a main starting point of segmentation. For example, this approach categorizes according to the level of repeat visitors (brand loyalty), or the chronological sequence of purchase by various groups. The latter is described as the theory of diffusion of innovation (Figure 5.2) and was first espoused by Rogers (1962).

Other dimensions are important. It is also possible to segment according to:

(g) Perception

Sometimes the market is segmented according to the values and perceptions held by the visitor which affects the things that they do or wish to do in their leisure time, the type of destination they prefer, etc. This assumes that people have different attitudes

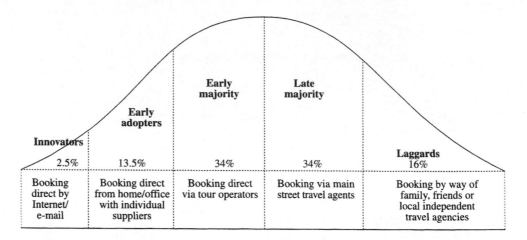

Figure 5.2 Adoption of tourism offerings: speed of diffusion into the market. *Source*: adapted from Rogers (1962: 162).

about types of holidays or tourism offerings available. Plog (1974), for example, refers to the adventuresome nature of allocentrics, seeking out destinations which are unspoilt and characterized by lack of tourism infrastructure.

(h) Personality

The idea that a buyer and brand personality can be matched has been progressed within other sectors of marketing, especially relating to fast moving consumer goods, but its application to the tourism sector has been limited. An example would be Club 18–30 where the choice of such a heavily branded holiday is projected specifically to reflect a fun-loving, outgoing personality. In a similar vein, segmentation is undertaken with regard to the degree of loyalty to the tourism offering.

(i) Usage

This approach is often practised in the accommodation and transport sectors where customers are segmented according to the level of usage from a light or infrequent use to regular repeated use. Companies target and reward customers according to their degree of usage. With regard to tourism destinations it is more common to segment according to whether it is a repeat visit or not. This is particularly important, as many destinations rely on returning visitors (Gitelson and Crompton, 1984: 31–4; Sampol, 1996: 339).

(j) Mulivariate segmentation

Most companies now segment the market by combining several segmentation variables such as age, socioeconomic background, geographic location and life cycle analysis. The two linked concepts of age and life cycle have been used extensively within the tourism market as patterns of consumption and types of holiday purchased vary considerably between the young-single segment, say 18–30, and the 55 plus age cohort.

For example, consider the senior tourism market in the USA and their propensity for international travel. One fifth of the US population is over 55, but in terms of international travel, however, one third are in that age group. Indeed, 47 per cent of long haul travellers are over 55. A quarter of international travellers over 55, from the USA, take four or more trips a year compared to 12 per cent of those under 55. Sixty one per cent of US seniors prefer independent travel rather than organized, guided tours (Hawkins, 1996).

(k) Multilevel segmentation

An associated concept is multistage or multilevel segmentation where an organization firstly segments according to geodemographics then subsequently segments in more detail using other variables. Many destinations in developing countries target European countries according to the number of visitors generated from each respective market. They then segment the market according to a number of variables. Australia targets the UK, for example, then segments according to trip purpose such as trip of a lifetime, visiting friends and relatives, perhaps cross referenced according to benefit segmentation, such as eco pursuit, or sun lust, etc.

5.2.2 Organizational segmentation

Business to business markets can also be segmented using a variety of criteria, which describe the characteristics of the companies within the business sector, such as size, and location, much in the same way as the Standard Industrial Classification (a technique used to classify companies by purpose and size) applies to other sectors. For example, conference buyers will profile destinations according to the size of venues, accessibility, level of facilities, image and appeal, etc.

At a micro level, companies might profile clients or other organizations according to patterns of buying, level of use, decision making processes within the company, etc. Thus, hotel groups will not only classify corporate clients according to the number of executives travelling on business, but also on the nature of the buying process. In a similar manner, destinations will segment tour operators in generating countries in accordance with their ability to generate business volumes or to create specialist packages.

When it comes to the hosting of major international events the buying process becomes very complicated, with a number of stakeholders involved, including political and economic institutions, the media and a host of companies. Such situations require custom made buying processes between buying organizations and pitching destinations. Such processes transcend usual segmentation processes.

5.2.3 Creating market segments

The process begins with the analysis of the marketing information outlined in Chapter 9. In this way, previous consumers and existing visitors can be defined accordingly, probably by way of some form of benefit segmentation. Then a company might also proceed to identify potential market segments to which it is able to offer a service or product. This would be based partly on an investigation of internal data but more likely on an examination of the wider marketing environment (using a PEST analysis, i.e. political, economic, social and technological analysis). This is not always possible, as companies might not have tourism offerings which match customer requirements. The development of both requires some refinement.

(a) Techniques

There are a number of techniques used to determine the most appropriate variables to use for segmentation purposes. Two often quoted techniques are:

- Automatic interaction detection – key purchasing variables are determined in a systematic ranking process, where a subset of a population of customers or potential customers is analysed according to lifestyles and geodemographic factors, etc.
- Cluster analysis – this is the reverse procedure where a group of individuals are analysed to find similarities using a simultaneous pairing process. This enables the researcher to bring together clusters of like customers, based on perhaps a series of uniform scales. The process is continued until a segment of customers or potential customers is identified (Saunders, 1994: 13–28). A statistical technique known as factor analysis is sometimes used to combine correlated variables into manageable clusters.

(b) Segmentation of the Finnish market

The following example (British Tourist Authority, 1995: 33–4) indicates how groups can be segmented and used in the formulation of strategy. In 1995 the British Tourist Authority (BTA) undertook the three steps below in the process of segmenting the Finnish market.

Step 1 Description of the segments

Using a range of parameters such as size of segment, demographic characteristics, financial status, attitudes and experiences, and accessibility the Finnish market was segmented by Gallup-Media Finland as shown in Table 5.4.

Step 2 Evaluation of the segments

Having ascertained the segments the BTA used a directional policy matrix to evaluate them against two main factors: how attractive are they and how easy are they to penetrate. The factors considered in assessing the degree of attractiveness were size of segment, return on investment, growth potential, seasonal and regional potential for long stays (as opposed to short stays) and interest in green tourism. Penetration factors included cost of reach, competition, knowledge, image of Britain, credibility of any potential message and partner support.

Step 3 Selection of appropriate segments

Five segments were prioritized and targeted accordingly in subsequent marketing campaigns in Finland:

- The generation of prosperity
  Age band 25–34

Table 5.4 Segmentation of the Finnish travel market

	Upper middle class	Lower middle class	Workers
Seniors	Active	Inactive	
Age 65+	259 000	366 000	
The Generation of War and Shortage Age 55–64	79 000	151 000	204 000
The Generation of Social Change Age 45–54	193 000	205 000	185 000
The Suburban Generation Age 35–44	254 000	265 000	216 000
The Generation of Prosperity Age 25–34	187 000	258 000	195 000
The Generation of Consumption Age 15–24	134 000	232 000	153 000
The Generation of Video Games Age 12–14	193 000		

Source: Gallup-Media Finland, 1994/United Magazines Ltd.

  Upper through to lower middle class
  Typically these people are couples/singles (no children)
  Located throughout Finland
  Segment size 445 000 people
- The suburban generation
  Age band 35–44
  Upper through to lower middle class
  Typically these people are parents with children aged 7–15
  Segment size 519 000 people
- The generation of social change
  Age band 45–54
  Upper through lower middle class
  Typically these people are couples/singles who have no children (or children who have flown the nest)
  Segment size 398 000 people
- Individual business travellers
- Group business travellers

The detailed segmentation of the Finnish market has enabled the BTA to target potential visitors more accurately.

5.3 TARGETING

A company which has segmented its market will then usually proceed to target those segments which it is best able to serve effectively and profitably. This involves a reappraisal of segments according to benefits, life styles and approachability.

The outcome is often that an organization decides to pursue one of three generic strategies, as outlined below.

5.3.1 Undifferentiated segmentation strategy

The organization decides that there is little basis for segmenting a market and develops a destination or tourism offering which it considers suitable for the entire market. This is sensible in some situations, such as the marketing of capital cities where the appeal is very broad. Nevertheless, individual enterprises, which make up a composite offering such as a destination, will segment their markets to meet the needs and desires of different visitors ranging from business segments to the school market.

5.3.2 Differentiated segmentation marketing

Most tourism businesses have adopted in one form or another a differentiated segmentation approach. In this approach several market segments are delineated and the core service offering is embellished accordingly, to suit the requirements of each specific segment. This occurs at many destinations where different features or sectors of a resort are targeted to different segments. It is also used widely by tour operators, such as segmenting markets for lakes and mountains, beach resorts or historic cities.

5.3.3 Concentrated segmentation marketing

The third segmentation approach is to segment smaller specialist segments which are associated with niche marketing. An organization aims to dominate a small market corner which others do not consider worthwhile pursuing. This is an approach adopted, for example, in the activity holiday market. There are hundreds of specialist tour operators offering bespoke services to those who enjoy canoeing, painting, birdwatching, etc.

5.4 POSITIONING

Positioning is the way in which a company, tourism offering, destination or country is viewed, in relation to other companies or organizations, by customer segments; for example, on a price-image range. The emphasis is on the word 'viewed'.

For example, according to the British Tourist Authority annual report (1996) Britain has a growing reputation as being a trendy place with stylish clothes, shopping, music and clubs:

> The BTA has worked hard on positioning the UK as a vibrant place, which is appealing to audiences who are not purely interested in countryside and heritage. Promotional campaigns in 36 countries are now extolling the virtues of bands like Oasis and Blur, and designers like Paul Smith and John Galliano.
>
> *(Leisure Opportunities, 1996)*

Positioning lies ultimately in the eyes of the consumer: it refers to how the market perceives the organization, rather than how it perceives itself. It has also been defined in terms of the way a company positions itself in the marketplace through its service offering and the communication of this to various market segments. This invariably relates to changing fashions and interests of consumer markets. Swallow Hotels, for example, won the best advertisement campaign by the Hotel Marketing Association for its 60-second TV burst which positioned it as a non-stuffy option to corporate hotels (*Marketing Week*, 1997: 27). Williams *et al.* (1996: 14–15) discusses this within the context of spa resorts:

> Indeed, often the image and market positioning of specific spas has rested as much on the reputation of their clientele as on the spa's products. As public values have shifted so have strategies of marketers; for instance in keeping with personal fitness and preventive health care, some spas have repositioned themselves in the marketplace by moving their focus from the treatment of ailments to the improvement and prolongation of health in a leisure environment.

5.4.1 The positioning task

Kotler *et al.* (1996: 244) suggest that the positioning task requires three key steps:

- Step one: identification of a set of competitive advantages to choose from, such as price, superior accommodation, speedy journey times, highly motivated and professional staff. This is often referred to as differentiation.
- Step two: prioritizing these advantages in order to select an optimum set. For example, a static and price sensitive market will prefer a positioning strategy which highlights value for money, offers regional departures for a standard supplement, etc.
- Step three: communicating and delivering the selected position to target segment(s). Once a position has been established it is necessary to project a clear and attractive image-position.

5.4.2 The problems of positioning

The major problems which come against companies in terms of positioning are:

- a lack of resources to sustain the position for any given length of time;
- a lack of clarity in terms of communication, thus leading to a mismatch between the image the company intends to project and that of the consumer segment;
- competitor assimilation which makes it difficult for the company to set out a pattern of differentiation. This might require a company to invest more resources in order to reposition either the image, or the actual offering, or both.

In terms of destinations, positioning is equally crucial. Even each country or region seeks differential advantage through positioning. A speaker at the 1996 Finance and Management of Wildlife Parks Conference in Tanzania argued that the strong point of African tourism is wildlife, which distinguishes Africa from its competitors. It was suggested that positioning the African continent as an eco tourism destination par excellence would provide the best chance of increasing its current 3.3 per cent share of international arrivals (World Tourism Organization, 1996).

Camison *et al.* (1994) have undertaken an interesting analysis using a matrix which plots market attractiveness (such as market size, profitability and degree of development) against competitive position (such as image, climate, environment, service quality, etc.). These criteria were previously developed by the Secretaria General de Turismo in Spain, and by the Generalitat Valenciana in Valencia. Camison *et al.* then adopt a portfolio analysis which indicates priority markets such as Third Age residential tourism, individual traveller tourism and non-residential Third Age tourism. In this way, it has been possible to suggest an appropriate postioning strategy for Valencia in order to reach attractive markets in which competition is not overwhelming.

5.5 STRATEGY DEVELOPMENT

The example above indicates how market segmentation is effectively used to target markets and to position an organization, or in this case a region, in the marketplace. The entire process is dependent on two key factors which require evaluation: the attractiveness of the market and, second, the competence of the organization to realize the potential of achieving success in accessing the segment(s).

5.5.1 Market attractiveness

Market attractiveness is primarily concerned with the size and potential spend of the market and, more importantly, the degree and intensity of competition. It is important for the tourism marketer to be aware of opportunities presented by emerging segments but also to take note of the level of competitor activity. It could be the case that a particular market is characterized by a number of well resourced aggressive competitors and this would make it a far less attractive market even if the market segment could be easily delineated.

5.5.2 Resources and capability

The second consideration relates to resource commitment and level of company capability. A company needs to access the level of resources required to exploit market segments. This is sometimes referred to as the 'marketing assets' of an organization, but the capability issue is much wider. It certainly includes dimensions such as the vision of the entire management team, the relationship with existing suppliers, the financial backing of the company, etc. Therefore, in order to take advantage of segmentation a company needs to be aware of the resource commitment required and whether a competitor can be outstripped in the process.

5.6 THE MARKETING MIX

Once an organization has positioned itself in the marketplace and formulated an appropriate strategy, the prime task is to plan a series of programmes or actions which can be implemented. These plans are usually unveiled within a framework known as the **marketing mix,** which is best defined as a set of tools available to the marketing manager to achieve a particular strategic direction or position. McCarthy (1960) first introduced four core elements of the mix, which he referred to as the four Ps – product, price, place and promotion.

Some authors still adhere to this basic structure as its simplicity is its major strength. Middleton (1994: 65–6), for example, argues that other elements which have been added to the original four are 'in fact all integral elements of travel and tourism products'. Cooper *et al.* (1993: 263) and Seaton and Bennett (1996: 19) take a similar position, suggesting that elements such as customer service are subsets of product design.

However, most services marketers now adhere to the augmented mix introduced by Booms and Bitner (1981). In reviewing the services marketing literature Palmer (1994: 31–2) comments that the four Ps 'have been found to be too limited in their application to services … this simple list fails to recognize a number of key factors that marketing managers in the service sector use to design their service output'.

The three additional dimensions which Booms and Bitner included are:

- **People.** The role of staff–customer interaction and service quality has become crucial to many organizations in the business of tourism. Hotels and airlines very often differentiate their offerings on this basis.
- **Physical evidence.** This refers to the nature of the design, aesthetics and ambience of surroundings of the service provision; for example, in hotels and restaurants, resort complexes, etc.
- **Processes.** The processes underlying service provision are very tangible to the customer in tourism as it is a high staff–customer contact business. Thus, processes such as hotel reception or travel agency booking systems are particularly pertinent.

The importance of the augmented mix in tourism is discussed in more detail in Chapters 10 and 14.

5.7 SUMMARY The principles of segmentation, targeting and positioning are inextricably bound together and can be considered to be the fundamental structures on which marketing strategy is built. There are numerous approaches to segmentation which require strict definition and measurement. With improved technology and specialization by a number of agencies, accurate segmentation is far more achievable than ever before. Ultimately, however, segmentation has to relate to what customer segments want.

It has been suggested that segmentation and positioning are more than technical decisions. They require a creative management input to establish segments which are based on judgement and intuition rather than pure functionality (Jobber, 1995) and, furthermore, are capable of growth (Peters, 1987). Hence, in some respects it could be described as an art. Marketers who modify traditional methods of segmentation in favour of identifying emergent segments, it is argued, might well be ahead of competitors. As a basis for positioning and targeting it is indispensable.

Segmentation and positioning form core elements in strategy formulation. In turn, a chosen strategy is unfolded by means of the marketing mix. The initial concept of the four Ps (product, price, place and promotion) is the subject of some debate as many service marketers now consider that it is more appropriate to refer to the augmented marketing mix which includes people, physical evidence and processes as being a more useful marketing toolkit in the tourism business.

REFERENCES

Booms, B.H. and Bitner, M.J. (1981) Marketing Strategies and Organization Structures for Service Firms. In *Marketing of Services* (eds J. Donnelly and W.R. George), American Marketing Association, Chicago.
British Tourist Authority (1995) *Market Guide – Nordic Region,* British Tourist Authority, London, pp. 33–4.
British Tourist Authority (1996) *Annual Report.* British Tourist Authority, London.

Camison, C., Bigne, E. and Montford, V.M. (1994) The Spanish tourism industry; an analysis of its strategies and efficiency and achievements gained from them. In *Tourism, the State of the Art* (eds A.V. Seaton *et al.*), John Wiley & Sons, Chichester.

Cooper, C., Fletcher, J., Gilbert, D. and Wanhill, S. (1993) *Tourism, Principles and Practice*, Pitman, London.

Frank, R., Massey, W. and Wind, Y. (1972) *Market Segmentation*, Prentice Hall, Englewood Cliffs, New Jersey.

Gitelson, R.J. and Crompton, J.L. (1984) Insights into Repeat Vacation Phenomenon. *Annals of Tourism Research*, **11**, 31–4.

Hawkins, M. (1996) Presentation given at the Second International Conference on Senior Tourism, Embratur, Recife 13–15 September.

Jobber, D. (1995) *Principles and Practice of Marketing*, McGraw-Hill, Maidenhead.

Kotler, P., Boweb, J. and Makens, J. (1996) *Marketing for Hospitality and Tourism*, Prentice Hall, Englewood Cliffs, New Jersey.

Leisure Opportunities (1996) Visits Rise to Trendy UK. *Leisure Opportunities*, 14–27 October.

Marketing Week (1997) Swallow Hotels Win Top Prize. *Marketing Week*, January 10, 27.

McCarthy, J.E. (1960) *Basic Marketing: A Management Approach*, Irwin, Illinois.

McDonald, M.B.H. and Dunbar, I. (1995) *A Step By Step Approach to Creating Profitable Market Segments*, Whitaker, London.

Middleton, V.T.C. (1994) *Marketing in Travel and Tourism*, Butterworth-Heinemann, Oxford.

N'Diaye, O. (1996) Presentation given to The Finance and Management of Wildlife Parks, World Tourism Seminar, Arusha 29 July–2 August.

Palmer, A. (1994) *Principles of Service Marketing*, McGraw-Hill, Maidenhead.

Peters, T.J. (1987) *Thriving on Chaos*, Macmillan, Basingstoke.

Piercy, N.F. and Morgan, N.A. (1993) Strategic and Operational Market Segmentation: A Managerial Analysis. *Journal of Strategic Marketing*, **1**, 123–40.

Ries, A. and Trout, J. (1982) *Positioning: The Battle For Your Mind*, Warner, New York.

Rogers, E.M. (1962) *Diffusions of Innovations*, Macmillan, Basingstoke.

Sampol, C.J. (1996) Estimating the Probability of Return Visits Using a Survey of Tourist Expenditure in the Balearic Islands. *Tourism Economics*, **2**(4), 339.

Saunders, J. (1994) Cluster Analysis. *Journal of Marketing Management*, **10**, 1–3, 13–28.

Seaton, A.V. and Bennett, M.M. (1996) *Marketing Tourism Products*, Thomson Business Press, London.

Smith, S.L.J. (1995) *Tourism Analysis*, 2nd edition, Longman, Harlow.

Williams, P.W., Andestad, G., Pollock, A. and Karim, B.D. (1996) Health Spa Travel Markets: Mexican Long-Haul Pleasure Travellers. *Journal of Vacation Marketing*, **3**(1), 12–13.

World Tourism Organization (1996) *Tourism Market Trends*. WTO, Madrid.

Marketing planning $\boxed{6}$

OBJECTIVES

This chapter explains:

- the levels of planning and their interrelationship;
- the benefits and disadvantages of marketing planning;
- the marketing planning process in tourism;
- the usefulness and limitations of analytical tools in the development of strategic options;
- the elements necessary to construct a marketing plan.

6.1 INTRODUCTION

Marketing planning is the process by which an organization attempts to analyse its existing resources and marketing environment in order to predict the direction it should take in the future. Warren (1966: 5) defines it as 'essentially a process directed toward making today's decisions with tomorrow in mind and a means of preparing for future decisions so that they can be made rapidly, economically, and with as little disruption to the business as possible'.

Why do companies plan? There is inevitably a delicate balance between achieving tomorrow's targets and planning what the organization needs to achieve in five years time. The case for planning, however, is well documented (Greenley, 1986; Jain, 1990; Leppard and McDonald 1987: 159–71; Piercy, 1991) and is adopted by the larger tourism firms (Athiyaman and Robertson, 1995: 199–205).

The list of potential benefits distilled from these works is as follows:

- It enables the organization to plan ahead with a greater degree of certainty.
- It documents aims, objectives and targets which can be reviewed in due course.
- In the right circumstances it engenders a culture which is forward thinking, innovative and can stimulate cooperation between functions.
- The process sharpens the degree of analysis applied by managers towards internal competencies and the external marketplace.
- The plan enables a company to think positively and flexibly about emerging markets in a proactive way (planning has also been criticized for inculcating an attitude of inflexibility!).

- The process encourages an organization to become market orientated rather than inward looking.

There have also been a number of reservations expressed about the marketing planning process which are summarized as follows:

- It can sometimes become an annual ritual with no consequence.
- It can possibly lead to inflexibility in approach.
- It is time consuming and can absorb a considerable amount of senior manager energy.

6.1.1 Corporate and marketing planning

A distinction is often made in the literature between the different levels of planning within an organization (Johnson and Scholes, 1989), but in reality such divisions are rarely so clear. Whereas corporate issues relate to the direction and strategies of the entire corporation, marketing planning concentrates on the way in which a company's resources are geared to the needs of the market or, more precisely, selected market segments. Nevertheless, corporate and marketing planning flow together, marketing being the power house which drives corporate direction.

6.1.2 Mission statements

The mission and direction of a company is firmly the remit of the chief executive and the board, which is charged with the responsibility of establishing appropriate goals and objectives for the entire corporation. For example, the Executive Board of Flughafen Frankfurt Main AG prepared a strategic blueprint in 1996, Vision 2000 plus, which it describes as 'a guideline for our staff of more than 12 000 professionals, from board room to baggage room, to follow every day'. The mission statement reads:

> Our objective is to maintain and expand our strengths as a high-performance international transport hub. To this end, we are further extending our top-quality and wide-ranging services. Wherever there is room for improvement we take assertive, customer-driven, flexible action.
>
> *(Gateway Frankfurt, 1996: 7)*

One of the most incisive mission statements is that projected by another German company, Siemens, which is summarized by Kotler and Armstrong (1996: 77). It refers to seven core statements regarding strategy, identity, entrepreneurial style, managers, executive decision making, new organization and strength.

The main directive statements of the corporate plan are usually referred to the strategic business units (SBUs) of a company for guidance and execution. They in turn establish business plans, including marketing strategies, which are then discussed with operational management. At this level tactical marketing or service plans are prepared which contain more detailed programmes of activity.

6.1.3 Levels of planning

The relationship between these planning levels appear quite hierarchical but they are often interlocking in terms of execution, feedback and driving forces underlying them. It depends both on the corporate culture and the power bases within an organization as to how well the planning process is executed and how effective the interaction is at all levels. For example, what might appear to be a string of good tactical ideas in Year 1 could well be crafted as a cornerstone of marketing strategy in Year 2.

Marketing is only one of a range of functional plans which direct the corporate entity. In larger tourism organizations there will also be human resource, operational and financial plans, for example. However, marketing plans form the core of corporate planning, for without a clear vision of existing and future customer requirements it is not possible to plan with any degree of accuracy other resource commitments. The differential levels and sequential approach to systematic planning which could be applied in a tourism organization is outlined in Figure 6.1. Detailed marketing operational plans would also include customer service, physical evidence and processes.

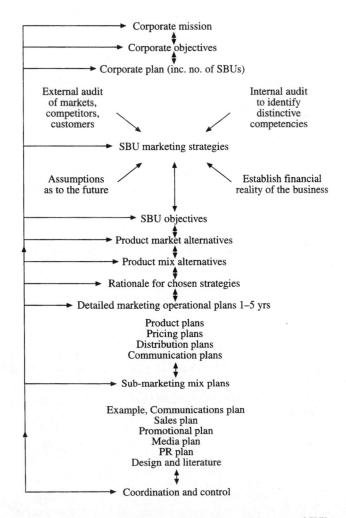

Figure 6.1 A strategic marketing planning model. *Source*: Atkinson and Wilson (1996).

6.2 THE MARKETING PLANNING PROCESS

The marketing planning process asks an organization to restate the following fundamental questions:

- What is our current position?
  Example: A hotel group which has ten medium sized hotels of which six are profitable and four of these are marginal performers.
- Where does the organization aim to be?
  Example: A hotel group with 12 medium to large scale hotels of which all are profitable.
- Which is the best route(s) to follow?
- *Example*: Sell eight of the current smaller hotels to finance an acquisition of another company with an appropriate portfolio of properties.
- How do we arrive at our preferred position?
  Example: Prepare detailed plans for disposal of existing assets, purchase of a new hotel group, corporate and brand restructuring, internal marketing, promotional campaign, and new market development with business clients.
- How should the plan be implemented?
  Example: The execution of detailed programmes of work such as establishing a project team to undertake disposals and acquisitions, devising a detailed internal marketing exercise to advise staff through the transitional period. This would be followed by a major external communications exercise with existing and potential customers.
- Have we arrived?
  Example: Monitoring the process and applying control measures where necessary. Have the sales of properties been executed to secure working capital towards the purchase of new hotels? Has there been minimal disturbance to the core customer base?

6.2.1 Objectives, strategies and tactics

It is important at the outset to clarify the difference between objectives, strategies and tactics.

(a) Objectives

Objectives refer to more specific goals or targets which an organization wishes to achieve within a given timescale. For example, the corporate goal of an organization might be to become a major pan-European tour operator. The objectives, therefore, would relate to the number of acquisitions necessary to achieve this longer term aim, the degree of market penetration necessary in each national market to achieve this position, etc.

(b) Strategy

Strategy refers to how an organization might achieve such objectives. It outlines a broad brush sketch of how the objectives will be met over a period of three to five years. Strategic decision making often requires a wide range of market information and a continuous appraisal of a changing environment. Otherwise, a strategy can be based on inaccurate or outdated information which is a route to disaster in a highly competitive marketplace.

(c) Tactics

Tactics follow from strategic frameworks but there are no hard and fast rules as to where strategy ends and tactics begin. As a rule tactics or programmes of work are about short term, narrowly focused marketing actions and are often specific in level of detail.

6.2.2 Corporate culture

Corporate culture refers to the way in which an organization progresses its main functions and more particularly the values underpinning them (Jain, 1990: 114–15).

There is another dimension, which Atkinson and Wilson (1996: 7) refer to as 'the wider domain of strategy'. They point to four elements of strategic thinking which should make an organization more resilient in the marketing environment:

- **Receptivity to new ideas.** A willingness to assess new ideas and concepts.
- **Future orientation.** Experimentation, innovation and longer term scenario building.
- **Nurturing of core competencies.** Creation of links between areas of competencies within a company, such as between research, development and marketing.
- **Developing positive attitudes to unexpected events.** The rethinking of strategic alternatives at times of crisis.

Given this type of injection of ideas, the marketing planning process should be one of the most stimulating driving forces within an organization. It allows marketers to not only consider the internal organization (i.e. its capability) but also the relationship between the organization and its markets. Good ideas are more likely to be tested in this type of managerial atmosphere. It should provide a training ground for developing a sharpened corporate culture where flexible planning and a degree of imagination are the hallmarks of the process (Hamel and Prahalad, 1991: 81–92).

6.3 THE MARKETING AUDIT

The marketing audit is 'the means by which a company can identify its own strengths and weaknesses as they relate to external opportunities and threats' (McDonald, 1995: 14). It involves an analysis of both the marketing environment, i.e. uncontrollable external variables, and the resource capability of the organization. It usually includes the following three key external dimensions (which the organization is unable to control).

(a) PEST (political, economic, social/cultural and technological) analysis

This is an examination of the broad macro trends in a country, a region, or on a world level in some instances. The PEST analysis has traditionally included:

- **Political factors.** These range from political factors in generating countries, such as the regulation of tour operators, to civil unrest in receiving countries, such as in Central Africa or the Middle East during the mid-1990s. There are also legal matters to consider, such as visas as an entry requirement to certain countries.
- **Economic factors.** These could include the effect of a tourist tax at hotels and airports on prices, or erratic exchange rates. There should also be an assessment of income distribution, levels of discretionary incomes available in generating markets, patterns of consumer spending power, emergence of home based spending opportunities, etc.
- **Social and cultural factors.** For example, there might be a trend towards environmentally sensitive holidays or healthy living which could affect the market. This also involves an analysis of trends such as changing family patterns away from the extended and nuclear family towards a higher percentage of single adult households. Furthermore, such structural changes are matched by the fragmentation of life styles rather than their convergence as some have predicted (Bremner, 1992: 29–32). This is happening in Europe and the USA in the late 1990s.
- **Technological change.** Improvement in tourism technology has generally stimulated markets. For example, the TGV train in France has re-awakened the market for medium distance travel by rail between cities. The development of computer reservation systems introduced on a worldwide scale has also changed the marketplace for booking holidays.

Wilson, Gilligan and Pearson (1992: 42) also include a fifth dimension, the ecological factor, which they refer to as natural resources, energy use, conservation and the implications of pollution which an organization needs to consider. This point is reinforced by several authors (Dembkowski and Hanmer Lloyd, 1994: 593–603).

(b) Visitor analysis (customer or passenger analysis)

A detailed analysis of customers or visitors is vital to the formation of a strategy, in that the organization needs to understand the size, structure and dynamics of the market, as well as the types of customer and their desires. It involves an assessment of:

- **Volume and value of current visitor/customer base.** For example, a museum will need to know the number of child, individual, family and senior citizen admissions, and value of spend on entrance, plus spending on goods and services bought on the premises.
- **Benefits sought.** Understanding the main motivational factors attracting different visitors to a museum, such as educational value, a venue to bring friends, loyal supporters, a place for hospitality meetings, etc.
- **Visitor profiles.** The characteristics of visitors by location, social class, lifestyle, etc. What proportion of visitors are local, regional or international?
- **Segmentation.** Can the overall market visiting the museum be readily segmented into discrete and measurable groups such as the individuals market, schools and groups, families, international specialists?
- **Nature of the buying process.** A review of the purchasing process. Is a visit made on impulse or planned as a special day out? Frequency of visit, peaks and troughs in demand, etc.

(c) Competitor analysis

Competitor analysis looks at:

- **The level of direct competition.** An analysis of competing museums or attractions with a similar mix of education and entertainment which could be a direct substitute to a museum in any locality. In some instances this might be on a national or international scale rather than at a local level. The first stage would involve a SWOT analysis (strengths, weaknesses, opportunities and threats). A SWOT analysis would be undertaken to assess each competitor, probably using ranking criteria in terms of resource availability, performance and strategic planning (including future investments) as well as an assessment of marketing mix activities.
- **Indirect competition.** A wider audit, conducted on a more general basis, of indirect substitutes such as home based entertainment or other forms of leisure activities, would also be applicable as they collectively constitute a considerable array of competition to travel.

The outcome of such a competitor analysis is to seek ways to gain competitive advantage 'by finding an aspect of differentiation that targeted customers will perceive as superior value and that cannot be duplicated by the competition' (Cravens, 1994). The two key aspects of differentiation are, first, non-price benefits such as how the visitor perceives a destination or a hotel in relation to the value offered by competitor offerings. The second element of differentiation is perceived price compared to competitors. Therefore, as Mathur (1992: 202) notes: 'The focus of competitive strategy is on the future, and on the triangular relationship between the customer, the offering and its competitors.'

6.3.1 Internal competencies

These are mainly controllable determinants which affect a company's competence and capability, such as the commitment, professionalism and training of staff.

Marketing objectives, strategies and tactics

This involves firstly an assessment of whether the museum is doing the right things (effectiveness) and secondly how well it is performing its marketing tasks (efficiency). For example, the museum might be positioning itself to an international market while its strengths lie in attracting a regional market. The measurement of the functional efficiency of such marketing campaigns is a completely different task. A selection of efficiency criteria are listed below:

- **Marketing information.** The degree of relevant and timely information available to the management team, for example about the museum and the nature of competing attractions.
- **Degree of marketing orientation.** This relates to an evaluation of whether the organization has in place appropriate structures to build a customer orientated culture through internal marketing, for example (which is explained in more detail in Chapter 12). Museums have in the past been criticized for being 'product based' rather than seeking ways of ensuring that visitor satisfaction is the priority. Therefore, this is a key area of discussion in the marketing of museums.
- **Level of marketing organization.** The audit should attempt to measure the effectiveness of the marketing organization, for example, the level of integration within the

company, degree of internal communication, and the sophistication of the marketing effort.

- **The execution of strategies and tactical plans.** The monitoring of the effectiveness of particular elements of the marketing mix. For example, does the museum have a welcoming reception (in terms of physical evidence) and sufficiently integrated processes for handling visitor enquiries, and encouraging visitor expenditure on site?

- **Value chain analysis.** In relation to competitor analysis Porter (1985) discusses the value chain, which he describes as 'the value a firm is able to create for its buyers that exceeds the firm's cost of creating it'. Value chain analysis refers to the way in which it is possible to disaggregate nine interrelated activities which enable a company to create value for their customers. Porter describes the five primary activities (those associated with production of the offering) and five support activities (those associated with the organizational matters). Figure 6.2 illustrates this.

  The more value that an organization can achieve in the process, while minimizing costs, will lead to competitive advantage if other organizations happen to achieve less. The technique applies to suppliers too. Value chain analysis therefore should be conducted throughout the supply chain. It is a concept that can be very aptly applied in the tourism business sector in that most tourism companies rely on a fairly complicated supply chain to deliver their service offering.

Therefore, the marketing audit allows an organization to assess its current position, but it does far more than this. It sows the seeds of strategic development by emphasizing an analysis of threats and opportunities. By analysing what others are doing, by giving due consideration to examples of best practice found elsewhere, and through an objective appraisal of its own capability, the organization will build or restructure its marketing strategy. This will, of course, take heed of the necessities of a changing marketing environment. Even in the worst scenario, with the isolated marketer working in an organization which is by nature reactive to the marketplace, the marketing audit process brings with it a strong case for change to be placed in the spotlight for discussion.

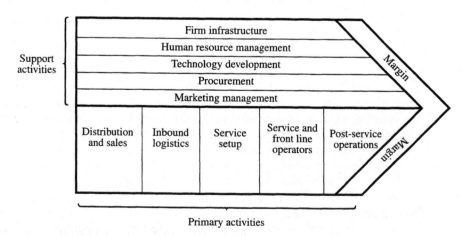

Figure 6.2 The hotel value chain. *Source*: Desinano and Vigo (1994). Copyright John Wiley & Sons. Reprinted with permission.

6.4 STRATEGY FORMULATION

The marketing audit should therefore lead to strategy formulation. While a marketing team might well undertake a SWOT (strengths, weaknesses, opportunities, threats) analysis at the beginning of the marketing audit, it is also likely that the findings will be revisited at a second stage of marketing planning as a prelude to strategy formulation. Conducted with rigour, it is a useful introductory management tool, as outlined in Table 6.1 which provides an analysis of the historic city of Canterbury.

There is, however, far more to strategic direction and strategy formulation than this elementary technique. One or more of the following analyses are usually undertaken during the process of strategy formulation.

6.4.1 Stakeholder and mission statement analysis

The marketer needs to understand the power structures of the organization in terms of its stakeholders, i.e. those people and institutions which have a stake in the organization, such as:

- visitors
- suppliers
- central, regional or local government
- financial backers (shareholders, banks and other similar institutions)
- pressure groups and trade organizations
- local community
- owners
- management and employees.

For example, a mission statement for a local-authority-owned attraction such as a pier or leisure centre will most probably reflect community aspirations equally or above financial returns. In contrast a profit-driven international tour operator will, above all other factors, emphasize market share and profitability. Thus, the objectives of each organization will vary enormously.

6.4.2 Market structure analysis

This takes into the account customer/visitor analysis and segmentation but attempts to analyse the dynamism and complexity of the market (rate of market entry, market fragmentation, trends) and the overall structure in terms of levels of competition and intensity. Thus, it is important to establish market boundaries, the degree of segmentation, the level of competition and the key driving forces, which give rise to market trends. In this way an organization can begin to indicate with confidence key success factors which either need to be incorporated or strengthened within the company.

6.4.3 Degree of competitor intensity

This forms part of the market structure analysis mentioned above but in recent years has become increasingly important in terms of strategic development. In some markets it is argued that a marketing strategy can only succeed if competitor reaction is anticipated with some degree of accuracy. Porter's analysis of the marketing environment provides an important framework for the understanding of competitive

Table 6.1 Canterbury SWOT analysis (1996)

Strengths

Internationally-known city name
A World Heritage Site (Cathedral, St Augustine's Abbey, St Martin's Church)
History, heritage and culture
High quality environment
Educational centre
Speciality shopping, restaurants, pubs
Theatre, sports facilities
Good street entertainment
Cosmopolitan atmosphere
Additional income from tourists
Park and ride strategy
Geographic location (easily accessible from London and Channel ports)

Weaknesses

Too many short stays (half a day or less)
Lack of visitor management strategy
Too small to be a long-term destination in its own right
Loss of independent retailers
Parking strategy poorly understood by the public
Poor rail service to and from London
Some negative attitudes towards visitors
One dominant visitor attraction
Quality of accommodation
Lack of interpretation
Coach park location/visitor access to the city

Opportunities

World Heritage Site – 14th century anniversary of St Augustine in 1997
Product development (new museums, new sports facilities)
Chaucer and other literary links
Develop short breaks/touring itineraries
Develop European links
Capitalize on North American links
Emerging coordinated tourism policy
Whitefriars redevelopment
Create festivals/events policy, to include licensing buskers
The developing partnership created by CCCI
Interpretation of the city, encouraging visitors to stay longer and see more

Threats

Slowness of recovery in the British economy
Increasing attractiveness of rival town shopping centres
Bluewater Park development
Poor local perception of the value of tourists
Poor understanding of the parking strategy
Aggressive marketing of other areas
Replacement of local, practical shops by souvenir shops
The sheer numbers of visitors, particularly young schoolchildren, alienating more mature visitors
    and local shoppers
The loss of the continental market if cross-Channel fares rise/currency fluctuations occur over
    which the city has no control
Product 'exhaustion'
Deteriorating city environment (graffiti, street traders)

Source: CCCI Business Plan 1996.

positioning and the development of strategy. Porter (1979: 136–45) suggests that there are five key forces which shape a market and the degree of competitive intensity. They are summarized in Figure 6.3, in relation to visitor attractions.

Porter argued that depending on the nature of the marketing environment and the resource capability of an organization, it can choose one of the three generic competitive strategies outlined below.

(a) Cost leadership strategy

The organization aims to reduce costs of production and distribution so that it can more readily compete on price if it wishes. This is a common strategy among major tour operators and travel agents vying for market share and leadership. Companies can reduce costs by progressing along what is known as the **experience curve**, in that the systems used to book and operate large volumes of customers, especially in the standardized packaged holiday market, are fine tuned to reduce costs throughout the organization.

The experience curve is not solely about economies of scale but also refers to the cumulative 'experience effect'. As a company increases its capability in delivering products and services through improved processes, technological advantage, and standardization, for example, it can lower costs. Obviously, to gain advantage in the market an organization has to move along the experience curve faster than its rivals.

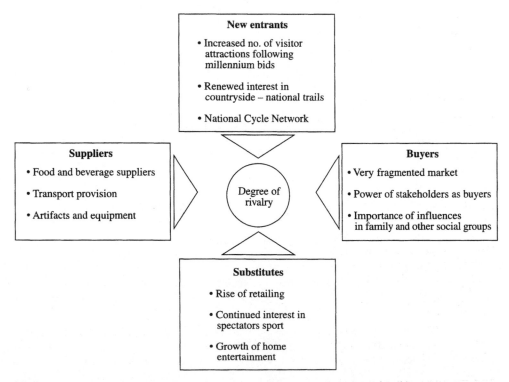

Figure 6.3 Porter's five forces: degree of competitive intensity. *Source*: adapted from Porter (1980).

This strategy enables market leaders to close small scale competitors. The UK travel agency business in the early 1990s offered a classic scenario when hundreds of small independent travel agencies closed in face of the competition of the large agencies, such as Lunn Poly and AT Mays, which were reaping the benefits of scale and experience.

(b) Differentiation strategy

This is a far more common strategy in tourism. The company or destination aims to achieve competitive advantage by specializing with regard to one or more aspects of the marketing mix which is particularly valued by the market. It can be seen in terms of a quality offering, service transactions, or in some instances by technological advance. Airlines compete on service differentiation and by placing a heavy emphasis on branding; ski resorts compete on the quality of snow and the special nature of the piste, for example.

(c) Focus strategy

Porter's third generic strategy is about focusing on one or more market niches. The aim of the strategy is almost total immersion in terms of one market segment by developing strong relationships with existing and potential customers. This allows a special service offering to be developed and therefore by cultivating a strong branding and premium pricing, barriers to entry can be erected. Tourism is replete with specialist companies pursuing niche markets, such as Backroads in the USA or Cycling for Softies or Headwater in the UK, which design exceptional tourism offerings at premium prices.

In contrast, Porter warned against being stuck in the middle, where there is no one clear strand of strategy. Porter's strategic framework has been widely accepted and many companies appear to pursue a low-cost differentiation strategy which combines two of the three generic options.

An alternative framework to Porter's is that developed by Snow and Hrebniniak (1980) which attempts to explain how hotels react to and affect their marketing environment. The approach is still based on the principles of competitor intensity. They present a number of strategic typlogies – defender, prospector, analyser/innovator and analyser/price defender.

Schaffer (1986) tested the typology by researching the approaches of 100 organizations in the hospitality sector. A similar framework was also used by Dev and Brown (1990: 269–82) to test the extent to which hotels' business activities are vertically structured (degree of control from centre over marketing and operational matters) in relation to the fit between their strategy and the degree of dynamism in the market environment. They concluded that as environmental uncertainty increases, those pursuing defender strategies also tend to increase vertical control. Those pursuing prospector and analyser strategies tend to use less vertical control. The framework was also utilized by Gilbert and Kapur (1990: 27–43) in their case study of four hotel groups (Penta Hotels Ltd, Forum Hotels International, Thistle Hotels Ltd and the Sheraton Corporation):

> These can be identified in the case study comparison. Penta's defender strategy can be gauged from the emphasis of the board on operating efficiency and quality

control without high prices. The prospector type organizations such as Sheraton utilize broad base strategic planning to experiment and respond to emerging trends. Companies such as Sheraton systematically develop and add new products in order to maintain or increase demand for their units.

6.5 PRODUCT PORTFOLIO ANALYSIS

Strategic decisions regarding which products and services to develop and which ones to divest (sell off or withdraw), and where to invest limited resources, is crucial to the organization. In terms of evaluating strategic objectives there are a number of management techniques used to assist the company in managing groups of products, services or brands. Of these the two better known are:

- the Boston Consulting Group growth share matrix, and
- the General Electric market attractiveness–competitive position model.

Both models have been useful in assisting companies in the development of objectives for product portfolio planning in general terms, although there is less evidence to suggest that the models can be applied to all marketing environments. While they have been subjected to much criticism, the important point is how the marketing manager or tourism officer can make use of them to improve decision making.

6.5.1 The Boston Consultancy Group growth share matrix

The matrix comprises four boxes on two axes (see Figure 6.4). The vertical axis indicates the growth rate of the market annually. For example, the lowest level of growth is zero and the highest level in this example is 20 per cent. The arbitrary dividing line between what the model assumes to be a high and low growth rate is 10 per cent. The matrix assumes that the growth rate can be equated to market attractiveness.

The horizontal axis indicates relative market share. It allows the marketer to plot the market share of each service product relative to its largest competitor, thus providing a yardstick for competitive strength. The division between high and low share is usually depicted as the numerical value 1. Thus, if the product in question has a market share of 60 per cent and the product's largest competitor has a 30 per cent share, this would be indicated as 1.5 on the horizontal axis. Conversely, if the product has a market share of 10 per cent and the product's largest competitor has a 20 per cent share, this would be less than 1, i.e. 0.5, on the horizontal axis.

A company would then plot all of its service offerings within the boxes as marked up in Figure 6.4. In this way, it is possible to measure the performance of each service product line in terms of cash flow. The assumption is that some services or products require large investments to stimulate growth or to build market share or leadership, etc., whilst others require little investment as they are established and produce both solid cash flows and profitability (defined as return on investment over a given period of time). The key is to maintain a balance.

In terms of setting strategic objectives it is argued that there are set patterns of response required according to each given situation. These are described as follows:

- **Problem children:** They require substantial investment, generate limited cash flows and therefore will offer either low or negative profitability. They are a

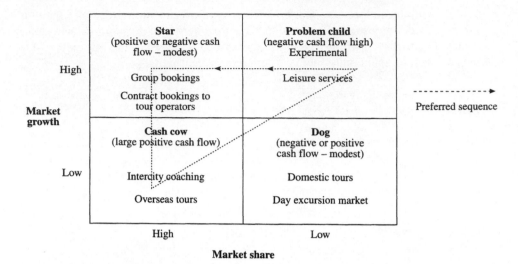

Figure 6.4 The Boston Consultancy Group matrix: coach operation example. *Source*: adapted from Henderson's growth/share matrix in Henderson (1970).

problem because a marketing team has to decide whether to increase investment to build the market share or to plan a withdrawal from the market, possibly harvesting (reduce resources, continue premium pricing) or divesting (delete it from the portfolio or sell it to another company). In some circumstances it might be possible to retain the service product for a niche market.

- **Stars:** Market leaders in growth markets are important to companies as they generate large amounts of cash but still require heavy investment to increase market share and to outstrip competitors. The main emphasis of strategy is to protect and nourish these through to mature markets.
- **Cash cows:** In mature markets, where growth rates have slowed, cash cows bring great returns without heavy investment. The objective is to maintain sales levels and hold the market share against competitors. The theory is that the cash flow accruing from these can be used to stimulate successful problem children.
- **Dogs:** In low growth markets there is still potential for profitability through positive cash flows but not for products with a relatively low share. Therefore, it is suggested that such service products should be harvested or divested depending on circumstances.

The portfolio has also been applied to the countries such as the work by Calatone and Mazanec (1991) in analysing Austria and Italy, see Figure 6.5.

Critique of the BCG matrix

One of the main frustrations about the BCG models described in textbooks is that unless you are in full possession of the data pertaining to a particular product or service portfolio and have similar data about near competitors in the marketplace, it is almost impossible to use in the way in which the consulting group intended. It has, however, been criticized on the following grounds:

(a)
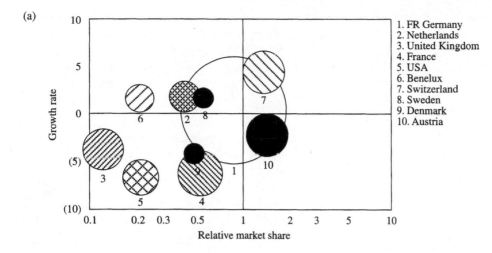

(b)
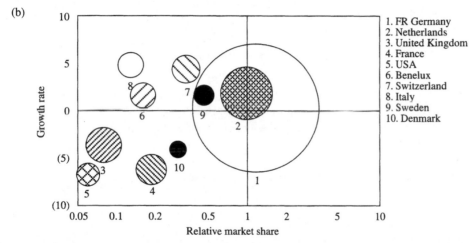

Figure 6.5 Portfolio models of (a) Italy and (b) Austria. Reprinted from *Annals of Tourism Research*, **18**, R.J. Calatone and J.A. Mazanec, Marketing Management and Tourism, p. 107 © 1991, with kind permission from Elsevier Science Ltd, The Boulevard, Langford Lane, Kidlington OX5 1GB, UK.

- The nature of the market is not defined precisely within the model.
- It ignores the dynamism of markets. What is the time period over which the market should be investigated? Some markets change rapidly, such as the fast food market, others are moving slowly such as country parks.
- The level of competitor activity has become increasingly important in most markets. For example, the degree of competitor reaction is not embraced in the model, and the related concept of market share does not substitute for the strategic dimension known as sustainable competitive advantage.
- Market growth rate only refers to one element of market attractiveness which includes other ingredients such as nature of competitors, potential size, and company capability.
- The matrix does not take into account the interrelationships between tourism offerings

which are so important in building strategy. Service offerings might be complementary or one product an essential component in developing another.

● As with the product life cycle, the model is deterministic in that the service position within one of the boxes demands a strategic direction which is well rehearsed from previous experiences. However, strategic direction also relies on marketing acumen and creativity which might suggest a risk strategy in given circumstances rather than the predictable route.

Whether or not the BCG matrix can still be an important tool in managing product/ service portfolios is debatable (Morrison and Wensley, 1991: 105–29). Much of the criticism relates to the relevance of a model which became widely adopted in the 1970s. Is it applicable to a marketing environment in which competitive dynamics are dominant? Nevertheless, marketers use such models in conjunction with a number of diagnostic techniques, some of which are quantitative, such as sales figures, and some of which are qualitative, such as Ansoff's matrix (see page 96). In terms of simplicity the BCG scores highly but should be used in conjunction with other tools be used as the only tool of analysis.

6.5.2 General Electric market attractiveness–competitive position (MA–CP)

The General Electric market attractiveness–competitive position model (developed by consultants McKinsey and Co. for General Electric) also employs a matrix format as outlined in Figure 6.6. The model is more sophisticated than the BCG matrix in that the concept of market attractiveness incorporates the findings of a PEST analysis, an assessment of the size and growth rate of the market, the strength of competitors and profitability potential, rather than just one factor – market growth.

The factors incorporated into **competitive strength** include differential advantage, cost maintenance advantages, distribution power and company standing as well as market share. Furthermore all factors included in the MA–CP are weighted according to importance in a particular market.

These weightings would then be allocated a score for each weighted factor. The sum of each product line is then plotted on the MA–CP matrix as shown in Figure 6.6. The relative position of each product line requires a different set of strategic objectives:

Area 1 Build, i.e. plan for growth in market share as both the market attractiveness and competitive strengths are high.

Area 2 Hold, i.e. set objectives to maintain market share in what is a far less attractive market but competitive strengths are high.

Area 3 This is the difficult area as competitor strengths and market attractiveness are less clear. Therefore, the strategy might be build or harvest.

Area 4 This presents a clear case of harvesting as both market attractiveness and competitive strengths are low.

Area 5 This involves deletion of the product line so that resources can be used to build elsewhere.

The MA–CP model offers greater potential for the tourism marketer than the BCG model but requires management expertise and agreement between colleagues as to the relative weightings of factors.

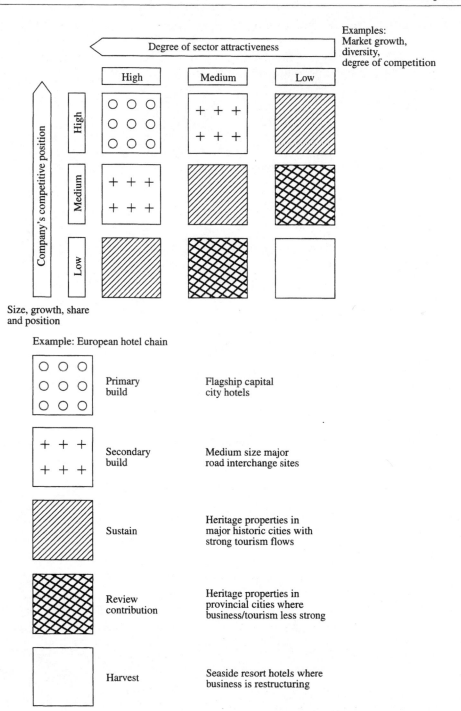

Figure 6.6 Example of a GEC model: company position/sector attractiveness matrix.

6.6 DIRECTIONAL TECHNIQUES

There are also a number of strategic directional models which are extensively used. Two of the most popular are outlined below.

6.6.1 The Ansoff matrix

This is probably the most commonly used of the strategic directional matrices and is named after the author who first devised the framework in the 1950s. The simple structure has been used extensively since. Figure 6.7 illustrates the application of the matrix within the tourism sector.

6.6.2 The Arthur D. Little matrix

A more comprehensive approach is provided by the Arthur D. Little matrix (named after the consultancy company) which has been adapted in Figure 6.8.

The appeal of such models is that they assist in simplifying the process of strategic direction. They enable the marketer to select a number of potential options which can be rebuilt into strategies which provide a framework for translation into tactical plans. In themselves, they do not provide solutions. They are simply tools of analysis which help to shape an appropriate marketing strategy for the company in a given market environment.

6.7 OTHER STRATEGIC OPTIONS

These models do not however cover an important area of strategic development in tourism, namely growth through alliances and joint ventures, acquisition and franchising.

| | **Markets** | | |
	Existing	New or adjacent	Other strategic directions
Existing	■ *Market penetration* • Tour operators discounting to increase market share • Airlines introducing loyalty schemes to retain existing passengers and repeat business	■ *Market development* • Airlines developing strategic alliances to gain territorial share • Destinations seeking new market segments	■ *Integration* • Strategic alliances • Franchising • Joint ventures • Acquisition (vertical and horizontal)
New or adjacent	■ *Product or service development* • Leisure centres at hotels • Integrated resorts being developed in Latin America/Australasia	■ *Diversification* • Waterfront regeneration – retailing and heritage zones • Festivals and events	

(left axis label: **Tourism offerings**)

Figure 6.7 An example of the Ansoff matrix. Strategic direction matrix: tourism offerings (products and services). *Source*: adapted from Ansoff (1957).

Stage of industry maturity

		Embryonic	Growth	Mature	Ageing
Competitive position	Dominant	Grow fast. Build barriers. Act offensively.	Grow fast. Aim for cost leadership. Defend position. Act offensively.	Defend position. Increase the importance of cost. Act offensively.	Defend position. Focus. Consider withdrawal.
	Strong	Grow fast. Differentiate.	Lower cost. Differentiate. Attack small firms.	Lower costs. Differentiate. Focus.	Harvest.
	Favourable	Grow fast. Differentiate.	Focus. Differentiate. Defend.	Focus. Differentiate. Hit smaller firms.	Harvest.
	Tenable	Grow with the industry. Focus.	Hold-on or withdraw. Niche. Aim for growth.	Hold-on or withdraw. Niche.	Withdraw.
	Weak	Search for a niche. Attempt to catch others.	Niche or withdraw.	Withdraw.	Withdraw.

Figure 6.8 The Arthur D. Little matrix. *Source*: adapted from Arthur D. Little (1974) in Wilson, Gilligan and Pearson (1992).

6.7.1 Alliances and joint ventures

Of all of the strategies for growth, alliances or joint ventures have been most prevalent. This has been particularly so in the airline business such as British Airways and American Airlines, Lufthansa and United Airlines or Delta, Sabena and Austria combining forces to increase share on the transatlantic routes (Kane and Conradl, 1997).

There has also been a degree of leasing and contracting out of services between suppliers, especially in the hotel sectors, where restaurants have been contracted out, and in transport operations, where food and beverage supply has been subcontracted to preferred companies as part of a wider alliance. These arrangements are sometimes referred to as **diagonal integration**. For example, Marriott have a deal with McDonald's to supply a fast food outlet in a selection of their hotels.

6.7.2 Acquisitions

The purchase of one company by another to secure new skills or market share is an option which is being considered by a number of larger companies seeking improved performance in a global market. This has certainly been the case in the international hotel market during the past two decades. In Europe, where the market has matured during this period, there has been some degree of consolidation through acquisition, including ITT Sheraton taking over the Italian based CIGA hotels, Forté taking over Meridien Hotels (which belonged to Air France) and then being taken over by Granada. Another example is the Thailand based Dusit Sindhorn acquiring the Kempinski group.

Consider for example the diversity of the French company Groupe Accor, which is involved in accommodation, food and beverage, reservation systems and transport. Table 6.2 illustrates its diversity in the global market.

Vertical and horizontal integration is also becoming increasingly common in the tour operator market. Consider, for example, the integration of Airtours as an organization, illustrated in Figure 6.9.

6.7.3 Franchising

Another way of gaining market share has been by way of franchising, which has been common in North America but less practised in Europe. Franchising relies on strong international or regional branding and strong adherence to the core values of the brand by the franchisee so that the delivery is as good as the brand expectation. The franchisor gains through strategic growth without major capital development expenditure, from fees, and marketing extension to new territorial areas. The franchisee gains an internationally recognized brand, clearly defined operational systems with a

Table 6.2 Groupe Accor: diversity

Division	Examples of companies
Hotels	Ibis Pullman Formula 1 Hotels PLM Azur Mercure Motel 6 Novotol
Travel agencies and intermediaries	Americatoins Astletours Croisières Paquet Wagons Lits Tourism
Restaurants and catering	B Burgers Café Rente Eurest Hexagone Pizza del Arte Relais
Car hire	Europcar
Railways	Wagons Lits – rail and ferry divisions
Tourism services	LV luncheon vouchers Other voucher services such as Ticket Restaurant, Vale despensas Académie Accor Resinter Société Touristique du Mont Blanc

Note: This is not an exhaustive list; it illustrates the wide ranging interests of the group.
Source: trade journals, company literature.

	UK operation	Scandinavia	North America
Distribution/ retailing	Going Places Late Escapes	Spies Shops Tjaereborg Ving	
Tour operation	Airtours Aspro Tradewinds	Always Saga Spies Tjaereborg Ving	Alba Sunquest
Airline operation	Airtours International	Premair	
Accommodation/Cruises	Sun Cruises	Sun Cruises	Sun Cruises

Figure 6.9 Airtours plc (vertical integration). *Source*: trade journals and company brochures, Airtours plc.

track record and back-up services ranging from marketing and training to technical support.

The main drawbacks for the franchisee is the initial capital outlay and the subsequent level of fees. The franchisor has the problem of maintaining quality control across a wide span of franchises. Some of the main franchising arrangements current in Europe are British Airways, McDonald's and several hotel groups.

6.8 STRATEGIC FRAMEWORKS

The tools are simply at hand to improve strategy development; it is essential to recognize the importance for the marketer of 'crafting' a strategy. There are a number of strategic frameworks adopted by organizations in tourism. They are summarized in Figure 6.10.

6.8.1 Market leader strategy

Crafting this type of strategy requires major skill and determination, for in most markets it is difficult to dominate in terms of volume and value of sales or bookings. Such power allows the company to establish benchmarks or standards in the market, to create barriers to entry, and to acquire or remove smaller competitors. It involves major resource commitment, a strong brand presence, a firm marketing orientation throughout the company and a flexibility to implement tactical plans to meet offensive actions by competitors. Innovation and cost reduction should run in parallel.

6.8.2 Follower strategy

Using this framework the company accepts that it might not be possible in the short term to become market leader so adopts a strategy which allows it to maintain a strong position in the market near to the leader. Thus, the company will hold a large market share and will adopt as a matter of course a similar strategic direction to the market leader, changing fast to match, or in some instances improving, the offering of the market leader. The strategy is dependent on intensive competitor intelligence, flexibility and speedily executed tactical campaigns. The ultimate goal will be to become a challenger to the market leader when market conditions permit.

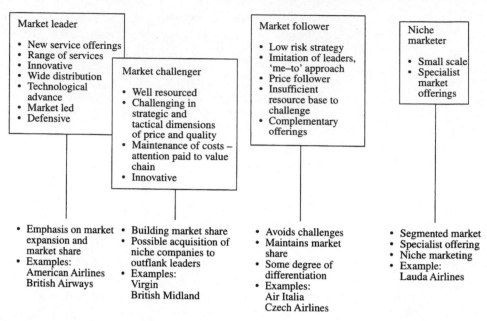

Figure 6.10 Strategic frameworks.

6.8.3 Me too strategies

This is a framework used when the company is not in a position to do otherwise, because of resource limitations. The aim is to maintain a firm position in the market-place by copying the strategy of the market leader in a diluted format. The firm will not be innovative and will be slower to respond to market changes, but nevertheless capable of staying within an outer zone of competition. The emphasis of the strategy lies in copying the successful formulae of market leaders in order to remain in the market.

6.8.4 Niche marketing strategy

This is adopted when a company or an organization appreciates that what it has to offer serves a limited number of market segments, or conversely that there is a limited market which can be readily served. The assumption lies in the fact that there will be limited competition. This is rapidly changing in the tourism sector as the range of substitute destinations is increasing.

6.9 SUSTAINING COMPETITIVE ADVANTAGE

Much of the discussion has focused on the need to devise strategies which offer competitive advantage. The main difficulty is then to sustain it. This requires a constant review of the marketing environment and an awareness of the competitive life cycle. Pioneers in the market tend to gain greater advantage through premium pricing than those who enter at a later stage. In turn, those companies entering later erode the base of the pioneer through competitor activity, but in some markets the pioneer manages to retain the leadership, market share and profitability. In some instances the differential and profits are eroded to a point where businesses, including one time pioneers, leave the market.

Sustainable advantage can also be maintained through an organization achieving extraordinary performance levels in relation to competitors, by adopting a marketing management philosophy which exudes excellence. Of all of the works in the field, the most influential has been that of Peters and Waterman (1982). They studied a number of companies and suggested that those who performed best in the marketplace showed evidence of the eight characteristics listed below. Despite minor criticisms of the work, it has provided an imaginative range of ideas for companies to consider when developing aspects of corporate culture in strategic development. The eight characteristics identified by Peters and Waterman are:

- A closeness to the customer, which they referred to as the 'smell of the customer'.
- Bias for action, in terms of the level of being proactive.
- Autonomy and entrepreneurship. The companies encouraged entrepreneurial activity and responsibility at all levels.
- Productivity through people. Enabling or empowering employees to develop high expectations and respond to peer group assessment.
- Hands-on, value-driven. Leadership spreads core values throughout the organization.
- Sticking to the knitting. Extension of activities should be based on existing competencies.
- Simple form, lean staff. Avoidance of complicated structures and increased layers of staff. Most staff are operational and know where the organization is going.
- Simultaneous loose-tight properties. Decision making happens within frameworks where core values are well understood.

6.9.2 Strategic wear out

The term **strategic wear out** is sometimes used to describe organizations which fail to maintain momentum and therefore sustain competitive advantage. It is brought about by a number of factors including:

- a succession of fast moving and innovative entrants to the marketplace;
- a lack of information on changing customer expectations;
- the pace of change of technological advancement;
- a lack of managerial capability;
- weak internal communications;
- a loss of control in the value chain.

6.10 IS THE MARKETING PLANNING PROCESS RELEVANT IN TOURISM?

Given the increasing complexity of the tourism marketing environment, the growth of international tourism, and the emergence of new patterns of tourism demand, those companies which fail to plan ahead will find it difficult to compete in the marketplace.

There is, of course, a distinction to be made between tourism planning, which refs to the way in which destinations develop tourism offerings for particular markets, and marketing planning, which focuses on how companies plan to meet the requirements of market segments.

In some respects they are similar, for they utilize similar rationales and techniques. The development of tourism offerings by a destination requires adherence to missions or vision statements, market intelligence, market disciplines and creativity in addition to organizational matters. At the same time, marketing planning demands certain types of lifestyle holidays which can only be satisfied at destinations. Tourism development is discussed in Chapters 17 and 20.

6.11 THE MARKETING PLAN

Once strategic options have been analysed, and direction and resource commitments established, an organization can devise a marketing plan which sets out how it will achieve the strategic objectives. The marketing plan usually spans three to five years and in many instances will be a rolling plan which is updated yearly to take account of changing circumstances.

6.11.1 Structure and content

Plans vary in size and structure but invariably include the following sections:

- **Marketing aims and objectives.** The plan will reflect the general aims of the corporate plan then relate more specific objectives to them.
- **Marketing information.** This will include the marketing audit discussed in Section 6.3, but also specifies marketing research required to investigate, for example, service improvement, new market development or consumer feedback.
- **Marketing strategy.** The main emphasis of this section will be to unfold in a rough manner the main directions of the company in terms of market attractiveness and competences. This will be presented in terms of a marketing mix plan.
- **Tourism offerings: service range.** This will include plans for each existing service offering, depending on the results of the analysis of the product or service life cycles, portfolio analysis and competitor analysis. It will also include plans for new developments and brand management.
- **Pricing plan.** The pricing strategy will reflect ways in which the organization relates price as a signal to markets and in relation to competitor offerings. Pricing strategy will take account of value chain analysis, product life and competitor life cycle implications for each brand and consumer perception of the degree of value/quality being offered. There might also be legal or distribution limitations to consider.
- **Communications plan.** This refers primarily to external marketing and is often the largest section of tourism marketing plans. The plan will incorporate a number of submix plans, including some or all of the following: image or brand creation or maintenance, publicity, sales management (or personal selling), advertising, public relations, sponsorship and direct marketing.
- **Internal marketing plan.** Increasingly plans refer to internal marketing of which the core concept is communication within the organization. This section will set

out how internal departments, quality circle groups and management teams can respond to make campaigns work well.

- **Distribution plan.** This varies enormously in the tourism business, as for most organizations it is a matter of bringing the customer to the service offering or destination. Therefore, the emphasis is on locational analysis when referring to hotels and visitor attractions, for example, as well as on the distribution or booking systems. Nevertheless, the distribution plan will invariably focus on the nature of the distributive system, ranging from direct sell to the use of extensive chains of travel agencies.
- **Customer service plan.** There will also be a section which relates to the way in which the organization wishes to recruit, train and improve its personnel, so that it can compete in terms of service provision. The emphasis on consumer service relates to one of the core theoretical constructs of services marketing – inseparability. Related concepts are service quality and the establishment of quality standards.
- **Process plan.** When discussing quality standards it is essential for the organization to integrate into the marketing plan a section on how processes can be improved to enable brands to be more accessible and consumed with ease. It is a classic case of adding perceived value to an offering while holding costs. The areas which this section covers will be improving information capturing systems, provision of information and ease of booking to improve conversions, processing of documentation, processing of visitors on site and improvement of retailing techniques.
- **Physical evidence: design, signage and facility development.** For many businesses in tourism physical evidence is of fundamental importance. Thus the nature of design standards for museums, attractions, retail outlets, hotels and visitor destinations becomes increasingly important if organizations are to seek competitive advantage.

The marketing plan will also often include two other sections relating to expenditure and revenue. They are:

- **Forecasting demand.** The plan will either set out as a separate section, or incorporate in the sales subsection of the communications mix, or in the service/brand section of the service mix, the levels of demand expected as a result of the marketing plan proposed.

   One of the most difficult tasks for marketers is to forecast demand with any degree of accuracy. A forecast relates to the estimate of anticipated visitor numbers or customers which an organization expects over a given time period. The main elements of forecasting are discussed in Chapter 7.
- **Marketing budgets.** Marketing managers have to plan budgetary expenditure in line with expected outcomes from their overall plans. This is a painstaking task, even when there are computerized spreadsheet analyses, which allow easier analysis of different levels of demand and revenues accruing from different marketing plans. Chapter 8 reviews the budgetary process in more detail.

6.12 SUMMARY Whilst the study of marketing planning has been extensive, there is a lack of empirical studies in general, but those which have been undertaken indicate that organizations fail to use many of the well known techniques discussed above (Greenley and Bayus, 1993: 155–72). This is particularly the case in tourism.

There is, however, a compelling case for planning within tourism marketing as a way of improving performance in what is a fast changing market. The problems in achieving sophisticated scanning mechanisms and frameworks for developing strategy should not be underestimated.

REFERENCES

Ansoff, I. (1957) *Strategies for Diversification*, Harvard Business Review, Sept.–Oct.

Atkinson, J. and Wilson, I. (1996) *Strategic Marketing: Cases, Concepts and Challenges*, HarperCollins, London.

Athiyaman, A. and Robertson, R.W. (1995) Strategic Planning in Large Tourism Firms: An Empirical Analysis. *Tourism Mangement*, **16**(3).

Bremner, B. (1992) A Spicier Stew In The Melting Pot. *Business Week*, 21 December, pp. 29–30.

Calatone, R.J. and Mazanec, J.A. (1991) Marketing Management and Tourism. *Annals of Tourism Research*, **18**, 101–19.

Cravens, D.W. (1994) *Strategic Marketing*, Irwin, Homewood, Illinois.

Dembkowski, S. and Hanmer Lloyd, S. (1994) The environmental value-attitude-system model: a framework to guide the understanding of environmentally conscious consumer behaviour. *Journal of Marketing*, October, **10**(7), 593–603.

Desinano, P. and Vigo, C. (1994) Developing information technology options in the hotel industry. In *Tourism, the State of the Art* (eds A.V. Seaton *et al.*), John Wiley, Chichester.

Dev, C.S. and Brown, J.R. (1990) Marketing strategy, vertical structure, and performance in the lodging industry: a contingency approach. *International Journal of Hospitality*, **9**(3), 269–82.

Gateway Frankfurt (1996) Foreword, in *Gateway Frankfurt*, Issue 1, Autumn.

Gilbert, D.C. and Kapur, R. (1990) Strategic Marketing Planning and the Hotel Industry. *International Journal of Hospitaliity Management*, **9**(1), 27–43.

Greenley, G.E. and Bayus, L. (1993) Marketing Planning Decision Making in UK and US Companies: an Empirical Comparative Study. *Journal of Marketing Management*, **9**, 155–72.

Greenley, G.E. (1986) *The Strategic and Operational Planning of Marketing*, McGraw-Hill, Maidenhead.

Hamel, G. and Prahalad, C.K. (1991) Corporate Imagination and Expeditionary Marketing, *Harvard Business Review*, July–August 81–92.

Henderson, B. (1970) The Product Portfolio. *BCG Perspectives*, p. 66.

Jain, S.C. (1990) *Marketing Planning and Strategy*, 3rd edition, South Western, Cincinnati.

Jobber, D. (1995) *Principles and Practice of Marketing*, McGraw-Hill.

Johnson, G. and Scholes, K. (1989) *Exploring Corporate Strategy*, Prentice Hall, Hemel Hempstead.

Kane, F. and Conradl, P. (1997) Brussels let rip in battle with BA, *Sunday Times*, 19 January.

Kotler, P. and Armstrong, G. (1996) *Principles of Marketing*, 7th edition, Prentice Hall, New Jersey.

Leppard, J. and McDonald, M.H.B. (1987) A re-appraisal of the role of marketing planning. *Journal of Marketing Management*, **3**, 159–71.

Leppard, J. and McDonald, M.B.H. (1991) Marketing Planning and Corporate Culture: A Conceptual Framework which Examines Management Attitudes in the Context of Marketing Planning. *Journal of Marketing Management*, **7**(3), 213–36.

Mathur, S.S. (1992) Talking Straight about Competitive Strategy. *Journal of Marketing Management*, **8**, 199–217.

McDonald, M.H.B. (1995) *Marketing Plans, How to Prepare Them, How to Use Them*, 2nd edition, Butterworth-Heinemann, Oxford.

Morrison, A. and Wensley, R. (1991) Boxing up or Boxed in? A Short History of the Boston Consulting Group Share/Growth Matrix. *Journal of Marketing Management*, **7**, 105–29.

Peters, T.J. and Waterman, R.H.W. (1982) *In Search of Excellence: Lessons from America's best run companies.* HarperCollins.

Piercy, N. (1991) *Market-led Strategic Change: Making Marketing Happen in Your Organisation*, Thorsons, London.

Porter, M.E. (1979) How Competitive Forces Shape Strategy, *Harvard Business Review*, **57**(2), 137–45.

Porter, M.E. (1980) *Competitive Strategy: Techniques for analysing industries and competitors*, Collier and Macmillan, Free Press.

Porter, M.E. (1985) *Competitive Advantage,* Free Press, New York.

Schaffer, J.D. (1986) Structure and Strategy: Two Sides of Success. Cornell HRA, February pp. 76–81.

Snow, C.C. and Hrebniniak, L.G. (1980) Strategy, distinctive competence and organizational performance. *Administrative Science Quarterly*, **25**, 317–36.

Warren, K.E. (1966) *Long Range Planning: The Executive Viewpoint,* Prentice Hall, Englewood Cliffs, New Jersey.

Wilson, R.M.S., Gilligan, C. and Pearson, D.J. (1992) *Strategic Marketing Management: Planning, Implementation and Control*, Butterworth-Heinemann, Oxford.

7 Demand forecasting

OBJECTIVES

This chapter explains:

- the principles of forecasting demand in tourism;
- some of the main techniques used by organizations in tourism; their main advantages and disadvantages;
- the application of forecasting to the marketing planning process.

7.1 INTRODUCTION

7.1.1 The principles of demand forecasting

One of the most difficult tasks for marketers is to forecast demand with any degree of accuracy. A forecast relates to the estimates or expected levels of demand set against time periods. Shearer (1994: 8) comments: 'A good forecast will meet the decision needs, give adequate lead time to implement policy, be accurate, cheap and easy to update.'

Forecasts are undertaken by a range of organizations for a number of reasons, but the literature refers mainly to econometric studies which seek to explain future total tourism demand (Sheldon, 1993: 13–20; Smeral *et al.*, 1992: 450–66; Witt, 1994: 516–20). Such forecasts help to set guidelines for strategic direction and form the basis on which more detailed appraisals of the way in which markets might develop. For example, Martin and Mason (1997) forecast that visitor attractions will need to investigate new technologies to succeed:

> New attractions like Sega World or the proposed Electronic Zoo are but the beginning of an industry in true virtual reality which will, in due course, outshine Disney World and CenterParcs in the creation of artificial environments. We counsel all operators to explore digital technologies now, so they are ready to exploit them when the new millennium dawns.

7.1.2 Two primary functions

This chapter outlines the main purposes and techniques available, rather than detailed methodologies and how to use them.

Forecasting has two primary functions:

- to enable resources to be allocated effectively to the marketing effort and at an operational level;
- to minimize risk when constructing future strategies.

In preparing a marketing plan forecasts are made for a number of purposes. They can range from short term predictions, such as tactical campaign planning by a major tour operator, to long term estimates of the demand for tourism to new destinations. Either way, they are based on an assessment of the marketing environment, the resource commitment to be made in providing a range of service offerings and the degree of competition. In its simplest form, forecasting is about establishing a base trend of past visitor numbers and extrapolating the data into the future, as below in Table 7.1, and as such is based on analysis of current trends and expert judgement.

Many businesses in tourism predict demand in this way but not with any degree of precision, because there are so many externalities affecting future demand. These can include rapid fluctuations in exchange rates, isolated acts of terrorism, or negative word of mouth marketing. They can all render forecasts inaccurate, even within the short term (Archer, 1987: 77–86).

7.2 FORECASTING METHODOLOGIES

There are two main sets of techniques, qualitative and quantitative.

7.2.1 Qualitative techniques

Qualitative techniques are those which seek to estimate future levels of demand, based on detailed subjective analysis. They might involve an analysis or interpretation of past and current data regarding a particular market, but the techniques base the projection of demand on knowledge of the market and expert opinion.

Qualitative techniques include:

(a) Sales staff estimates

Some companies seek the opinion of their sales staff as to the direction of the market. For example, a sales team working for a large hotel group might be able to feed back a possible picture of the market.

Table 7.1 European seniors are forecast to travel more

	1990 actual	1995 estimate	2000 forecast
Domestic trips	142 m	185 m	255 m
International trips (within Europe)	38 m	51 m	67 m
International trips (outside Europe)	3 m	5 m	7 m
Total trips	183 m	241 m	329 m

Source: World Tourism Organization (1996) from the presentation of consultant John Seekings, Aviation and Tourism International.

Advantages

1. The main advantage is that sales staff are close to the customer. They can feed back qualitative views about what customers think.
2. They also have a reasonably accurate idea of how competitors are performing.
3. The feedback is likely to be current.

Disadvantages

1. The main disadvantage is that the views will be imprecise and possibly conflicting between staff.
2. It will be particularistic, i.e. based on those who proffer a view rather than on an assessment of a wide range of opinion.

(b) Senior management opinion

Management teams and external consultants are often asked to submit their views about the future of the market. Research reports also tend to rely heavily on expert opinion about the future direction of a market. In some instances, panels of experts are gathered to deliver opinions about the market.

Advantages

1. It brings together expert opinion from those who are often close to the state of the art.
2. Furthermore, discussion with suppliers, internally within the organization and with competitors at trade gatherings, can assist in providing a qualitative forecast of future demand.

Disadvantages

1. It is difficult to quantify the trends and the opinion will be subjective.
2. If the opinion is gathered at a management meeting then it might be the case that senior managers or some experts might dominate the discussion at the expense of other contributions which might be equally valid.

(c) The Delphi technique

A more sophisticated approach is the Delphi technique. It involves obtaining expert opinion about the future prospects for a particular market without the experts actually meeting or necessarily knowing at any stage the composition of the panel. The methodology requires at least two responses from a panel to a formal questionnaire or set of related questions. After the first round, the responses are collated and a summary of the responses fed back to all panel members independently. In light of this feedback, they are asked to respond to the questions again to see if they want to rethink their response, given an appreciation of other points of view.

Advantages

1. Green, Hunter and Moore (1990: 111–20) argue that it has two advantages over other approaches to expert opinion. First, 'the method can aim at gaining a more candid response to the unknowns under consideration. A less personal, corporate opinion would possibly be given if responses were publicly attributed to the individual, as is often the case in a conference situation.'

2. Second, given that there is little or no contact between panel members there is likely to be less peer group pressure. This reduces the level of bias in the predictive process.
3. It is a non-statistical method which lends itself to long range forecasting.

Disadvantages
1. According to Taylor and Judd (1989: 95–9) the main limitation is the problem of selecting panel members. Unless the panel members reflect a wide range of expertise in the business the results could well be biased.
2. Another major problem is attempting to keep the panel committed through what can be a lengthy period. A panel can become unrepresentative if too many respondents drop out at the first stage.

(d) Buyers' intention survey

An organization might simply commission a consultancy to undertake a survey of what buyers will be looking for in the future for their organizations or customers. This type of technique is used in the conference market and sometimes to evaluate how product managers in tour companies think about future destinations.

Advantages
1. The main advantage is that it brings rich qualitative comment from key buyers.
2. It allows a dialogue between supplier and customer in the process.
3. It provides current opinion.

Disadvantages
1. It is a very expensive methodology.
2. Some buyers might feel less inclined to comment on the basis that the nature of discussion is commercially confidential.

(e) Scenario planning

Long term or broad brush scenario planning is undertaken by larger organizations, such as hotel or airline companies. It is a systematic attempt to predict what the future market environment will be like in 10–25 years time and what the likely impacts will be on the company. It involves the examination of a series of trends and patterns of behaviour, such as by governments, and multinational companies. For example, will governments across the world continue to privatize utilities in most states?

This tends to be a precarious activity in that on a global scale there are so many imponderables. Could the break up of the ex-Soviet Bloc have been predicted, for example, or that previously unstable regimes in the Far East could develop as accepted tourism destinations? There will always be unpredictable elements which political risk analysis or disaster planning techniques can not foresee.

Nevertheless, it is feasible to sketch out future scenarios regarding the use of finite resources, demographic predictions, regional development analysis and cultural value systems. A multinational hotel group might, for example, plan a staged approach to hotel development in developing countries initially on the basis of a scenario exercise.

Moutinho (1992), for example, presented an interesting paper at a Tourism in Europe conference where he predicted the way in which tourism will develop by the year 2030. He set out possible changes in consumer behaviour, supply sectors and technology, and concluded by saying that:

> To cope with future tourism planning, management and research, tourism professionals need to be renaissance thinking men and women. The need to imagine, perceive and gauge the future are paramount professional attributes of tourism professionals of tomorrow ... 'we must not expect the expected!'

Advantages
1. Scenario planning exercises are useful in the preparation of contingency or survival plans in the event of certain scenarios coming to fruition, especially when considering rapidly changing patterns of consumer behaviour.
2. Prepare an organization for major disasters such as earthquakes, or environmental catastrophes.

Disadvantages
1. They have been criticized for being too general to be applied with any degree of accuracy.
2. They are time consuming to prepare.

7.2.2 Quantitative techniques

Quantitative techniques rely on analysis of past and current data, in some instances simply projecting future demand in line with past trends; in other cases unravelling casual determinants which may alter in the future. There are a number of well tested methods used, most of which require a degree of statistical ability. A brief description is provided below of the techniques and their advantages and disadvantages. Marketing managers need to be conversant with the range of techniques and what they indicate but very often the statistical formulae are now incorporated into computerized packages. Further discussion of methodological issues are provided in the references.

(a) Time series, non-causal

These involve the forecasting of future demand on the basis of past trends. Historic data is collected for collation on a graph. The vertical axis is the measure of tourist demand such as visitor arrivals at an attraction, sales of holidays, etc., while the horizontal axis is usually the unit of time such as per hour, day, month or year. A line is fitted to the data and extrapolated to forecast future demand. In reality data reflect a more erratic pattern of demand for all manner of reasons. Demand might fluctuate because of seasonality, a promotional campaign, weather, or competitor intrusion. This might result in a biased estimate. Such fluctuations tend to be smoothed by using one of the following techniques:

- **Moving average.** This technique involves taking the average of, for example, the last three values in a set of data, and using this average as the new value.
- **Exponential smoothing.** This applies more weight to the most recent points or

values and less weight to older data. Single exponential smoothing is employed to reduce forecast error. It does this by correcting the last period's forecast by a proportion of last period's error. Other more complex smoothing methods are sometimes used to take into account sudden upward or downward trends such as those brought about by seasonality.

- **Trend curve analysis.** This method involves plotting data, for example bookings, against time on a graph, then proceeding to find a curve of best fit. The model is then used to extrapolate data for the future. The shape of the curve can, for example, be linear, exponential or quadratic, and so on. Therefore, you will find a variety of equations used to explain the trend curve.
- **Regression analysis.** This is the method used to correlate the dependent variable such as visitor demand with the independent variable, for example a given time period. The analysis involves a degree of calibration by way of least squares estimates. Using historical data it enables the marketer to predict new values of demand for expected future values of the independent variable. The coefficient of correlation may also be used to test how well the estimated regression line fits the historical data. In other words, it tests the accuracy of the model as a predictive tool.

Advantages of time series methods
1. They are both easy and inexpensive to compute.
2. The collation of the data necessary for the computation is straightforward.
3. The information can be presented with clarity in a graph form.

Disadvantages of time series methods
1. Time series models assume that demand will grow at a constant rate based on past trends. This renders them inaccurate as markets change so rapidly.
2. They are unable to take into account variables which can cause change in demand, such as erratically fluctuating exchange rates.
3. They are inappropriate for medium to long term forecasting and often this is the requirement for the marketing plan. Thus, assumptions about and interpretation of the market are vital if the trends are to be meaningful to the marketer, even when analysing the short term.

(b) Causal methods

These methods attempt to show, by using regression analysis, how some measure of tourism demand is influenced by selected variables other than time. There are a number of techniques.

Simple regression
This is used to illustrate how demand varies with a single variable such as price of a holiday. In a similar way to trend curve analysis, demand is plotted against the variable using historical data. Using a statistical method known as linear least squares, the line of best fit is drawn and an appropriate equation used to generate a satisfactory model for future forecasts.

Advantages
1. It is easy to use and inexpensive.

2. Only two sets of data are used and therefore obtaining the information is usually feasible.
3. Unlike trend curve analysis a variable is used to explain change in demand.

Multiple regression

Multiple regression is used to demonstrate the influence that a number of variables have on a demand forecast, and how changes in those variables will affect demand. Multiple regression uses essentially the same methodology as simple regression, but more than one variable is used to explain demand. Using a mathematical formula, a relationship is established between demand, for example short breaks, and selected variables such as prices and discretionary income.

To estimate future demand, projected discretionary income and price levels are substituted into the mathematical formula for the given year. The relationship between these variables and the forecast variable (usually demand) is expressed as an equation. Historical data is then used to test the validity of the method. If it is found to work with an acceptable degree of accuracy it will be used to forecast future demand.

Advantages
1. The use of more variables enables a greater degree of accuracy. There are, however, limitations as to how many variables can be used.
2. The method can be used to predict the consequences of possible future changes in variables.

Disadvantages
1. With the increase in variables, the relationships are obviously more complex and there is a greater margin for error.
2. The expenditure on data collection and computation increases substantially.
3. The models cannot be presented graphically and are therefore less easy for non-specialists to grasp.

(c) Computer simulations

Trend curve analysis and multiple regression are combined mathematically to give a computer model which simulates tourism demand. Historical data is used to calibrate the model before using it for forecasting. The data needs to be accurate but sometimes the models are used for longer term complex forecasting.

Software such as Regression Analysis of Time Series (RATS) and Time Series Processor (TSP) are used, as is SPSS-X (a commonly used statistics package). Other commercial forecasting packages such as Orion and Forecast Plus are also available.

7.3 SUMMARY   Organizations need to be aware of the pitfalls of all forecasting methodologies, and wherever possible try a number of techniques to verify the responses. Qualitative techniques are prevalent but have the major drawback of subjectivity. As Makridakis (1986) notes:

> Humans possess unique knowledge and inside information not available to quantitative methods. Surprisingly, however, empirical studies and laboratory experiments have shown that their forecasts are not more accurate than those of quantitative methods. Humans tend to be optimistic and underestimate future uncertainty. In addition the cost of forecasting with judgmental methods is often consistently higher than when quantitative methods are used.

Quantitative forecasting offers a greater degree of accuracy. Econometric forecasting is more promising than time series models in that it anticipates the impact on the variable to be forecast of possible changes in the causal variables. Nevertheless, Witt (1989: 164) comments:

> Forecasting future events precisely is impossible because of the uncertainty which inevitably attaches to the future. A forecasting system therefore cannot be expected to eliminate future uncertainty, only reduce it.

This is a crucial point: forecasting helps to reduce very costly mistakes, for example where estimates of demand for tourism offerings are grossly underestimated or exaggerated. There is a strong case for a mix of qualitative and quantitative methods to secure accurate estimates.

REFERENCES

Archer, B.H. (1987) Demand Forecasting and Estimation. In *Travel, Tourism and Hospitality Research* (eds J.R.B. Ritchie and C.R. Goeldner), John Wiley, New York.

Green, H., Hunter, C. and Moore, B. (1990) Assessing the environmental impact of tourism development, Use of the Delphi technique. *Tourism Management*, June, pp. 11–120.

Makridakis, S. (1986) The art and science of forecasting. *International Journal of Forecasting*, **2**, 17.

Martin, B. and Mason, S. (1997) Baby Boom. *Leisure Management,* January, **17**(1), 34–7.

Moutinho, L. (1992) Tourism: The Near and Future from the 1990s to 2030s or Sensavision TV to Skycycles. A paper presented to the Tourism in Europe Conference, The 1992 Conference, Durham, 8–10 July.

Shearer, P. (1994) *Business Forecasting and Planning*, Prentice Hall, Hemel Hempstead.

Sheldon, P.J. (1993) Forecasting Tourism: expenditures versus arrivals. *Journal of Travel Research,* **XXXII**, 13–20.

Smeral, E., Witt, S.F. and Witt, C. (1992) Econometric Forecasts: Tourism Trends to 2000. *Annals of Tourism Research,* **19**, 450–66.

Taylor, R. and Judd, L. (1989) Delphi Method Applied to Tourism. In *Tourism Marketing and Management Handbook* (eds S. Witt and L. Moutinho), Prentice Hall, New York.

Witt, S.F. (1994) Forecasting international tourism demand: the econometric approach. In *Tourism Marketing and Management Handbook* (eds S.F. Witt and L. Moutinho), Prentice Hall, Hemel Hempstead.

World Travel Organization (1996) World Travel Organization News, No. 4, November.

8 Planning: budgets

OBJECTIVES

This chapter explains:

- the importance of budgets in tourism marketing;
- different types of budgetary methods;
- the use of budgets as control mechanisms;
- examples of how budgets are constructed.

8.1 INTRODUCTION

As part of the overall marketing planning task, marketing managers calculate the level of expenditure necessary to execute a plan. Financial considerations can be of short term nature, such as putting together costings for a six month promotional campaign, or longer term, such as the expenditure associated with a five year strategic plan. The prime purpose of the budget is to evaluate the level of spend necessary to achieve the proposed objectives and targets set out in the plan. A marketing plan is therefore incomplete without a budget.

8.2 THE MAIN PURPOSES OF A MARKETING BUDGET

The marketing budget serves the following purposes:

- It is a numerical representation of the marketing commitment. A crucial element is the cost of implementation in relation to sales or bookings revenue. Thus, if a budget of £500 000 generates £5 million of revenue, the ratio would be expressed as 1:10, i.e. every £1 spent on marketing yields £10 revenue.
- It is a form of monitoring and control to ensure that the marketing effort yields the expected amount of revenue within a given time period. Significant variances in actual revenue or costs can be problematic.
- The marketing budget should ensure that the pricing strategy is based on profitability (or a surplus) in the longer term and break even in the short term. In effect, marketing is an additional cost, as is operational delivery. These costs accumulate to form costs of sales. Pricing can only be determined if costings are accurately known.

- Territorial growth or acquisition strategies involve investment decisions which in turn have an impact on budgetary structure. This in turn affects the net value of the business, i.e. its value in the marketplace.

8.3 METHODS OF BUDGETING

There are a number of methods adopted by organizations but in essence they fall into two broad approaches: the percentage of sales method and the objective and task method.

8.3.1 Percentage of sales method

The first method relies entirely on management judgement as to setting an acceptable budget within the context of expenditure in the entire organization (Balasubraman and Kumar, 1990). It is very often calculated on the basis of previous marketing plans, based on growth of the market, and market share. The marketer is therefore dependent on information about the relationship between marketing spend and sales in previous years.

Many companies therefore set a budget based on a percentage of sales, say between 3 and 10 per cent of sales revenue, which is set aside for marketing. This is sometimes referred to as the **concept of affordability**. Companies also seek benchmarks to follow. They observe what others spend within the sector to ascertain a normal rate, which is sometimes referred to as **comparative parity**. If the normal rate happens to be 12 per cent, then the company concerned will aim for a similar figure. Within a given sector it is common to find that companies allocate a similar amount to marketing expenditure in line with their competitors.

There are two fairly substantial criticisms of this approach. First, it assumes that the level of sales revenue should determine marketing expenditure, when in reality the logical exposition would be that marketing effort determines a level of revenue. The second criticism is that according to the percentage of sales formula, marketing budgets should be reduced when sales revenue is falling. This is not always the best approach. Given a particular set of circumstances such as intense competition, the opposite would be appropriate, i.e. increase marketing expenditure to hold a position.

8.3.2 Objective and task method

This approach is more systematic in that it allows a company to take into account a number of objectives, rather than simply increased revenue (Stewart, 1995). The marketing team establish the tasks required to meet the objectives of the plan, cost each element, then total them to achieve an overall budget.

This approach invariably leads to larger sums of marketing expenditure. Many organizations begin with this type of approach, then adjust the final allocation so that it falls within a ceiling imposed by the board. Thus, once again the budgetary decision reverts to the underlying concept of affordability. This is a polemical topic within an organization, particularly one which follows an overall strategy of cost reduction. An interesting study by the WTO (1995) compared the budgets and marketing plans of national tourism organizations, indicating major variations between levels of expenditure. The results suggest that most government sponsored organizations tend to follow the objective and task methodology as modified by political expediency. In this respect it is interesting to note that convention bureaux and national tourism organizations often seek data from their competitors to illustrate that they are under resourced for the task expected of them.

8.4 CONSTRUCTING BUDGETS

Once a total budgetary level has been determined, the main task relates to reassessing the allocation of the budget between cost centres, service offerings, or according to each task area, such as marketing research or public relations, or in some instances between main elements of publicity and generating markets.

One of the most difficult tasks is to obtain an appreciation of the different elements of cost required to pursue a campaign. Invariably, the marketer will have to rely on the provision of professional and production services, such as the price of a design for a campaign, print, renting of exhibition space and distribution of leaflets (see Figure 12.3 for an illustration).

8.4.1 Examples of budgets

Here are several examples adapted from case studies which indicate the variation in size of budget according to the nature and components of the campaign or tasks. They are based on current examples, but are not attributed to any organization, as budgetary matters tend to be of a confidential nature. They illustrate, however, the varying levels of resources available to tourism marketers and the approaches adopted to reach different market segments.

Example 8.1 presents a budget expenditure associated with the development of a new visitor attraction in relation to expected visitor numbers. It stresses the importance of relating expenditure to estimated revenue.

Examples 8.2 outlines estimated marketing expenditure of an historic city, which outlines the breakdown of a hypothetical budget.

Example 8.3 illustrates how a budget can be used to monitor effectiveness. Baker (1996: C33) refers to a database marketing campaign seeking to generate enquiries for short breaks. A database of 65 000 product names were chosen of people who have previously shown an interest in tourism and who lived within a reasonable catchment area. The campaign costs are shown in the example.

8.4.2 Problems encountered in constructing budgets

There are a number of dilemmas when constructing budgets:

- The difficulty for many tourism marketers is that the budget expenditure in year one might not reap the desired outcomes within the time frame of the plan. There can be a time lag of at least one season between the diffusion of a campaign message and a response from the market.
- It is often difficult to apportion exact amounts of expenditure to each different tourism offering. A tour operator might promote a range of 10 to 12 different types of holiday in a general publicity campaign, knowing that of the 10 holidays on offer, four sell very well and the others simply break even. It is not always possible to allocate precisely costs to a particular brand or area of marketing activity.

Example 8.1 Costings for a new transport related visitor attraction.

	Walk-up visitors	Group travel	Educational	Promotional events	Corporate	Other income[2]	Total
Visitors							
Visitor numbers	200 000	10 000	10 000	50 000	25 000	–	295 000
Entrance charges income[1]	£600 000	£30 000	£30 000	£150 000	£75 000	£150 000	£1 035 000
Retail income[3]	£300 000	£15 000	£15 000	£75 000	£37 500	–	£442 500
Net retail income	£100 000	£5 000	£5 000	£25 000	£10 253	–	£145 253
Catering revenue[4]	£400 000	£20 000	£20 000	£100 000	£50 000	–	£590 000
Net catering income	£200 000	£10 000	£10 000	£50 000	£25 000	–	£295 000
Subdivision totals							
Gross income	£1 300 000	£65 000	£65 000	£325 000	£162 500	–	£1 917 500
Net income	£900 000	£45 000	£45 000	£225 000	£110 253	£150 000	£1 475 253

Notes

1. Tickets vary according to adult, concessionary, group and family.
   Average per head is £3.00.
2. Using facilities for filming/promotional purposes.
3. Assumption that average retail spend per head is £1.50.
   Retail margin 30 per cent (after cost of sales and VAT).
4. Assumption that average catering spend per head is £2.00.
   Catering retail margin 50 per cent (after cost of sales and VAT).

Marketing budget	summary (£)
Originating/Design[1]	25 000
Media advertising	35 000
Exhibitions	8 000
Public relations	5 000
Print	20 000
Misc. promotions	6 000
Market research	10 000
Travel and subsistence	8 000
Events	15 000
Contingency	5 000
TOTAL[2]	132 000

1. Improve/build on existing 'brand' identity.
2. This represents a ratio of 1:11, i.e. every £1 spent on marketing yields £11
   net income.

● With destination marketing there is often no direct measurement of a campaign
   which promotes all aspects of a destination, rather than simply core visitor attractions, or selected accommodation.

8.5 BUDGETS AS MONITORING TOOLS

Measuring actual performance against estimated results is a perennial pastime of marketers. Rightly or wrongly they are judged by the level of bookings, passengers on
board, or visitors through the shop, and the revenue this brings. This is, however, far
too narrow a perspective when considering the marketing role in the context of corporate
vision. Analysis of sales or bookings on a regular basis allows an organization to
adjust the plan accordingly in the short term and to reallocate resources where necessary.

Example 8.2 The marketing budget of an historic city, 1997/8.

Advertising	Target market		Expenditure
Tourist board guides	Overseas visitors		£2000
Local advertising	Local community		£500
Radio Times /regional newspapers	Regional/short breaks		£3000
Travel trade manuals	Travel trade		£2500
		Subtotal	£8000
Exhibitions			
Domestic trade fairs			
British travel trade fair			£1000
Other travel fairs			£2000
Shopping precincts	Short breaks		£1000
Origination of new displays	market/day visitors		
Overseas trade fairs			
ITB (Berlin)	Holidays		£1000
Vakantie (Netherlands)			£1000
World Travel Market (joint venture)			£3000
		Subtotal	£9000
Publicity and promotion			
Brochure	Mainstream market		£5000
Travel trade material	Travel trade		£1000
Visitor attraction leaflets	Day market		£2000
Personal selling (expenses)			£500
		Subtotal	£8500
Joint marketing schemes			
Overseas tourism partnership	Overseas		£3000
Historic cities partnership	Short breaks		£1000
Conferences promotion	Business		£1000
Festive campaigns	Day visits		£3000
Other joint marketing initiatives	Day/short breaks		£3000
		Subtotal	£11 000
Public relations			
Familiarization visits (press)			£1500
		Subtotal	£1500
Monitoring and review			
Annual visitor survey			£3000
		Subtotal	£3000
Contingency funds		Subtotal	£2000
Total budget			**£42 000**

8.5.1 Ratio analysis

The analysis of financial data to assess how effective a marketing plan has been usually involves the calculation of a number of ratios. Ratio analysis is commonly used to assess the relationship between two financial variables, primarily to assess the current performance of the business, both internally and with competitors. Figure 8.1 highlights the key performance ratios.

Example 8.3 Mailing costs and response rates. *Source*: Baker (1996).

Total mailed 65 000

List rental	£7 150.00
Printing: £20 per '000	£1 300.00
Postage: £130 per '000	£8 450.00
Freepost reply: £200 per '000	£1 314.00
Total cost	£17 214.00
Response	6 570
Response percentage	10.1%
Cost per reply	£2.62

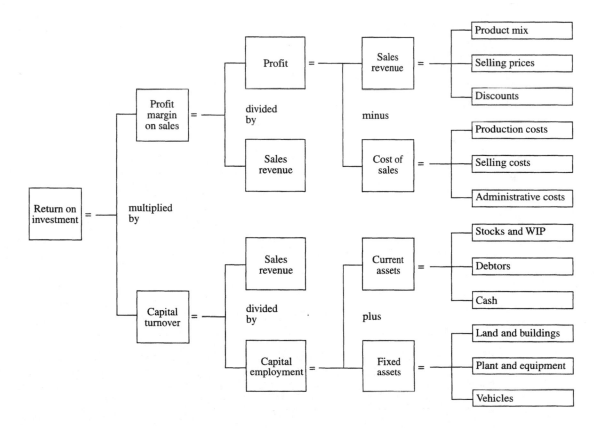

Figure 8.1 Constituents of return on investment. *Source*: Wilson, Gilligan and Pearson (1992).

Middleton (1994: 159) suggests that there are four specific ratios which are useful to marketers when evaluating the results of a plan or campaign:

- ratio of total marketing expenditure:total sales revenue;
- ratio of total marketing expenditure:gross contribution;
- ratio of total marketing expenditure:net profit;
- ratio of total marketing expenditure: unit cost of production.

8.5.2 Unit performance

Budgetary control allows comparison across outlets and can highlight very quickly if a unit is not performing well for internal rather than external reasons. For example, a staff team might be disgruntled about their work at a fast food restaurant and pass this feeling onto customers. The results will show clearly as revenue drops. The variance will show in relation to other units and remedial action can be taken.

8.5.3 Internal liaison

In theory the process of constructing budgets is meant to bring the finance and marketing teams together, to devise more finely tuned plans in subsequent years. In reality there is always a balance between financial monitoring and risk taking. This requires the skills of both departments but can lead to tensions.

8.6 SUMMARY The marketer needs to be conversant with elementary budgeting. It is an essential task to plan marketing expenditure and compare this with expected revenues. Tourism marketers use a variety of techniques to establish budget levels but the most appropriate is the objective and task method. While this is adopted by many organizations, the approach is invariably modified by the need to hold or reduce costs.

Tourism marketers also need to build in to the marketing planning process budgeting as a form of monitoring and control so that actual sales or visitor spend can be assessed against expected demand. This usually requires continued liaison with sales administration and finance sections.

REFERENCES

Baker, J. (1996) A Lesson in Database Marketing – The English Tourism Example. *Insights*, November, C29–C38.

Balasubraman, S.K. and Kumar, V. (1990) Analysing Variations in Advertising and Promotional Expenditures: Key Correlates in Consumer, Industrial and Service Markets. *Journal of Marketing*, **54**(2), 57–68.

Middleton, V.T.C. (1994) *Marketing In Travel and Tourism*, Butterworth-Heinemann, Oxford.

Stewart, D. (1995) Allocating The Promotional Budget: Revisiting The Advertising and Promotional Sales Ratio. A paper presented to the Marketing Education Group Conference, Salford University, July.

Wilson, R.M.S. with Gilligan, C. and Pearson, D.J. (1992) *Strategic Marketing Management*, Butterworth-Heinemann, Oxford.

World Tourism Organization (1995) *Budgets and Marketing Plans of National Tourism Administrations*, WTO, Madrid.

Marketing research in tourism $\boxed{9}$

OBJECTIVES

This chapter explains:

- marketing information systems;
- the uses of secondary and primary research;
- marketing research methodologies, their advantages and limitations;
- marketing research as an aid to decision making in tourism.

9.1 INTRODUCTION

Marketing managers need to possess timely and accurate information in order to plan both market and service development. They also need market information in order to be proactive, for example, in terms of positioning a company or brand in the market. This could not be more apposite in tourism marketing as both the consumer and competitive environment tend to change within short time frames. Furthermore, as Chisnall (1986) notes, there should be a two way flow between the organization and its external environment. This has become critical, for example, in terms of computer reservation systems and the symbiotic relationship between airlines, hotels groups and car rental companies. The importance of a similar flow of information within an organization forms an integral part of the internal marketing process.

9.2 MANAGEMENT INFORMATION SYSTEMS

Management information systems, often known as MIS, describe a variety of information networks which are adopted by organizations. A subset of this is the marketing information system (sometimes referred to as MKIS). Lancaster and Massingham (1993: 276) define the MKIS as:

> a system used to generate and disseminate an orderly flow of pertinent information to marketing managers. Marketing research is concerned with the task of generating information, whereas the MKIS is focused on managing the flow of information to marketing decision makers.

A marketing information system comprises a series of networks rather than necessarily a library of information stored in one location. Different departments within an organization generate data for a variety of reasons. It is quite common to find the sales department of a hotel group storing information regarding customer enquiries, conversion rates from calls to bookings, and length of stay per visitor. The finance department, on the other hand, will record details regarding how consumers pay, the level of spend per visitor and other pecuniary details. The MKIS is meant to bring dispersed data, such as this, together in a way that makes sense to the marketer and in a format which can be used effectively. For example, by analysing these two discrete sources of information a hotel might find that executives on corporate accounts spend less across the bars and restaurants than non-corporate account clients from small to medium sized companies. This would signal the need for a more detailed examination to ask why and how the hotel can gain from the trend. Whatever the system it should be designed to ensure that the available data is both comprehensive and digestible, i.e. in a format that the tourism marketer can easily interpret. In larger organizations such as Quantas Airlines or Thomas Cook, where there are major flows of information, there is often a systems department or Marketing Intelligence unit to manage such processes. Such a unit determines the type of information available and the level and frequency of provision appropriate. The approach makes sense as marketing information is both a costly and perishable commodity.

9.3 MARKETING RESEARCH

Marketing research is the systematic collection and analysis of data relating to the provision of products and services. Defined more formally it is:

> the function linking the customer and public to the marketer through information used: to identify and define marketing opportunities and problems; to generate, refine and evaluate marketing actions; to monitor marketing performance; and to improve the understanding of the marketing process.
>
> *(American Marketing Association, quoted in Kotler et al., 1987)*

9.3.1 Purposes of marketing research

The main purposes of marketing research are threefold:

● to inform and hence improve decision making at all levels;
● to minimize the degree of uncertainty when making risk-laden decisions such as an evaluation of the potential of a multimillion pound holiday complex;
● to allow an organization to develop a market forecasting system based on market intelligence.

There are other reasons which are seemingly less obvious but nevertheless important:

● Marketing research is conducted to establish closer contact with customers in a formal way. It is a visible demonstration of interest in customer needs expressed in an objective manner.
● It allows an organization to focus attention on specific but crucial issues which require resource commitment. Therefore, marketing research can be used to prepare a case at operational management level to support a project requiring resource commitment at board level.

Given that the potential application of marketing research in tourism is wide ranging it is surprising that it is not employed extensively (Horner and Swarbrooke, 1996: 444).

Nevertheless, marketing research has become more important during the past decade, certainly among the major international companies. It has, for example, become a recognized core of any feasibility study. Consultants and developers undertake marketing research to assess the potential of particular resorts, or when evaluating specific sites for development such as a hotel, visitor attraction or retail complex.

Furthermore, marketers at hotels, visitor attractions or in tour operation increasingly seek data, both of a continuous and *ad hoc* nature, about patterns of consumer behaviour. Furthermore, national tourism organizations seek to coordinate research ranging from attitudinal surveys to the measurement of large scale tourism flows.

9.3.2 The research process

The marketing research process (more specifically market research exercises) follows a series of logical steps. Whilst different researchers have identified a varying number of stages involved, the following steps appear to be universally accepted. Figure 9.1 illustrates the key steps in the process.

(a) Problem identification and definition

Firstly, the aim and scope of the research needs to be established. This leads to a more detailed set of objectives which focus on the problem(s) to be solved. They are often represented as a series of hypotheses (i.e. testing assumptions as a starting point of an investigation) to be addressed during the process. Consider a possible case of market development. A marketing executive might wish to test the assumption that over 55s are now more interested in activity holidays than previously, but are seeking gentler pursuits such as walking and cycling.

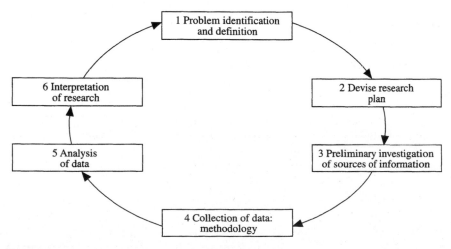

Figure 9.1 Key steps in the marketing research process.

(b) Devise a research plan

The second step would be to determine a research action plan, if only to draft time scales and levels of resource available. In reality, this stage is almost certainly undertaken in parallel with the next one. Until there is clearer idea of the nature and availability of secondary data the plan cannot be finalized. At the second time of drafting, the plan would include both secondary and primary research necessary, the methodology to be adopted and whether the research will be undertaken in house or by an external agency.

In the example above, the research activity might relate to an examination of an activities package which potential elderly customers might prefer. The research would provide a clearer picture, for example, prior to a test market of a possible package break for next season. A market research budget of £8000 might be allocated for the project. Given tight time scales and a low budget, the scope of the investigation would have to be limited. In such circumstances, an executive might decide to undertake the desk research first then commission an agency to survey existing clients in the 55 plus age group.

(c) Preliminary investigation of information sources

A review of existing sources of information, both internal and external, would assist in the process of sharpening and focusing objectives. It enables the marketer to decide whether primary research is essential or simply desirable. This initial review feeds the methodology section of the plan. In the example of the over 55s' market, the executive would most probably analyse internal data about existing customers, their age profile, preferred destinations, etc., in order to understand patterns of behaviour better. He or she would also possibly buy in external reports from companies such as Keynote or Mintel as well as looking at other sources of intelligence such as the English Tourist Board's *Insights* intelligence service.

It is probable that there will be a need for more detailed primary research because the study is about customer motivation and buying intentions. The executive might decide to issue a tender for a marketing research exercise, say on a budget of £6000 (the £2000 having been spent on commercial reports). The brief would outline the task in hand.

(d) Collection of data

Determining data requirements is difficult on two counts. First, it is necessary to make a judgement as to whether the collection of primary data is necessary or not. The second question relates to a decision about which type of data would be most useful, and obviously within the budgetary constraints of the project. This relates to the methodology to be adopted. Very often a marketing research company will test the method by using a pilot survey.

In the case of the tour operator, the marketing research agency would perhaps decide to hold six focus groups (a qualitative technique featuring discussion groups) in different parts of the country (at an estimated cost of £650 per focus group, amounting to £3900) and then to sample a potential client database by telephone interview given that time schedules are tight (at an estimated cost of £8 per interview, amounting to £2000).

(e) Analysis of data

This would depend entirely on the methodology chosen, whether qualitative or quantitative. For example, a focus group analysis will invariably require a written interpretation of attitidunal statements recorded at the time of the discussion. In contrast, the analysis of 250 responses to a telephone survey will more than likely involve processing previously coded survey forms using a computer software package.

This raises an important practical issue which often confounds those undertaking research for the first time. There is a need to anticipate the analysis required when designing (and costing) a survey. That is why a pilot questionnaire should be tested. This enables the researcher to check that not only do respondents understand the questionnaire but that the coding is functional.

(f) Interpretation and research presentation

Interpretation of results so that the organization can make best use of the data is an important part of the process. Results need to be presented in a summary format, represented visually wherever possible, and referring to a more detailed information breakdown if required. In the 55 plus survey, the results might show a divided opinion among respondents as to whether they really like the concept of activity holidays and then if they do, which ones are preferred. The report might indicate a very undecided and fragmented market and the executive might decide to put the development of a new package on hold until next year.

9.4 SOURCES OF INFORMATION

9.4.1 Desk research

Desk research (sometimes known as secondary research) relates to information which has already been collected for another purpose. It often suffices. Vital information about the marketing environment such as market size and structure, consumer trends, etc., will usually be available in a variety of government and trade reports. In terms of global data, the most comprehensive source is the World Tourism Organization's Online Statistics Service covering some 200 countries and territories. Furthermore, the company will most probably have a considerable amount of internal data (sales records, financial transactions) on existing customers. Table 9.1 outlines the major sources of information available in the UK for tourism marketers.

Limitations
External secondary research is essential to the researcher in tourism but it is equally important to a marketer in a company. Practitioners offer a number of salient points about desk research:

1. Selecting the information
   There is usually more information rather than less available. Therefore, it is essential to develop a clearly defined framework focusing on the objectives of the exercise. While the initial stage of an investigation will be by necessity broad, narrowing the scope of the research activity is a prime task. This can be done by selecting key documents to analyse in the first instance. Essential information includes:

Table 9.1 Major sources of information

Sources of external published data	Type of information available
International organizations, world data and other regional/country trends	• World Tourism Organization: the most authoritative source of international tourism data. There is now an online interactive statistics service: www.world-tourism.org • United Nations: statistical yearbooks • OECD: tourism policy and international tourism in OECD member countries (annual) • European Union: European marketing data and statistics, such as Eurobarometer
United Kingdom government sources	• Major surveys based on General Household Survey, Social Trends, Transport Statistics, Overseas Visitor Survey, International Passenger Survey • Special commissions reporting back on findings or departmental reports such as 'Competing With The Best' 1995, main departments are Employment and Heritage
Tourist boards	Major surveys including: • UK Tourism Survey – annual survey sponsored by all tourist boards, comprehensive coverage • UK Day Visits Survey – sponsored by a variety of organizations and published by the Countryside Recreation Network • Other tourist board surveys including Sightseeing in the UK, numerous local visitors surveys, etc. • *Insights* published by English Tourist Board
Intelligence gathering agencies	The main sources of tourist information are: • Economist Intelligence Unit – *Travel and Tourism Analysis* • Euromonitor – consumer series and other reports • Keynote – many reports feature aspects of tourism • Mintel – wide range of tourism reports • Commercial data on companies in tourism such as Directory of Multinationals, Datastream, Kompass, etc. Many of these are to be found on CD-ROM.
Trade press	Periodicals such as *Leisure Opportunities* and *Travel Trade Gazette*
Newspapers	Reports in quality papers
Trade and academic journals	• F&S Index which abstracts trade journals on a worldwide basis • Major journals such as *Annals of Tourism Research, Journal of Travel Research, Tourism Management*, etc.
Professional organizations	Reports from meetings such as The Tourism Society
Specialist consultancies	Major consultancies prepare reports for clients which sometimes become public

• market volume – the total number of bookings or sales in the market;
• market value – the monetary value of the sales;
• market structure – the number and level of competitors;
• trends – the direction of the market;
• consumer segmentation – different types of customers;
• consumer profiles – their characteristics and how they buy.

2. Verifying data sources

It is important to verify sources of information. What is the credibility of the organization collecting the data and for what purpose?

3. Checking the methodology

   The degree of accuracy of data is also important, the reason for it being collected and the methods used. It enables an assessment of the value of the data. This is very apparent when working with comparative data across countries or regions of the world. Comparisons are notoriously difficult as data is gathered in different ways for different purposes. For example, the emerging states in Eastern Europe have been in recent years attempting to seek a degree of coordination about a unified statistics system. They have established a Commonwealth of Independent States (CIS) Statistics Committee (World Tourism Organization, 1996: 13) to coordinate the work.

4. Over-generalizing

   There is also a danger in generalizing about a market from particularistic studies. An in-depth report on one country in South East Asia does not mean that a similar pattern is occurring elsewhere in the region. When data is limited there is a temptation to generalize about a region based on the scant information which is available.

5. Time lags

   One of the major drawbacks of secondary data is that it is often dated. In a fast moving market such as tourism this can be a serious limitation.

6. Syndicated research

   Syndicated research which is collected on behalf of a group of companies or as a service to the sector by a specialist marketing research or intelligence agency is often overlooked as a rich source of material.

9.4.2 Primary reseach

In some cases, either because the secondary data is limited, dated or not verifiable, it is necessary to undertake what Crouch (1984: 67) describes as 'made to measure' research. This involves establishing a research framework to obtain new data about an aspect of the business or market. It becomes a more prominent subset of the marketing research plan as researching primary data is an expensive pursuit.

9.5 RESEARCH METHODOLOGY

In terms of methodology the main distinction lies between qualitative and quantitative techniques in tourism marketing. Whilst other marketing research approaches are used, such as observational techniques, they are rare. Techniques tend to be divided into qualitative and quantitative methods.

9.5.1 Qualitative research

Qualitative techniques are used to probe areas if a deeper insight is required, such as in motivational studies, including attitudinal or perceptional issues. The aim of qualitative research is to elicit detailed material, such as attitudes towards a tourism offering, but in no way can it be described as a representative sample of a given population. Despite this limitation, qualitative studies are highly regarded in the business. As Veal (1993) notes:

Table 9.2 Main research techniques

Qualitative

• In-depth interviews	Used to ascertain detailed attitudinal views
• Group discussions	Used to ascertain attitudes about new services, branding, etc. Commonly used technique.
• Group discussion with experts	As above
• Delphi technique	Forecasting technique primarily
• Participant observation	Researcher joins respondents in discussion or activities

Quantitative

• Omnibus surveys	Widely used method of obtaining survey data
• Postal surveys	Self-completion surveys
• Exit surveys	Self-completion on existing attractions for example
• Diary response	Respondents are requested to maintain a diary of activity and expenditure
• Telephone survey	Tele-research is becoming a more common approach to surveying
• Face to face interview	Improves the quality and targeting of research

Much qualitative research is based on the belief that the people personally involved in a particular (leisure or tourism) situation are best placed to analyse and describe it in their own words – that they should be allowed to speak without the intermediary of the researcher.

They can be used as an exploratory approach to a major quantitative exercise in some instances.

(a) In-depth interviews

An interviewer would be briefed to discuss a topic or topics, usually on a face to face basis, with a small number of respondents, using a guideline for discussion but allowing a free flow approach rather than structured questions and responses. This would allow for more natural and unguarded responses.

For example, a few years ago a major long haul tour operator was interested to find out why potential customers sought their brochures but then did not book. An initial review suggested that there might be some failing with the publicity material. A researcher was briefed to visit approximately 15–20 customers to discuss their attitudes towards travel, their approach to buying travel packages and in particular why they were not buying the client company's tours. The respondents were without exception in the AB socioeconomic category, mainly retired or semi-retired, and viewed travel as an enjoyable pastime.

They were found to be very knowledgeable about destinations, and about most company packages, including those supplied by the client company. The researcher found that the customers regarded the company highly in all aspects, including the literature provided. Price was the only barrier to purchase: the company was perceived as being too expensive. Having used the company's publicity as a guide, the respondents proceeded to make other arrangements for travel in order to economize. On the basis of the in-depth qualitative research, the company reformulated its offering to overcome the perceived major barrier.

(b) Group discussions

This is frequently used to ascertain attitudes to new services, products, branding and endorsement, or to uncover underlying beliefs about destinations. The methodology is straightforward. Members of the discussion group are selected to reflect a market and geographical spread. Respondents are invited to a hotel in their town of residence, to join say 8 to 12 other respondents and a moderator. The moderator (usually a psychologist) guides the discussion and records the session on tape. The emphasis is on informality so that people can freely and openly respond to the ideas presented for discussion. This might include discussing a proposed brand name of a new holiday package, the components of a holiday package, or the type of celebrity that might be associated with a promotion. The results might then be used as a basis for structuring a quantitative research exercise. The respondents are given a small honorarium as recompense for attending.

(c) Group discussion with experts

This is similar to the above except that a group of experts are gathered together to discuss issues. The experts might be a group of buyers from tour operators, hoteliers, or tourism officers.

(d) The Delphi technique

The Delphi technique was discussed in Chapter 7 as a forecasting technique. It is also used for wider marketing research exercises. First developed by the Rand Corporation for technological forecasting, it has since been used in tourism as a way of eliciting expert opinion with some degree of objectivity (Seaton and Bennett, 1996: 108). The aim is to encourage a group of experts to evaluate a complex issue by consensus without actually meeting face to face. The process begins with the selection of a panel of experts and this is considered to be the most critical element, achieving a dedicated, mixed and genuinely knowledgeable panel (Taylor and Judd, 1994: 95–9). They do not meet nor do they know who their colleagues are at this stage. A questionnaire is devised and sent to the panel. The results are evaluated by the moderator of the research and a second questionnaire is issued allowing respondents to rethink through their first responses again in light of comments fed back to them from the first stage. The aim is to achieve a degree of agreement about each topic without the peer pressure associated with expert meetings.

The main advantage of the technique is that it can provide an objective view about the subject being discussed at a reasonable cost (Green, Hunter and Moore, 1990: 111–22). The limitations are that it depends very much on the panel and whether they can be pursuaded to collaborate through what can be a lengthy process. The summary of the first questionnaire results may also be biased by the researcher(s).

(e) Participant observation

The technique of participant observation is not used extensively in tourism market research. This is where the researcher gathers information about a process or pattern of behaviour, by participating in it at the same time as recording observations.

9.5.2 Quantitative techniques

There are a wide range of techniques available to tourism marketers and marketing researchers to choose from. The methodologies have benefits and disadvantages according to specific situations. For example, postal questionnaires are relatively cheap but few respondents are willing to reply to long questionnaires. Response rates are often low.

Quantitative research refers to the collection and analysis of statistically verifiable data involving the diligent use of sampling techniques. The underlying principle is that by surveying a **representative sample** the marketer will be able to apply the findings of the sample survey to the entire market, simply because the respondents to the survey are thought to be representative of the entire population being researched. Table 9.3 summarizes the sampling techniques available and offers a guide to sample sizes.

Survey methods

These are sometimes referred to as contact methods, and include the following:

Omnibus surveys

This is a method which involves companies sharing space on a questionnaire survey. A respondent will therefore be asked about a number of issues ranging from weekly household purchases, to eating out or holiday taking. For example, the types of questions given in Example 9.1 are sometimes used in omnibus surveys.

Omnibus surveys are well established and offer a cost effective method of initiating quantitative research without incurring heavy costs. There are specialist services

Table 9.3 Sampling plans

Sampling techniques	Examples
Probability samples	
Simple random sampling	Selecting from Acorn, or census data
Stratified sampling	Selecting from different market segments
Cluster sampling	Selecting pockets of respondents in urban areas
Non-probability samples	
Convenience sampling	Sampling at city centre locations only
Quota sampling	Selecting 18–25s only

Calculation of sample size for 95% (i.e. margin of error ± 5 per cent)

Population	Sample size required
100	80
200	132
500	217
1 000	278
2 000	322
5 000	357
10 000	370
100 000	383

Example 9.1 Examples of questions in omnibus surveys: likely client would be a tour operator.

- Where have you been on holiday in the last 2 years? Please tick

  ☐ England   ☐ Scotland   ☐ Wales

  ☐ Europe   ☐ USA   ☐ Elsewhere

  Reason: Verification of existing holiday taking.

- What type of holiday do you prefer?

  ☐ Camping/caravanning

  ☐ Self-catering

  ☐ Hotel

  ☐ Winter sun

  ☐ Winter snow

  ☐ City breaks

  Reason: Preference of type of holiday.

- Are you considering a trip to any of the following within the next 12 months?

  ☐ Australia   ☐ Latin America

  ☐ Asia   ☐ South Africa

  ☐ Far East   ☐ USA

  Reason: Evaluation of trends in long haul market.

---

available from companies such as CAPIBUS (RSL), BRMB or NOP. Some offer specialist travel surveys, for example, of business travellers.

Postal surveys (self-completion)

This is the most common form of survey. A respondent is sent a questionnaire, usually with instructions, a pledge of confidentiality and a reply-paid envelope. The major problem with this technique is the low rate of return despite organizers offering prize draws to stimulate return. It is not unusual to achieve a response rate of less than 10 per cent. It can also be expensive to issue a reminder questionnaire to those who fail to send in a return by the required date.

In situ or exit surveys (self-completion)

Self-completion questionnaires which seek customer feedback are becoming more common in hotels, at visitor attractions and to a lesser extent among transport operators. The classic example is the self-completion questionnaire provided by companies to assess customer satisfaction. See Figure 9.2.

Diary response

An uncommon self-completion technique is the use of a diary issued to the respondent before he or she travels or begins a holiday. The diarist is expected to record places visited, activities undertaken and the amount of spend per day.

Please place your completed questionnaire in the collection box, located within the outlet were you made your purchase. Pens can also be obtained from this point.

	Very Poor	Poor	Average	Good	Very Good
Firstly, how would you rate us on the following?					
Friendliness, courtesy of staff	☐	☐	☐	☐	☐
Range and variety of food/drink/ refreshments	☐	☐	☐	☐	☐
Atmosphere/ambience	☐	☐	☐	☐	☐
Cleanliness	☐	☐	☐	☐	☐
Quality of food/drink/refreshments	☐	☐	☐	☐	☐
Speed of service	☐	☐	☐	☐	☐
Value for money	☐	☐	☐	☐	☐
To summarise, how would you rate your visit to this outlet?	☐	☐	☐	☐	☐

Would you visit this outlet again if visiting the airport in the future? Yes ☐ No ☐

| Date of visit   /   / | Time of day   am/pm |

Food/drink items purchased:

Amount spent: £

What do you think we should be concentrating on most to improve our operation?/Further comments

_____
_____
_____
_____
_____

What is your reason for being at the airport today?

leisure/ traveller ☐   business traveller ☐   dropping off or collecting passengers ☐   working at airport ☐   other reasons ☐

If travelling, what is your flight number? [   ]

How long would you anticipate spending at this terminal today?

less than 1 hour ☐   1 to 2 hours ☐   2 to 3 hours ☐   other [hrs]

How many times during the last 12 months have you visited/used this terminal?

first time ☐   twice ☐   3–10 times ☐   more than 10 times ☐

How often do you visit this outlet when visiting the airport?

first time ☐   seldom ☐   often ☐   each time ☐

How many people are in your party? [   ] How many are under 18? [   ]

Please tick:

Male: ☐   Name [   ]

Female: ☐

Age group: Address [   ]

Under 18 ☐   [   ]

19–24 ☐   [   ]

25–34 ☐   [   ]

35–44 ☐   [   ]

45–54 ☐   [   ]

55–64 ☐   Postcode [   ]

65+ ☐

Would you mind telling us your occupation? [   ]

Please note, should you have a serious complaint, please contact the manager on duty to allow us to deal with the problem immediately.

If you do not wish to receive any future promotional literature please tick ☐

Thank you for your help

Figure 9.2 Customer comment card. *Source*: Select Service Partner Airport Restaurants Ltd.

Telephone survey

As the level of household telephone ownership has increased almost to saturation level in most European states, telephone research surveys have become more common. Using computerized scripts, telephone researchers are able to input the responses to the survey questions as the respondent speaks. These systems are sophisticated in that they guide the interviewer through complicated questionnaires with ease. This makes it a far more cost effective technique than previously and offers the advantage of speed. The main disadvantages are calling back respondents, which increases costs.

Face to face interview

The face to face interview is the most common personal interview technique used in many countries. The interview can be conducted in the home, at the airport, or at any given tourism destination. The use of an interviewer has a number of advantages especially when questionnaires are unstructured (i.e. the questions are open ended, rather than closed questions requiring yes/no responses, scales, etc.), long, complicated, or where there are sections which invite comment, for example, about likes and dislikes. Furthermore, an interviewer can prompt the interviewee if there is no immediate response. Advantages are high response rates, complete questionnaires, rich anecdotal comment and the accurate selection of respondents when seeking quotas. Disadvantages are cost and interviewer bias.

9.6 QUESTIONNAIRE DESIGN

The most difficult task for the market researcher is the design of a questionnaire, although there are a number of computerized packages which can assist in the process of questionnaire design such as SNAP. A questionnaire usually requests three key levels of response:

- identification (name, address and telephone);
- classification (socioeconomic group, lifestyle, frequent-infrequent traveller);
- subject data (core information being gathered).

The layout and presentation of a self-completion questionnaire is of vital importance when considering response rates. The questionnaire has to be easy to understand and complete, and should also be visually attractive if higher response rates are to be encouraged. Therefore, questions need to be formulated with clarity, using unambiguous language and avoiding bias.

Most questionnaires comprise mainly closed questions where the respondent is given a limited choice of possible answers to tick, usually dichotomous (yes or no response) or multiple choice. At the end of the questionnaire, there might be one or two open-ended questions where a more free flow comment is expected. Scaling has become an important technique in quantitative surveys. It allows a gradation of opinion to be expressed regarding certain aspects. The question areas are usually drawn from more comprehensive qualitative work. Of importance is the Likert scaling technique where positive and negatives are given equal weighting. Other scaling techniques are semantic differential scaling, alternative attitude positions and diagrammatic scaling.

Open ended questions allow greater expression on the part of the respondent, but are not used as much as closed questions, mainly because they add little more and are far more time consuming to process and interpret. Table 9.4 shows the variety of question techniques used and possible bias.

9.7 EFFECTIVE USE OF MARKETING RESEARCH IN DECISION MAKING

The final aspect of marketing research is interpretation and presentation of findings. The material has to be in a format that will allow a marketing manager to make a

Table 9.4 Questionnaire design
(a) Question formulation: points to remember

1 Avoid poor question construction by avoiding
   (i) ambiguity,
   (ii) lack of mutual exclusiveness,
   (iii) lack of meaningfulness,
   in the questions.
2 Follow a logical sequence in the questioning.
3 Keep questions as simple as possible.
4 Avoid complex words or phrases.
5 Avoid words which would be unfamiliar to respondents.
6 Avoid leading questions and emotionally loaded words which would appear to respondents as hinting at the answer required.
7 Avoid questions that the respondents' background, experience etc. does not equip them to answer correctly.
8 Do not use questions, or choice of answers, where one answer may appear to respondents to confer some status to them, or make them appear to have a higher standing than they do. (The interviewees will tend to pick that answer whether it is true or not in their case.)
9 With all questions provide a space where respondents can answer 'don't know'. (If this is a genuine view, encourage them to select this answer rather than guess at an answer or give an incorrect one.)
10 Avoid questions that tax the memory too much (or which respondents do not wish to answer because they think it belittles them).
11 Avoid too wide a choice of answers.
12 Do not narrow the choice so that answers are not fully representative of the main possibilities.

(b) Common causes of bias in research results

1 Use of a faulty sampling frame.
2 Sample incorrectly drawn for the purpose.
3 Non-representative sample used.
4 Sample too large (so much data provided as to confuse or hide the true significance).
5 Sample too small and results may not be statistically significant.
6 Failure to cover some important market segment.
7 Non-response (either respondents not willing or able to answer, or selected respondent not at home or available for interview).
8 Unintentional interviewer bias (through researcher over-stressing a word or question).
9 Answers resulting from the questions posed.
10 Lack of precision or accuracy in the research.
11 Misinterpretation or incorrect analyses of responses.
12 Use of too many open-ended questions or too many choices with multiple-choice ones.
13 Unintentional incorrect response; no use made of control questions.
14 Ambiguity in questions or some other part of the research.
15 Unavoidable bias.
16 Faulty processing of data/information.

Source: Foster (1984).

decision about the market or a product. Otherwise, it will remain on the shelf.

In 1994, the then director of the Gladstone Pottery Museum in Stoke-on-Trent decided to commission marketing research as part of an overall marketing audit. When the results were available, he provided a checklist of actions against each main finding as a way of stimulating discussion among staff as to how to progress matters. Below are a number of the findings and the actions he recommended:

Finding: Approximately 70 per cent of visitors were over 40.

Action: Development and publicity should target children and families.

Finding: 41 per cent of visitors came from the West Midlands.

Action: Target more day visitors from within a 60 mile radius.

Finding: 73 per cent declared the Gladstone to be excellent or good value for money.

Action: Should be in excess of 85 per cent. Indicates that visitor satisfaction level is too low, and that prices should not be increased for the time being.

Finding: 49 per cent of visitors would have liked a guided tour, 49 per cent would not.

Action: Guided tours are a restrictive method of interpretation. The problems of visitor circulation and site interpretation should be overcome by establishment of the Family Fun Trail, the Gladstone Host Scheme and first person live interpretation.

Finding: Pre- and post-visit perceptions of the relative importance of the different elements of the visitor experience were listed. This revealed a number of areas for action.

Action: More demonstrations, hands-on opportunities. Improved audiovisual introduction required. Shop and catering need major work.

Source: Gladstone Pottery Museum (1994).

The Gladstone Pottery Museum proceeded to address the key issues which visitors had raised with a marked improvement in subsequent years of both levels of visits and the trading accounts.

The above example points to the need to use research findings in a proactive way. It is equally important to prepare a succinct synopsis of the research, so that managers, staff and others can see at a glance the major trends and to give a brief interpretative note.

Table 9.5 illustrates a major exercise underlining the importance of providing summaries which can be easily interpreted by the researcher.

Marketing research is an underestimated element of the marketing management function. For it to be used as an effective tool, managers need to be proactive in their application of findings.

Table 9.5 A survey of the opinions of departing summer visitors to South Africa, January and February 1994

Under Satour's auspices, research was done during January 1994 and February 1994 into the opinions of departing summer visitors to South Africa. This synopsis distils highlights from the survey, which included all types of visitors, namely, holiday makers, visitors to friends and family and business visitors; departing from Jan Smuts and DF Malan international airports.

Topic	All Visitors	Holiday Visitors	Friends & Family Visitors	Business Visitors	Comment
Total number of visitors:	5535 (100%)	2511 (45%)[1]	1659 (30%)[1]	1311 (24%)[1]	VFR component is losing share to both Holiday and Business sectors.
Country of origin:					
UK	26%	26%	38%	20%	UK is prominent in all sectors. Findings
Germany	19%	25%	18%	10%	consistent with previous research,
North America	9%	8%	9%	18%	except for more business visitors
Far East	8%	6%	3%	12%	from the UK. (North America and Far East slightly under-represented in sample)
Sources consulted prior to visiting					
Word of mouth or experience	61%	53%	77%	50%	Findings consistent with last summer, except for
Promotional	25%	38%	16%	15%	slightly more reliance on Promotional Efforts.
Length of stay (days)	19.5	18.1	24.21	15.5	Overall trend is for shorter visits. Trend continues.
Longest portion of stay: place	Cpt 4.5	Cpt 4.5	Cpt 4.7	Jhb 5.6	For the first time Cape Town is the most frequently
& type accom. (days)	Hotel 6.4	Hotel 6.7	Friends 10	Hotel 9	used destination with Jhb in second place. Jhb & 'Friends' lost popularity to Cape Town & hotels.
Total spend per person	R8 206	R8 760	R6 891	R10 325	Includes airfare.
– Airfare	R3 461	R3 301	R3 031	R5 389	Spend in SA is up from winter '93, but down from
– Income to SA	R4 745	R5 459	R3 860	R4 936	summer '93. The drop is attributable to a shorter stay.
Spend per pers/day (excl air)[2]	R244	R280	R164	R367	
Opinions about SA in general[3]					
Liked most about the country:	Scenery	Scenery	Climate	Scenery	Climate 2nd & Wildlife 3rd choice. This survey's results are typical of summer preferences.
Expectations not met by:	African cultures	Available facilities	Available facilities	African cultures	Consistent with previous surveys. 'Diversity' also does not have widespread appeal.
Is SA good for tourists?	82% ✓	84% ✓	87% ✓	75% ✓	Slightly less positive than previous summer.
Will you refer SA back home?	82% ✓	81% ✓	55% ✓	78% ✓	In line with last summer.
Is service in SA good?	60% ✓	66% ✓	58% ✓	53% ✓	Although only 60% of responses are positive about service, this survey continues in slowly improving trend.
Is personal safety good?	40% ✓	47% ✓	48% ✓	30% ✓	This survey showed a better rating than all previous surveys, mainly due to including Cape Town.
Opinions about facilities in SA:[3]					
Accommodation liked best:	National parks	National parks	National parks	National parks	National parks are consistent favourites.
Are hotels good?	75% ✓	76% ✓	79% ✓	72% ✓	3 in 4 tourists positive about hotels.
Is care hire good?	68% ✓	71% ✓	69% ✓	62% ✓	Consistent with previous years.
Are airports good?	51% ✓	55% ✓	52% ✓	43% ✓	Slightly better than previous years due to JSA refurbishing.

Note
[1] Due to overlap, together with other purposes for visit, these will sum to over 100%.
[2] Excludes airfare but includes other pre-paid expenses.
[3] ✓ denotes percentage of 'yes' votes

In summary, tourists were largely satisfied with their visit. Only six percent of visitors said they would probably not recommend South Africa to acquaintances at home. Most responses were fairly consistent for all international regions represented, as well as for the airports surveyed.

Source: South African Tourist Board (SATOUR)

9.8 SUMMARY Marketing research is a vital component of the marketing approach within a company. It enables a company to identify market segments, the needs and wants of these segments, and to measure the levels of satisfaction achieved through marketing interaction.

The tourism marketer has to decide how much information can be gleaned by reviewing existing data collected for another purpose. Desk research can yield an incredible amount of accurate information. Furthermore, companies are usually a storehouse of information about existing customers. It simply needs to be brought together in a marketing information system. There are occasions where continuous or *ad hoc* primary research has to be undertaken, perhaps when introducing a new tourism offering. As primary research is a time consuming and relatively expensive item in the budget it is important to brief marketing research agencies carefully in order to achieve an effective solution to the issue at discussion.

Market research is not a substitute for decision making but it assists in the process of minimizing risk in the management process. Within the tourism sector, marketing research is not used extensively beyond the large scale international companies and some governmental organizations. There is a strong case to be made for more research activity in this field.

REFERENCES

Chisnall, P.M. (1992) *Marketing Research*, 4th edition, McGraw-Hill, Maidenhead.

Crouch, S. (1984) *Marketing Research for Managers*, Longman, London.

Foster, D. (1984) *Mastering Marketing*, 2nd edition, Macmillan, Basingstoke.

Green, H., Hunter, C. and Moore, B. (1990) Assessing the environmental impact of tourism development – use of the Delphi technique. *Tourism Management*, **2**, 111–22, June.

Horner, S. and Swarbrooke, J. (1996) *Marketing Tourism, Hospitality and Leisure in Europe*, Thomson, London.

Kotler, P., Armstrong, G., Saunders, J. and Wong, V. (1996) *The Principles of Marketing*, Prentice Hall, Hemel Hempstead.

Lancaster, G. and Massingham, L. (1993) *Marketing Management*, McGraw-Hill, Maidenhead.

Seaton, A.V. and Bennett, M.M. (1996) *Marketing Tourism Products*, International Thomson Business Press, London.

Taylor, R. and Judd, L. (1994) Delphi method applied to tourism. In *Tourism Marketing and Management Handbook* (eds S. Witt and L. Moutinho), Prentice Hall, New York.

Veal, A.J. (1992) *Research Methods for Leisure and Tourism, A Practical Guide*, Longman.

World Tourism Organization (1996) *WTO News*, (**4**)13, WTO, Madrid.

10 | The tourism offering (services product)

OBJECTIVES

This chapter explains:

● the relationship of service planning to market planning;
● the concepts of core and augmented services and the tourism offering;
● the distinction between service offerings and brand management;
● the concept of the service life cycle;
● the importance of new service development in tourism.

10.1 INTRODUCTION

When discussing consumer behaviour in Chapter 3 the conclusion reached was that people gain core benefits from purchasing either physical products, such as a washing machine, or from intangible services, such as insurance or travel. On both counts the core benefits attributed to the exchange are intangible and in tourism this is almost always the case. Therefore, why do tourism marketers hold to the conceptual framework and terminology applied to the manufactured product when tourism is ostensibly an intangible core offering?

10.2 UNDERLYING PRINCIPLES OF SERVICES MARKETING

In discussing the marketing of tourism most writers (Middleton, 1994; Gunn, 1988; Lewis and Chambers, 1989) do not distinguish between product and service; they refer to the 'tourism product' assuming that products and services are virtually synonymous. As discussed in Chapter 5, the assumption is that all elements of the augmented marketing mix – people, physical evidence and process – are subsumed under the banner of the product. Kotler, Bowens and Makens (1996: 274), for example, define a product as:

> anything that can be offered to the market for attention, acquisition, use or consumption that might satisfy a want or need. It includes physical objects, services, places, organizations, and ideas.

This approach appears to be incongruous with existing service marketing literature which suggests an alternative approach. In Chapter 2 the discussion centred on the framework of services marketing, especially the five defining and distinguishing principles which are equally applicable to the business of tourism. It is worth restating them again briefly:

- Intangibility – services do not have tangible characteristics so cannot be displayed and tested by the intending customer;
- Perishability – services cannot be stored;
- Heterogeneity – it is difficult to standardize services as there is potential for variability;
- Inseparability – when services are sold, performance (or production) and consumption are simultaneous;
- Lack of ownership – services cannot be owned in the same way as products, as they are intangible and ephemeral.

10.2.1 Symbolic associations

There are two other dimensions which are significant in the discussion. Jefferson and Lickorish (1991: 67) allude to one when describing the tourism product as: '... a collection of physical and service features together with symbolic associations which are expected to fulfil the wants and needs of the buyer.'

It is the ingredient 'symbolic associations' which highlights the degree of intangibility of a service offering in tourism and is conspicuous by its absence in other sectors.

Secondly, the concept of inseparability has an important bearing on the discussion. Most products are manufactured separately from the point of consumption but invariably tourism service offerings are performed by the service provider and enjoyed by the customer simultaneously. This high degree of contact is at the core of the discussion.

Therefore, whether service provision in tourism should be categorized under a generic heading of 'product' is debatable. It is hard to imagine that it should be, either in terms of a standard definition or as a framework of analysis. It is difficult, for example, to conceive that the provision of holidays can be equated to the marketing of heavy capital plant, or white or brown goods.

There is now a considerable research base suggesting that tourism provision should be categorized as a service. This spans twenty years from the early work of Rathmell (1974) as developed by Shostack (1977) and Grönroos (1984). Palmer (1994: 124–8) redefines the 'service product' as a core service. He reaffirms the concept as a bundle of intangible core benefits and secondary service facilities. This constitutes a mix of tangibles and intangibles, including branding, processes, accessibility, quality, packaging and features.

Some components of tourism are clearly tangible items, such as souvenirs, food and beverages, but most are not. The focus, therefore, should be on the collection of intangible benefits which provide the core offering. There is perhaps a need to rethink both the terminology and the application of service management in tourism.

10.2.2 Product or service offering?

Consider, for example, the presentation of product levels by Kotler *et al.* (1996: 274). They suggest that there are four levels of product in the hospitality sector:

- **The core product.** This inner zone is described as the core benefits, which are clearly distiguishable from product features. For example, the core benefits of visiting a hotel's leisure centre might be to feel physically good, or to heighten esteem.
- **The facilitating product.** This is a combination of goods and services which enable the visitor to buy the core product, for example, telephones and booking systems.
- **The supporting product.** These are considered extras: they add value to the core product. They are not essential like facilitating products, but allow tourism suppliers to differentiate from their competitors, for example, complimentary inflight newspapers and drinks.
- **The augmented product.** According to the authors this includes 'accessibility, atmosphere, customer interaction with the service organization, customer participation, and customers' interaction with each other.' They are peripheral to the core product.

There is, of course, a distinction between levels of service offered as part of the overall augmented product and how the service element is actually delivered, which is discussed in Chapter 14. What is described as the overall product concept is reflected in Figure 10.1, but does it describe adequately the service offering in tourism?

Smith (1994: 582–95) has designed an alternative model, laying stress on the term 'generic tourism product', i.e. the facilitation of travel and activity of individuals away from their usual residence. The model comprises elements of the product and the process by which those elements are assembled. It also includes what the author refers to as the role of human experience, or what is described elsewhere as the service encounter. The diagrammatic representation of the generic tourism product, illustrated in Figure 10.2, 'is not a simple combination of the five elements, but the result of synergistic interaction among all the components'.

The six elements are:

- The physical plant, such as a site or natural resource, weather and infrastructure, and the design standards applied to the built environment.

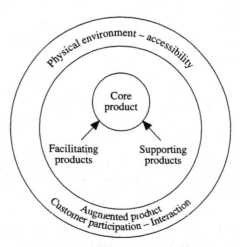

Figure 10.1 Presentations of the service product. *Source*: adapted from Grönroos (1987).

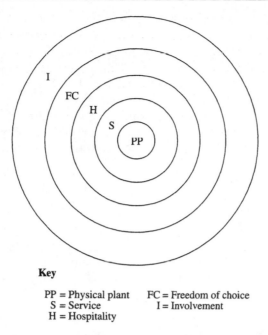

Key

PP = Physical plant   FC = Freedom of choice
S = Service   I = Involvement
H = Hospitality

Figure 10.2 The generic tourism product. *Source*: Smith (1994). Reprinted with kind permission from Elsevier Science Ltd.

- Service refers to the tasks required to meet the needs of tourists such as in a hotel or airline facility. It is the technical element of service provision.
- Hospitality refers to the way in which service is provided, i.e. the something extra that makes a visitor feel good. It is distinct from the technical competence of service provision.
- Freedom of choice refers to the notion that the visitor has some degree of choice in order for the experience to be satisfactory. It is the trigger to relaxation and allows some degree of spontaneity.
- Involvement refers to the underlying services marketing principle of simultaneous performance or consumption mentioned earlier. It involves participation and some degree of engagement.
- The sixth dimension of the model is the tourism product process. Resources are used to create tourism infrastructure and intermediate processed inputs, known as tourism facilities, but this is still a commodity. The final refinement is provided by the customer; the outcome is the 'personal experiences' which Smith refers to as 'intangible but highly valued experiences such as recreation, business and social contacts'.

Smith deduces from this reasoning that the tourism product and process are inseparable, but the terminology and the perspective utilized is one derived from a production orientated approach, which emphasizes outputs and phases rather than consumer benefits and outcomes. It is the terminology of the industrialization of services:

> Tourism products, however, do not exist until a consumer journeys to a point of production and actively gets involved in the final phase.
>
> *(Smith, 1994: 592)*

An alternative view would be to argue that the benefits to the consumer are delivered *only* if the service provider(s) and customer(s) are central to the model. Service interaction is central to the process rather than being represented at the periphery as in the model provided by Kotler *et al*. Atmosphere and customer-performer interaction at the service encounter are integral to the core offering.

Therefore, the concepts of core and augmented product are one and the same in tourism because of the underlying principle of inseparability, i.e. consumption and provision occur at the same time and place. The core bundle of benefits accrue from the degree of satisfactory interaction. A modified framework set out below illustrates the point. It places the service offering within tourism as a central component rather than one viewed as a periphery.

10.2.3 Tourism offering

A further consideration about the tourism product, which is perhaps more accurately described as a tourism offering, is its composite nature. Seaton and Bennett (1996: 112–13) point to the wide application of the term product across tourism sectors, from accommodation providers to destinations, commenting:

> This diversity is matched by an even greater diversity of component features specific to each tourism product sector which need to be considered and managed in providing individual products for particular markets.

The composite nature of a hotel, for example, might include accommodation, meeting rooms, a public bar, restaurant, leisure centre and swimming pool, all of which can be purchased as a collective service offering or bought separately such as booking a meeting room only.

There is invariably a balance between intangible-tangible benefits dependent on each specific offering, but in tourism the core benefits and service interaction almost

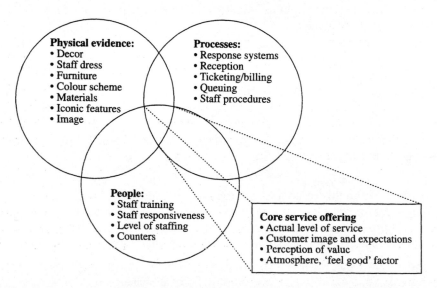

Figure 10.3 The tourism offering: a modified framework.

always dominate (Sasser *et al.*, 1978). Therefore, they constitute a tourism offering which can be defined as a combination of services which deliver primarily intangible, sensual and psychological benefits but which also include some tangible elements.

10.3 SERVICE (OR PRODUCT) LIFE CYCLE

The literature on the management of products has focused primarily on the concepts of the product life cycle and portfolio analysis (Wilson, Gilligan and Pearson, 1992: 293). Very little has been written specifically about the service life cycle. The classic product life cycle theory assumes that products have a limited life, during which they pass through a number of stages from introduction to decline. The theory has been built on a foundation of empirical studies which focus on physical products but is criticized on the grounds that the S curve in reality rarely fits the idealized progression presented in textbooks (Doyle, 1976: 1–6). There have been far fewer applications to tourism offerings with the exception of the tourism life cycle (Butler, 1980) and (Cooper *et al.*, 1994: 89–91). Figure 10.4 outlines the service life cycle (adapted from the product life cycle and exhibiting a modified S curve). Associated with this model is the theory of diffusion of innovation (Rogers, 1962; Brown, 1991: 190–1), which argues that different groups of people have a propensity to consume a product or service at different stages of its development. Thus, when a new service is introduced to the market, a small number of innovators will try it, eventually followed by a large group of the market known as early majority. The categories are listed below and the theory assumes a normal distribution curve, rather like the product life cycle:

> Innovators 2.5 per cent
> Early adopters 13.5 per cent
> Early majority 34 per cent
> Late majority 34 per cent
> Laggards 16 per cent

Whilst the theory is very plausible there has been little work undertaken in tourism to verify the pattern of adoption. More than likely the pattern will vary according to each offering. It is possible to marry the diffusion of innovation theory to the product life cycle model as illustrated in Figure 10.4. According to the classic theory, each stage of the life cycle necessitates a different strategy to maximize sales and profits.

One of the major applications of the product or service life cycle (PLC) has been as a diagnostic tool in developing future strategies for the market. It draws attention to the need to plan the next stage(s) of product or service development. Thus, in the introduction stage, the priority is often to create awareness and the trial of the tourism offering. In the growth stage, it would be to increase market share. Ultimately, most products or services come to the end of their life cycle and consequently there is a need to plan new tourism offerings for the market to replace those withdrawn.

Hence, there is a link to a second core concept of product or service management, of the product portfolio, which refers to the capability of a range of products or services to bring cash into a company, or alternatively to drain cash from a company. The aim is to retain a balanced portfolio. A more detailed appraisal of product portfolio analysis is to be found in Chapter 6.

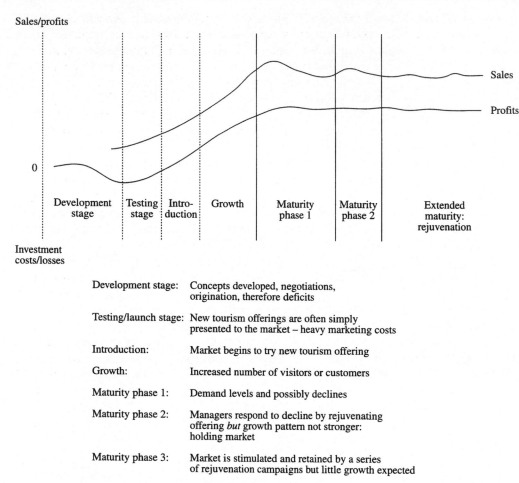

Development stage: Concepts developed, negotiations, origination, therefore deficits

Testing/launch stage: New tourism offerings are often simply presented to the market – heavy marketing costs

Introduction: Market begins to try new tourism offering

Growth: Increased number of visitors or customers

Maturity phase 1: Demand levels and possibly declines

Maturity phase 2: Managers respond to decline by rejuvenating offering *but* growth pattern not stronger: holding market

Maturity phase 3: Market is stimulated and retained by a series of rejuvenation campaigns but little growth expected

Figure 10.4 The service life cycle in tourism.

10.3.1 Criticisms of life cycle concept

Practitioners accept in general terms that the product or service life cycle is simply one of many tools which assist managers to plan ahead. The theoretical basis of the concept has been criticized on the following grounds:

● While early authors suggest that products follow a pattern of growth and maturity, the S shaped curve is not inevitable. This is true of tourism offerings too. For example, many tourism offerings have a steeper growth rate and shorter life cycle (rapid growth, slow slump) than the classic curve implies, such as tourism events and other visitor attractions. On the other hand, many tourism offerings appear to be in the maturity stage permanently. Classic offerings such as Paris or New York city enjoy a succession of rejuvenation campaigns to freshen the market. This makes the generalized theory less acceptable, for many tourism offerings do not readily fit the neatly portrayed framework.

● The second major criticism is that using the PLC as a diagnostic and prescriptive tool without recourse to other techniques can lead to problems. The PLC can direct managers to devise inappropriate strategies. For example, a curve which follows a scalloped pattern, as several visitor attractions or hotels do, might indicate to a marketing manager that a harvesting strategy is required, i.e. cutting back on market investment of a service and harvesting revenue. On the contrary, a detailed appraisal of the marketing environment might suggest a boost to extend the growth phase, i.e. to take an opportunity for an extended growth period. In this respect, the life cycle is not a 'fait accompli'. Therefore, in most cases it would be more appropriate to describe the PLC as a result of determined management strategy, rather than a consequence of other factors.

- The main difference is that when a tourism offering reaches the maturity stage it is very rarely allowed to be withdrawn. The pattern is one of rejuvenation. The life cycle should be redrawn as a scalloped pattern of demand in the long term. There seems to be a succession of new service offerings, scheduled at planned intervals, so as to stimulate a pattern of recycling. Thus, theme parks invest in new rides, improved processes and enhanced levels of customer service, in order to extend the maturity stage in perpetuity. The strategy is one of life cycle extension through an agglomeration of new product and service attributes. Palmer (1994: 144–5) argues that there is a stronger case for a more rigorous approach to service deletion, which applies very much to tourism. He presents a product-retention index which could be used to provide a more systematic approach to service deletion, highlighting such factors as the contribution to profits, alternative opportunities, etc.

- It would be wrong, however, to suggest that this is a rule, for there are a number of exceptions. For example, consider the fate of the circus or travelling fairs which no longer hold the appeal of 50 years ago. They illustrate all of the signs of the decline stage – low or negative profitability, lack of investment for renewal and improvement, limited marketing, negligible customer service and indeterminate image.

- Emphasis tends to be placed on the development of the product or service when it should be placed firmly in the context of the changing nature of the market, and trends in consumer behaviour, i.e. there is a case for developing more strongly the concept of the market life cycle.

- The concept has been extended to destination marketing in the form of the tourist area life cycle, which takes into account elements of the product and market life cycles. The model has been subject to considerable criticism (Cooper *et al.*, 1994: 89–91) on the grounds that the generalized model should not be used as a predictive tool.

The fundamental question remains as to whether the life cycle concept can be applied to tourism with any degree of confidence. The original theory was developed with physical products in mind and therefore does not readily lend itself to service concepts. Despite a cautionary note about the lack of empirical research (Cowell, 1984), the validity of the concept applied to services has not as yet been tested with any rigour.

10.4 SERVICE RANGE

In a similar manner to the way in which a food manufacturer offers a product range, tourism organizations tend to offer a service range. It is the counterpart to a product line. For example, a hotel group is able to provide differential offerings to various market segments, most of which are available at all hotels within the group. Inter Continental Hotels and Resorts, founded under the aegis of Pan American Airways in 1946 and now owned by the Saison Group of Japan, provides a range of service offerings, such as the Six Continents Club for regular customers which includes membership priviliges (upgrade to superior room, fresh fruit and mineral water, special check-in desk or area, late check-out, single rate for double occupancy), Global Leisure Options and Corporate Rate portfolio and Club Inter Continental for businesses. The core service offering of luxury accommodation, quality restaurants, recreational facilities and strong personal service presented by Inter Continental is available to all guests but the brand range adds benefits, and hence value, to match different customer expectations. In tourism, the brand range tends not to be wide, possibly three or four brand variations in most instances.

10.5 BRAND MANAGEMENT

Branding is about establishing the identity of a tourism offering in the minds of consumers or visitors. It has been defined as:

> a distinctive name or symbol which identifies a product, or set of products, and which differentiates it from its competitors.

> *(Cooke, 1996: A101)*

Cooke lists the attributes associated with a successful brand:

- It can be a name, symbol or both and is well known.
- It is unique and cannot be copied, especially by competitors.
- It is reflective of the consumer's self image.
- It represents the intangibles of a product.
- It informs and influences a consumer at the point of consumption.
- It provides the foundation for all marketing activity.

In essence it is about adding value to what would otherwise be a service with no name; long haul travel becomes Bales, Cox and Kings, Kuoni, The World of Difference. As a marketing tool branding was first used to great effect by pioneer tourism companies such as Thomas Cook, the Great Western Railway and P&O Ferries.

A brand signals to the potential customer a set of expectations about a holiday, travel journey, hotel or visitor attraction. The value might relate to authenticity, freedom, adventure or supremacy over other offerings. The distinction between a proprietary brand (i.e. the same as a manufacturer's brand such as Heinz baked beans) or an own-label brand such as a supermarket branding does not exist in the same way as in the fast moving consumer goods market, where there are supermarket or distributor brands such as Spar or Aldi. In the tourism sector, however, a similar position applies where the components of the holiday are supplied by a variety of companies but promoted under the brand umbrella of the tour operator, such as Kuoni or Thomson.

De Chernatony (1993: 173–4) points to five key reasons why there has been renewed interest in brands, reasons which are appropriate in the tourism sector:

- a growing awareness of the value of brands as assets;
- shift to below-the-line communications in light of increasing prices of advertising;
- the power of retailers and own brands;
- breaking down of trade barriers in Europe;
- greater awareness of global competition.

10.5.1 Brand personality

The concept of brand personality is sometimes used to describe the characteristics of the brand which evoke customer association with it. Brand personality includes all aspects such as psychological values associated with a brand such as luxury, reliability or excitement, and these are created by a mix of visual representation as well as, for example, by word of mouth marketing. In the final analysis a brand image exists in the minds of the customers as well as the marketer.

De Chernatony also argues that the core dimensions which make up the personality of a brand can be represented in two dimensions. The first is brand functionality such as consistency and reliability which is paramount in transport provision, for example. The second dimension is the brand dimension which appeals to emotive desires such as the romantic or exotic appeal of a destination. Furthermore, he points to the need for marketing managers to understand the evolutionary nature of a brand, particularly with reference to the way in which brands as planned by marketers engender positive mental pictures in the minds of consumers, intermediaries and employees (Bull and Oxley, 1996: 240). The British Airways re-branding exercise in 1997 is a classic example of this, where a strategic drive for global presence has necessitated a change in image.

10.5.2 Brand strategy

Branding strategies vary considerably. Some prefer corporate brands to dominate, others allow individual brands to flourish. For example, organizations such as McDonald's, Disney and the Virgin Group emphasize the overall corporate brand in a global arena, whereas other companies stress brand individuality, such as the short haul tour operator Air Travel Group which offers up-market European packages such as Magic of Spain, Magic of Portugal as well as a Sky Shuttle and Italian Flight Centre brands.

(a) Strategic value

The strategic and financial value attributed to strong brands is well recognized. Following the acquisition of Forté Plc by Granada Plc early in 1996, the parent company restructured the Forté Hotel division into three distinct brands, Le Meridien Hotels and Resorts, Forté Posthouse and Forté Heritage. The brand personality of Le Meridien focuses on European style quality hotels situated throughout the world, ranging from Portugal to Mauritius. In contrast Forté Posthouse refers to the UK's largest branded hotel chain catering primarily for the business market. The Forté Heritage collection comprises characterful hotels, often historic inns which are replete with antique furniture and endearing features such as log fires and traditional food. These three brands have very different brand personalities and are positioned in specific market segments accordingly.

(b) Brand building

The question of brand building in intensively competitive global markets is one which is acutely pertinent for tourism suppliers. King (1991: 5–12) argues that brand building for a service based company will need to reflect the need to present a strong company (rather than service offering) image. This will involve understanding that consumers are now different, that service brands are easily copied, that points of contact between the brand and stakeholders are diverse and that discriminators are based on people not things. Given this, he considers that companies will have to place greater emphasis on staff as brand builders and organizational matters as well as effectively communicating strong brand ideas.

10.5.3 Branding destinations

The question as to whether a tourism destination, which is in effect a multi-faceted composite offering, can be branded in the same way is the subject of further discussion. Several destinations have adopted a strong brand image such as that of the English Riviera (Torquay, Paignton and Brixham), Barcelona or Florida but several writers argue that it is difficult to apply a brand for the following reasons:

- The destination is a composite offering features many brands.
- It is difficult to mould a brand personality based on a living and dynamic community.
- In such circumstances it is virtually impossible to control a brand identity.

10.5.4 Themes

There might be a confusion between the term branding and theming. The latter is a divergence of an attraction, destination or event towards one particular topic or indulgence. While the term has been applied mainly to theme parks (Robinson, 1996: D15–D21) such as Camelot and Port Aventura, the technique has been used by destinations such as Las Vegas and New Orleans. Some destinations now build campaigns on the basis of films or television series having been filmed on location in the vicinity. Australia gained considerable recognition from the film 'Crocodile Dundee' and South Dakota attracted visitors with the screening of 'Dances With Wolves' (Riley, 1994: 453–8).

10.6 DEVELOPMENT OF TOURISM OFFERINGS

The theory of product or service development rests on the pivotal argument for new products or services to replace those which have reached the end of their life cycle. A literature review reveals a detailed discussion of the factors underlying innovation and new product launches in the marketplace (Johne and Snelson, 1988; Nystrom, 1985). What determines success in the process has also been subject to debate. Hart (1993: 23–41) provides a critique of several studies which measure success in terms of financial (assets, sales) and non-financial (design, technological) criteria. Her conclusions, based on initial review and additional primary research, indicate a need for further work in the field:

If research is to throw light on new product success, for the benefit of both the academic and business community, it must clearly show what types of product development strategies and processes will result in what *types* of success. Not only is success multi-dimensional, even *within* dimensions, the dynamic interrelationships are far from properly understood.

In some respects the stress on the term 'new product development' is a misnomer. In reality, very few new products or services are actually new to the world; they mainly constitute modifications to existing products or service offerings, or a repackaging of core brands, such the Sheraton Hotels' Body Clock Cuisine which is designed to help long haul travellers adjust to new time frames and to combat fatigue. Lufthansa's recent introduction of organic food for business class travel on North Atlantic flights is a similar example of service modification, rather than entirely new to the world offerings.

10.6.1 Reasons for development

New service development is considered equally necessary for service companies to survive. There are, however, a number of key reasons why companies introduce new tourism offerings which are summarized below:

- build recognition as an innovator in the market;
- provide a new tourism offering to develop a market;
- proactive territorial expansion through a new or modified offering at a destination;
- defensive action to challenge competitors;
- imitate the success of another organization;
- take advantage of technological breakthroughs;
- to reposition, i.e. to fit consumer requirements more accurately.

The development of new tourism offerings tends to be stimulated by both proactive and reactive strategies, although much of the growth in the market relates to imitation and repositioning of tourism offerings. Very little could be classified as concepts or innovations entirely new to the market. Those organizations which do have a proactive strategy tend to have a real commitment and resource base to plan a succession of new products or offerings. This is very much the case in the visitor attractions sector where updating and addition is commonplace. For example, the White Cliffs Experience at Dover launched in the mid-1980s was given a £1.2 million refurbishment programme in 1997. The Roman Encounters section was much improved with the introduction of interactive puzzles and challenges (Leisure Opportunities, 1996) which are considered more appealing to younger visitors. In this respect, most companies could be defined as imitative in approach (sometimes referred to as 'me too' strategies) in that they adapt good ideas which have worked well elsewhere.

In the tourism sector the development of new service offerings can be classified as outlined in Table 10.1.

10.6.2 The development process

The commonly acknowledged eight stage process brought together by Booz, Allen and Hamilton (1982) is cited by several writers (Crawford, 1985). In reality many organizations simply do not have the time or resources to progress systematically through these stages. They often resort to a shorter method of trial and error, where

Table 10.1 Development of new tourism offerings

Categorization	Comment	Example
• Entirely new tourism offerings	'Movie' induced tourism packages	'The Piano', New Zealand 'Field of Dreams', USA
• New to destinations	This refers to the addition of a new facility in a tourism resort	Port Aventura, a major theme park established near Salou, Spain in 1996. New concept for Spanish market
• Technological breakthrough	The use of interactive computerized information and reservation systems in direct marketing	Internet
• Repackaging and positioning	The reformulation of the brand and associated core benefits to meet more accurately changed consumer requirements	Development of indoor sun centres to attract all year visitation in northern European resorts
• Service enhancements	Emphasis on upgrading service levels and delivery associated with a given tourism offering	Butlins and Pontins holiday centres have invested heavily to upgrade accommodation facilities and services to meet the expectations of customers

good ideas are subject to a brief screening before being tested in the market. The time from the inception of an idea to positioning in the market might be less than three months. The test market will be undertaken during the first and sometimes last season. The eight steps are summarized below:

- **Idea generation.** Ideas generated by customers, staff and external marketing agencies present any given company with a stream of potential opportunities.
- **Screening.** Many of the ideas might well prove to be interesting, but only a small percentage will survive an initial screening exercise to assess whether they are sufficiently commercial to progress. The types of question asked at this stage relate to potential markets, how the idea fits with existing service offerings, the likely level of resource required to develop the idea, etc.
- **Concept testing.** The idea is then formulated into a tourism offering or a set of related offerings which might suit a market segment or segments. The concepts will be tested by way of qualitative research, possibly in discussion groups or following in-depth interviews to ascertain whether potential customers envisage benefits and contemplate purchasing any of the offerings.
- **Business analysis.** Those that appear to be attractive to the market will then be subject to a more detailed market analysis. This allows the company to assess the market size, potential sales and revenue against development and launch costs. The use of sensitivity costing will be applied at this stage, where a series of adjustments are made to factors such as price, packaging and customer take-up, and revenue implications evaluated. On this basis a minimum and maximum revenue potential will be projected.
- **Service development.** Once the tourism offering has been developed to this level the aim will be to minimize the time to bring it to the market. With manufactured goods, there might be a considerable amount of product testing at this stage to ensure, for example, the quality of the components, the safety of equipment, etc. In service development there is often a similar testing of the offering. For example, a

new package holiday in North Africa might rely on local suppliers who supply transfers from airports to resort locations. The potential subcontractors might have different standards and these will have to be harmonized, probably through discussion with each respective local supplier, and probably at each location concerned.

In the business to business sector selected 'close' companies will probably agree to test a service, for example, a modified computer reservation system. Probable minor technical or user problems would be teased out at this stage.

- **Market testing.** This often involves a partial launch of a new offering on a limited basis for the new season to assess the level of demand and to allow sufficient scope to effect remedial work if required. Then, the offering can be rolled out in a second season to a wider market. The problem with this approach is that it allows competitors the opportunity to encroach at an early stage for, unlike manufactured products, service offerings are easy to imitate.
- **Commercialization.** The latter stage accepts that the tourism offering has succeeded in achieving acceptable results during an intial test period and will need to be launched on a wider scale.

The traditional step format provides a useful guide but is rarely pursued in tourism marketing with such rigour for the trial and test marketing method is found to be a far less bureaucratic approach to market and service development. Furthermore, several studies refer to brand launching and how lead times to test a service or product are being cut in order to get to the market faster (Bose and Khanna, 1996). The exception, of course, are multimillion pound projects which involve extensive feasibility studies directing attention to locational, marketing and financial aspects in considerable detail.

10.7 SUMMARY   The term 'tourism or service offering' is preferred to that of 'tourism product' because, in tourism, service interaction and symbolic associations are the very core of the process. They are essentially intangible and differ considerably from what has traditionally been described as a manufactured product.

The management of tourism offerings, better known as brands, requires an understanding of both the market and service life cycles. The key aim is to match the development of tourism offerings to fit the nature of the marketing environment. The new product development model provides some guidance, but in reality many companies do not systematically commit themselves to all steps as they have limited resources, or the market is moving with too much rapidity.

REFERENCES

Booz, Allen and Hamilton (1982) *New Product Management for the 1980s*, New York, Booz, Allen and Hamilton Management Consultancy.

Bose, A. and Khanna, K. (1996) The Little Emperor, A Case of a New Brand Launch. *Marketing and Research Today*, November, 216–21.

Brown, R. (1991) Managing the 'S' Curves of Innovation. *Journal of Marketing Management*, 7, 191–2.

Bull, N. and Oxley, M. (1996) The Search For Focus – Brand Values Across Europe. *Marketing Research Today*, November, 240.

Cannon, T. (1994), New Product Development. *European Journal of Marketing*, 12(3), 48–64.

Cooke, P. (1996) The Branding and Positioning of Tourist Destinations. *Insights,* November, A101–A106.

Cooper, C., Fletcher, J., Gilbert, D. and Wanhill, S. (1994) *Tourism Principles and Practice,* Pitman.

Cowell, D.W. (1984) *The Marketing of Services,* Butterworth-Heinemann, Oxford.

Crawford, C.M. (1985) *New Products Management,* Irwin, New York.

De Chernatony, L. (1993) Categorizing Brands: Evolutionary Processes Underpinned by Two Key Dimensions. *Journal of Marketing Management,* **9,** 173–4.

Doyle, P. (1976) The Realities of the Product Life Cycle. *Quarterly Review of Marketing,* **1,** 1–6.

Grönroos, C. (1984) *Strategic Management and Marketing in the Service Sector,* Chartwell-Bratt, Bromley.

Grönroos, C. (1987) Developing the service offering – a source of comprehensive advantage. In *Add Value to Your Service* (ed. C. Suprenant), American Marketing Association, Chicago page 83.

Gunn, C.A. (1994) *Tourism Planning,* Taylor and Francis, New York.

Hart, S. (1993) Dimensions of Success in New Product Development: an Exploratory Investigation. *Journal of Marketing Management,* **9,** 23–41.

Jefferson, A. and Lickorish, L. (1991) *Marketing Tourism, A Practical Guide,* Longman.

Johne, A.F. and Snelson, P. (1988) Marketing's Role in Successful Product Development. *Journal of Marketing Management,* **3,** 256–68.

King, S. (1991) Brand Building in the 1990s. *Journal of Marketing Management,* **7,** 3–13.

Kotler, P., Bowen, J. and Makens, J. (1996) *Marketing for Hospitality and Tourism,* Prentice Hall, Upper Saddle River, New Jersey.

Leisure Opportunities (1996) White Cliffs Get a Facelift. *Leisure Opportunities,* 9–22 December, p. 2.

Lewis, C.C. and Chamber, R.E. (1989) *Marketing Leadership in Hospitality.* Van Nostrand Reinhold, New York.

Middleton, V.T.C. (1994) *Marketing in Travel and Tourism,* Heinemann, Oxford.

Nystrom, H. (1985) Product Development Strategy: An Integration of Technology and Marketing. *Journal of Product Innovation Management,* **2.**

Palmer, A. (1994) *Principles of Service Marketing,* McGraw-Hill, Maidenhead.

Rathmell, J. (1974) *Marketing in the Service Sector,* Winthrop Publishers, Cambridge, Massachusetts.

Riley, R.W. (1994) Movie-Induced Tourism. In *Tourism:The State of the Art* (eds A.V. Seaton *et al.*), Wiley, Chichester.

Robinson, K. (1996) Themed Attractions – Variations on a Theme. *Insights,* November, p. D15–16.

Rogers, E.M. (1962) *Diffusion of Innovation,* Free Press, New York.

Sasser, W.E.R., Olsen, P. and Wyckoff, D.D. (1978) *Management of Service Operations: Texts, Cases, Readings,* Allyn and Bacon, Boston.

Seaton, A.V. and Bennett, M.M. (1996) *Marketing Tourism Products,* ITP, London.

Shostack, G.L. (1977) Breaking Free From Product Marketing. *Journal of Marketing,* **41,** April.

Smith, S.L.J. (1994) The Tourism Product. *Annals of Tourism Research,* **21**(3), pp. 582–95.

Wilson, R.M.S., Gilligan, C. and Pearson, D.J. (1992) *Strategic Marketing Management: Planning Implementation and Control.* Butterworth-Heinemann, Oxford.

Pricing 11

OBJECTIVES

This chapter explains:

● the principles of pricing;
● different approaches to pricing strategy;
● the distinction between pricing strategy and tactics;
● the integration of pricing and other elements of the marketing mix in tourism;
● the relationship between price and quality in tourism provision.

11.1 PRINCIPLES OF PRICING

Of all of the elements of the marketing mix, pricing appears, on first consideration, to be the most straightforward. In reality, pricing can become a complex task requiring adherence to all other elements of the marketing mix. **Price** is the term used to describe what customers actually pay in exchange for the benefits accruing from a product or service. Therefore, it should not be confused with the term **cost** which is the level of resource commitment necessary to provide a service or product. This is often described in terms of unit cost of provision. In this respect, it is the only ingredient in the marketing mix which generates revenue, as the other elements are expenditures.

Pricing has become an increasingly important element in the marketing mix, mainly because of the intense competition in many domestic as well as international tourism markets. The issue of international pricing has gained attention given the increasing number of long haul destinations and the varying fortunes of countries brought about by external factors, such as civil unrest or natural disasters. Pricing is therefore important for both public and private sector organizations in tourism.

11.1.1 Perception

The most important factor is consumer perception of price. If consumers choose not to buy, because the offering is perceived to be of lesser value than the asking price, then bookings or visits will decline. If price is low in relation to value offered, then demand will be difficult to manage and revenue loss could be substantial. Maintaining a balance between the two is the main task facing the marketer.

The key to understanding pricing in the service sector, it is argued, is to understand consumer perception of the price-quality dimension. This, of course, is not as easy as it might seem given that each particular market segment attributes different values to service offerings. A major study in Canada reviewed by Stevens (1994: 44–8) suggests that there are strong links between price, quality and the degree of competitiveness of a destination or country. Stevens concludes that other factors in the marketing mix (such as image and accessibility) are more important than price in determining a holiday destination but that pricing becomes more important in people's minds when they are actually on vacation. The main findings of the study are summarized below:

- price and quality perceptions are closely linked;
- value is more important than price;
- many product attributes are more important than price in selecting a destination;
- this and other studies have found that the residents of a country are more critical of their own country's tourism products;
- price perceptions are visitors' subjective reality;
- the cost of getting to a destination does influence the overall price of the trip and visitors do distinguish between the overall price of the trip and the price of individual goods and services;
- prices take on increasing importance as visitors decide what they will do or buy on a trip;
- Canadians are more price sensitive and are more influenced by prices than travellers in the USA, UK, France, West Germany and Japan;
- Japanese and West German markets are very demanding of quality;
- visitor perceptions of quality and prices are influenced by past travel to a destination;
- more affluent and older travellers are less price-sensitive and place greater emphasis on quality;
- potential travellers are more price-sensitive: however, they place a greater importance on other quality factors;
- quality services appear to be a key to repeat visitation and to attracting potential visitors.

A research exercise undertaken in New Zealand provides similar conclusions to the Canadian study. The study concurred that perceptions of price, rather than actual prices, is a fundamental consideration for the marketer. Lawson, Gnoth and Paulin (1995: 3–10) revealed in the New Zealand study that tourists' awareness of prices for attractions and activities was low; visitors had little idea about actual prices. Furthermore, the total amount of variance between different segments, such as between independent and package holidaymakers, was found to be equally low.

11.1.2 The law of supply and demand

Classic economic theory of supply and demand points to an inverse relationship between the price charged and the quantity ordered. In constructing a supply and demand curve it is recognized that for any given tourism offering an equilibrium price can be reached, i.e. where price is acceptable to both consumer and supplier. This is illustrated in Figure 11.1.

Whilst accepting this fundamental principle, tourism economists appreciate the complexity of factors affecting patterns of demand which affect such analysis:

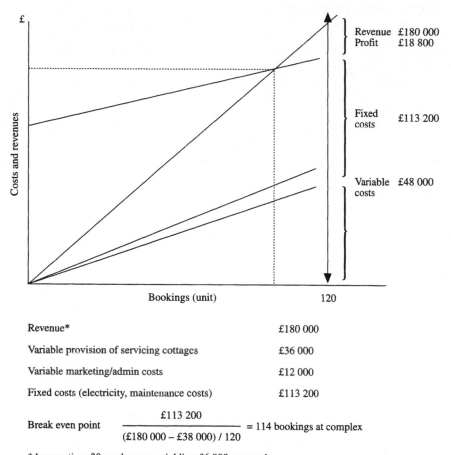

Figure 11.1 Equilibrium pricing: holiday cottage complex (12 units).

The 'law' of supply and demand suggests that the relationships between supply and demand are inexorable, a change in one results in a change in the other. In some cases this is no doubt true, but other forces, such as advertising, marketing skills and human motivation – with all of its intricacies and convolutions – exert tremendous influence on what people 'supply' and 'demand' ... Thus while the laws of supply and demand utilise the disclaimer that other things must be equal in order for the laws to work, in the reality of the business world things are not equal.

(Lundberg, Stavenga and Krishnamoorthy, 1995: 33–4)

There are a number of other important issues. In developed countries tourism is a much sought after service offering. A significant proportion of the population now demand an annual holiday, and some seek several breaks per year. As the level of discretionary income rises in an economy so does demand for tourism offerings. The concept of taking a holiday is no longer perceived as a luxury item (with the exception of long haul travel); it has achieved a higher priority in household expenditure.

11.1.3 Price elasticity of demand

Another important point to note is that while many tourism offerings are price sensitive (i.e. the level of demand is sensitive to price changes), mainly because of readily available substitutes, some are not. Those in the latter category tend to be at the luxury end of the market where supply is limited and associated status is high. In such cases, price elasticity of demand is said to be inelastic, so premium prices can be charged without a proportionate fall in demand. This is sometimes known as the Veblen effect, after the early twentieth century theorist who used the phrase 'conspicuous consumption' to describe the phenomenon. The concept of price elasticity, or the degree of responsiveness of customers to movements in prices, is crucial in determining price levels. Each tourism offering will have a different price elasticity of demand and the marketing manager needs to be aware of this.

11.2 FACTORS WHICH SHAPE PRICING STRATEGY

As well as analysing consumer perceptions and buyer behaviour the tourism marketer has to be cognisant of a number of internal and external factors which establish parameters when formulating a pricing strategy. They are much wider than the standard indicators of financial performance.

The influencing factors are summarized below:

- **Overall marketing policy and objectives.** Pricing is integral to position. Given the intangibility of tourism offerings, price signals to the customer an expectation about what is being sold.
- **The price–quality relationship of the company's range of service offerings, especially with regard to the market life cycle.** In particular, price is associated with quality, the expectation being that the more a customer pays, the higher the expected quality. A similar connotation is value, where customers invariably expect higher quality than the price they pay.
- **The uniqueness of the tourism offering and strength of brand.** Tourism marketers use premium pricing when they are selling a unique or an unusual type of experience, or when a brand holds great value.
- **The potential to reduce costs through effective use of the value chain within the company and in terms of suppliers.** Many companies look to reduce costs in the supply of tourism services so that it allows greater flexibility in pricing.
- **The structure of the market and the company's position in the marketplace.** Positioning is important in that companies with a large share of the market tend to lead with pricing while competitors follow their pricing structure.
- **The degree of competition.** The level of competition within a market can lead to parity pricing, price following or price warfare depending on the nature and intensity of competitors.
- **Government involvement in the market.** Governments impose taxes, levies or retail price maintenance mechanisms which affect the market.
- **Currency exchange rates.** The fluctuation of currencies between countries can lead to international pricing policies which build in safeguards against erratic movements of exchange rates.

External factors such as government taxation or fluctuating exchange rates can be of critical importance. Take, for example, the influence of government on pricing. Wason (1996: A31–9) illustrates the likely improved performance of hotels in the UK if the rate of value added tax were lowered. The levy of some form of tourism tax is not an uncommon form of government imposition which affects pricing. For example, in Zimbabwe tourism authorities levy 2 per cent on hotel bills, and many airports throughout the world service a levy, known as a departure tax. There is also consideration of environmental pricing by local authorities or destinations to assist in enhancement of tourism environments. The different methods are set out in Table 11.1. One interesting study is that undertaken by Rogers (1995) which investigated the pricing practices of English tourist attractions. The study concluded that 'price decisions are multifaceted and complex, requiring more than one approach to be used'.

Table 11.2 illustrates the primary influences on pricing.

11.3 APPROACHES TO PRICING

There are four broad approaches to pricing.

11.3.1 Cost-based pricing

Many companies use either full cost pricing or marginal (direct) cost pricing to achieve their goals. For example, if a visitor attraction has a cost structure as outlined below it would decide to charge the minimum entrance price possible given the full costs. There is no mark-up as such because the attraction seeks to make a surplus when visitors spend on site. The problem arises with this method, when visitor figures are predicted to decline, as has been the case for many attractions in recent years. In terms of full cost pricing the attraction would have to increase prices in relation to the

Table 11.1 Pricing methods of enhancing tourism environments

Method	Purpose	Price	Impact on demand	Supply	Examples of application in tourism/leisure
Taxes/ charges	Meet social costs	Higher	Reduced	Reduced	• Air/water pollution • Noisy sports • Bednight tax to fund destination environmental improvement
Subsidies	Increase social benefits	Lower	Increased	Increased	• Retention of heritage artifacts, e.g. historic buildings • Maintenance of rights of way
Licences	Reduce usage	Higher	Reduced	Reduced	• Use of fragile resources • Congestion at scenic attractions
Investment	Enhance environmental quality	Indeterminate (probably lower)	Indeterminate	Increased	• Improved technology, e.g. energy efficiency in buildings • Provision of new or enhancement of existing tourism resources • Hotel development incentives

Source: Goodall and Stabler (1992).

Table 11.2 The primary influences on pricing decisions

Category	Costs		Competitors' prices		What market will bear		Other		Total responses	
	No	%ᵃ	No	%ᵃ	No	%ᵃ	No	%ᵃ	No	%ᵃ
Size										
Small	18	58	9	29	14	45	2	6	43	139
Medium	14	42	7	21	25	75	1	3	47	142
Large	11	55	3	15	16	80	2	10	32	160
Total responses and as % overall sample	43	51	19	23	55	65	5	6	122	145
Ownership										
Private individuals	8	33	8	33	15	62	0	0	31	129
Partnerships	3	60	2	40	3	60	0	0	8	160
Private ltd company	6	85	3	43	5	71	0	0	14	200
Public ltd company	4	80	1	20	3	60	0	0	8	114
Trust or charity	17	53	5	16	23	72	2	6	47	147
LAs/govt	3	37	0	0	4	50	3	37	10	125
Other	2	66	0	0	2	66	0	0	4	133
Total responses and as % of overall sample	43	51	19	23	55	65	5	6	122	145
Type of attraction										
Historic house	5	25	5	25	15	75	2	10	27	135
Museum	20	65	7	23	17	55	1	3	45	145
Heritage centre	2	25	1	13	6	75	1	12	10	125
Farm/park	6	60	4	40	6	60	1	10	17	170
Other	10	66	2	13	11	73	0	0	23	153
Total responses and as % of overall sample	43	51	19	23	55	65	5	6	122	145

Notes: ᵃbased on responses against number of concerns within category size, ownership category and type category.
Source: Reprinted from *Tourism Management*, **16**(3), H.A. Rogers, Pricing practices in tourist attractions, page 221. © 1995 with kind permission from Elsevier Science Ltd, The Boulevard, Langford Lane, Kidlington OX5 1GB, UK.

changing cost structure in order to break even (level of sales required to balance costs and revenue). However, the higher the price the less attractive the venue will be to potential visitors. This position is outlined in Table 11.3.

Some companies use a mix of full cost and marginal pricing based on the level of fixed overheads and the degree of fluctuation of demand. This approach takes into account a number of factors, especially the ability of different market segments to pay, the degree of seasonality and the need to offer a contribution to high fixed costs. Marginal cost pricing directs attention to those costs which rise as the number of customers increase, rather than the fixed costs. Thus, the pricing approach does not reflect the total unit cost of provision (fixed plus variable or directly attributable costs). It takes into account only the additional costs in providing the additional use of the facility or service offering.

For example, a coach operator in the low season might have days when part of the fleet is barely utilized. The full cost of running a 50 seat coach for a one day excursion to a historic city 100 miles away might be £240, the marginal cost £175. If seats are each priced at £8 assuming a loading of 30 passengers, the operator will just manage to break even at £240. However, at that price in winter, it might appear a little expensive to marginal passengers so the traffic manager will price to achieve a return on the

Table 11.3 Museum pricing policy

	Year 1	Year 2	Year 3
Direct costs per visitor (staff, on-site demonstrations, etc.)	£1.50	£1.50	£1.50
Fixed costs (buildings, displays, etc.)	£400 000	£400 000	£400 000[1]
Estimated number of visitors	100 000	80 000	70 000[2]
Cost per visitor			
Direct costs (heating, cleaning)	£1.50	£1.50	£1.50
Fixed costs (£400 000 ÷ number of visitors)	£4	£5	£5.71
Gives full costs	£5.50	£6.50	£7.21
Price (per adult)	£5.50	£6.50	£7.20[3]

Notes

[1] Assumption that good housekeeping holds both direct and fixed costs.

[2] During recessionary times – decline in demand. No extra marketing activity.

[3] Full cost means that prices rise as cost of servicing each visitor rises.

direct costs. Assuming a loading of 30, seats can be priced at £5.80 to cover direct costs (£174), and therefore be more attractive to the market.

Thus, while the price does not attempt to cover full costs it will allow operating costs to be met and possibly a contribution to overheads or fixed costs. This type of pricing is commonplace in tourism. It relates to the fundamental principle of perishability, i.e. seats on coaches and trains, hotel bedrooms, etc., cannot be stored. Therefore, pricing to cover marginal costs of operation plus a contribution to overheads is appropriate at times when demand is traditionally low.

11.3.2 Competitor-based pricing

The second approach is common in intensely competitive areas such as the short haul package holidays market. Many tour operators, for example, are currently pricing in line with competitors to stay in the market. They use tactical short term incentives to gain a differential edge.

The market leader will set the pricing structure and other companies will take a lead from this, i.e. they are price takers. This is sometimes referred to as going rate pricing. For example, the bed and breakfast market in any given area often follows this pattern. Only those who have a special location or offer the unusual can price differently to the majority. This type of pricing structure can lead to stability in the market.

The opposite occurs when companies begin to price aggressively to gain market share, as such situations have a tendency to edge towards price warfare and instability. The issue is then one of long term sustainability, for profit margins are continually under pressure as a result of the price war. Eventually one or more of the competitors fall out of the market. One example is the continuing price war between Le Shuttle and the channel ferry operators such as P&O or Stena in their attempt to hold market share. Despite continuous setbacks, the Channel Tunnel continues to gain market share mainly by using pricing as a fundamental incentive to encourage trial by customers who would otherwise have used the ferry (Dyer, 1995).

11.3.3 Competitive tendering

Competitive tendering is an increasingly important method of pricing in tourism. In the provision of catering services, coaches and other operational components, the supplier or contractor seeks sealed tenders from a number of companies. While most of the bids include a qualitative dimension many decisions are made primarily on price, i.e. the lowest bid wins the contract. The exception tends to be in the consultancy and marketing research sector where quality is deemed more important than price. Here, companies are asked to submit proposals within a price range and the bids are judged primarily on the level of analysis, creativity and practical application, and presentation of the proposal, although in reality reputation and level of contact is equally relevant (Morgan, 1991).

11.3.4 Market-driven pricing

This approach accepts that pricing should be highly integrated with other aspects of marketing strategy. Price, positioning and promotion are three key interlinking factors which require careful coordination. For example, the selection of target markets and offering a differential advantage are the hallmarks of premium pricing strategies. Many niche market operators in tourism price this way. They ensure that there are few real substitutes to their offering and project an image of it that has distinct appeal. This is often the case at the launch of a new venture before competitors have had an opportunity to imitate the offering. Thus, market driven pricing is very much about what the market will bear in given marketing environments.

11.4 PRICING STRATEGIES

The four broad approaches have a bearing on the crafting of a pricing strategy. There are, of course, numerous other factors such as market evolution, company resources and market structure. When all of these factors are taken into consideration, the company can build a pricing strategy which fits best within the overall marketing strategy.

The task becomes far more complicated when pricing on an international basis. Crouch (1992: 643–64) argues that studies investigating the effect of income and price on the demand for international tourism offer very varied results. There appears to be no firm universal relationship between price elasticity and the demand for travel; it depends on a number of determinants which vary according to each specific situation.

A number of strategic pricing frameworks are explained below.

11.4.1 Premium pricing

This strategy requires tight integration with all aspects of the marketing mix. It is usually adopted, for example, by up-market, specialist tour operators, hotel and resort complexes who trade on reputation, bespoke service and exclusivity. Reduction of price is tantamount to repositioning. It would perhaps only be included as part of a corporate package or loyalty scheme to encourage occupancy at times of lesser demand. Price in this strategy simply reinforces other aspects of the mix. Examples include specialist activity holidays, luxury cruises and highly rated restaurants.

11.4.2 Skimming pricing

Skimming the market is a pricing strategy which companies use when the tourism offering is relatively new to the market and the level of competition low. It allows the marketer to build a premium package which adds value, but not cost, so that the buyer is enticed to purchase at high prices therefore enhancing the price margin. Inevitably, competitors seize the opportunity to enter the market with a number of close substitutes and this forces the pioneer company to review the skimming strategy. The introduction of villas at newly developing resorts, for example, allows the owner to charge premium prices but this position soon becomes untenable as second stage development brings an increased range of properties.

11.4.3 Market penetration

This is probably the most common pricing strategy adopted in the world of tourism, pricing to gain market entry and share. Most new wine bars, clubs, resort complexes and visitor attractions, when new to the market, price to attract trial purchase and to establish strong word of mouth marketing. The assumptions are that most customers in the market are price sensitive and will be seduced by an offer which brings good value. Second, where there are numerous indirect and direct substitutes, sharpened pricing is necessary to maintain share. The promenades of the Mediterranean provide classic example where there are dozens of restaurants and bars to choose from within such close proximity. In some cases price bundling is adopted where an inclusive price means that wine and coffee are added as part of a value package at the table.

11.4.4 Differential pricing

This strategy assumes that different market segments will pay different prices for a similar bundle of core benefits. Pricing in this context is more dependent on season (or the peaks and troughs in the week), location and differing levels of service. Most hotel groups and airlines adopt this type of strategy where business and exclusive travellers (segments which have been traditionally price inelastic) are offered the same core benefits as other customers (who show a tendency to price inelasticity). For example, all passengers would be offered a flight between Hamburg and Rome, but pricing emphasizes the additional benefits offered such as levels of on-board service. Such benefits might be marginal in terms of cost, especially in comparison to fixed cost allocation. They are nevertheless significant in terms of customer perception. A mid-market provincial city hotel is another classic example. Consider the tariff schedule in Table 11.4.

11.4.5 Survival pricing

This is where competitive or market circumstances dictate that pricing has to maximize cash flow in the short term. It is simply a case of generating working capital to survive. Liquidity problems affect many small traders in tourism at any given time. Problems are usually exacerbated when there is a major upheaval in the market, such as the Gulf War which affected many European hotel businesses in the early 1990s.

Table 11.4 Yield management in hotels. Medium sized hotel located in a provincial city with established tourism trade, Central Europe. Available rooms 140, annual average occupancy 68 per cent, sales of rooms 34 748 (140 × 365 × 68%)

Customer segment	% of room sales per year	Rate achieved per night	Room sales (volume)	Revenue
Corporate clients	30	Corporate rate £60	10 424 × £60	£625 464
Business clients (individuals)	25	Rack rate £70	8687 × £70	£608 090
Groups (mainly weekends)	20	Group rate (offered Fri–Sun only) £30	6950 × £30	£208 488
Package short breaks	10	Wholesale price £35	3475 × £35	£121 625
Individuals (pleasure)	15	Negotiated individually but averaging £60	5212 × £60	£312 732
			Total revenue	£1 876 399

Possible projections could be made based on yield management as follows:

$$\frac{\text{Number of nights sold} \times \text{actual average room rate}}{\text{Room nights available} \times \text{room rate potential}} = \text{yield}$$

11.4.6 Harvesting pricing

Harvesting is pricing to reap the benefits of previous marketing investment as a service offering reaches its decline stage. It involves little marketing expenditure, simply selling an existing service to a dwindling but loyal market at a relatively premium price. It is rare in tourism as most offerings are rejuvenated or relaunched during early decline stage. An example might be a traditional hotel which has managed to maintain a clientele without upgrading or investment.

11.4.7 Preventing market entry

Companies sometimes adopt a strategy which seeks to create barriers to entry through predatory pricing. This involves pricing artificially low (even below break even point) to prevent a rival or potential competitor seeking entry into a particular market. The likely response depends on the capability of the rival(s). In terms of oligopolistic pricing where a group of companies are threatened by a new market entrant, it is a most effective deterrent. However, the arrival of Freddie Laker or Virgin Airlines on transatlantic air routes have illustrated how short term predatory pricing can lead sometimes towards a price war. In such circumstances, prices spiral to a point well below the expected customer value and supplier return on investment.

11.5 TACTICAL PRICING

Some writers argue that pricing is best used as a flexible, tactical tool which can be adapted to support other elements of the marketing mix. This is particularly the case in fast moving markets where competitor activity dictates speedy responses.

Tactical pricing refers to the following areas:

● price cutting of holiday packages at short notice;

- discriminatory prices to increase demand during traditional troughs such as winter in northern European seaside resorts, or during the week such as hotels on Sunday nights;
- discounts for early booking, inclusive packages for families, etc.;
- intensive group discounts to secure high volume;
- loyalty schemes offering free holidays for regular travellers.

As tactical campaigns reappear with familiarity the question is whether companies have now moved to a position where the main thrust of their strategy is a succession of interrelated discounting techniques. It is being used to hold position against severe competition such as in the airline and hotel business sectors. This type of offensive marketing strategy is designed to outrank the offer of a competitor by a combination of price cutting and adding value. It sometimes involves decoy pricing which involves severe price discounting on one service line to distract competitors from other service offerings. It can also be reinforced by advance publicity, where discounts and offers are rushed to the market in advance of competitors. UK tour operators have competed in recent years by offering substantial discounts for early bookers, or by inclusive insurance policies, inclusive duty free provision, as early as possible before the next main season. For example, brochures were launched in May 1997 for the 1998 season.

11.6 PRICE–QUALITY DIMENSION

The relationship between a brand, quality and pricing has generated considerable discussion in recent years. The argument is that branding helps a company to maintain a stable pricing policy, because the brand reflects a statement about the quality of the offering. The positioning of a tourism offering on a price–quality matrix can be a useful method of deciding where a company should target its branded offering and at what price. It depends so much on the marketing environment.

11.7 SUPPLIER PRICING

One area which has not been investigated in any detail is the pricing strategies adopted by suppliers in bringing together composite service offerings to the market. Tour operators and travel agents have highly skilled teams of negotiators who source tourism goods and services as part of supply chain management. The criteria that suppliers adopt, in terms of pricing components, depends on a number of factors, such as the level of competitive activity in the market, and the long term investment between suppliers and the company concerned, which are becoming increasingly important in relationship marketing.

There is also an important factor of seasonality and pricing in this context. American wholesale tour operators, for example, buy in hotel rooms in Caribbean resorts at very low prices during the low season. When surveyed in 1993, Caribbean Hotel Association members indicated that 57 per cent of room revenues came from wholesalers. While several expressed concern that prices were low, they also pointed to a reduction in their marketing costs, particularly in terms of distribution (Kimes and Lord, 1994: 70–5).

The discussion applies equally to internal marketing where hotels and coach operators belonging to a parent group might be expected to bid for work which has been secured by the corporate group. The bidding process involves both a tendering process and the pricing quality dimension.

11.8 THE PRICING OF PUBLIC GOODS

Tourism involves both public and private sector provision of services and in particular, the use of public goods has been defined by Lumsdon and Swift (1995):

> Public goods in terms of the tourism sector, for example, include scenery, climate, architecture, flora and fauna all of which are viewed as 'free' heritage of a country. Ironically, it is these 'goods', albeit intangible in many respects that constitute the major appeal for visitors to a holiday destination.

This presents a problem to marketers in the public sector, for in the past such facilities have been provided free of charge or at a low price acceptable to visitors and residents. The case has been presented that all visitors to such facilities should pay a commercial price. In many countries the thought of charging for the use of public amenities is anathema. Consider the attitude of British people to being charged for using a public convenience! Suggestions that walkers should be charged to use rights of ways which have been established across countries throughout Europe over the centuries has also stimulated considerable consternation.

In developing countries the issue has another dimension. Those managing areas of natural or ecological sensitivity are increasingly looking to pricing as a mechanism of environmental protection on two counts. If the land is given economic value, by virtue of being used for tourism purposes, it is less likely to be claimed for other purposes, such as the felling of timber or extraction of minerals. Second, as demand to visit such areas has increased considerably, one of the most expedient ways to reduce visitation to a manageable level is to introduce an entrance charge, so that marginal users cease to visit. This is a controversial area worthy of more detailed exploration.

It has been the subject of debate in terms of national reserves and parks throughout lesser developed countries. Tanzania, which has some of the largest and best known reserves in the world, experienced considerable growth in entrances to parks in the 1980s, particularly in the most famous reserve, Serengeti. With the introduction of commercial charges in the early 1990s, the pattern of revenue has changed considerably, and demand has stabilized in the short term.

11.9 SUMMARY   Pricing is an integral part of the marketing mix in tourism but perhaps not the most important. Nevertheless, in determining pricing strategies tourism marketers have to be aware of consumer perceptions, propensities to travel and the degree of competitor activity. For the commercial organization the key issues will be parity pricing, which seeks to add value and customer service, to encourage improved relationships with customer segments. Such schemes as all inclusive package deals and loyalty programmes are adopted by many organizations, but these are currently considered to be less appropriate at destinations.

Those charged with the operational management of resorts and areas which are currently classified as public goods and hence falling within the realm of public choice, have a difficult task. Pricing policies to enhance the environment, or in some cases protect it, can prove to be very successful in reducing marginal customers, but there will always be a political edge to the introduction of such schemes.

REFERENCES

Crouch, G.I. (1992) Effect of Income and Price on International Tourism. *Annals of Tourism Research*, **19**, 643–64.

Dyer, G. (1995) Eurotunnel to change fares in price war with ferries. *Financial Times*, 11 October.

Goodall, B. and Stabler, M. (1992) Environmental Auditing in the Quest for Sustainable Tourism: The Destination Perspective, Durham, 8–10 July.

Kimes, S.E. and Lord, D.C. (1994) Wholesalers and Caribbean Resorts. *Cornell Hotel and Restaurant Administration Quarterly*, **35**(5), 70–5.

Lawson, R., Gnoth, J. and Paulin, K. (1995) Tourists' Awareness of Prices for Attractions and Activities. *Journal of Travel Research*, **34**(1), 3–10.

Lumsdon, L.M. and Swift, J.S. (1995) Urban Tourism: A Latin American Perspective. Paper presented to The Urban Environment: Tourism conference at South Bank University, September.

Lundberg, D.E., Stavenga, M.H. and Krishnamoorthy, M. (1995) *Tourism Economics*, John Wiley & Sons, New York.

Morgan, N. (1991) *Professional Services Marketing*, Heinemann, London.

Rogers, H.A. (1995) Pricing practices in tourist attractions. *Tourism Management*, **16**(3), 221.

Stevens, B.F. (1992) Price Perceptions of Travelers. *Journal of Travel Research*, Fall, 44–8.

Wason, G. (1996) Effective Tourism Policy, *Insights*, English Tourist Board, September, A31–9.

12 Communications mix

OBJECTIVES

This chapter explains:

- the principles of communication;
- internal and external communications;
- the applicability of different elements of the promotional mix in the tourism sector;
- the interface between design, print and publicity;
- the different approaches to the construction of a promotional plan and budget.

12.1 INTRODUCTION

There is perhaps a useful distinction to be made between the promotional and communications mix, one that is not entirely clear in the current literature. The former tends to be used primarily when referring to external promotional activity, whereas the latter encompasses external and internal promotional activity.

Most texts refer to external marketing communications as the promotional interface between the company and its suppliers, retailers, stakeholders and customers. It is a two way process and one which also involves a flow of messages between customers and between customers and intermediaries, as well as directly with the company. This is not simply formalized communication, but includes word of mouth marketing (Haywood, 1989: 55–67). It is therefore a complex process. Marketing communications which take place within an organization should also be included, for this forms part of the internal marketing process, one which companies are coming to recognize as increasingly salient in achieving a competitive edge (Berry, 1981: 33–40).

12.2 THE PRINCIPLES OF COMMUNICATION

The literature reflects a long standing interest in explaining the principles of the communication process which takes place between the sender(s) of a message and receiver(s) (Chisnall, 1985; Delozier, 1986). The most commonly adopted generalized model comprises four components – the sender, message, medium and receiver. It is outlined in Figure 12.1.

The theory presents a scenario where the message is prepared for a prospective audience or market in symbolic form, i.e. a combination of visual representation, copy or numbers. This process is referred to as **encoding**. In its simplest format, a destination might prepare textual and pictorial references which present a selective set of positive intangibles about the place. The message is then transmitted by way of a suitable medium which could range from a brochure to a global television advertising campaign. The receiver hears, sees or even smells the message in some cases (scratch and sniff techniques are well developed in other markets).

The major concern of the marketer at this stage is that the message is not distorted in the process by what is termed 'noise'. For example, a TV advertisment showing Florida on television at the same time as a news item referring to a devastating hurricane sweeping through the region would fail to convey a convincing message.

The process then involves the customer **decoding** the message, i.e. the way in which the message is filtered or internalized. Thus, the message might be received in the way in which it is intended by the sender. For example, the classic approach is that a potential holiday maker sees pictures of sandy beaches, music in the streets and smiling faces of local people at a destination and is persuaded to make an enquiry about the pictorial paradise. On the other hand the message might become distorted or be dismissed as unacceptable. The model also implies some degree of feedback but this very much depends on the medium used and the nature of the message transmitted.

You will also find in the literature a number of references to how communication, or in many instances, advertising, works. There are a number of very similar explanations. The models invariably assume that customers follow a number of predetermined stages commencing with awareness and progressing to purchase which are known as buyer states of readiness.

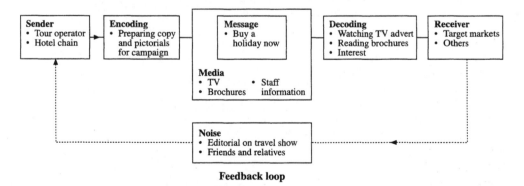

Figure 12.1 The principles and process of communication.

AIDA
Awareness
Interest
Desire
Action

ATR
Awareness
Trial
Repeat buying

Figure 12.2 Traditional communications models.

12.2.1 Limitations of the theory

The simplicity is, of course, immediately appealing but fits uneasily with consumer behavioural models outlined in Chapter 3, which suggest that the customer has an interactive role both in terms of involvement with the sender and in terms of filtering messages. For example, the potential holidaymaker may look favourably on a number of tour operators because they project an image which suits his or her lifestyle. On closer inspection of the promotional material, the idea of a holiday with one of these companies could be rejected on a number of grounds, such as over packaging, concern about particular destinations, etc.

Another criticism is that the theory tends to focus on the process of conversion, from a state of awareness to that of purchasing a tourism offering, whereas the objectives of communication are far wider. They might, for example, correct misconceptions rather than seeking conversion, or heighten awareness of potential customers, without giving a specific call for action. Table 12.1 lists the major uses of advertising within this context.

12.2.2 Awareness, trial and reinforcement

A variation of the theory is that customers move from awareness to trial and then reinforcement, known as the ATR model. The main emphasis lies with the aspect of reinforcement. In the tourism sector it is likely that both models are applicable in different circumstances. How might this work?

Consider the following example. The potential holidaymaker becomes aware of a new destination having read a travel editorial in *La Vanguardia* or *The European*, possibly about a farm holiday in Umbria, Italy. He or she is prompted to 'phone the information line provided in the advert on the same page. On receiving the brochure or video about the holiday the customer's interest is then sufficiently aroused to make a direct telephone enquiry, but probably not before asking friends and relatives about the destination. This leads to desire and action, which in the case of buying a holiday,

Table 12.1 The potential uses of advertising: tour operator

Rationale	Techniques
Attract interest • enquiries to add to database • direct sales • renew interest.	Brochures Coupons or adverts in magazines TV advertising (e.g. Direct Holidays)
Generate awareness of • new destinations or packages • remodelled packages • price discounting campaigns, special offers.	Brochures and TV campaigns which highlight new features Children free holidays Early booking – TV advertising
Influence travel trade • influence wholesalers and retailers.	Advertising in trade magazines such as *Travel Trade Gazette* to back up incentives, sales promotion campaigns
Reinforcement	Advertising in brochures to reinforce position in relation to competitors and to reassure existing customers

is a major step. It is beyond simply expressing a level of interest, both in psychological terms and the commitment of finance. A booking is made. From this point onwards the advertising task is one of reinforcement, i.e. to ensure that the customer feels that he or she has done the right thing and, second, to secure a repeat visit. This type of holiday buying process reflects the sequential approach to purchase through several states of readiness.

In contrast, at a destination, a multitude of attractions, restaurants and bars advertise directly to achieve awareness and trial, many at the level of the sandwich board on the street. The level of risk in terms of trial on the part of the customer is minimal. Given such a low involvement purchase, consumers will make a choice very easily in these circumstances (Jones, 1991: 167–9). In this case the ATR model might be more applicable.

12.2.3 Branding

The communications mix is so important in terms of the development of brands. Branding offers a tried and tested route to securing repeat purchases through some degree of brand security. Hotel groups such as Accor, Hilton and Marriott aim to sustain competitive advantage through brand loyalty, both in terms of reinforcement and loyalty schemes. Branding, as a way of differentiating the services of one supplier from another in terms of name, logo and other identifying features, forms an important component of the communications mix.

12.3 COMMUNICATIONS STRATEGY

The objectives, strategy and nature of a communications campaign depend on a number of factors. Seaton (1994: 334–5) refers to promotion, for example, as one way of influencing demand to best effect. He suggests that there are eight possible states of demand, adopting a framework developed by Kotler (1973: 42–9):

1. No demand. Promotion is of no use in this situation unless the offering is repackaged.
2. Latent demand. There is no offering available, but promotion is an integral part of satisfying demand once a facility is introduced.
3. Faltering demand. Promotion can be used to reposition a tourism offering.
4. Full demand. Capacity has been reached and promotion is used simply to maintain existing demand.
5. Irregular demand. Promotion can be used as a tool to even demand.
6. Overfull demand. Demand exceeds supply and promotion can be used to shift demand in time and spatially.
7. Unwholesome demand. Where demand is considered socially or physically damaging, promotion is used to educate the market.
8. Negative demand. There is little promotion can do to shift demand when segments of the population indicate outright dislike of the offering.

Any communications strategy will not only take into account the service offerings or brands but will also decide how best to communicate these brands to respective market segments. This requires an examination of the organization's range of brands and how they are currently positioned to meet the perceptions of different market segments. In particular, how can the company's offering be differentiated from close competitors both in terms of benefits and possibly features?

The direction of strategy development will also take into account the degree of pre-consumption priming required. For example, with new tourism offerings there is a need to educate visitors about how to obtain the best from their trip, or how to use a facility more effectively. In tourism, given the importance of word of mouth marketing, it is also necessary to consider post-consumptive evaluation in order to reinforce the decision to travel.

Therefore the strategy will embrace the stages outlined in Sections 12.3.1 to 12.3.9.

12.3.1 Segmentation of targets

The first stage is to define with some degree of precision the target audience(s) and the benefits they seek. For example, a campaign to attract visitors to Australasia from Europe might define the key segments outlined in Table 12.2.

12.3.2 Define aim of campaign and objectives

The overall campaign might seek to create awareness in the market. For example:

● Positioning a country or a destination as – a special holiday (a cruise to Antarctica)
                                         – an inexpensive break (a camping holiday in France)
                                         – a unique experience (the Orient Express);
● specifying benefits accruing from activities (Kenyan safari holidays);
● symbolic branding (e.g. the Viva Espana campaign);
● 'bettering' the competition (e.g. airlines specifying differential levels of service).

In some instances, a campaign might be designed to improve misleading or negative views such as the destination Rio de Janeiro in Brazil countering views about crime and pollution in the city. In other cases, the communications mix might simply be utilized to retain existing custom such as British Airways television advertising campaigns.

12.3.3 Establish a budget

A budget tends to be based on two methods.

(a) Percentage of sales technique

The first method is the percentage of sales technique (say 5 or 10 per cent of sales

Table 12.2 Benefit segmentation: Communications plan

Segment	Benefits
Consumer markets – examples	
UK 25–55 couples VFR segment	Visiting relatives and touring
Euro youth 18–35 singles and couples	Adventure across Australasia
Trade markets – examples	
Specialist tour operators	New destination to add to portfolio
Travel agencies	Awareness of new offering – incentivize travel agencies

revenue) being devoted to the communications mix. It is usually based on a judgement of the level of spending in previous years or what competitors are spending.

(b) Task and objective technique

The second method is the task and objective technique. In this case the budget is constructed according to the level of resource needed. For example, the budget in Figure 12.3 illustrates the level of expenditure required for a communications campaign to promote a new regional walking trail in the UK.

12.3.4 Decide on core message(s)

Establishing a style, a branding position if appropriate and maintaining the integrity of a campaign is a vital element. This is especially the case when the communications strategy involves originating new brands or identities. For example, the repositioning of Torbay (comprising Torquay, Paignton and Brixham) as a continental style resort required an entirely fresh approach in the 1980s, one which featured a stylized palm tree.

12.3.5 Internal marketing

During the past 20 years there has been a growing interest in the concept of internal marketing (Sasser and Arbeit, 1976; George, 1990: 63–70; Piercy and Morgan, 1991). It has been defined by Berry (1981: 272) as 'viewing employees as internal customers, viewing jobs as internal products that satisfy the needs and wants of these internal customers while addressing the objectives of the organization'.

As part of the overall process of internal marketing it is argued that employees need to be consulted as to the best way to develop and unfold marketing campaigns. Furthermore, if front line staff (those interfacing with the customer) are to satisfy customers, they have to be fully conversant with the objectives of a plan, the benefits the customer will receive, in addition to the benefits the company and employee gain. Furthermore, internal marketing means that background staff also need to be aware of the campaign and how they can best support front line staff. Therefore, an important element is an appropriately targeted internal marketing communication structure.

Many campaigns now include essential briefing and feedback sessions with staff concerned within the organization. This is to ensure that they are both aware of the nature of the campaign and exactly what is expected from them in the communications process. It also allows continuous feedback. For example, when a hotel group launches a new service offering it will most probably devise a 'training kit' which includes a video, briefing sheets and examples of the promotional elements to be seen or heard by the customer. This kit will be presented to managers of hotels and other senior staff in the company by the marketing team or their marketing agency. Each manager (or other appropriate member of staff) will then be given a kit to take back to their hotel so that they in turn can brief all staff.

12.3.6 Development of tactical programmes

Tactical programmes should be developed for each element of mix. The strategy will specify the appropriateness of a number of submixes, as follows:

	Year I £	Year II £
Walking route elements		
Trail furniture & implementation	8000	
Interpretation boards (10)	4000	
Contingency	2000	
Maintenance programme		2000
Marketing & promotion		
Branding – corporate identity	2000	
Creation of trail brand and logo. Preparation of an information sheet on how to use it in other publications		
Artwork/bromides/adverts	800	200
Artwork and bromides, copy describing the trail which can be used for adverts or provided to traders to use on their own publicity material		
Waymark discs	500	
Design and production of waymark discs for use on trail		
Full colour leaflet – 20 000	2000	1000
A4, folded to third A4, (6pp) which explains what and where the trail is, its appeal and how to access and use it, plus how to obtain further information. Intended for distribution through tourist information centres		
Walkers pack – 5000	4000	
Pack with route cards. Saleable item outlining the trail		
Walkers welcome kit – Folders	600	
Traders kit; this would comprise a folder, the walkers pack, leaflets, information sheet, sticker etc., and additional information. It would be given to all traders who have been briefed and agree to welcome walkers		
Window stickers	100	
To be used by traders to reassure walkers		
Public transport/access/accommodation leaflets – 2000	600	600
Leaflets giving advice to walkers on using public transport to access trail plus listing of accommodation provision		
Information bulletin	200	200
A one colour briefing sheet for interested organizations i.e. for local communities		
Public relations & launch costs	2000	2000
Target magazines – Country Walking, Trail Walking and one quality weekend paper.		
Organization and implementation of launch		
Photography	500	
Research and provision of prints which reflect target groups walking trail. Photos of most attractive/scenic areas		
Media costs	2000	500
Costs of placing paid-for advertisements in chosen publications		
Community liaison & monitoring	1000	
To arrange meetings, prepare briefing sheets and maintain a register of volunteers who will check the route on a regular basis		
Training & business advice	3000	
To implement two Welcome Host training programmes which incorporate use of 'Walkers Welcome Pack'		
Business development		2000
In Year II there is likely to be a need to assist in the development of walking packages plus other marketing advice		
Total	**£33300**	**£8500**

Figure 12.3 The costing of a campaign to launch a newly established walking trail.
Source: Simon Holt Marketing Services, Gatley, Manchester. Data adjusted to maintain

- Publicity
- Advertising
- Public relations
- Direct marketing
- Sales promotion
- Personal selling

Depending on the nature of the tourism offering, the organization will decide on a schedule and the sequencing of the submixes. For example, many destinations focus on publicity, public relations and advertising; time share complexes on personal selling; tour operators on off-the-page advertising.

12.3.7 Specify media channels

Depending on the submixes chosen, it is essential to choose media channels to reach selected target audiences – television, press, posters, cinema, radio, computer networks. For example, destinations with wide appeal might choose television coverage in key generating markets during pre-season booking months. This is known as a **demand pull** campaign. Tour operators wishing to sell their particular packages at that destination might concentrate on providing publicity and incentives to core travel agencies, i.e. a much narrower focus. This is referred to as **demand push**, i.e. the intermediaries stimulate demand through recommendation.

12.3.8 Launch campaign and implement schedule

Most communication strategies adopt a staged approach, which brings a campaign to a climax at the launch, to achieve maximum appeal from all of the chosen submix elements.

12.3.9 Monitor and evaluate effectiveness

Most strategies include a degree of monitoring so that customer and trade feedback can be taken into account as the campaign unfolds. In some instances, this allows a fine tuning of the campaign effort. Public relations activity might be more effective than anticipated, demand pull techniques might be working, but not demand push, etc.

12.4 CAMPAIGN STYLE AND MESSAGE

Marketers need to be aware of the interface between design and marketing in the creation of a creative campaign. There is as yet little research in this area, and certainly not in the tourism sector (Wilson, 1994). Most organizations in tourism have a department or section involved in spearheading the marketing function but it is unlikely that they will have an in-house design team. Therefore, the trend is towards organizations hiring specialist design skills to create a campaign style, a brand, etc. This might range from a major global advertising agency such as J. Walter Thompson to a small design house. The skills required to originate a design are:

- two or three dimensional design, the visuals;
- copy writing;
- creative photography;
- production capability: scanning, printing, audio/visual presentations, computing software houses, etc.

In the past, much of these skills were provided entirely by an advertising agency and the client–agency relationship was managed by an account executive. Increasingly these specialisms, such as copy, photography and media buying are bought in as required. The task required of the account executive is to bring those skills together in an acceptable sequence and schedule within the budget limitations.

The creative flair lies with the art director or the principal designer of the marketing agency. This is the core to any communications strategy, for unless the copy, visuals and layout come together effectively to offer a distinctive image or strong selling appeal to the potential customer, the results will be poor. The process usually involves the design of a corporate, company or service brand, described by King (1991: 5) as,

> using all the company's particular assets to create unique entities that certain consumers really want; entities which have a lasting personality, based on a special combination of physical, functional and pyschological values; and which have a competitive advantage in at least one area of marketing (raw materials/sourcing, product/design/patents, production systems, supply/sales/service networks, depth of understanding of consumers, style/fashion, and so on.

The brand is obviously far more than a logo and identity, but as such brand identity hinges on the visual representation of such core values. That is why major airlines and hotel groups lay such great stress on corporate design manuals, so that there can be little or no variation in the way in which the company and its service offerings are depicted by design agencies and others. Marketing managers or the communications manager are the guardians of the integrity of the brand. There has been little criticism of this dimension of the communications mix.

12.4.1 Imagery

There is another issue which relates to imagery and that is how such companies portray the service offering or destination, rather than the company image or brand. The major source of criticism relates to the representation of the destination. The projection of the stunning, or iconic and ethnic stereotypes, it is argued, often portrays an image of a destination which is not truly representative of any given place. Among the critics are Selwyn (1993: 117–37) and Wilson (1994), both of whom question the ethics of projecting unbalanced or manipulated images of destinations in the developing world. As Crick (1989: 329) observes: 'One cannot sell poverty, but one can sell paradise.'

It is a question that tourism marketers need to address in terms of brand or destination building. More confident customers, who are becoming increasingly intolerant of offerings which are not presented in a balanced, 'worldy wise' way, will become increasingly disaffected from promotional tools currently being used, rendering them ineffective in the long term.

12.5 COMMUNICATIONS TECHNIQUES

The range of techniques which can be used are summarized below.

12.5.1 Publicity (published material)

Publicity is sometimes expressed, in the widest sense, as the sum of all public relations work undertaken by an organization. Practitioners also refer to the range of printed material as publicity. For most tourism organizations, the main piece of printed literature is the brochure. This might well be supplemented by other pieces of material such as a video, or audio tape, but the brochure usually reigns supreme as the cornerstone of a campaign.

A campaign might include a number of core pieces of material. This would include a general explanatory leaflet, which is designed to create awareness and interest. It might present to prospective customers a number of calls to action such as 'phoning for a brochure or contacting a travel agent. The brochure, in contrast, is designed to provide the level of detail necessary to consider purchase; it is the counterpart of the direct mail catalogue. It is especially important in that tourism is about selling intangibles. The brochure attempts to tangibilize the key benefits.

In the trade sector travel trade manuals are the counterpart to the brochure for the buyer of group travel. They contain more technical detail about features such as meeting rooms, etc., and are often supplemented by material designed for the consumer market.

As mentioned above, there have been a number of criticisms of the use of promotional techniques in tourism particularly by Mayo and Jarvis (1981) who describe how 'pockets of paradise' are presented to markets in generating countries. There have also been a number of articles critically appraising representations of people and other cultures in brochures, notably Mellinger (1994). Gilbert and Houghton (1990) have undertaken a preliminary study in brochure design, and more recently, work has been undertaken by Dann (1996: 61–83). His findings are particularly interesting as they provide an insight into brochure design. He analysed 11 summer holiday brochures (5172 pictures featured on 1470 pages). The main emphasis of the research was to analyse the use of people in the visual representation. One quarter of the pictures featured no people (a representation of tranquillity and getting away from it all). By far the largest category were holidaymakers (usually depicted in groups of two or three) enjoying themselves at a destination. This, argues Dann, reflects the view of normative segregation between hosts and visitors. The visuals depict visitors enjoying themselves. In contrast, less than 10 per cent of pictures depicted local people. From this initial study, Dann suggests that we need to reappraise more closely the way we depict holidays in brochures.

12.5.2 Advertising

Advertising has been defined as 'any paid form of non-personal presentation of products, services or ideas by an identified sponsor' (Foster with Davis, 1994: 167). The distinction between advertising and other forms of communications is that advertising is paid for. It therefore allows the company or an advertising agency to create and transmit a message to a target audience with the minimum of distortion.

Advertising still accounts for a major slice of most tourism marketing budgets and is the primary form of communication for many organizations.

The advertising submix includes:

- audio visual advertisements for TV and radio;
- press adverts for newspapers, and magazines;
- poster advertisements;
- joint advertising where brand identities (such as logos) are associated with a destination.

The advertising campaign will involve the origination of advertisements, possibly some pre-testing, media planning and evaluation of effectiveness. Much of the discussion in recent years has focused on the effectiveness of advertising techniques (see below).

12.5.3 Public relations

Public relations is a systematic approach to maintaining goodwill between an organization and its various publics. In this respect it is a corporate activity reflecting the desire to bring about a mutual understanding between an organization and its publics. Public relations stimulates some form of dialogue or feedback and possibly some degree of modification of view as a result. This is referred to as two way symmetrical public relations by Grunig and Hunt (1984). It also is a well used technique employed within the communications mix and within this context is subsumed under marketing as such, although this is a point of contention between practitioners.

Tourism organizations are increasingly using public relations, possibly because of the greater social and environmental pressures on companies which are articulated more now than previously. For example, many destinations rely heavily on public relations activity rather than advertising because it is argued that, managed in a strategic way, public relations can be more effective. The result can be positive 'soft' coverage of a tourism offering or destination in an editorial context. This is not always the case. For example, the *Sunday Times* (22 September, 1996) reported that an increasing number of tourists are going to Venice to commit suicide, chronicling that over 50 had killed themselves in the previous year. The old adage that any news is good news might not apply in this case.

Furthermore, much of tourism development involves discussion between government, local communities and a range of commercial interests and public relations as a technique can be used to good effect in such circumstances.

The types of techniques used are:

- Press releases or press packs, which include accompanying printed publicity material, including compact discs or videos.
- Editorials or features. These can emphasize negatives rather than positives thereby completely rejecting the intended message of the sender. This problem of distortion is a major disadvantage.
- Press conferences, as at major travel exhibitions.
- Presentations at trade and public meetings and political gatherings.
- Familiarization trips or provision of detailed text and photographs for journalists, travel writers, corporate buyers or intermediaries.
- Preparation of positive information for other interested publics such as students, or charities seeking sponsorship or reduced travel costs, etc.

- Intensive telephone activity, or interviews with media at times of crisis in order to stem negative imagery.

12.5.4 Direct marketing

In Chapter 5 we discussed the role of segmentation and the creation of databases which can be used for marketing purposes. Direct marketing is used extensively in service marketing sectors such as finance, insurance or professional services and increasingly by tourism organizations. It involves organizations contacting targeted customers by way of a variety of media, including response printed advertisements, door to door visits, the telephone, television and radio, mail and computerized systems, to evoke a direct response.

The rise of direct marketing is partly a response to a continuing fragmentation of markets and partly to advances in computer software which has reduced the cost of information systems. Direct marketing often allows more accurate targeting of market segments than other forms of communication.

Database marketing

The core of direct marketing activity is an accurate and well maintained database which often includes contact addresses, and characteristics about the customer such as type and frequency of holiday activity. A degree of sophistication of detail allows effective targeting of existing loyal customers for any given holiday company.

Increasingly companies and some tourist authorities create databases from enquiries, sales promotion activities, or competitions at exhibitions. Several consultancies specialize in data capture and the creation of consumer and business lists, for example, of school parties and group travel organizers. These can be rented and they often provide fulfilment and handling services for campaigns, which feature mailing of brochures or other items. Patron (1996) argues that lowering computer costs and increasing data will lead to integrated marketing which centres on the marketing database. This is illustrated in Figure 12.4

Database marketing (DBM) is the powerhouse of the process. It stresses the need to match the information gathering system of an organization to the complexity of the marketplace (Fletcher *et al.*, 1994: 133–41). DBM focuses on data acquisition, classification and analysis for marketing purposes. The principal benefits are summarized by Lewington *et al.* (1996: 329) as:

- improved accuracy in terms of market segmentation, which can strengthen the marketing mix decision making;
- on-line market research which relates consumer characteristics to purchasing behaviour, thus allowing improved market modelling;
- improved measurement of marketing plan performance.

Companies establish a generic database management system which comprises three elements – the database, the market modelling process and a mechanism for performance measurement (feedback). DBM is provided as a framework which organizations can build on, as shown in Figure 12.5.

The English Tourist Board has been developing database marketing for the domestic tourism market, which assumes that continued direct contact by the board can

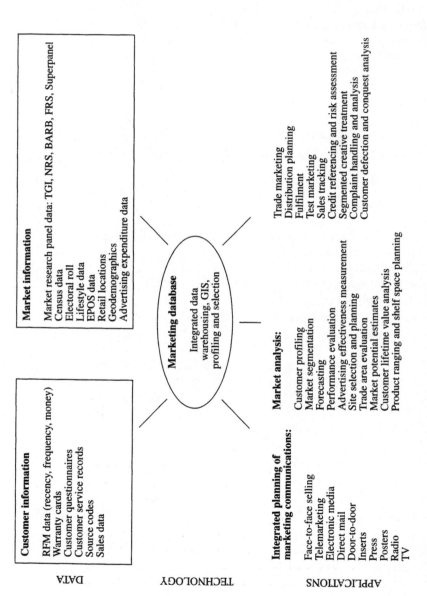

Customer information

RFM data (recency, frequency, money)
Warranty cards
Customer questionnaires
Customer service records
Source codes
Sales data

Market information

Market research panel data: TGI, NRS, BARB, FRS, Superpanel
Census data
Electoral roll
Lifestyle data
EPOS data
Retail locations
Geodemographics
Advertising expenditure data

Marketing database

Integrated data
warehousing, GIS,
profiling and selection

**Integrated planning of
marketing communications:**

Face-to-face selling
Telemarketing
Electronic media
Direct mail
Door-to-door
Inserts
Press
Posters
Radio
TV

Market analysis:

Customer profiling
Market segmentation
Forecasting
Performance evaluation
Advertising effectiveness measurement
Site selection and planning
Trade area evaluation
Market potential estimates
Customer lifetime value analysis
Product ranging and shelf space planning

Trade marketing
Distribution planning
Fulfilment
Test marketing
Sales tracking
Credit referencing and risk assessment
Segmented creative treatment
Complaint handling and analysis
Customer defection and conquest analysis

DATA

TECHNOLOGY

APPLICATIONS

Figure 12.4 The marketing database of the future. *Source:* Patron (1996).

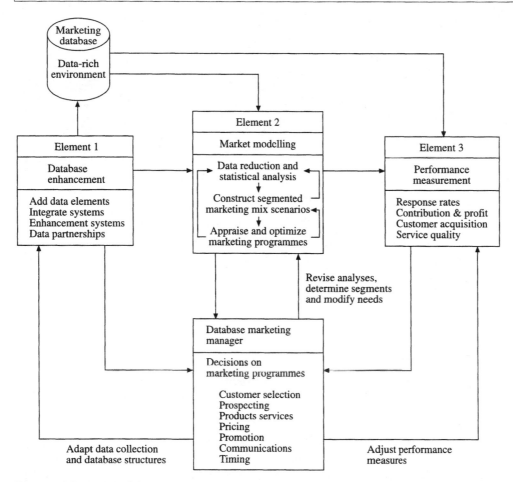

Figure 12.5 Model of database marketing. Reprinted from 'Harnessing the power of database marketing', *Journal of Marketing Management*, Vol. 12, 1996, page 334, by permission of the publisher. © The Dryden Press, Harcourt Brace & Company Ltd. All rights reserved.

improve loyalty to taking domestic holidays. The process of establishing a national tourism consumer database is explained by Baker (1996: C29–C38) and she sets out a model for development (Figure 12.6). The benefit of this database approach is its low cost.

Of all of the methods mentioned above, direct mail is still the most important in western economies, although in the USA telemarketing is becoming more popular. Most campaigns tend to relate to a domestic market only but major concerns such as American Express, airlines and international visitor attractions, such as Disney World, generate multicountry promotions.

While telemarketing is more prevalent in the business to business sector, there is some evidence of its use in tourism. Hotels and timeshare consortiums use telemarketing to find new customers as well as to update files on existing customers. It is a low cost form of communication which allows some degree of feedback but it has also been criticized for being intrusive and therefore offering limited conversions or subsequent enquiries.

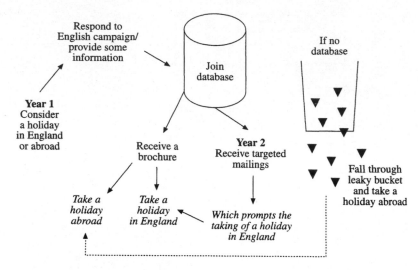

Figure 12.6 The English tourism marketing model. *Source*: Baker (1996).

12.5.5 Sales promotion

Sales promotion is also known as **below the line activity**. It comprises a series of techniques which can be used collectively or independently to stimulate demand. This involves two basic approaches: intermediary push or consumer pull. The techniques focus on offering impulse incentives to purchase, such as competitions, discount vouchers, or by other similar methods. Examples of the various sales promotion techniques used are listed in Table 12.3.

The 1980s saw a rapid growth in the use of sales promotion in the UK and elsewhere (Schultz, 1987: 17–27). One estimate is that global expenditure in 1990 accounted for 39 per cent of total marketing expenditure (*Financial Times*, 1989: 13). Peattie and Peattie (1993: 255–69) summarize eight key reasons why companies have moved towards using sales promotions:

- Rising prices and advertising 'clutter' – the argument that consumers are becoming desensitized to mass media advertising.
- Sales promotion becoming 'respectable' – increasing professionalism and use by market leaders.
- Increased impulse purchase – retailers are responding to greater impulse buying.
- Shortening time horizons – intensive rivalry and accelerating product life cycles make fast moving sales promotion campaigns look worthwhile.
- Micro-marketing approaches – as a response to more fragmented markets.
- 'Snowball' effect in some markets – in markets where competitions are prevalent, suppliers have to follow suit.
- Manageability – other elements of the mix can be unwieldy in comparison.
- Measurability – while it is still not easy to measure success, it is possible to track results with some degree of precision.

There are some problems of wider definitional issues, for example, in some North American texts sales promotion is used to express the entire communications mix. In

Table 12.3 Sales promotion techniques in the tourism sector

Technique	Explanation	Example
Consumer Market		
Trial offers using coupons	Customers collect coupons when purchasing a product or service allowing free or low-cost trial of tourism offering	Eurostar and *The Sunday Times*
Self-liquidating offers	Provision of branded merchandise such as T-shirts, etc., within overall price of holiday or visit or as a low-cost extra	Many specialist holiday companies offer T-shirts or other items of clothing as an integral part of the package, either way seen as revenue earner
Loyalty collection schemes	The customer collects points when spending on the company's products or services	Most airlines now have loyalty schemes, for example, Iberia or KLN
Competitions	The use of competitions are often to build awareness and more often to create databases for future marketing activity	
Displays	These are often used by tour operators or destinations to reinforce a campaign with travel agents	Window displays, travel agencies and hotel reception areas
Sampling	Used frequently at exhibitions to tangibilize destinations, such as food and beverages typical of a location	Travel fairs
Merchandising	Presentation of small gifts such as confectionery, pens through to expensively branded products which reflect the quality of a tourism offering	Reception areas, travel agencies and at travel fairs

other instances it is described as a range of tactical techniques to stimulate sales. This is a limited view of sales promotion, for many companies now view it in a strategic way. For example, the provision of customer or trade incentives is considered vital to the ongoing success of many communications strategies. Air Miles has been one of the longest running strategic sales promotion campaigns in the UK, but many others have now followed the success formula.

Sales promotion in tourism is best described as a set of associated techniques which when combined, offer customers or intermediaries enhanced incentives to buy or to remain loyal to a particular brand. They are distinguished by their use primarily at the point of purchase. While many of the techniques are used in isolation and at a tactical level they can be brought together as a longer term strategic campaign. The sales promotion submix includes exhibitions, intermediary and consumer incentives, merchandising and sampling.

(a) Exhibitions

Exhibitions offer an opportunity to bring targeted buyers and sellers from both consumer and business to business sectors together in a competitive arena. The main advantages of exhibitions are that they provide a forum for sales leads, contact with influencers, gathering competitor intelligence and image building (Browning and Adams, 1987: 31–6; Dudley, 1990). During the exhibition tour operators can source potential destinations to develop, hotels can test reservation systems, destinations can launch new tourism offerings and everyone has the opportunity to watch closely what others are doing next season. In terms of effectiveness, there is a dearth of information available. The main travel exhibitions of Europe are indicated in Table 12.4.

(b) Intermediary and consumer incentives

These include loyalty schemes and competitions for consumers and increased commission (overrides) for travel retailers. There is a continuing debate as to whether competitions incentivize customers or devalue a brand (Bawa and Shoemaker, 1987: 370–76). They have been used more frequently with intermediaries to good effect but there are fewer examples of customer based schemes written up in the research literature. Peattie and Peattie (1993: 255–69), in reporting a three year study involving the analysis of 2600 competitions, argue that when executed in a sophisticated manner, competitions can reap considerable benefits such as increases in sales, smoothing of demand, database building, idea generation, point-of-sale and public relations opportunities, etc. This suggests that sales promotion used in a strategic way, rather than as a series of *ad hoc* tactical campaigns, can gain longer term benefits. The loyalty schemes certainly appear to be more strategic in terms of establishing long term consumer loyalty, but there is a need for more research activity in this field.

(c) Merchandising

The use of point-of-sale material, such as window displays and brochure dispensers to enhance a brand image is common in tourism especially in travel agencies and information offices. They are essentially short term, in that much of the material is geared for one season or pre-season period only.

Table 12.4 The main travel exhibitions of Europe

Exhibition	Venue	Month	Comment
MITCAR	Paris	October	Coach operator segment in France
World Travel Market	London	November	Worldwide travel and tourism sector
Brussels Travel Fair	Brussels	November	Travel trade
Ferien	Vienna	January	Austria's largest holiday fair – influence from Eastern Europe
Vakantie	Utrecht	January	Dutch travel consumer exhibition
Matka	Helsinki	January	Finland's major travel fair
Fitur	Madrid	January	Spain's premier travel show – interest from Latin America
Ferie	Copenhagen	January	Large exhibition in Nordic region
BIT (Borsa Internazionale de Turismo)	Milan	February	Italy's major show
ITB	Berlin	March	World's leading international travel trade event
TUR	Gothenburg	March	Nordic region's major travel and tourism fair

(d) Sampling

Sampling is used at exhibitions and trade fairs. Potential customers are offered a taste of food or beverage from a destination, or are presented with a small artisan gift which is representative of the area.

Such techniques make up the core of sales promotion. They have been used both at a tactical level, primarily to boost sales of a product or service in the short run, but increasingly companies are investigating ways of integrating sales promotion into longer term strategic plans.

12.5.6 Incentive travel

Travel is also often used as an incentive to sell other goods and services. For example, brand loyalty to a product is rewarded with travel offers. In some instances, these are joint ventures, such as the dream holidays offered by television game shows throughout the world. There are also a number of specialist incentive travel companies which arrange holidays for executives who are being rewarded by their companies for outstanding results.

12.5.7 Personal selling

Personal selling is used to describe the face to face promotion of goods or services which is directed towards obtaining a sale or booking. In tourism, personal selling is a valued technique which is used in a variety of ways by visitor attractions, hotels and destinations. It is particularly important in terms of the travel adviser and customer in the travel agency sector. Given that production and consumption often take place at the same location there is also an opportunity for operational staff to sell additional offerings. A good waiter or waitress, for example, can encourage a return visit to a restaurant.

12.5.8 Sponsorship

The relationship between sponsorship and sports or events tourism has become increasingly important in recent decades. The benefits accruing from such joint promotional activities are dependent on a number of factors which are discussed in Chapter 17.

Sponsorship is, however, being adopted by companies as well as destinations. First Choice, for example, sponsored weather programmes on television in 1996/7. The travel agency group Going Places sponsored the popular series Blind Date and Radisson Edwardian Hotels agreed a deal to support the Society of London Theatres in 1997.

12.6 MONITORING AND EVALUATION

The process and evaluation of communication methodology has been extensively researched (Coulson-Thomas, 1983). In summary there are a number of issues which apply equally to tourism as to other business sectors. The first level of assessment relates to an early reappraisal of what the strategy is attempting to achieve and whether or not this is feasible. Prentice (1994: 375–9), suggests that:

the evaluation of promotional campaigns may have four objectives:

1. To test by recall how promotion has informed the potential tourist.
2. To test the overall awareness of the potential tourist of the destination or company.
3. To test by additional research how past behaviour has been reinforced.
4. To test by sales research how the campaign has affected bookings or visitor numbers.

A common approach is to test the effectiveness of the message or creative design before the launch of a campaign. It might then be possible to test the respective channels to be used. Therefore, in terms of design and understanding of the key messages, there will most probably be some degree of pre-testing with focus groups.

There will also be evaluation of the media channels as to their effectiveness in any particular campaign. This might involve a number of similar measures such as the reach, i.e. the number of people who read a paper or view television, or the relative numbers having an opportunity to see an advertisement (OTS). This could include such indicators as television ratings at different times, or the cost per thousand in reaching target audiences.

Post-testing of a campaign might include an assessment of sales or bookings, the number of press stories featured in newspapers and magazines, or marketing research exercises relating to awareness or changed attitudes. These will involve questions regarding recall of a message, recognition, image projection and actual use or visitation.

Tourism organizations test the effectiveness of public relations in a fairly elementary way. They measure the exposure, in terms of column square centimetres achieved in printed material, or listening and viewing time on the radio and television, and calculate the price of advertising to achieve similar coverage. It becomes more complex when the quality or value of the audience is evaluated. As with advertising effectiveness, research econometrics modelling is used to isolate the effect of public relations from other variables in the marketing mix:

In general, econometric models work at the brand or firm level, using time-series data to relate a brand's market share to its marketing efforts (and those of its competitors).

(Duckworth, 1996, p. 30)

Ultimately, as with all methodologies, it depends on the objectives set by the client.

12.7 SUMMARY The tourism organization has to be conversant with the theories of communication and how they might be applied to any given marketing campaign. In setting out a campaign plan it is necessary to give consideration to both external promotional and internal marketing campaigns.

While the most important promotional materials still tend to be the brochure and printed material, increasingly organizations and destinations are turning to direct marketing and using improving technologies such as the Internet. Videos and CD-ROMS are also beginning to replace traditionally presented print as publicity tools.

The chapter explores other promotional techniques including public relations, sales promotion, incentive travel and sponsorship. In many instances, these are techniques which are enjoying increased success within the more conventional framework of above-the-line communication techniques such as advertising.

REFERENCES

Baker, J.D. (1996) A Lesson in Database Marketing – The English Tourism Marketing Model. *Insights*, ETB/BTA, Vol. 8, November, C29–38.

Bawa, K. and Shoemaker, R.W. (1987) The Effects of a Direct Mail Coupon on Brand Choice Behaviour. *Journal of Marketing Research*, **14**, 370–76.

Berry, L. (1981) The Employee as Customer. *Journal of Retail Banking*, **11**(1), 33–40.

Browning, J.M. and Adams, R.J. (1988) Trade Shows: An Effective Promotional Tool for the Small Industrial Business. *Journal of Small Business Management*, **26**(4), 31–6.

Chisnall, P.M. (1985) *Marketing: Analysis, Planning, Implementation and Control*, McGraw-Hill, Maidenhead.

Coulson-Thomas, C.J. (1983) *Marketing Communications*, Heinemann, Oxford.

Crick, M. (1989) Representations of international tourism in social sciences: sun, sex, sights, savings and servility. *Annual Review of Anthropology*, **18**, 307–44.

Dann, G. (1996) The People of Tourist Brochures. In *The Tourist Image* (ed. T. Selwyn), Wiley, Chichester.

Delozier, M.W. (1986) *The Marketing Communications Process*, McGraw-Hill, Maidenhead.

Duckworth, S. (1996) Market modelling: any common threads. *Admap*, December, 30.

Dudley, J.W. (1990) *Successful Exhibiting*, Kogan Page, London.

Financial Times (1989) Worldwide Marketing Expenditure 1989, 30 November, 13.

Fletcher, K., Wheeler, C. and Wright, J. (1994) Strategic Implementation of Database Marketing: Problems and Pitfalls. *Long Range Planning*, **27**(1), 133–41.

Foster, D. with Davis, J.E. (1994) *Mastering Marketing*, Macmillan, Basingstoke.

George, W.R. (1990) Internal Marketing and Organizational Behaviour: A Partnership in Developing Customer-Conscious Employees at Every Level. *Journal of Business Research*, **20**, 63–70.

Gilbert, D.G. and Houghton, P. (1990) An Investigation of the Format, Design and Placement of Tour Operators' Brochures. A paper presented to Tourism in the 1990s, Durham, Sept., pp. 80–8.

Grunig, J.E. and Hunt, T. (1984) *Managing Public Relations*, Holt, Rheinhart Winston, New York.

Haywood, K.M. (1989) Managing Word of Mouth Communications. *Journal of Services Marketing*, **12**, 55–67.

Jones, J.P. (1991) Over Promise and Under-delivery. *Marketing and Research Today*, August, 167–9.

Kotler, P. (1973) The major task of marketing management. *Journal of Marketing*, **37**, October, 42–9.

Kotler, Bowen and Makens (1996) *Marketing for Hospitality and Tourism*, Prentice Hall, Upper Saddle River, New Jersey.

Lewington, J., de Chertatony, L. and Brown, A. (1996) Harnessing the Power of Database Marketing. *Journal of Marketing Management*, **12**, 329–46.

Mayo, E. and Jarvis, L. (1981) *The Psychology of Leisure Travel, Effective Marketing and the Selling of Travel Services*, CBI, Boston.

Mellinger, W. (1994) Toward a critical analysis of tourism representations. *Annals of Tourism Research*, **21**, 756–79.

Morgan, N. (1991) *Professional Services Marketing*, Butterworth-Heinemann, Oxford.

Patron, M. (1996) Direct Marketing. *Admap*, October, p. 22.

Peattie, K and Peattie, S. (1993) Sales Promotion – Playing to Win. *Journal of Marketing Management*, **9**, 255–69.

Prentice, R. (1994) Sales promotion in tourism, In *Tourism Marketing and Management Handbook*, Prentice Hall.

Rafiq, M. and Pervaiz, K.A. (1993) The Scope of Internal Marketing: Defining the Boundary Between Marketing and Human Resource Management. *Journal of Marketing Management*, **9**, 219–32.

Sasser, W.E. and Arbeit, S.F. (1976) Selling Jobs in the Service Sector. *Business Horizons*, June, 61–2.

Seaton, A.V. (1994) Promotional strategies in tourism. In *Tourism Marketing and Management Handbook*, Prentice Hall.

Selwyn, T. (1993) Peter Pan in South-East Asia: views from the brochures. In *Tourism in South-East Asia* (eds M. Hitchcock, V.T. King and M.J.G. Parnwell), Routledge, London.

Shultz, D.E. (1987) Above or Below the Line? Growth of Sales Promotion in the United States. *International Journal of Advertising*, **6**, 17–27.

Wilson, D. (1994) Unique by a thousand miles: Seychelles tourism revisited. *Annals of Tourism Research*, **21**, 74–92.

Wilson, I. (1994) *Marketing Interfaces*, Pitman, London.

13 Distribution in tourism

OBJECTIVES

This chapter explains:

- the nature of distribution channels within the tourism sector;
- the effectiveness of alternative channels in the determination of channel strategy;
- the roles of tour operators and travel agencies.

13.1 THE PRINCIPLES OF DISTRIBUTION

The principles which underlie the establishment of distribution channels in tourism are much the same as in other markets. However, there is one fundamental difference: in most sectors we refer to the distribution of goods from manufacturing centres to markets whereas in tourism the opposite occurs. The distribution channel in tourism enables the customer to be enticed to the destination.

In the world of fast moving consumer or industrial goods markets the emphasis is often placed on logistics and transport. In tourism, it lies with the flow of promotional material and information about tourism offerings; it is a brokerage of intangible offerings. Therefore, given the nature of service marketing, i.e. the underlying principles of intangibility, perishability and simultaneous consumption and provision, the distribution channels which have grown up to serve tourism markets differ to those found in other sectors.

There is, of course, an essential component of passenger transport without which tourism could not exist but this chapter is devoted to distribution channels in the sense of accessing the marketplace. It includes both the tour operator as a service developer but also as an intermediary. It also focuses on the travel agency and a plethora of other specialist agencies such as tourist information centres and city bureaux. The aspect of intermediaries in the corporate business sector is addressed in Chapter 4.

13.2 THE ROLE OF TRAVEL INTERMEDIARIES

The way in which potential customers are attracted to a particular destination or tourism offering is determined by a multiplicity of factors. The role of intermediaries in the process can be summarized as follows:

- Presentation of a wide range of travel opportunities to the customer.
- Provision of information on crucial aspects at the pre-purchase stage such as price, availability and other dimensions.
- Offering a comprehensive range of ancillary (sometimes specialist) services such as sourcing of additional facilities or information.
- Allowing easy access to the supplier.
- Enabling speedy reaction to market conditions given the perishable nature of the tourism offering.
- Bringing economies of scale for the supply chain (especially long haul destinations).
- Offering feedback to the supplier of tourism offerings which would not otherwise be feasible from distant markets.

13.3 CHANNELS OF DISTRIBUTION

The alternative channels of distribution are illustrated in Figure 13.1. They range from direct distribution to longer chains of supply.

There is no one dominant channel. Domestic holidays tend to be arranged directly by the customer throughout the world. The customer will more than likely book directly with a venue at a destination. The customer will then proceed to arrange their own transport requirements to and from this location.

In most countries, short to medium haul holidays are arranged on behalf of a customer by a travel agent or similar organization such as a business travel house. Short haul travel is invariably bought as a package from a travel agency but also directly from the tour operator. This has considerable implications for certain destinations. For example, Mallorca which is a favourite with the British family market (*Sunday Times*, 13 January 1997) is extremely reliant on a small number of tour operators to generate demand. It is estimated that 65 per cent of UK visitors to Mallorca are handled by tour operators such as Airtours, Cosmos, First Choice (Air 2000) and Thomson (Britannia Airways) and that 75 percent of all air traffic comprise charter flights organized by north European operators (Rojas, 1994). Mallorca is not untypical in this respect.

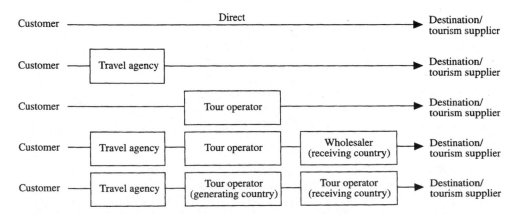

Figure 13.1 Channels of distribution.

13.3.1 Channel strategy

For the marketing manager in tourism the crucial decision is which channel(s) to choose in order to achieve an effective market coverage. There are a number of recognized factors which affect channel selection.

(a) The nature of the market

The essential point is an understanding of how the market, or markets in any given country chooses to buy a holiday. For example, in Spain the concept of direct response using the press would be far less successful than Germany. In the former, the level of readership of newspapers is notoriously low and in the latter high, offering a potentially suitable medium for direct marketing. In southern Europe the travel agent as an adviser and broker is a more strongly entrenched concept in society than in north European countries, so in some instances the use of agencies would be an important consideration.

(b) Resource commitment

One of the major problems for lesser known destinations or small niche tourism suppliers is that they are unable to afford the distribution costs of supplying brochures and paying a sufficiently attractive commission to obtain extensive coverage by a chain of travel agencies in generating markets. They will have to seek other, possibly less effective, ways of reaching the customer, or become involved in an alliance with a tour operator based in the generating market.

(c) Cost

Given the increasing fragmentation of many markets, companies are increasingly seeking to restructure their value chains to reduce costs of provision at every stage, including distribution. This process has been fuelled by vast improvements in technology, which enables more suppliers to reach more niche markets than in past decades.

(d) Competitor activity

This is a major area of contention between tour operators in the UK market where vertical and horizontal integration, as well as the formation of alliances, has led to tightly focused supplier owned distribution channels.

13.3.2 Degrees of intensity of distribution

Any given distribution strategy would also need to take into account the degree of intensity envisaged:

- **Intensive distribution.** This would provide a wide coverage in most generating markets. For example, many tour operators aim for total coverage, for if they are not represented in a travel agency, they know that a close substitute will be offered to a customer instead.

- **Selective distribution.** Some tourism offerings are specifically designed for selective markets or are premium priced. They are therefore targeted to such markets through specialist tour operators, or by way of focused direct marketing activities. Activity holidays or long haul exotic holidays are distributed in this way. Eurostar tickets were originally distributed through a handful of outlets but in 1997 the strategy altered to increase to well over 11 000 distribution points.
- **Exclusive distribution.** This is rare in tourism but some destinations or tourism offerings, such as island retreats or luxurious hotel complexes, are promoted in the same way as works of art. The buyer is invited to join an exclusive set of customers. In this respect, the very appeal is social esteem generated by association with other select guests.

Once a company or organization establishes a channel strategy, the relationship between supplier and distributor should focus on establishing an effective campaign suited to each particular generating market. This might involve different levels of commitment within each market. The role of the tour operator and travel agency are crucial to the entire process but there is a shifting emphasis toward direct communciation.

13.4 ROLE OF DISTRIBUTORS

There are two primary organizations which provide the key role of accessibility: tour operators and travel agencies. Secondary distribution methods include business travel houses and direct booking systems.

13.4.1 Tour operators

The tour operator brings together the essential elements of a holiday, such as transport, ground handling (luggage forwarding, transfers, etc.) and accommodation, as well as additional features, such as visits to attractions in some circumstances. The pioneer in the UK was Thomas Cook, who began to organize tours by rail in the 1840s, through to the company's illustrious steamship tours in the 1920s. Tour operation (sometimes referred to as tour wholesaling in North America) has been the linchpin of distribution of tourism development ever since. This is particularly important for the internationalization of suppliers in developing countries:

> The tour wholesaler acts as a catalyst of demand – he interprets the market needs of his clients and packages these needs into destinations. His influence on the direction of demand is particularly significant to long haul, relatively expensive, destinations, i.e. most developing countries.
>
> *(Jenkins, 1991)*

(a) The package holiday

During the boom years of tourism, from the 1960s through to the 1980s, the package holiday became the most prevalent form of tourism offering in the international travel scene. The EC Package Directive (90/314 of 13 June 1990) defines a package holiday as 'the pre-arranged combination of not fewer than two of the following when sold or offered for sale at an inclusive price and when the service covers a period of more than 24 hours or includes, overnight accommodation, other tourist services not ancillary to transport or accommodatio§§n and accounting for a significant proportion of the package'.

As the tourism market grew in north Europe so did the importance of the easy to digest and consume package holiday. The most important point is that tour operators made such packages accessible to all market segments through a range of distribution channels. It still remains an important aspect of the tourism business. Serving a mass market is as important now as in the 1960s, but tour operators are conscious that the market environment is moving away to less packaging (Commission of the European Communities, 1991; Poon, 1993: 9–11).

Tour operators vary in terms of what they offer, their size, direction and territorial interest. The major tour operators are situated in generating countries such as the USA and in northern Europe. Mainstream operators include Thomsons and Airtours in the UK, and ITS and Neckermann in Germany. However, a number of large transport operators have tour operating subsidiaries such as the German Railways and British Airways, etc. A number of tour operators have grown up especially to serve specific segments such as Club 18–30 targeting young people and Elderhostel (USA) for older age groupings. Many tour operators have also been established to serve a specialist market. They might cover a specific territory for activity holidays, such as Journey Latin America, or special activities such as Backroads (USA) and Activtours (Netherlands).

Most tour operators often grow from a clearly defined home market, such as Club Méditerranée in France, into other markets to include Japan, the UK and USA. In a similar manner, companies such as Tjaerborg have grown to serve the Scandinavian market, then expanded through northern Europe. In the case of small tour operators they invariably sell direct, but with larger organizations they use a range of channels, such as travel agents as well as direct marketing.

The key tasks in putting a package together for a market are outlined in Figure 13.2.

(b) Tour operator consortiums

In many parts of the world there are also consortiums which act both as a network and a proactive lobbying group to protect the interests of their memberships such as the European Tour Operators Association (ETOA) in Europe and the United States Tour Operators Association (USTOA) in the USA. The consortiums are also involved in marketing ideas to potential clients by organizing workshops and trade trips.

13.4.2 Travel agencies

The retail travel agent is primarily in business to advise and sell a range of holidays and other tourism offerings to potential and existing customers. They do not gain title to the services offered and hence the use of the term agent. In return for selling a tourism offering they receive a commission which usually ranges from 8–12 per cent of the sale price of a given holiday or travel ticket. The level of contribution from each service offering indicates that the sale of inclusive tours is still very important. Mintel, in evaluating the turnover of the top five travel agencies in the UK, estimates that 37% of revenue accrues from inclusive tours, 36% from business travel and 14% from independent travel. The remaining 13% accounts for insurance commissions, currency transactions and interest.

Activity	Year 1					Year 2												Year 3									
	Aug	S	O	N	D	Jan	F	M	A	M	J	J	A	S	O	N	D	Jan	F	M	A	M	J	J	A	S	O
Research																											
• Review market performance	×	×																									
• Forecast market trends	×	×																									
• Select and compare new and existing destinations			×	×																							
• Determine market strategy				×	×																						
Capacity planning																											
• Tour specifications						×	×																				
• Negotiate with and contract suppliers								×	×	×	×																
Financial evaluation																											
• Determine exchange rates											×	×															
• Estimate future selling prices											×	×															
• Finalize tour prices													×														
Marketing																											
• Brochure planning and production							×	×	×	×	×	×															
• Brochure distribution and launch													×	×													
• Media advertising and sales promotion														×	×	×											
• Market stimulation											×	×															
Administration																											
• Recruit reservation staff										×	×																
• Establish reservation system														×	×												
• Receive reservations by telephone and viewdata															×	×	×	×	×	×	×	×	×	×	×	×	×
• Tour accounting and documentation																×	×	×	×	×	×	×	×	×	×	×	×
• Recruit resort staff																			×	×	×						
Tour management																											
• Customer care at resort																						×	×	×	×	×	×
• Customer correspondence																							×	×	×	×	×
• Payment of suppliers																							×	×	×	×	×

Figure 13.2 Developing holiday packages. Tour operating cycle for a summer programme abroad. *Source:* Cooper, Fletcher, Gilbert, Wanhill (1993). Reprinted by permission of Addison Wesley Longman Ltd.

Currently, margins are tight and turnover is dependent on inclusive tours and business travel respectively, with other services bringing far smaller contributions. The concept of the experience curve, i.e. an increased market share relative to competitors which leads to the creation of economies of scale, is appropriate in this context. Not only is it a matter of increasing the volume of sales of tourism offerings across branches that improves commercial return, but also the wider experience applied across all activities of the business, which leads to greater profitability.

The travel agent is expected to supply information, offer travel advice, sell ancillary services, collect payment, and administer the holiday and travel bookings. In some cases, the travel agent might also offer post-travel services such as the exchange of foreign currency, etc. In theory, travel agencies offer impartial advice. In practice, many travel agency chains in the UK are increasingly tied to a tour operator and this has become a critical issue. The level of vertical and horizontal integration has meant that travel agencies have a tendency to recommend preferred tour operators. For example, the tour operator Airtours took over the Pickfords travel agency business in 1992 and Hogg Robinson in 1993, to form a newly branded Going Places in 1993. Such concentration meant that Airtours has created market leverage by virtue of its spend and size in the marketplace. It has been criticized on the grounds that Going Places operate a preferential policy of offering Airtours holidays rather than those of their competitors.

This is a general criticism raised against all of the leading tour companies involved in vertical and horizontal integration and is the subject of continued debate. In terms of marketing strategy, however, it is one of the few options open to the companies in a restructured marketing environment.

With the concentration of travel agencies there has also been an increased intensity in terms of sales promotion techniques applied at the wholesale and retail level, especially targeted to travel agency staff. A representative from a tour operator will not only make a quarterly visit to brief staff on new service offerings, but will also stress incentives to achieve higher personal sales bonuses, enhanced commission for volume sales (known as overrides), or competitions where travel and cash prizes are offered. Such sales promotions can rarely be matched by other small scale tour operators.

Even the racking of brochures is subject to intense competition with many travel agencies seeking payment for premium 'opportunity to see' positions in the shop. In these circumstances, it is difficult to describe the travel adviser as entirely objective in the traditional sense of a brokerage. The shrinking independent travel agent sector in the UK argues that its only marketing advantage over the major chains is that it can offer objective and specialist advice to the customer. This remains true of travel agencies in some countries where the customer still views the travel clerk as a personal adviser. In reality, the UK high street travel agency remains in business because of three perceived consumer benefits: low pricing and discounts, close proximity and well informed and helpful staff.

13.4.3 Business travel houses

There is a distinction between consumer based agencies and business travel houses in terms of direction, skills and level of service. Major companies, such as American Express or Wagonlit, and a number of smaller travel companies, such as Ayscough Travel or Business Routes, specialize in providing corporate travel. Each business account might be worth between one and five million pounds in turnover per annum. The purchase of business travel is different in that not only will the end user specify what he or she wants, but there will be at least one other person involved in authorizing the transaction and processing the order. Therefore, the business travel house has to understand the roles of those involved, the regulations which apply and the processes to be absorbed for each particular client. The discussion of the theoretical framework of organizational buyer behaviour, such as the buyphases (the stages which the organization progresses through before purchasing services) and buyclasses (the nature of the purchase from risk laden new tourism offerings to routine buy) apply in this sector. For a more detailed review refer to Chapter 4.

13.4.4 Direct booking systems

Another dimension is the rapid ascendancy of direct booking systems. There has been a surge in the provision of information and direct booking using enhanced communications systems, known as on-line systems. The same technology which has renewed the role of the travel agency is now available directly to the customer. Tour operators, hotels and other suppliers offer a direct channel to potential customers which means that with little or no effort a holiday can be booked from the home.

13.5 INFORMATION TECHNOLOGY

The catalyst has undoubtedly been the application of information technology (acquisition, storage and retrieval of information) to tourism distribution systems (Barras, 1986: 161–78). It has enabled timely information to be made available to all levels of the distribution system regarding availability and occupancy of facilities at any given time. This is vital when the offering is both perishable and intangible. Furthermore, it has enabled thousands of suppliers from around the globe to connect into computerized reservation systems. The major problem for the tourism marketer is that many of the systems have been designed for specific purposes or sectors and do not interrelate entirely. Buhalis has mapped the interconnections between reservation systems and the major global distribution systems which are illustrated in Figure 13.3. Many of these systems have been designed as a second stage development of major airline computer reservation systems (CRSs) (Bennett, 1993: 259–66). The aim is eventually to incorporate access to a wider range of other services.

Most systems are screen based. The development of view data or videotex such as teletext has served to stimulate the market. Most travel agencies now use interactive systems, mainly those provided by Istel and Midland Network Services which enable on-line holiday, hotel and airline, car hire and other services to be accessed. The major systems are outlined in Table 13.1.

The continuing development of CRS provides the cutting edge of competitor activity in tourism (Boberg and Collinson, 1985: 174–83; Bruce, 1994: 455–8). There has been some debate about the way in which the airline systems favour the service offerings provided by each particular parent group. It is obviously a cost effective way of sustaining marketing advantage as is the code sharing arrangement between airline companies which are now in alliance. This means that a smaller airline offering a link to a major hub will receive the same code as a major airline route across the Atlantic, for

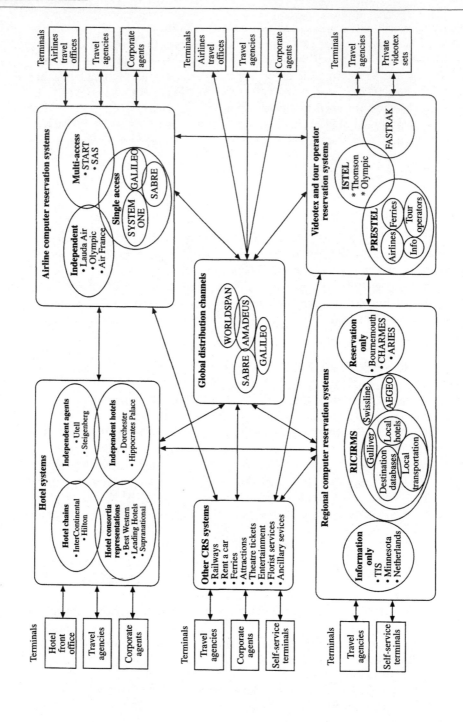

Figure 13.3 The complexity of the computer reservation systems. *Source:* Buhalis (1994). Copyright John Wiley & Sons Limited. Reproduced with permission.

Table 13.1 Computer reservation systems worldwide

Name	Owner(s)	% ownership
Sabre	American Airlines	100
System One	Continental Airlines	100
Worldspan	Delta Airlines	38
	Northwest	31.6
	TWA	35.7
	Abacus	5
Gemini	Air Canada	–
	Canadian Airlines	–
	Galileo International	30
Amadeus	Air France	33.3
	Iberia	33.3
	Lufthansa	33.3
Galileo	United Airlines	38
	US Air	11
	Air Canada	1
	British Airways	14.7
	Swissair	13.2
	KLM	12.1
	Alitalia	8.7
	Olympic	1
	TAP	1
	Aer Lingus	1
	Australian Airlines	1
START	Lufthansa	30
	Deutsche Bundesbahn	30
	TUI Hannover	30
	Amadeus	10
Infini	All Nippon Airways	60
	Abacus	40
Fantasia	Qantas Airways	50
	Ansett Airlines	25
	Air New Zealand	25
Abacus	Cathay Pacific	13.5
	Singapore Airlines	13.5
	Malaysian Airlines	13.5
	China Airlines	13.5
	Royal Brunei Airlines	13.5*
	Dragonair	2.5*
	Silk Air	2.5
	Worldspan	4.5*
	Infini	13.5
	Philippine Airlines	9.5*
Axess	Japan Airlines	100
Southern Cross	Qantas Airways	50
	Ansett Airlines	25
	Air New Zealand	25

Source: Seaton and Bennett (1996).

*Estimate.

example. Thus, a flight from the UK to the Americas using KLM will involve a transfer from England to Schipol, Amsterdam via Air UK. The alliance means that the code used on the CRS will be the same and therefore will be illustrated as a single routing rather than a route with a connecting flight and two different codes, which is afforded a lower ranking on the CRS. The marketing edge is compounded in another important way. Seaton and Bennett (1996: 431) comment:

> Affiliated to the CRS is the RMS (revenue management system) which is unshared for good reasons. It is the intelligent counterpart of the CRS monitoring sales and calculating fares accordingly. Given the fact that competing airlines are in the CRS, the RMS will monitor them too and use that information in its fares calculations. All of this gives the CRS owner an unprecedented competitive advantage in the marketplace, or, as some might argue, an unfair advantage.

Travel agencies have also adopted expert systems (Hruschka and Mazanec, 1990: 208–27) which assist the travel adviser to find suitable offerings to meet the needs of the enquiring customer. Such systems are currently separate to CRS but research is being undertaken to merge such systems so that customer profiles and supplier offerings can be assessed by the expert system, to assist the travel adviser to select options which might suit.

To a lesser extent, destination marketing has been developed using similar computerized systems (Sussmann, 1992: 209–15). Tourist information centres have been slow to develop systems and there have been problems in networking between such centres, which are often financed by local government and are not entirely convinced by the need to network as such.

13.5.1 The Internet

The Internet (or the Net) describes a global netscape of computers that are connected as an open market, known as the World Wide Web. The Internet allows tourism organizations access to potential markets at a much lower cost than using other distribution channels. The Internet is as yet an untried marketing tool but commentators suggest that it will become more important in future years. Archdale (1996) cites six examples of marketing activity using the 'Net':

- airline seat auctions
- hotel reservations
- airlines CRS
- publishers of guidebooks
- destinations
- new directions such as business travel advice.

13.6 PHYSICAL LOCATION

There is another aspect of distribution which is sometimes described as locational analysis. Many hotel and resort groups, such as Accor or Hyatt for example, plan with precision the distribution of their facilities throughout the world. The same applies to restaurant and fast food suppliers, such as McDonald's or Burger King. They use locational analysis to determine best sites in capital and provincial cities and resorts throughout the world. The extension of facilities is afforded either through generic growth, franchising (McDonald's), or through alliances or consortiums, such as the Best Western consortium.

As international tourism grows so will the intensive competition for prime sites in newly developed destinations, rejuvenated water-fronts and integrated resorts. This will prove something of a challenge for marketers seeking global territorial expansion in order to increase overall share.

<table>
<tr><td>13.7 SUMMARY</td><td>While the principles of distribution are similar to other markets there is one major difference in tourism. The customer has to be enticed to travel to the destination. This has led to a sophisticated set of distribution channels which convey a wide range of information and tourism offerings to a mass market.

The major intermediaries are the travel agent and tour operator as well as international carriers. These organizations have invested heavily in the past decade to develop computerized reservation and booking systems to make buying holidays both easy and accessible. The pace of technological change has provided a marketing edge for some tour operators, not only by way of the high street retail outlets but also through direct marketing systems.

Distribution issues also include locational analysis and this is increasingly important in the development of new resorts of the rejuvenation of cities as tourism destinations.</td></tr>
</table>

REFERENCES

Archdale, G. (1996) The Internet in Context, *Insights*, English Tourist Board, September.

Barras, R. (1986) Towards the theory of innovation in services. *Research Policy*, **5**(4), 161–78.

Bennett, M. (1993) Information Technology and Travel Agency: A Customer Service Perspective. *Tourism Management*, **14**(4), 259–66.

Boberg, K.B. and Collinson, F.M. (1985) Computer Reservation Systems and Airline Competition. *Tourism Management*, September, 174–83.

Bruce, M. (1994) Technological Change and Competitve Marketing Strategies. In *Tourism Marketing and Management Handbook* (eds S.F. Witt and L. Moutinho), 2nd edition, Prentice Hall, Hemel Hempstead.

Buhalis, D. (1994) Information and Telecommunications Technologies as a Strategic Tool for Small to Medium Tourism Enterprises in the Contemporary Business Environment. In *Tourism, the State of the Art* (eds A.V. Seaton *et al.*), John Wiley & Sons, Chichester.

Commission of the European Communities (1991) Final Report Project 409/90. The Evolution in Holiday Travel Facilities and in the Flow Inside and Outside the European Community.

Cooper, C., Fletcher, J., Gilbert, D. and Wanhill, S. (1993) *Tourism: Principles and Practice*, Addison Wesley Longman, London.

Hruschka, H. and Mazanec, J. (1990) Computer-Assisted Travel Counselling. *Annals of Tourism Research*, **17**, 208–27.

Jenkins, C.L. (1991) Tourism Policies in Developing Countries. *Managing Tourism* (ed. S. Medlik), Butterworth-Heinemann, Oxford.

Poon, A. (1993) *Tourism, Technology and Competitive Strategies*, CAB International, Wallingford.

Rojas, M. (1994) *El Turismo en las Islas Baleares*, Jorvich s.l., Palma.

Seaton, A.V. and Bennett, M.M. (1996) *Marketing Tourism Products*, International Thomson Business Press, London.

Sussmann, S. (1992) Destination Management Systems: the Challenge of the 1990s. In *Progress in Tourism, Recreation and Hospitality Management* (ed. C. Cooper), Vol. 4, 209–15.

14 The augmented marketing mix

OBJECTIVES

This chapter explains:

- the importance of people, processes and physical evidence in the provision of tourism offerings;
- the principle of service quality and techniques of measuring service quality;
- the processes and systems for customer service;
- the importance of physical evidence in services marketing.

14.1 THE PRINCIPLES OF THE AUGMENTED MIX

In Chapter 5 we introduced the concept of the augmented marketing mix as developed by Booms and Bitner (1981). The conclusion drawn was that whilst the four elements of the marketing mix provide a useful structure for marketing implementation, there is a need to strengthen the approach through the inclusion of three other elements: people, processes and physical evidence. Figure 14.1 outlines how the elements of the marketing mix interrelate. The three elements of the augmented mix are often analysed separately but nevertheless are interdependent elements of the marketing management process. They also integrate with other dimensions of the marketing mix such as distribution and communication as determined by the marketing plan.

14.2 SERVICE CULTURE: PEOPLE

The constant interaction between the guest and service provider in tourism means that the employee often represents the company to the customer. Therefore, the issue of staff presentation, customer interaction and levels of satisfaction with the service encounter is crucial in tourism. The extent to which responsibility for staff recruitment, training and motivation is shared between marketing, operations and human resources depends on the organizational structure and culture. The organizational culture may be defined as:

> a set of assumptions or an ideology shared by members of an organization. These assumptions are used by people to identify what is important and how things

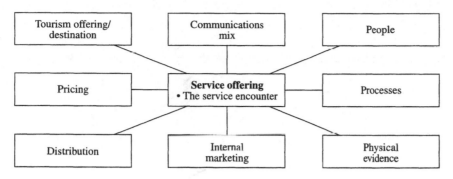

Figure 14.1 The augmented marketing mix.

work in that company. When these assumptions become formalized, rules for behavior are established so that people know how to act.

(Tidball, 1988, p. 63)

Thus, it is argued that the service culture within an organization is not the province of the marketing team alone; it is a responsibility for all staff.

14.2.1 Service encounter

For tourism marketers, however, the core of the service element is the interaction between those supplying the tourism offering and the customer. This is known as the service encounter, described by Carlzon (1987) as 'the moment of truth'. Customer satisfaction can only be achieved if appropriate processes are designed to ensure that the service encounter meets customer expectations. The result has been described as customer delivered value, which is the difference between total customer value and total customer cost (Kotler, Bowen and Makens, 1996: 343–4). Many tourism providers compete on this basis; service delivery has become the linchpin of marketing strategy. Managers in tourism will vouch that it is easier to specify than execute.

Tourism marketers have to balance the cost of improving the core service in relation to what the consumer considers to be valuable and hence worth paying a higher price for. There is some incremental empirical evidence to illustrate that those companies who are perceived as being quality providers show improved results in terms of profitability. The Profit Impact of Market Strategy study (PIMS), which was developed in the early 1980s, indicates that quality, as measured in comparison to competitors, is the single most important factor affecting performance (Buzzell and Gale, 1987: 103–34). It has to be noted that PIMS involves mainly manufacturing industries, so the findings will be less valuable in the services sector.

14.2.2 Service quality gaps

It is difficult to discuss the service offering without introducing the issue of quality, which has been defined as:

> the totality of features and characteristics of a product or service that bear on its ability to satisfy a stated or implied need.

(British Standards, 1987)

The characteristics of service quality are summarized in Table 14.1. In terms of

Table 14.1 Determinants of service quality in the tourism sector

Determinant	Care features	Examples
Reliability	Consistency of performance and dependability Getting it right first time Keeping promises	• Airlines ensuring that the baggage arrives on same flight as passenger at same destination • Waiters bringing the ordered dishes to the right table • Providing a taxi transfer from the airport to accommodation as promised in the brochure
Responsiveness	Willingness and readiness of employees to provide service Timeliness of service	• Responding to a customer enquiry on the same morning or afternoon • Transport operations keeping to timetable
Competence	Existence of required skills and knowledge especially in contact personnel	• Tourist information staff knowing exactly where places are located and how best to arrive there
Access	Ease of contact	• Hotel groups answering the telephone within 4 or 6 rings • Tourist information centres being located near major flows of visitors and open seven days a week
Courtesy	Respect and consideration, friendliness	• Visitor attraction staff helping families to enjoy their day without being over familiar
Communication	Informing customers in language they can understand; explanation of service offered	• Coach driver assuring passengers that the party will reach the ferry in good time
Credibility	Trustworthiness, believability and honesty	• Travel agent offering advice about long haul travel
Security	Freedom from danger, risk or doubt	• A hotel providing safes for expensive items
Understanding the customer	Making the effort to understand customers' needs	• Hotel reception staff making guests feel welcome on arrival
Tangibles	Physical evidence – facilities and appearance	• Entrance to a country park being designed to encourage exploration on foot rather than by car

services the entire quality issue is about a customer's expectation of what should happen and to what extent these expectations have been met during the service process.

There are problems for the tourism marketer in specifying service quality and this can lead to a quality gap or gaps. Grönroos (1983: 48) explains that there are four potential gaps between service expectations and delivery:

- **Gap 1 Management misjudges customer perception**
  A mismatch between a manager's perception of service quality and the expectations of the customer might occur when service levels are being specified. For example, the management team at a hotel might decide that provision of a newspaper at the bedroom door is not required whereas the guest values this addition.
- **Gap 2 Lack of development**
  This is where managers are aware of customer expectations but there is simply not the management will to implement what is necessary, either through ignorance, lack of vision, limited resources, or adoption of a strategy such as harvesting where management is not concerned with the long term future.
- **Gap 3 Poor delivery**
  The management understands the levels of service desired by the customer and

specifies an appropriate set of standards. However, the staff involved deliver the specified level of service poorly, possibly because they are insufficiently trained.

- **Gap 4 Unrealistic expectations**
  A gap between customer expectations and service provision is sometimes present simply because pre-purchase promotional material projects unrealistic levels of service which cannot in reality be delivered. This can also be a case with lapsed expectations. A hotel with a great reputation could be bought out by another company which has far weaker standards. Retention of past customers would be difficult in such circumstances.

- **Gap 5 Service gap**
  This represents the difference in any given situation between expected and perceived quality. It is a culmination of the first four gaps and provides a clear indication of the degree to which service quality exists in a tourism organization.

Hooley (1993: 315–35) presents a case for extending the use of gap analysis in service provision to include other dimensions, such as the perceptual, design or marketing intelligence gap as a way of analysing the relationship between specification and customer satisfaction or delight.

14.2.3 Service delivery

Much subsequent discussion in the literature has been about how the gaps can be measured, and minimized. It has focused on customer expectation of service quality at the service encounter rather than simply assessing eventual outcomes. For example, the primary benefit of a coach trip to a local market might be the pleasure of shopping. The overall experience, however, could be marred by poor driving or lack of communication between driver and passengers en route.

14.2.4 Servqual

Parasuraman, Zeithaml and Berry (1985: 41–50) set out ten criteria to enable managers to evaluate both the experience and the outcome of a service encounter. They are listed below:

1. Access. Is the service provision easily accessed from a convenient location?
2. Reliability. Can the customer rely on the service?
3. Credibility. Is the company and its staff trustworthy?
4. Security. Is the service risk laden?
5. Customer empathy. Does the service provider understand customer expectations?
6. Responsiveness. How speedily do staff respond to requests and problems?
7. Courtesy. How friendly and courteous are staff?
8. Competence. Do staff have the appropriate skills and knowledge?
9. Communications. Is the service provision described with clarity?
10. Tangible. How well presented are the tangible aspects of service such as physical layout, decoration, staff uniforms?

From this initial framework of analysis and further empirical work Parasuraman, Zeithaml and Berry (1988) developed a scaling device known as Servqual, which uses five core criteria – reliability, responsiveness, courtesy, competence and tangibles – to measure customer expectations. The methodology asks respondents to grade their expectations on a seven point scale for each criteria. Subsequently customers are asked to evaluate the actual service enjoyed by an organization. Given the results, it is argued that management can identify gaps in provision of delivery and the outcomes.

This has proven to be a useful tool for tourism marketers and has been developed in other respects such as in hotels (Saleh and Ryan, 1992: 163–8). Furthermore, Histoqual, an adapted form of the Servqual model, has been tested as a method to evaluate perceived quality of heritage attractions (Frochet, 1996: 119–32).

Nevertheless, the Servqual methodology has also been subject to some criticism, mainly on methodological grounds:

- The original use of positive and negative statements cause confusion among respondents (Carman, 1990: 33–57).
- The ultimate measurement of quality is based on scoring performance minus the evaluation score by the client. Subsequent studies have indicated that simply measuring perception of performance gives a good evaluation (Fick and Ritchie, 1991: 2–9).

One area of discussion worthy of pursuit is the distinction between efficiency and effectiveness in the delivery of quality. In terms of operation, a holiday centre might wish to book the same number of guests in a new season but with four less staff than in previous years to look after the guests. Costs will be reduced and the level of productivity should therefore rise, but response times to visitor enquiries might be slower. How can this be measured?

This is the type of quality dilemma faced by many organizations in tourism, especially given the nature of fluctuating demand. Service quality can fall dramatically when staff are overwhelmed by a surge of demand. The scenario is increasingly one of competitive pressure. Companies often respond by holding or reducing costs while extolling the values of increasing quality and delivery to the customer. The argument simply does not add up; it would seem contradictory. The answer lies in the fine tuning of service expectations to core customer values, thereby selectively reducing those aspects which add cost and not value or vice versa.

By monitoring service encounters it is possible to design service delivery systems which guide the interactions between front line and support staff, between staff and consumers pre-delivery (for instance, when on the 'phone), during delivery, post-delivery, and between staff and suppliers. This is referred to by Shostack (1977) as service blueprinting which is about bringing together elements and interactions in service delivery which make it work for customers and brings profitable transactions to the organization. But service delivery is as much about processes as people.

14.3 SERVICE PROCESSES

This is one element of the marketing mix which receives less attention, possibly because it is as much an operational matter as a marketing task. The adoption of processes which add value to the tourism offering without incurring major cost disadvantages are beneficial to the customer and the organization. It is an essential part of the value chain.

What exactly do we mean by the term processes in tourism marketing? They are ways of undertaking transactions, supplying information, advising customers and providing services in a way which is acceptable to the consumer and effective to the organization. As mentioned earlier, the responsibility for introducing such processes lies primarily with operational management but it also falls within the realm of marketing. In order to introduce a process which is of real benefit, there needs to be a thorough understanding of customer wants and patterns of behaviour.

Such processes are commonly found in tourism as part of the service encounter. For example, they include booking systems for transport and accommodation, the use of smart cards for payment, design of queuing systems at visitor attractions. They are designed to assist interaction between staff and customers at the critical points of contact. Marketing research is paramount in this respect.

In designing a process a balance has to be maintained between functionality, security, aesthetics and ease of use by the customer. This is not always possible and there can be difficulties. In the mid-1990s, train operating companies within British Railways introduced a new door locking mechanism to many carriages in order to enhance passenger safety. While the new system worked well in terms of improving safety it was a difficult task informing passengers about the system. People were used to the old system of opening a door independently on arrival at a station without a central locking device. A special publicity campaign was required to advise and educate customers about the new system.

There are, however, an increasing number of examples where organizations use promotional techniques to advise customers about processes to expect when consuming the service. Disney World (Florida), for example, run a pre-season direct marketing campaign where potential customers can send for a 'Holiday Planner' video explaining how to obtain the best from a visit.

14.3.1 Critical moments

However, the involvement of the customer from pre-consumption stage through to post-visit feedback is not commonly practised. Process techniques appear to have been applied primarily to visitor flows at attractions, interpretation techniques, signing and transportation systems, etc. The marketer needs to anticipate customer needs and reactions at all stages of the process including during critical moments of the service encounter. Palmer (1994: 152–3) notes, for example, the large number of likely interactions between an airline and its passengers, from pre-sales through to baggage reclaim – at least 20 transactions for one flight.

Shostack (1977: 37–47) introduced the concept of 'blueprinting' to assist marketers to design complex processes. She pointed to the need to view processes in a holistic way, plotting in diagrammatic form (similar to critical path analysis) the sequencing of tasks to meet the requirements of customers. Blueprinting also allows the marketer to evaluate which tasks are more critical (as perceived by customers) and which are prone to failure. Furthermore, it enables the tourism marketer an opportunity to recover mistakes and to turn complaints into repeat business.

14.4 PHYSICAL EVIDENCE

In the services sector the environment in which the service is delivered is often more important than with the provision of goods. Physical evidence is significant because of the underlying principle of simultaneous provision and consumption.

Tourism marketers therefore become involved with design and architectural consultants to ensure that design standards bring to a location a desired atmosphere. In terms of developing areas of a resort such as a historic waterfront, a restaurant quarter or a historic core, the importance of design outweighs many other marketing considerations. It is the element of creative flair which can make a facility sufficiently attractive to visit or not. This is sometimes referred to as a 'sense of place'.

In a similar manner, restaurants, hotels and visitor attractions are concerned to provide tangible cues as to the level of service provided. The seating, decor, staff uniforms and musical background combine to signal to the customer the nature of the establishment. An interesting study by Saleh and Ryan (1992: 163–8) on client perceptions of hotels indicated that tangible components of hotels are important to guests including interior and exterior aesthetics of the buildings. It argues that the physical components of a hotel should not be underestimated despite current emphasis on intangible benefits such as customer staff interaction.

There is obviously a trade off between functionality as far as the supplier is concerned and aesthetic guidelines. In terms of processing visitors, a reception area often retains the sharp edge of efficiency so that intending visitors can be processed speedily and queues avoided. At theme parks, queuing has become something of an art form with entertainers and fast food stalls making queuing almost an experience in its own right rather than an absolute negative.

Several studies, including Jones and Lockwood (1989) suggest that in the hotel sector the level of customer satisfaction is based on an optimal quality level of tangible and intangible elements, a point also verified by Saleh and Ryan (1992: 163–8). The relationship has been expressed in a matrix adapted in Figure 14.2 to fit tourism services rather than just hotels.

In terms of the implementation of the marketing mix in tourism these three dimensions are at the very core of the tourism offering.

Characteristics of the experience

Nature of the contact		Tangible	Intangible
	Product	The product Facilitating goods Information	Atmosphere Aesthetics Comfort
	Service	Actions Process Speed Script	Warmth Friendliness Care Service

Figure 14.2 Hotel quality matrix. *Source*: Lockwood *et al.* (1992) after Jones and Lockwood (1989). Reprinted by permission of Addison Wesley Longman Ltd.

14.5 SUMMARY The augmented marketing mix is a useful tool in that it directs the marketer to a wider view of the tourism offering from pre- to post-consumption activity as defined in Chapter 2. The interrelationship between all elements of the mix is crucial but the special emphasis which is placed on the service encounter in tourism means that the augmented mix is central to the marketing effort rather than at the periphery as sometimes presented in previous studies.

REFERENCES

Booms, B.H. and Bitner, M.J. (1981) Marketing Strategies and Organization Structures for Service Firms. In *Marketing of Services* (eds J.H. Donnelly and W.R. George), Chicago, American Marketing Association.

British Standards (1987) *BS 4778: Quality Vocabulary: Part 1 International Terms, Part 2 National Terms,* British Standards Institution, London.

Buzzell, R.D. and Gale, B.T. (1987) *The PIMS Principles: Linking Strategy to Performance,* New York, Free Press.

Carlzon, J. (1987) *Moments of Truth,* Ballinger, Cambridge, Massachusetts.

Carman, J.M. (1990) Customers' Perceptions of Service Quality: an Assessment of SERVQUAL Dimensions. *Journal of Retailing,* **66**(1), 33–57.

Fick, G.R. and Ritchie, J.R. (1991) Measuring Service Quality in the Travel and Tourism Industry. *Journal of Travel and Tourism Research,* Fall, 2–9.

Frochet, I. (1996) Histoqual: The Evaluation of Service Quality in Historic Properties. A paper presented to the Tourism and Culture Conference, Northumberland, September 14–17.

Grönroos, C. (1983) *Strategic Management and Marketing in the Service Sector,* England, Chartwell-Bratt.

Hooley, G.J. (1993) Market-Led Quality Management. *Journal of Marketing Management,* **9**, 315–35.

Jones, P. and Lockwood, A.J. (1989) *The Management of Hotel Operations,* Cassell, London.

Kotler, P., Bowen, J. and Makens, J. (1996) *Marketing for Hospitality and Tourism,* Prentice Hall, Upper Saddle River, New Jersey.

Lockwood, A. *et al.* (1992) Developing and maintaining a strategy for service quality. In *International Hospitality Management* (eds R. Teare and M. Olsen), London, Pitman.

Palmer, A. (1994) *Principles of Services Marketing,* McGraw-Hill.

Parasuraman, A., Zeithaml, V.A. and Berry, L.L. (1985) A Conceptual Model of Service Quality and its Implications for Future Research, *Journal of Marketing,* Fall, 41–50.

Parasuraman, A., Zeithaml, V.A. and Berry, L.L. (1988) SERVQUAL: multiple item scale for measuring consumer perceptions of service quality. *Journal of Retailing,* **64**(1), Spring.

Saleh, F. and Ryan, C. (1992) Client perceptions of hotels. *Tourism Management,* June, 163–8.

Shostack, G.L. (1977) Breaking Free from Product Marketing. *Journal of Marketing,* **41**(2), April.

Tidball, K.H. (1988) Creating a Culture Adds to Your Bottom Line. *Cornell Hotel and Restaurant Administration Quarterly,* May, 63.

15 Relationship marketing

OBJECTIVES

This chapter explains:

- the underlying principles of relationship marketing;
- the appropriateness of the concept in tourism marketing environment;
- the links between relationship marketing and quality.

15.1 INTRODUCTION

Relationship marketing as a concept has evolved against a background of rapid change in purchasing behaviour. Increased consumer consciousness, availability of information technology, databases and a backlash against unsophisticated marketing methods have led to the development of marketing strategies which focus on customer action rather than consumer passivity. Berry (1983: 25–8) and Gummeson (1987: 10–20) have identified relationship marketing as a way in which quality service and interpersonal interactions can be managed to sustain customer involvement in the longer term. It is characterized by the following:

- building long term sustainable relationships with customers;
- creating mutual benefit through interaction and individualized contact;
- developing value added and profitable relationships with customers.

15.1.1 Key benefits of relationship marketing

Reichheld and Sasser (1990) have listed some of the key benefits of relationship marketing within the service environment:

- Revenue growth as a result of repeat purchase and increased purchase over time by the regular customer. Also, increased revenue because of referrals from existing to new customers.
- Decrease in costs of attracting and acquiring new customers and from efficiencies of serving more experienced customers.
- Increase in employee retention as job satisfaction grows, which in turn helps to reinforce customer loyalty to members of the organization, decrease in the costs of hiring and training and increase in productivity and speed of service.

The difference in the new and old approaches to marketing are summarized in Table 15.1.

15.2 DEVELOPMENT OF RELATIONSHIP MARKETING

It could be argued that relationship marketing has developed as a response to the following:

● Critiques of traditional marketing concepts. Drucker (1955: 52) made it abundantly clear that 'there is only one valid definition of business purpose: to create a customer' but the emphasis of the traditional transactional approach to marketing through to the creation of relationships between buyer and seller only became an important issue in the 1980s (Peters and Waterman, 1982).
● Since the widespread adoption of McCarthy's four Ps (product, place, price and promotion), marketing theory has built on this simplistic framework almost in a mechanical format. As discussed in Chapter 14, increased interest in services marketing from the mid-1970s onwards has brought about a criticism of the four Ps as being too limiting in scope (Payne, 1994: 25). The emphasis placed on relationships between suppliers and supplier and customer has grown out of this fundamental criticism.

15.2.1 Focus on quality management

There has also been a focus on the issue of quality management. This developed initially from research in the industrial manufacturing sector and Japanese firms were the first to recognize its value in terms of competitive advantage. They adopted total quality management (TQM) programmes almost as a matter of course. The success of these initiatives led to the principles being adopted in all sectors including tourism.

Table 15.1 New approaches to tourism marketing

Traditional transactional marketing	New relationship marketing	Examples
1. Emphasis on single transaction	Key aim is to retain customers	● Loyalty schemes ● Attention to detail
2. Appeal of destination as an offering	Appeal of benefits in relation to lifestyle	● Tracking systems ● Promotion of lifestyle holidays
3. Short time scale	Longer time scale	● Customers are for life
4. Less emphasis on the service quality	High emphasis on service quality	● Much higher investment in staff training e.g. airlines
5. Limited customer commitment	High involvement	● Education of customer as to expectations ● Encouraging customer commitment through branding and information
6. Moderate customer contact	High customer contact	● Customer encouraged to participate in entire process of booking a holiday
7. Quality related to operations	Quality paramount throughout	● Quality checks and systems care

Source: adapted from Christopher, Payne and Ballantyne (1991).

TQM provided the answer to achieving both cost efficiencies and customer satisfaction by getting it right first time. Relationship marketing is in many respects a progression from the focus on quality. Like TQM, it aims to provide quality beyond customer expectations. The disciplines needed for relationship marketing are illustrated in Table 15.2.

15.2.2 Increased customer orientation

Both the expansion of the traditional marketing mix into the area of service delivery and the focus on quality management have been prompted by the increased recognition that 'customers are not targets, they are assets that must be nurtured and developed' (Naumann, 1995: 167). This revision challenges traditional concepts of consumer buying behaviour in terms of a simplistic-stimulus to response approach.

It has therefore been suggested that relationship marketing can become a strategy for dealing with the active, participating consumer. Kuoni, the Swiss based long haul travel specialist, was one of the first tourist companies to adopt such an approach. Their custom-made holidays which rely on the sophisticated technology of a complex booking system have provided a solution to customers wanting an interactive personalized approach to booking holidays. It has provided a clear market advantage. They are, in essence, offering a direct dialogue with their customers.

15.2.3 Customer retention

The increased emphasis on customer dialogue has proven to be economically valuable too. A survey in 1995 by the communications giant AT&T showed a direct correlation between customer satisfaction levels and movements in sales figures (*Marketing*, 1995: 35). There is now widespread acceptance that the retention of a loyal customer is more profitable in the long term than attracting new customers. This has forced companies to focus even more on providing consistently sound products and services which meet as precisely as is feasible possible customers needs. Pepper and Rogers (1994: 4–7) argue that 'the future is one to one', estimating that the cost of acquiring one new customer at £20 is expensive in contrast to retaining a current customer at a cost of only £4. They have proven a positive correlation between the level of investment and the close personal relationships of buyer and seller. Costa (1996: 35) argues

Table 15.2 The disciplines needed for relationship marketing

Product marketing model		Relationship marketing model
Focus on the product	→	Focus on process for serving customers
Define the target group	→	Feed and nourish the relationship
Set brand objectives	→	Extend respect and value to customers
Opportunity comes from analysis	→	Opportunity comes from synergy
Focus on brand benefit	→	Develop and refresh relevance
Create strategic advertising	→	Open the doors for dialogue
Operate against a brand plan	→	Improvize to sustain the relationship
Driven by a marketing group	→	A pervasive interdisciplinary attitude

Source: Costa (1996).

that marketing managers need to move from a single 'hook' to multiple hooks which she terms to 'velcro' the customer. Table 15.3 explains the approach.

15.2.4 Behaviourist theory

Relationship marketing is couched in a theoretical framework of behaviourist theory. The assumption is that interaction with another individual brings greater trust, commitment and benefits in a relationship. The result is that people are more likely to remain loyal to the relationship if a sense of mutual bonding is fostered on both sides.

Bennett (1996) suggests that this sense of mutual partnership enables the buyer and seller to develop a 'win win' situation where both sides benefit from working together to satisfy each other's needs, instead of constantly playing out a game of win or lose with each other. In the tourism sector, this explains why retail travel agents are now often referred to as travel consultants and why conference managers at hotels aim to foster the idea of mutual responsibility for the success of the conference. The emphasis is on the shared nature of the transaction.

Beaton and Beaton (1995: 55–70) take the concept further in describing relationship marketing as a series of interactions between buyer and seller which can be likened to a personal relationship. They highlight stages as initial discovery, courtship, investment and interaction in the relationship, then bonding and forsaking of others. Emphasis is duly placed on the concept of commitment within the process, arguing that as loyalty increases in a relationship the stronger it becomes and the less likely it is for each side to search for other partners. By measuring the level of this commitment, the position and value of players in the relationship can be assessed. In this way a company can identify their most important customers in terms of levels of commitment and repeat visits.

Those who argue on a functionalist basis, however, would refute the tenor of the argument on the grounds that the rationality of the decision making unit would still not succumb to the irrationality of a deepening relationship between client and supplier.

15.3 EFFECTIVE RELATIONSHIP MARKETING

The main objective of relationship marketing is to encourage customer loyalty and profitability. The two main tools used to achieve this are the focus on the firm's

Table 15.3 Customer retention – from 'hook' to 'velcro'

'Hook'		'Velcro'
Single benefit	→	Multiple benefits
Single-minded	→	Many-sided
Repeat consistently	→	Consistently surprise
Fixed for the long-term	→	Flexible for the short-term
Differentiates vs. competitor	→	Engages the customer
Presents a positioning	→	Surrounds with inducements
Focuses on transaction	→	Builds towards relationship
Simple for memorability	→	Complex for involvement

Source: Costa (1996).

markets and on a firm's quality procedures which involves including all elements of the augmented marketing mix. The following approach outlines how relationship marketing can be used in the tourism sector.

15.3.1 Identification of markets

It is necessary to identify both internal and external markets which may affect how an organization can provide a high quality service and therefore effectively market to their customer base. One traditional approach has been to identify stakeholders and assess their expectations. In terms of asking the question 'What constitutes an excellent company?' Doyle (1991: 115) argues that too much attention has been given to unidimensional measures such as earnings per share and too little to longer term stakeholder measures. Figure 15.1 outlines the major stakeholders that could be involved in the provision of a tourism offering. Governments, Customers and the Community are the most important of these stakeholders.

Christopher *et al.* (1991: 8) identify five markets which need to be specifically targeted for relationship development in a firm's strategy.

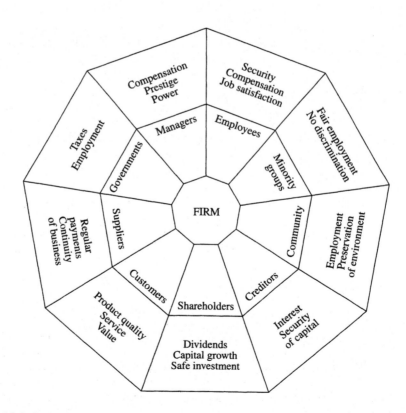

Figure 15.1 Stakeholders and their expectations.
Reprinted from 'What are the excellent companies?', *Journal of Marketing Management*, Vol. 8, Page 112, by permission of the publisher. © The Dryden Press, Harcourt Brace & Company Ltd. All rights reserved.

(a) Customer market segments

This is the most important market that needs to be targeted through the marketing mix, by using people (staff) and processes to convert existing customers into advocates of the company. The ultimate aim, according to the theory, is to take them beyond customer satisfaction to a stage of customer delight. However, it is important to define which markets are the most profitable within this context as customer delight could spell negative returns. Kotler *et al.* (1996: 352) suggest these are a 'person, household or company whose revenues over time exceed, by an acceptable amount, the company costs of attracting, selling and servicing that customer'. This is based on 'lifetime revenues and costs, not profit from a single transaction'. The Alton Towers theme park 'Fun Club', for example, seeks to build a relationship with young people through to adulthood.

(b) Supplier markets

In this market the new approach is referred to as 'co-makership' where the customer and supplier work together to ensure a service fits the customer's needs and quality specifications. This relationship is based on mutual benefits and obligations and brings more reliability and efficiency than a situation where client and supplier disagree over price. Co-marketship is often at its best when public and private sectors join forces to develop new tourism offerings.

(c) Referral markets

This market increasingly needs to be satisfied as it often acts as an intermediary between firm and customer, such as in the conference market where agencies or venue finders conduct the search process initially for the client and may have more knowledge about the market and substantial purchasing power.

(d) Influence markets

These markets have to be retained to ensure macro-environmental factors work in favour for the company. They therefore could include regulatory, financial and governmental bodies. A venue's catering facilities would, for example, be checked by the Health and Safety Officer. Similarly, coach companies will have to observe safety regulations when transporting school groups.

(e) Internal/employee markets

The importance of the employee in building good customer relationships dominates much of the literature on relationship marketing. Internal marketing within organizations touches human resource management, operations management and marketing. Recognizing that people are a firm's greatest asset has led many large corporations to develop more complex and effective internal communication systems and employee retention schemes.

Commitment at top management level is necessary for this, and ultimately focus on employee retention can improve efficiency between departments, decrease turnover of staff and increase staff loyalty to the firm. Ultimately this will help to increase profits as customers are attracted and retained by trusted known suppliers. Unfortunately tourism traditionally has a very poor reputation for its human resource policies. High staff turnover, seasonal demand and long unsociable hours have meant tourism providers have often employed workers who are underskilled, with few motivations above financial gain. More advanced organizations with the tourism sectors are seeking to invest more in staff to overcome the negative imagery associated with the business.

Successful identification and servicing of all these markets will only help a service provider to retain customers if the quality of product corresponds to the claim of marketers. Therefore, quality of the tourism offering is paramount.

15.3.2 Quality

It is difficult to define exactly what terms of reference a firm can use to assess quality. The most commonly used term is total quality management (TQM) which refers to the need to surpass customer expectations. Discussions have focused around functional, technical and perceived quality. In terms of a marketing perspective Hooley (1993: 319) provides a workable definition:

> Quality is concerned with supplying superior benefits in the opinion of the customer. Thus, the pursuit of quality is the pursuit of greater customer benefit.

Given the underlying principles of services marketing it is not surprising that the issue of service quality has been the subject of continued discussion in the business. In particular, potential difficulties in measuring quality have been addressed. This is especially with regard to a service encounter where the customer forms part of the delivery process.

(a) Servqual

The most often quoted model of the measurement of service quality in this sector is known as Servqual, devised by Parasuraman, Zeithaml and Berry (1988) and discussed in more detail in Chapter 14.

However, claims that Servqual can be applied universally to every service encounter have been criticized, with most theorists agreeing that service encounters are so process specific that comprehensive standards are hard to establish with accuracy.

(b) Quality solutions in the corporate market

One way to look at how quality can be used to achieve a competitive advantage has been outlined by Payne (1994: 220). He suggests that one should look at 'quality solutions' to problems in order to rectify a position to a point where a customer perceives sufficient value has been obtained. 'Service support', which provides added features to the process, although not essential to the purchase, does provide added value to the customer. A combination of quality solutions and service support should achieve the desired result of delighting the customer and surpassing their expectations.

An example of this within the conference sector would be a venue offering quality solutions in the form of technical facilities, number of rooms available and packages on offer. The service support would constitute itself in the warm welcome of the delegates on arrival, the efficiency of the venue in dealing with customers with special needs and the overall helpfulness of the conference staff. A Peter Rand Group survey identified that 92 per cent of organizations agreed that service is the most important factor transforming a satisfactory venue into an 'outstanding' one (Martins, 1991: A103).

Service quality and training are inextricably linked within the tourism sector. The evolving 'relationship marketing' strategies which embrace both total-firm quality management and to some extent Servqual style monitoring is certainly permeating into major hotel groups. Jarvis, of Jarvis Hotels, has suggested that hotels should 'become obsessive and fanatical about quality' (Martins, 1991). In this respect, quality has been recognized by the large hotel chains as an important source of competitive advantage. For example, Hilton International have introduced Meeting 2000, a service developed after research and user consultation into needs and problems on the conference organizer's agenda. It provides a full conference meeting package for the customer, including help and advice with registration, audiovisuals and technical needs, catering and room requirements, for example. It is designed to foster relationship marketing, through, for example, training, quality, service, research and consultation into customers' needs.

Hotel award schemes have been introduced to indicate levels of quality, with some degree of criticism by the travel trade media. They perceive them as focusing primarily on physical and functional factors and not accounting for service levels and unquantifiables. It has been commented that 'quality is a personal subjective measure and cannot be substituted by the views of a hotel's inspector' (Callan, 1990: 45). There are therefore doubts whether judgemental benchmarking could work in this sector.

(c) Benchmarking

Despite criticisms, the hospitality sector has moved towards some degree of quality benchmarking. This is essentially a management technique which allows companies to compare how well they are performing vis-à-vis their competitors. In 1996 regional tourist boards and associations in the UK discussed setting up a national quality assurance scheme for the conference sector. Its aim was to consult widely on the practicality of forming such a scheme. A commission has initiated independent research among UK and overseas marketing buyers and the Meeting Industry Association working party with a view to developing a model for tackling measurement of service quality (Meetings and Incentive Travel, 1996).

The ultimate aim of the service provider is to combine marketing and quality strategies to attract loyal customers to use their services. Mulitinational hotel chains, for example, promote their standardized quality packages across countries and cultures as a major selling point to attract corporate accounts.

(d) Loyalty

Loyalty represents the commitment part of a relationship. It is the transformation of the customer into a long term supporter. The most fashionable and commonly used method of encouraging customer loyalty and repeat business in the tourism sector is the promotion by the supplier of loyalty schemes.

Customer loyalty programmes in the organizational and business travel sector have flourished since the introduction of strategic concepts, such as Air Miles, proved to be a beneficial incentive to repeat purchase (that 'win win' situation in its best form).

However, several multinational hotel chains have realized that the cost of administering frequent stayer programmes are outweighed by the benefits in generating long term business. Hilton International, for example, allows travellers to collect both Air Miles and hotel points and maintains this is one of its key reasons for holding its market share. In the last five years, loyalty schemes have increasingly been seen as the answer to sustaining competitive advantage. In 1996 alone two important accommodation suppliers in the UK – Forté Posthouse and the Grand Heritage Hotels group – launched frequent stay incentive schemes. Eurostar also initiated its own frequent traveller scheme in November 1996, enabling customers to enjoy benefits of faster check-in facilities, discounts and access to luxurious waiting lounges. Loyalty schemes are also being introduced as a competitive weapon between airlines.

However, it has recently been argued that loyalty schemes should not be seen as the entire answer to establishing relationships and encouraging repeat custom from organizational buyers. Do perceived benefits of loyalty programmes therefore really attract repeat purchases or merely act as sales promotion exercises? The Henley Centre (Sigrid de Mul, 1995: A15) suggests that people often see loyalty schemes as a mere promotion and not as a dialogue between customer and supplier as relationship marketing strategies seek to achieve. Loyalty offers, it is argued, may just attract price sensitive customers rather than loyal repeat users: 'the essential mistake in creating a loyalty strategy is to confuse a short term promotional objective with a long term retention programme'. Perhaps therefore, it is essential, as with the success of the Marriott and Hilton programmes, to ensure that these benefits reward in the short term, have a credible delivery system and appreciate in the long term. Such rewards, however, are not enough to encourage loyalty and establish a relationship between client and supplier. Success is based, according to Ranby (1995: A51), on frequent customer contact. He notes that when Consort Hotels limited their loyalty scheme mailing to two instead of four per year, membership lapsed and research showed customers also belonged to other schemes.

There is a danger that such schemes become a necessity and that suppliers will have to initiate new ways to retain customers and gain a competitive advantage. Loyalty schemes are also only successful if the product/service itself is of a sufficiently high quality to warrant repeat visits. Otherwise, they are rendered simply as a short term tactical tools with no lasting benefit to either party.

Relationship marketing is a way of doing business. It emphasizes longer term strategy rather than short term tactics and is as an orientation rather than simply another adjunct to the marketing mix. The next decade will prove its worth to the marketer.

15.4 SUMMARY   Relationship marketing has developed in the last decade as a way of enhancing service levels and quality to increasingly discerning customers. It would be inaccurate to describe it as a set of discrete tools; it is a way of doing business that invests in establishing long term relationships and confidence.

The focus of relationship marketing has been on increased customer orientation and participation, total quality management and strategies to sustain loyalty through incentives. In this way, tourism companies from hotels chains to tour operators have sought to increase their customer retention rate and hence their profitability.

REFERENCES

Beaton, M. and Beaton, C. (1995) Marrying Service Providers and their Clients. *Journal of Marketing Management*, **11**(1–3), 55–70.

Bennett, R. (1996) Relationship Formation and Governance in Consumer Markets. *Journal of Marketing Management*, July.

Berry, L.L. (1983) Relationship Marketing. In *Emerging Perspectives in Services Marketing* (eds L.L. Berry, L. Shostack and G. Upah), American Marketing Association.

Callan, R. (1990) Hotel Award Schemes as a Measurement of Service Quality. *International Journal of Hospitality Management*, **9**(1), 45.

Christopher, M., Payne, A. and Ballantyne, D. (1991) *Relationship Marketing*, Chartered Institute of Marketing Professional Development Series.

Costa, J.D. (1996) A new marketing model for a new advertising reality. *Admap*, January, 33–5.

Doyle, P. (1992) What are excellent companies? *Journal of Marketing Management*, **8**, 101–16.

Drucker, P.F. (1955) *Practice of Management*, Heinemann, London.

Gummeson, E. (1987) The New Marketing: Developing Long-term Interactive Relationship. *Long Range Planning*, **20**, 10–20.

Hartley, J. and Witt, S. (1991) Conference and Function Cancellation and Customer Goodwill. *International Journal of Hospitality Management*, **10**(1), 35.

Hooley, G.J. (1993) Market-Led Quality Management. *Journal of Marketing Management*, **9**, 315–35.

Kotler, P., Bowen, J. and Makens, J. (1996) *Marketing for Hospitality and Tourism*, Prentice Hall, New Jersey.

Martins, C. (1991) Meetings Marketing for Hotels and Destinations. *Insights*, English Tourist Board, March, p. A103.

Naumann, E. (1995) *Creating Customer Value*, Thomson Business Press, London.

Parasuraman, A., Zeithaml, V.A. and Berry, L.L. (1988) SERVQUAL: Multiple Item Scale for Measuring Consumer Perceptions of Service Quality. *Journal of Retailing*, **64**(1), Spring.

Payne, A. (1994) *The Essence of Services Marketing*, Prentice Hall, New Jersey.

Pepper, D. and Rogers, M. (1994) Building Loyalties Via One to One Marketing. *Business Marketing*, **79**(8), 4–7.

Peters, T.J. and Waterman, R.H. (Jnr) (1982) *In Search of Excellence, Lessons from America's Best-Run Companies*, Harper and Row, New York.

Reichheld, M.J. and Sasser, W.E. (1990) Zero Defections: Quality Comes to Services. *Harvard Business Review*, September/October, **68**(5), 105–11.

Ranby, D. (1995) The Loyalty Scheme Panacea, *Insights*, English Tourist Board, September, A51.

Sigrid de Mul, S. (1995) The Tourism and Leisure Industries in Need of a Personal Touch. *Insights*, English Tourist Board, July, A15.

16 Tourism supply sectors

OBJECTIVES

This chapter explains:

● an overview of the supply sectors in tourism;
● the different marketing environments facing organizations;
● the relationship between supply sectors.

16.1 INTRODUCTION

This chapter differs in format from the others. It provides an overview of the supply sectors which make up the business of tourism but does not include tour operators and travel agencies. They are introduced as an area of study in Chapter 13 on distribution. The marketing of tourism destinations of course brings most of the elements of the tourism supply sector together as a tourism offering to the visitor. In this respect they are inextricably linked together. This is what makes the marketing of a tourism offering both complex and challenging.

Each supply sector has, however, developed within its own marketing environment. For example, the airline business competes very much on a regional or global basis, and in contrast most small scale accommodation providers operate at a destination level. The sectors reviewed are listed below:

● accommodation
● entertainment
● events
● catering
● visitor attractions
● retailing
● transport operators.

Each section defines the sector, provides some indication of scale and scope and discusses some of the key issues facing marketers within the sector.

16.2 THE ACCOMMODATION SECTOR

16.2.1 Definition

Accommodation providers include all establishments whose primary aim is to provide overnight accommodation, either on a commercial basis or as a service to members, such the International Youth Hostels Association. Accommodation providers are primarily in business to service the needs of the staying visitor, but usually provide other facilities which are directed to residents, or day visitors such as a health club, public bar or restaurant. Notwithstanding this, their primary purpose for trading is to provide accommodation.

The accommodation sector appreciates that a hotel or a guest house does not constitute the prime motivation for travel to a destination. In this respect accommodation provision enjoys a derived demand. There are some exceptions to the rule when the accommodation offers something special or unique. For example, golfers will travel to the Gleneagles Hotel in Scotland almost as a modern day pilgrimage. The Paradores of Spain bring to visitors fine accommodation in historic buildings. The primary marketing task of all accommodation providers is to understand the expectations of their guests and meet them accordingly. These will obviously vary between market segment and level of accommodation but elements of the marketing mix, such as service provision and physical evidence, are underlying factors for success.

16.2.2 Hotels

(a) *Key issues*

Hotels are mainly in business to supply overnight accommodation to a range of customer segments including business and pleasure travellers and in some instances health or pilgrimage tourists. They vary enormously in size from 20 to 500 bedrooms and from basic facilities to luxury suites. Table 16.1 provides an analysis of the hotel market in Australia. Like many other worldwide destinations, the key issues are the balance between market segmentation, customer needs and level of supply. The level of provision of luxury and economy hotels, the diversity of the market mix, the cyclical pattern of demand in the week and the nature of advance booking systems, are all issues which the hotel marketer needs to address.

(b) *Marketing strategy*

Go and Pine (1995: 361–2) argue that in terms of devising strategies marketing managers will have to take note of six trends which are 'driving the direction and speed of the hotel industry':

- The slow growth of demand and increase in many substitute offerings in industrialized countries and rapid growth in newly industrialized countries.
- Increasing consciousness of the price-value by customers.
- Simultaneous rise of the short break and long haul market segments.
- Rise of corporate mergers and acquisitions.
- Trend of internationalization through geographical expansion and global distribution systems.
- Shortage of skilled and semi-skilled labour.

Table 16.1 Analysis of Australia's hotel market characteristics, 1994

Percentage	Total	Luxury	First class	Economy
Source of business				
Domestic[a]	71.6	72.2	71.9	70.8
International	28.4	27.8	28.1	29.2
Total	**100.0**	**100.0**	**100.0**	**100.0**
Nationality of international guests[b]				
Asia (excl Japan)	24.2	8.8	32.4	21.3
USA and Canada	23.1	32.0	19.0	23.8
Japan	20.4	36.0	19.7	16.7
Europe (excl UK)	16.7	9.2	16.6	19.7
UK	12.2	9.2	10.2	13.9
Africa and the Middle East	2.4	3.3	1.4	2.8
Central and South America	1.0	1.5	0.7	1.8
Total	**100.0**	**100.0**	**100.0**	**100.0**
Market mix				
Business travellers	30.9	18.8	36.9	29.5
Independent tourists	26.3	38.0	22.5	24.2
Tour groups	13.3	6.6	11.1	18.7
Conference delegates	13.0	25.4	12.0	9.2
Government officials	6.9	0.8	6.3	10.7
Other categories	9.6	10.4	11.2	7.7
Total	**100.0**	**100.0**	**100.0**	**100.0**
Room nights sold by day of week[c]				
Sunday	9.6	11.1	9.2	9.7
Monday	15.8	13.0	15.4	16.6
Tuesday	15.3	13.4	15.7	16.1
Wednesday	15.7	14.0	16.3	16.0
Thursday	15.9	13.5	17.0	15.9
Friday	14.1	16.6	13.3	13.3
Saturday	13.6	18.4	13.1	12.4
Total	**100.0**	**100.0**	**100.0**	**100.0**
Advanced reservations				
Percentage of advance reservations	91.2	91.9	91.6	89.9
Composition of advance reservations				
Direct	48.3	65.8	52.9	36.0
Own reservation system	10.6	8.0	8.8	13.8
Independent reservation system	4.7	2.4	4.6	5.7
Travel agents	16.1	11.4	15.9	18.0
Tour operators	13.3	7.8	9.1	20.9
Other	7.0	4.6	8.7	5.6
Total	**100.0**	**100.0**	**100.0**	**100.0**

[a] Includes New Zealand.

[b] Nationality of international guests is presented as percentages of total international guests.

[c] This represents room nights sold on specific days of the week as a percentage of annual room nights sold. For example, for the total sample group, 9.6% of room nights sold over the survey period were sold on a Sunday.

Source: Australian Hotel Industry Survey of Operations 1995. Horwath Asia Pacific. Quoted in *Travel & Tourism Intelligence*, 1996.

Furthermore, Middleton (1994: 277) suggests that there is a need to give consideration to five key areas which impact on the marketing task: choice of location, evidence of peaks and troughs in demand, influence of room sales on profits, low variable costs of operation, and focus on bookers, not occupancy levels. These are discussed below.

(c) Locational analysis

Traditional hotels and accommodation provision are hostage to the site chosen in past times, which might not meet current market desires. For example, many of the great Victorian hotels of Europe were established near major rail terminals. As zones around many stations have deteriorated in recent decades, this presents an image problem for such hotels. Fortunes might change with the steady revitalization of a long distance European rail network, but in other countries where rail networks are still in decline, prestigious hotels suffer. Many small to medium sized hotels in north European seaside resorts which were once popular in Victorian times have been sold at substantial capital loss, because demand has dwindled to a level which necessitates withdrawal from the market. Walker (1995) explains this by quoting from Dries de Vaal, a partner at the Touche Ross consultancy:

> There is a whole raft of British stock in the wrong place or in poor condition or of the wrong type. Some of the traditional British resorts, particularly the seaside, are no longer competitive. It doesn't matter if the sun shines or not, it has the wrong tourism structure and poor facilities which people don't want any more. People won't accept that type of hotel in that kind of environment. If we are to compete effectively, we need a new product.

In contrast there has been substantial development of hotels at airports, on major holiday routes, at new resorts in developing countries and in the centres of emerging commercialization where business tourism is set to increase. Rogers and Slinn (1993: 117–18) suggest a framework for site selection of tourism facilities such as accessibility, climate and geography, and management preferences, for example. They also point to the following specific factors:

- transport networks
- space requirements
- zoning/character of environs
- services available and needed
- people flows/demographic analysis of catchment area
- land and building costs.

Central zone sites have a premium because of the potential to increase guest numbers throughout the year. In European capital cities, for example, the highest average occupancy level in 1994 was 79.6 per cent (Walker, 1995). Nevertheless, hoteliers found it difficult to yield revenue from room rates, which have been decreasing at 1.5 per cent per annum. The traditional markets of Europe and North America are virtually saturated, and both occupancy and revenue optimization is difficult to achieve.

(d) Market development

Growth can be achieved in two ways. The first way is by a combination of customer retention and gaining market share from other competitors in the markets. However, in many saturated markets there is little scope for such market retention.

Many hotel companies, such as Inter-Continental, have therefore chosen a market development strategy. The main thrust of the marketing strategy has been to target newly industrializing countries through partnerships with governments, anxious to accelerate the growth of tourism. Nicaragua, for example, is offering a ten year tax incentive package to international hotel groups to develop sites in newly developing resort areas.

The approach of the multinational hotel sector is far more selective now than it was in the boom years of the 1980s, when investment packages were being created everywhere. The common belief was that inflation would drive up real estate prices. In reality, recessionary trends in the early 1990s have meant less hotel construction in many parts of the world, although there are notable exceptions, such as in Asia, where 150 hotels were due to be completed in 1997–98, primarily in Malaysia, Indonesia and Thailand (Croston, 1997: 12–13). In the context of developing hotels in Asia, Schlentrich and Ng (1994: 403) consider that hotel developers need to pay specific attention to the following factors:

● the political risk associated with any given country;
● the regulation of foreign investment;
● taxation and repatriation of profits;
● the degree of crime and corruption, and bureaucracy;
● the level of government support for tourism development;
● infrastructure;
● the availability of construction materials and produce supplies when complete;
● restrictions on foreign workers, and internal laws relating to training and employment;
● existing and potential ecological problems.

The main concern for the hotel marketer is first and foremost the image of the destination and the specific area where the hotel is located. The second issue is the staffing

Table 16.2 Analysis of world hotel business by region, 1992

Percentage	All hotels	Africa and Middle East	Asia and Australasia	North America	Europe	Latin America
Source of business						
Domestic	47.0	18.2	33.6	85.3	47.4	53.5
Foreign	53.0	81.8	67.4	14.7	52.6	46.5
Total	**100.0**	**100.0**	**100.0**	**100.0**	**100.0**	**100.0**
Percentage of repeat business	**36.7**	**32.7**	**32.9**	**41.0**	**35.5**	**47.1**
Composition of market						
Government officials	3.9	11.3	4.6	6.5	1.8	4.9
Business travellers	33.6	38.6	30.7	28.5	37.4	32.6
Tourists (individuals)	24.6	9.4	27.4	26.1	22.9	24.8
Tour groups	17.4	13.6	20.1	7.8	16.6	23.4
Conference participants	11.3	7.8	7.5	22.9	12.1	8.2
Others	9.2	19.3	9.7	8.2	9.2	6.1
Total	**100.0**	**100.0**	**100.0**	**100.0**	**100.0**	**100.0**
Percentage of advance reservations	**84.4**	**78.8**	**87.1**	**84.2**	**86.4**	**73.8**

Source: Horwath International Worldwide Hotel Industry, 1993. Quoted in *EIU Travel and Tourism Analyst*, No 2 (1994).

and corporate culture in terms of service provision. Some authors have been critical of this process, arguing that developing countries are locked into an unequal trading agreement. Lea (1988: 12), for example, comments:

> Transnational hotels ... are characterized by certain features which are responsible for their successful invasion of Third World destinations.
>
> 1. They seldom invest large amounts of their own capital in the Third World, but seek funds from private and governmental sources locally, thus minimizing risk.
> 2. Associated infrastructure like new roads and power supplies are essential in resort development and are similarly funded through local sources or via foreign loans.
> 3. A viable visitor flow is ensured through worldwide marketing campaigns.
> 4. Transnational corporations participate in the profits of their Third World hotels through charging management fees, limited direct investment, and various licensing, franchise, and service agreements.
>
> In all such cases the ability of the parent company to withdraw from these arrangements puts it in a controlling position.

(e) Design standards

Another important consideration which affects the task of the marketer is the design standards applied to hotels. Accommodation developers have been criticized for the excesses of functionality at the expense of design integration with surroundings. Many accommodation centres dating from the 1960s and '70s are considered to be unfashionable and in some instances decidedly ugly. This is particularly the case with Mediterranean resorts which expanded rapidly at this time. It is also the case with planned economies where aesthetic considerations were afforded a very low priority.

Increasingly, planning authorities throughout the world are strengthening regulations which ensure compliance with vernacular architecture, by specifying maximum heights of buildings, materials to be used, preferred styles, etc. Cities and more progressive tourism authorities are seeking state of the art design and contemporary flair to enhance the image of the destination.

(f) Interior design

Interior design is often understated as a part of the promotional mix in tourism. The degree of symbolism signaled by decor and layout of service provision is a function of design capability, style, resource commitment and spatial dimensions.

The trade-off between functionality and aesthetic richness is not always diametrically opposed, but there are implications for the marketer if the balance between the two is biased in either direction. Furniture and fittings also add value, but only if the guest values them. A study published by the IHA (1988) indicated that while customers increasingly expect higher standards, many facilities can be designed for the guest to serve themselves such as a mini-bar, multi-use television, etc., while low valued services can be reduced to hold costs.

In recent years there has been a shift towards the franchising out of some catering provision. There has, however, been an enhancement of other facilities such as health and fitness centres.

(g) Cyclical nature of demand

The patterns of demand for different accommodation providers varies enormously according to type, purpose and locality. In the case of a business hotel in a provincial city, the rooms can be sold Mondays to Thursday nights throughout the year for business purposes, therefore one of the first objectives will be retention of business patronage. The second objective will be to seek alternative markets to boost weekend trade. The task is far more difficult for the owner of a camp site in a temperate climate where the season might range from 12 to 20 weeks at the most. Even the most imaginative of promotional techniques or penetrating pricing techniques will not stimulate demand during the coldest months.

(h) High fixed costs

The provision of accommodation is invariably a high fixed cost project (perhaps with the exception of a camping site), with many schemes falling into the multimillion pound range. It is estimated, for example, that a hotel will take 12–15 years to bring a return on investment. This is often reflected in the pricing structure which necessitates multilevel pricing.

(i) Occupancy and bookers

Middleton (1994: 278–9) highlights the importance of gross profit on the sales of rooms and therefore presents the case for marketing emphasis to focus on sale of rooms, rather than on ancillary facilities, such as catering, where profit margins are lower. In the past there has been a pre-occupation with occupancy levels, but as Middleton indicates the focus should be to target prospective customers, especially bookers, i.e. those who have made a firm reservation. For hotels or conference centres which specialize in meetings and sales conferences the buyer has to be of supreme importance.

(j) Sustaining competitive advantage

The direction in hotel marketing is towards the use of computer aided yield management systems (such as Holiday Inns' Revenue Optimiser) which highlight the value of each customer transaction rather than volume related goals, i.e. seeking highest yield by maximizing sales of rooms to highest spenders.

Hotels and other accommodation providers will have to become increasingly flexible in their approach to the market. Go and Pine (1994: xvi) comment:

> ... contemporary key issues for most hotel companies are how to organize, integrate, and manage their activities in order to respond to global competition, and how to modify approaches to suit local application.

For tourism marketers facing increasing competition, it means that companies will seek to sustain competitive advantage by making best use of their portfolio properties and company competencies to reap economies of scale. Perhaps more importantly, to sustain any advantage there will be a need to build quality through the integration of staff and finely tuned processes so that customer retention is high. This might be difficult for those that have not yet reached a stage where marketing orientation is attuned to their corporate culture. Renaghan (1993) describes the position as follows:

> It is easiest to think of international hospitality firms as occupying a point on a line with sales anchoring one end and marketing anchoring the other end. Hospitality firms would be placed somewhere along the continuum based on the degree to which their culture, values and activities emphasize one or the other orientation. Firms that emphasize revenue generation through sales, pursuing promotion as the primary vehicle for accomplishment, would be placed towards the sales end. Firms that emphasize revenue generation through loyalty and repeat business, by satisfying customer needs through the offering of distinctive products and services, would be placed towards the other end. I suggest that most international firms would be placed towards the sales end ...

16.2.3 All inclusive resorts

Key issues

The combination of accommodation, catering, recreation and entertainment at an all-inclusive price is not new. The early concept of the British holiday camp in the 1930s has proven to be quite resilient, despite changes in the market. The Butlins and Pontins holiday centres of the 1990s still manage to maintain high levels of occupancy as do the new inclusive accommodation complexes such as CenterParcs and Oasis. The concept is also popular in mainland Europe, shown by the spectacular success of Club Mediterranée in the 1960s in the French market and Robinsons serving the German market. By far the largest company is Club Med based in France, followed by Robinsons, Club Aldina and Club Calinera in Germany. There is an increasing number of companies emerging in Mexico and the Caribbean.

The degree to which the holiday is all inclusive depends on each company, but the appeal to the customer is the perceived value of a holiday where there are no extras. Poon (1993: 54) concludes that 'the superior performance, profitability and innovativeness of all-inclusive resorts suggest that they will continue to be a very powerful force in the travel and tourism industry. The experience of the Caribbean bears this out.'

16.2.4 Timeshare complexes

Key issues

The other major international growth trend has been in timeshare provision, i.e. where a customer buys a one- or two-week time slot in an apartment. The 1970s and '80s saw the rapid growth of timeshare complexes provided by a multitude of developers at resorts throughout the world, but mainly in the Mediterranean and North America. In the 1990s the major thrust of the marketing effort has been in the provision of timeshare exchanges, to enable timeshare owners to try other premises throughout the world. The marketing techniques used are primarily direct marketing to a club membership or affinity group.

16.3 ENTERTAINMENT

16.3.1 Definition

Entertainment is an underrated sector in tourism. A broad definition would include all forms of art and culture which is on show or performed for the public. This varies from street theatre to art galleries, folk clubs to rock concerts. Thus, it is much wider than the traditional approach to the marketing of the arts. It also includes cinemas and casinos (Leiper, 1989: 269–75) or similar multipurpose entertainment complexes, which are fast becoming tourism offerings in rejuvenated quarters of cities. For example, the Centro Oberhausen near Düsseldorf in the Ruhr Valley is a retail and entertainment complex based on old steel mill sites; it includes a nine screen Warner Bros cinema, an 11 000 seat arena, a Planet Hollywood restaurant and Centropark children's activity park, barbecues and badminton courts as well as retail outlets.

The fusion of entertainment, retailing and recreation means that marketers will have to reposition such complexes within the overall appeal of the city tourism destination. It also makes it difficult for the market to be evaluated in terms of value or volume attributable to entertainment, rather than retailing or eating out.

16.3.2 Key issues

The key issues facing marketers of the arts are not entirely related to tourism. The creation of arts programmes are often targeted primarily to local people but some entertainments are planned to entice visitors to attend. One of the major issues for the arts marketer in this context is the need to market to stakeholders, rather than potential end users. Therefore, the marketing effort concentrates on achieving political and financial support from local authorities and grant aiding organizations, as well as revenue from guests. In this way, a theatre or dance company can present a performance of specialized art which would not otherwise be commercially viable. The second area of marketing interest is within the realm of sponsorship of productions.

16.4 EVENTS

16.4.1 Definition

Destinations have begun to market events for a number of reasons:

● to heighten image such as in the garden festivals in Britain where transforming industrial sectors gained a new lease of life through repositioning as a major event location;
● to expand the tourism season. The classic example has to be the Blackpool Illuminations;
● to engage the interest of local people;
● to attract overseas visitors with a specialist interest.

The marketing of events relates to the ephemeral. Events are therefore not the same as visitor or arts attractions which are of a more permanent nature; they have an intentional finite span (Thomas, 1993: 19). Therefore, events marketing is somewhat different in that the benefits tend to be wide ranging, from corporate prestige and individual status to sheer hedonism. As with other tourism offerings, an event is an amalgam of tangibles and intangibles, but the imagery and delivery is inextricably tied to the destination where it is held.

There is a major difference between the organization of small scale community directed festivals and major international events. With regard to the thousands of small scale events organized throughout the world, research findings (Getz and Frisby, 1988; Mayfield and Crompton, 1995) point to a lack of marketing orientation on the part of the organizers. Ritchie (1984: 2–11) classifies events into those which are significant and others based on local themes, customs or activities. The former he refers to as hallmark events, which are divided into seven categories:

- world fairs and expositions such as the World Travel Market in London;
- unique carnivals and festivals such as Rio de Janeiro carnival;
- major sports events such as the Olympic Games, the World Cup, etc.;
- cultural and religious festivals;
- historical milestones such as American Independence Day;
- classical commercial and agricultural events;
- major political events.

16.4.2 Key Issues

Getz (1990: 125–37) discusses the nature of special events in tourism. He distinguishes special events from other types of attractions in the following way:

- special events are open to the public;
- their main purpose is celebration or display of some theme;
- they occur once a year or less frequently;
- they have pre-determined opening and closing dates;
- permanent structures are not owned by the event;
- the programme consists of one or more separate activities;
- all activities take place in the same community or tourist region.

He argues that special events are increasingly being 'viewed as an integral part of tourism development and marketing plans' especially mega-events (for example, the Olympic Games) which have the potential to heighten image and achieve economic gain. The onus is on the word 'potential'. The estimation of demand for mega-events is notoriously difficult (Evans, 1996: 91–8). Table 16.3 indicates the current forecasts for the Millennium Festival at Greenwich. Evans notes that such estimates can be inaccurate because of factors such as promotional hype, the economy and even the weather. The benefits of such events have to be weighed against disruption factors. There also needs to be an evaluation of environmental and social impacts incorporated into pre-event evaluation. Figure 16.1 indicates the potential demand stimulated by a mega-event such as the Olympic Games. The projections for increased demand for tourism if the Olympic Games are hosted in Cape Town are substantial and are certainly three times more than existing visitation.

Roche (1993: 1–19) argues that there are two models of event planning processes, one which fits the pattern of rationality and the other which is described as the 'political approach'. He points to the influence of urban leadership, societal change and non-rational planning in event production processes.

Table 16.3 Median forecast of visitors to British Millennium Festival, Greenwich 1999/2000

Target market	Segment Size 000s	Pull through factor	Penetration rate %	Repeat Visit factor	Market Share 000s
Local population	980	1.00	35	3.20	1100
Regional pep.	5810	1.00	25	1.50	2170
London day visitors	10200	1.25	18	1.00	2300
Domestic tourists	5400	1.50	25	1.10	2220
Overseas tourists	7800	1.50	15	1.10	1930
Educational groups	5000	1.25	28	1.10	1890
Business tourists	3800	1.00	10	1.02	390
Total	38990				12000

1. Population figures – OPCS, 1991/Census;
2. Local includes Greenwich and three adjoining south London boroughs (Bromley, Bexley, Lewisham); Region represents the rest of Greater London;
3. London Day Visitors (London Tourist Board/UKTS, 1992);
4. Domestic and Overseas Tourists – (LTB, 1992);
5. Educational Groups (School rolls – London/South-East catchment);
6. Business Tourists (LTB, 1992).

16.4.3 Segmentation of events

Segmentation is also less clear, as in some instances both arts and certain events have wide ranging appeal, while others offer specialist appeal. Table 16.4 highlights the aspect of segmentation of the marketing of an international festival.

16.4.4 Sponsorship

Events are increasingly associated with sponsorship and this complicates the marketing process. For example, Euro '96, which was held at several stadia in the north of England, involved multimillion pound sponsorship. Canon, Carlsberg, Cola-Cola, Fujifilm, JVC, Mastercard, McDonald's, Opel/Vauxhall, Philips, Snickers and Umbro each paid £3.5 million for the exclusive rights to advertise and sell their products inside the stadia. The estimated global TV audience was 6.9 billion (Abel and Long, 1996: 18). The destinations which hosted the events gained from the TV coverage but the multifaceted nature of the sponsorship made it difficult for tourism marketers seeking to develop destination imagery.

Other issues which face the marketer of a destination are the lack of research about the benefits and disadvantages of events, the multiplicity of motives of stakeholders in event management, the power base of events organizers and the degree of competition between rival destinations. The entire process of course depends on the scale and scope of an event and how it is evaluated within the overall strategy for tourism development.

16.5 RESTAURANTS AND CATERING

16.5.1 Definition

The term restaurant covers a very broad range of food service provision but primarily refers to the eating-out market. Catering is a much wider term which relates to all

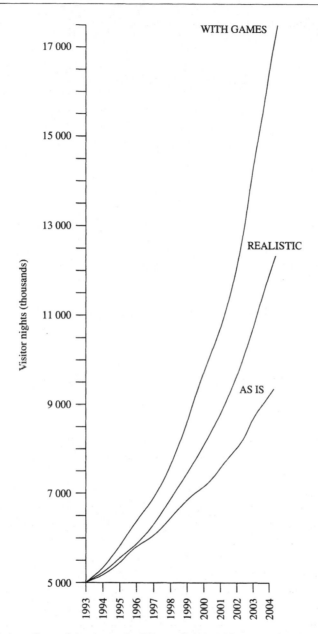

Figure 16.1 Western Cape visitor growth. *Source*: South African Tourist Board.

types of retail and wholesale providers of food and beverages to the tourism sector. It is an important sector as witnessed by many visitor surveys which point to visitor enjoyment of local cuisine, restaurants, bars and inns.

Table 16.4 Segmentation of events

Type of event	Markets/Scale
Annual festivals • Cultural • Musical	Regional markets Small scale
Sporting events	Major national, European or global events Medium to large scale
Political events	Summits and similar major events Medium scale
Mega-events	Sporting or musical e.g. Olympic Games Large scale

The supply sector can be segmented into the eating-out sector such as restaurants and the take-out food service. Powers (1995) notes that while the structure of the market in the USA is relatively stable, there has been a trend away from eating in formal settings, and an increase in fast food and take-away offerings.

In the USA, the National Restaurant Association estimated the values shown in Table 16.5 in 1994. The internationalization of the North American food service has been an important feature in the tourism sector in terms of styling of venues, service processes and marketing. A major global trend has been established. It amounts to a roll-out programme of fast food outlets, of which McDonald's is undoubtedly the world leader, with outlets from Delhi to Moscow. It is estimated that 22 million people eat at McDonald's worldwide (Lyon, Taylor and Smith, 1994: 95–9) and that the hundreds of generics which copy the formula have spawned a new dimension to urban living. It is increasingly common to see several of the multinational fast food chains grouped together in the central zones of most resorts.

The success of the standardized offering and operational concept of delivery has been praised by some authors, such as Kotler, Bowen and Makens (1996) but subject to criticism by others such as Ritzer (1993). The main thrust of his argument is that the management philosophy and principles behind McDonald's is being copied throughout the services sector, especially the provision of 'homogeneous products, rigid technologies, standardized work routines, deskilling, homogenization of labor (and customer), the mass worker and the homogenization of consumption'. There certainly has been a growth in the number of international restaurant chains offering

Table 16.5 Supply segmentation: catering

Types of outlet	US$ (millions)	Percentage of market
Restaurants and fast food outlets	187.7	68.2
Institutes' own catering	31.0	11.3
Contracts and caterers	20.2	7.3
Service in hotels and motels	15.5	5.6
Other	20.8	7.6

Source: adapted from data collected by the National Restaurant Association.

standardized formats such as TGI Fridays, Planet Hollywood and Fatty Arbuckles, as well as the growth of theme bars at airports and major retail shopping centres.

Within the hotel sector, there has been an important shift in recent years to contracting out to restauranteurs. The main reasons behind this decision, in an area which has been traditionally positioned as a central feature, are to cut costs in an intensely competitive market, to improve quality or to provide a speciality feature (Wexler, 1993: 69–72). There is, of course, an important business to business market in the provision of catering services to restaurants and hotels provided by such companies as Gardner Merchant.

16.5.2 Key issues

The key issues for the marketer will be to introduce strategies which prioritize customer retention by adding value in the light of intense competition between international giants on the high streets of resorts. This also means that service provision will become crucial to the marketing process.

16.6 VISITOR ATTRACTIONS

16.6.1 Definition

Human attractions are either natural or artificial resources which feature facilities of interest, education and entertainment. They are essentially there to be consumed by the visitor, although the consumption of sensitive landscapes is extremely contentious. MacCannell (1976: 41) defines an attraction as 'an empirical relationship between a tourist, a sight and a marker – a piece of information about a sight'. Thus, three elements combine to become a phenomenon known as a tourism attraction (Leiper, 1990: 371).

The primary appeal of any destination is the image creation. This in turn is based on its mix of attractions which combine to form the core appeal or offering. These might range from natural landscapes or features which have worldwide appeal to small scale museums which are of limited appeal even to the resident population.

16.6.2 Nature reserves and country parks

There is a distinction to be made between those attractions which need to be conserved from development – wildlife reserves, sensitive environments or historic sites and monuments – and other attractions. In such cases the main aim of management will be philanthropic, i.e. conserving a particular aspect of our past or an endangered environment for future generations. Berry (1996) comments:

> Most heritage attractions are products which by definition cannot change much. Examples include: country houses (French châteaux, George Washington's country home in Virginia), town houses (Fairfax House in York), and city palaces, for example in Istanbul in Turkey … They are competing against modern attractions which include aquaria and other increasingly popular 'conservation' attractions which are able to change their product.

Thus, many visitor attractions are developed mainly with entertainment value as the main benefit for the consumer. They, of course, seek a commercial return on assets and can modify or develop their offering accordingly. There are implications for the marketer in terms of conservation.

First, consider the marketing of sites such as country parks or national reserves. Marketing in such cases should be about management of demand in line with the overall objectives of conservation. Marketers become involved in developing strategies to generate revenue from visitors without damaging the core features. It is not always an easy task as there are political considerations, mainly issues of funding management and security measures to stop poaching, despoiling of the landscape and over-visitation. For example, the national parks of Costa Rica, one of the world's richest sources of biodiversity, have the dilemma of widening access to meet the demands of more visitors but within serious budgetary constraints.

16.6.3 Museums and galleries

There are estimated to be approximately 2500 museums in the UK which attract over 110 000 visitors per annum (Davies, 1994). Both national and local government tend to become involved in the funding of museums and galleries, which house national treasures, simply because they reflect the culture of the country. The degree of public ownership affects both marketing strategy and tactics in the following ways:

- The site chosen for a museum might be significant, perhaps in terms of someone's birthplace or a reuse of an old artisan's works, but not all sites are chosen for accessibility or attractiveness. There has been a recent trend in Europe and in North America to build museums or galleries into regeneration projects, for example the Tate Gallery at Albert Dock in Liverpool.
- Public stakeholders often regard a museum or attraction as a place which should be open to both residents and visitors at no charge. Pricing plays little or no part in the strategy and therefore it is difficult for potential visitors to value its worth. Contributory revenue will be expected from ancillary services such as a shop or cafeteria, whereas in commercial terms the enterprise would stand or fall by entrance charges.
- The third influence is that there is often an uneasy balance between curatorial conservatism regarding displays and artifacts and the role of the marketer in presenting the museum as a visitor attraction. There will most probably be a degree of antipathy between the custodial staff and a marketing officer as to the positioning of the museum to existing and potential visitors. The argument has been particularly acute with regard to the interpretation of historic buildings and monuments, which is sometimes referred to as the 'heritage industry' (Hewtson, 1987). He argues that historical fact and presentation is being distorted to meet the needs of commercialism.
- The final factor is that marketing expenditure is likely to be set in accordance with stringent budgetary frameworks determined by a parent authority. Museums and local authority based attractions are renowned for the paucity of their marketing budgets.

16.6.4 Theme parks

Definition

The marketing of major visitor attractions such as theme parks follows a more conventional pattern. Theme parks can be defined as 'an amusement park that has themed attractions, be it food, costumes, entertainment, retail stores or rides' (International Association of Amusement Parks and Attractions cited in Loverseed, 1994). Market segmentation can be somewhat different in that the school and group market is of prime importance. In the USA, theme parks, although accounting for only 8 per cent of attractions, dominate the market in terms of visitor numbers, generating an average attendance of 3 374 500 per annum according to the International Association of Amusement Parks and Attractions. This compares with an average attendance at amusement parks of 565 300 per annum and 230 800 for water parks during 1993.

Whilst the North American market for the theme park sector has reached maturity with approximately 160 million visits to Canadian and US parks, the European sector is still in growth, as shown in Table 16.6.

Marketers of major visitor attractions aim to both innovate and diversify in terms of the provision of new rides, experiences and improved systems to maintain market share. The level of competition in the UK is expected to increase as newly funded projects supported by the Millennium Commission encourage increased provision. In 1995 there were over 80 new visitor attractions opened against 32 closures. Some of the major new entrants have gained market share rapidly such as Legoland in Windsor, targeting 1.4 million visitors, and Segaworld in London, expecting 1.7 million visitors per annum.

16.6.5 Key issues

The key issues facing man-made and natural attractions will be to manage demand in order to ensure that there is little long term damage to the site. These are the issues which confound managers of attractions throughout the world from the Egyptian Pyramids and the Acropolis in Athens to the major game parks of Central Africa and the ecotourism hot-spots of Belize, Costa Rica and the Galapagos Islands in Ecuador. There is a need for more urgent action to manage demand at a level

Table 16.6 Europe's major attractions (selected sites over 1 million visitors)

Attraction	Estimated visitor numbers (1995)	
Disneyland Paris	10 700 000	Paid entrance
Notre-Dame, Paris	10 000 000	Entrance free
Pleasure Beach, Blackpool	7 300 000	Free
British Museum, London	5 700 000	Free
Köln cathedral, Germany	3 500 000	Free
Alton Towers, UK	2 800 000	Paid entrance
Port Aventura, Spain	2 700 000	Paid entrance
Tower of London	2 600 000	Paid entrance
Legoland, Denmark	1 300 000	Paid entrance

Sources: Trade magazines, public relations material.

which will sustain these attractions without incurring long term damage. Marketing can play a decisive role in this context, through appropriate promotional campaigns and judicious pricing strategies.

The key issues facing commercial visitor attractions will be the need to encourage repeat visits in a market which is becoming increasingly mature and saturated. This might involve a combination of investment in new technologies, service processes and loyalty schemes. Either way, throughout Europe, millennium initiatives and the rapidly growing home entertainment market will present the visitor attraction sector with major challenges. In other parts of the world (except North America) the visitor attraction market is very much in a growth stage, but marketers will have to take heed of cultural differences.

16.7 RETAILING

16.7.1 Definition

In contrast to the other elements in tourism, the retail sector sells goods and services, but mainly the former. Retail outlets and some specialist quarters are becoming important as a stimulator of tourism demand.

The distinction between utility and leisure shopping has become more sharply defined in recent years, with the growth of out-of-town supermarkets and specialist high street shops offering a distinct contrast in many countries. The concept of retail centres, however, is in ascendancy. This is where developers incorporate attractions and entertainments alongside retail outlets. Visitors can combine shopping with rides and eating out to make a day outing. The most successful of early schemes was West Edmonton Mall in Alberta, Canada, which includes approximately 800 shops, 100 restaurants, a water park, fantasy land and amusement park.

Tourism destinations in Northern Europe have begun to include regeneration projects, purpose-built shopping complexes, or the development of artisan quarters to attract visitors who are motivated by shopping for fashionable items. They have been targeted to both residents and day visitors mainly, but also have secondary appeal to staying visitors. The development of retailing in relation to transport terminals has also been the subject of recent research. Increasingly, transport providers and terminal owners are testing the potential of retailing for their passengers.

Another aspect is the industrial tourism market. This has stimulated the demand for factory and retail centres. The core concept of visiting a place of work to witness at first hand how a product is made spans a wide range of businesses, from coffee plantations in Colombia to breweries such as Pilsner Urquell, Pilzen, in the Czech Republic. The latter concern has a shop and restaurant on site and plans to roll out several of them in major European centres. Industrial tourism forms a small sector, but one which has maintained a stable position within the overall portfolio of many destinations.

16.7.2 Key issues

The relationship between retailing and tourism is becoming stronger, as retail outlets realize that visitors through their doors mean additional revenue and tourism officials recognize that fashionable shopping outlets attract higher spending visitors. The key tasks for the marketer will be to ensure that the visitor experience is maintained at a high level, for problems such as petty crime and security in such retail zones has become a major issue in North America.

16.8 TRANSPORT OPERATORS

16.8.1 Definition

Transport is a highly competitive sector which includes every conceivable option from the rickshaw ride to an extensive international network of scheduled flights. The main forms of transport are listed below:

- **Walking and cycling:** Sustainable transport options; walking is important for visitors when exploring most destinations. There are also horse-drawn carriages and rickshaws.
- **Private vehicles:** The car is the most important form of transport for short to medium distance journeys (also includes car hire).
- **Road passenger transport:** This ranges from local buses to long distance coaches. This is of declining importance in tourism. Taxis are included in this category.
- **Rail transport and fixed track:** This includes trams and metros in cities, local rail, inter-urban and long distance trains. Not important in tourism for short distances but gains in importance over medium to long distances.
- **Water:** Ferries and water buses for local journeys. Cruise liners.
- **Air:** Scheduled and charter flights.

There are seven fundamental points regarding the provision of transport facilities for tourism:

- Most transport provision is not geared solely for tourism and in many instances local transport systems are designed for residents or freight transport.
- Without transport tourism could not exist, for it is a movement of people away from their daily existence at their home and in the neighbourhood that is a distinguishing feature.
- Transport infrastructure is essential for most transport systems to function. The infrastructure is primarily in public ownership although there has been a sweeping tide of privatization and deregulation across the globe in recent years. Thus, many rail systems have been privatized, including the rail track, and in some countries highways are being financed in partnership with private sector companies. Transport terminals such as airports reflect a high fixed cost and are large business enterprises in their own right. For example, London Heathrow handled 10.5 million passengers on 192 000 air transport movements in 1965 and approximately 50 million passengers in more than 400 000 air transport movements in 1995 (Chataway, 1996: 3).
- The marketing of transport systems is similar to other tourism sectors, in that the main task is to manage the peaks and troughs of demand and to segment the market with painstaking accuracy. Like the accommodation sector, competition from other modes and between modes is intensifying.

- Despite privatization government involvement is likely to remain, given that the free market approach to transport continues to generate unacceptable levels of congestion and pollution. This is a worldwide problem fuelled partly by tourism.
- Deregulation of airlines will continue as governments review protectionist policies (Wheatcroft, 1994: 3).
- There is a sector which markets the transport facility primarily as a tourism attraction. The steam railways of Britain and the mountain railways of Switzerland are classic examples. Table 16.7 lists transport as tourist attractions.

16.8.2 Marketing airlines

In developing marketing strategies, many airline companies exhibit a similar pattern of behaviour. The past ten years have witnessed a significant increase in strategic alliances. KLM and Northwest Airlines, British Airways and American Airlines, Lufthansa and United Airlines have all formed alliances, thereby linking regional or domestic networks to long haul routes. This is especially the case with transatlantic routes, an issue discussed in greater detail in Chapter 8. This has led to a concentrated provision in both the scheduled and charter airline market in the UK, as shown in Table 16.8.

To a lesser extent franchising has been used to expand influence. For example, British Airways franchises routes to Brymon and Manx airlines.

16.8.3 Coaches and railways

As with airlines, the major external impacts on this market in Europe and elsewhere in the world have been the deregulation of services and wholesale privatization of both coach and railway companies. Within Europe the development of an intercity level of fast services between major centres is holding market share between rail and airlines. The TGV train in France is also gaining share, as is Eurostar. Eurolines has created a demand for longer distance coach travel between cities across Europe, in the development of a strongly branded service offering.

Some marketing strategies include cross-company promotions for tourism purposes. Inter Rail, for example, is organized by a consortium of European railway

Table 16.7 Transport as tourism

Transport mode	Explanation	Examples
Cruise liners	The basis of the holiday is the use of a cruise liner as a floating hotel, which takes the passenger to exotic locations	P&O Cruises; Carnival Cruise Liners
Rail based holidays/ steam railways	The key motivational factor is travel by train, unusual railway lines and scenic splendour	Orient Express; rail passes – Switzerland; the Little Great Trains of Wales
Tour bus or coach	Use of local bus and coach network to explore cities and countries	Guide Friday city bus tours; Greyhound in the USA
Ferries/local water-based transport	Use of local ferries, trip boats, narrow boats, etc.	Baton Rouge in Paris; Cross-Channel ferries; Hoseasons boating holidays
City/walking/cycling tours	Walking and cycling exploration of cities or countryside areas	City walking tours of London or York; Vienna bike tour

Table 16.8 The UK air travel industry, 1991–96

	Passengers m	Index	£bn	Index	Average price £	£bn at 1991 prices	Index	Average price £
1991	55.5	100	7.0	100	126	7.0	100	126
1992	62.7	113	7.3	104	116	6.9	99	110
1993	65.8	119	8.5	121	129	7.6	109	116
1994	71.0	128	11.7	167	165	10.2	146	144
1995	75.0	135	13.1	187	175	11.1	159	148
1996 (est)	79.0	142	14.6	209	185	12.1	173	153

Source: CAA/Mintel.

operators. In the coach market, Eurolines offer a similar package as a consortium of coach operators. National Express franchise many routes throughout the UK to regional coach operators.

16.8.4 Ferries and cruise liners

The ferry market is increasingly moving away from being a provider of transport to becoming a visitor attraction in its own right. Both Stena and P&O have introduced imaginative campaigns to hold patronage against the Channel Tunnel, but are losing share despite price discounting on a heavy basis. It is likely that as market share decreases there will be some degree of consolidation. Throughout the world, thousands of ferry operators have repositioned to meet the needs of the tourism sector by increasing facilities on board and stopping at more destinations en route. The ferries to the Greek Islands, or those serving the Western Isles of Scotland, fall into this category.

The cruise liner sector is growing fast as the market image is changing to meet the lifestyle of more moderate income earners. Carnival Cruises in the USA, for example, repositioned to provide lower cost, shorter and more fun-based cruises. In contrast, other major companies, such as P&O and Fred Olsen Lines, have invested heavily in a new fleet to meet the needs of an affluent client base. Table 16.9 illustrates the growth of the cruise market in the UK.

16.8.5 Key issues

The key issues facing passenger transport marketers are the perennial ones of capacity, planning and perishability. It will become intensely difficult for those who do not enjoy the benefits of investment in computerized booking schemes which enable late bookings. Airline companies are moving towards automatic ticketing and even no ticket systems in the USA and to a lesser extent in Europe. The railway and coach sector is again experiencing a period of acquisition and alliance and this will continue throughout the world in the wake of deregulation and privatization.

The provision of infrastructure for road transport will become increasingly problematic, as countries and intergovernmental agencies fear the consequences of unbridled growth of traffic. Tourism is one of the major generators of car traffic, with approximately 75 per cent of all holiday trips being undertaken this way. Increasing regulation will attempt to hold or reduce this in cities and seaside resorts.

Table 16.9 Cruise holidays as a percentage of the total overseas holiday market, 1989–95

	Total overseas holidays m	Index	Cruise holidays m	Index	Cruises as a % of total
1989	21.9	100	0.168	100	0.8
1990	21.3	97	0.187	111	0.9
1991	20.6	94	0.193	115	0.9
1992	23.1	105	0.229	136	1.0
1993	24.5	112	0.265	158	1.1
1994 (est)	26.2	120	0.302	180	1.2
1995 (est)	29.3	134	0.362	215	1.2

Source: IPS/Mintel 1996.

16.9 SUMMARY   The marketing issues facing many tourism sector suppliers relate to the underlying principles of service marketing. Increased intensity of competition, customers demanding higher quality and the increasing power of global companies will mean that marketers will have to become more sophisticated in their approach to the marketplace. There is much to learn from comparing the different approaches adopted by the different sectors which make up the tourism business.

REFERENCES

Abel, S. and Long, A. (1996) Event Sponsorship: does it work? *Admap*, December.

Berry, S. (1996) The Changing Economics of Heritage Tourism: Who Pays and Who Benefits. Proceedings from Tourism and Culture Conference, Northumberland, September 14–17.

Capetown 2004 Olympic Bid Committee (1993) *The Essence of Cape Town's Bid.*

Chataway, C. (1996) Airports in the 21st Century. *The Proceedings of the Chartered Institute of Transport in the UK,* **5**(4), December.

Croston, F. (1997) Continental Bed and Breakfast. *Leisure Management*, January, **17**(1), 12–13.

Davies, S. (1994) *By Popular Demand: A Strategic Analysis of the Market Potential of Museums and Art Galleries in the UK,* Museums and Galleries Commission, London.

Evans, G. (1996) The Millennium Festival and Urban Regeneration – Planning, Politics and the Party. A paper presented to the Tourism and Culture Conference, Northumberland, September 14–17, 91–8.

Getz, D. and Frisby, W. (1988) Evaluating Management Effectiveness in Community-Run Festivals. *Journal of Travel Research*, **27**, Summer, 22–7.

Getz, D. (1990) *Festivals, Special Events and Tourism*, Van Nostrand Reinhold.

Go, F.M. and Pine, R. (1995) *Globalization Strategy in the Hotel Industry*, Routledge, London.

Hewison, R. (1987) *The Heritage Industry, Britain in a Climate of Decline*, Methuen, London.

IHA (1988) Hotels of the Future: Strategies and Action Plan, Paris: International Hotel Association.

Kotler, P., Bowen, J. and Makens, J. (1996) *Marketing for Hospitality and Tourism*, Prentice Hall, Upper Saddle River, New Jersey.

Lea, J. (1988) *Tourism and Development in the Third World*, Routledge, London.

Leiper, N. (1989) Tourism and Gambling. *Geo Journal*, **19**(3), 269–75.

Loverseed, H. (1994) Theme Parks in North America, *The Economist Intelligence Unit, Travel and Tourism Analyst*, No. 4, London.

Lyon, P., Taylor, S. and Smith, S. (1994) McDonaldization: A Reply to Ritzer's Thesis, a discussion paper in *International Journal of Hospitality Management*, **13**(2), 95–9.

MacCannell, D. (1976) *The Tourist: a New Theory of the Leisure Class*, Schocken, New York.

Mayfield, T.L. and Crompton, J.L. (1995) The Status of the Marketing Concept Among Festival Organizers. *Journal of Travel Research*, Spring, 14–22.

McGuffie, J. (1993) CRS Development in the Hotel Sector, *Economist Intelligence Unit, Travel and Tourism Analyst*, No. 2, London.

Middleton, V.T.C. (1994) *Marketing in Travel and Tourism*, Butterworth-Heinemann, Oxford.

Poon, A. (1993) All Inclusive Resorts, *Economist Intelligence Unit, Travel and Tourism Analyst*, No. 2, London.

Powers, T.F. (1995) *Introduction to Management in the Hospitality Industry,* 5th edition, Wiley, New York.

Prentice, R. (1993) *Tourism and Heritage Attractions,* Routledge, London.

Renaghan, L.M. (1993) International Hospitality Marketing. In *The International Hospitality Industry, Organizational and Operational Issues* (eds P. Jones and A. Pizam), Pitman, London.

Ritzer, G. (1993) The Mcdonaldization of Society: An Investigation into the Changing Character of Contemporary Social Life, Pine Forge Press, Newbury Park.

Roche, M. (1993) Mega-Events and Urban Policy. *Annals of Tourism Research*, **21**, 1–19.

Rogers, A. and Slinn, J. (1993) *Tourism: Management of Facilities,* Pitman, London.

Schlentrich, U.A. and Ng, D. (1994) Hotel Development Strategies in Southeast Asia: The Battle For Market Dominance. In *Tourism, The State of The Art* (eds A.V. Seaton *et al.*), Wiley, Chichester.

Thomas, C. (1993) Garden Festival Wales, *Insights,* English Tourist Board, November, p. C19–31.

Walker, C. (1995) Hospitality Industry Revival? *Insights*, English Tourist Board, London, pp. A61–6.

Wexler, M.S. (1993) Who does the cooking? *Hotels,* May.

Wheatcroft, S. (1994) *Aviation and Tourism Policies: Balancing the Benefits,* Routledge, London.

17 Marketing destinations

OBJECTIVES

This chapter explains:

● the principles of marketing destinations;
● the composite elements which make up the destination;
● the theory of the tourism area life cycle and its limitations;
● the various marketing techniques applied to tourism destinations.

17.1 INTRODUCTION

The term destination has been applied to a country, a region within a country a city or coastal resort. The marketing task is similar in all cases in that it concerns:

● the development of tourism offerings to appeal to various markets;
● drawing on special appeals for promotional purposes;
● management of demand;
● monitoring social, economic and environmental impacts resulting from the development of tourism.

17.2 THE PRINCIPLES OF DESTINATION MARKETING

To understand the principles of destination marketing it is important to comprehend what is meant by the term tourism destination. The tourism destination comprises a number of elements which combine to attract visitors to stay for a holiday or day visit. There are four core elements: prime attractors, built environment, supporting supply services, and atmosphere or ambiance. They are outlined in Table 17.1.

Within this context, Garnham (1995) describes the elements which constitute a sense of place, such as architectural style, natural setting, use of local building materials, cultural diversity, societal values and public environments.

It would, therefore, be misleading to define the destination as a composite product, for this implies that it can be marketed as a packaged bundle of benefits in the same way as a fast moving consumer item. As the major appeal to the visitors revolves around prime attractors and cultural attributes of the host community, the offering is far more complicated than that of a product. In this respect, the elements of the

Table 17.1 Characteristics of a destination

	Comment	*Example*
Prime attractors	The main attractors which appeal to the visitor and which differentiate one destination from another, some of which are international, others appealing to a country or on a regional basis	Acropolis in Athens; Pyramids in in Egypt; Niagara Falls, USA; Taj Mahal, India
Built environment: physical identity	The physical layout of a destination including waterfronts, promenades, historic quarters and commercial zones. Major elements of infrastructure such as road and rail networks, plus open spaces and communal facilities	Boston Waterfront; London Docklands; Venetian canals; Roman Quarter in Paris
Supporting supply services	Essential facilitating services such as accommodation, communications, transport, refreshment and catering, entertainment, amenities	Essential at all destinations
Sociocultural dimensions	Cultural attributes – bridges between past and present, the mood or atmosphere ranging from sleepy to vibrant. The degree of friendliness and cohesion between the host community and visitors	Chaotic transport of Delhi, India; the salsa music of La Habana, Cuba; the friendliness of the Greek islands

destination mix are in most cases inherited from previous generations. They can be classified as external factors which the marketer is not in a position to control. Furthermore, the mix between public and private sector provision make traditional approaches to branding and service range planning difficult to apply. The other main difference is that the visitor also becomes part of the overall appeal (or otherwise), especially given the changed patterns of behaviour of visitors when at a destination. They form an integral part of the contemporary destination:

> Tourist destinations – resorts, sights, heritage centres and even entire countries – are all places removed from the everyday concerns that revolve around the home, the family and work, at least as far as visitors are concerned. The tourist experience is thus marked as distinct in both spatio-temporal terms and also in the kinds of behaviour both expected and indulged in.
>
> *(Meethan, 1996, p. 179)*

17.2.1 Three key influences

In summary there are three constituent elements which affect the degree of control (or lack of it) in the marketing of a destination. These elements affect the formulation of principles underlying destination marketing. Admittedly, the marketer might be able to encourage the way in which the built environment is developed. He or she may also be able to affect the management of demand. Nevertheless, three powerful influences shape the form of tourism marketing at most destinations: natural resources, climate and culture.

(a) Natural resources

The natural resources endowed on destinations often form the primary attraction(s) which stimulate visitor interest. They range from sandy beaches and tropical jungle to high level mountain paths or spas. The landscape is a crucial factor for most destinations throughout the world and for the most part it is considered a 'public good'. This means that it belongs to the people of the country in which it is situated and in theory does not have a commercial value as such. At many destinations there is no direct charge to view such priceless assets, they simply come as part of the package. Obviously, the degree of exploitation and commercialization of such 'free goods' is the subject of controversy. In some cases, what were traditionally public goods to be enjoyed by all have been developed into commercial enterprises. The great spas of the world, such as Baden Baden in Germany, or the shores of the Dead Sea in Israel provide a good example:

> The traditional spa still focuses on cures, some tapping the earth's inner geology, exploiting thermal muds or waters, others exploiting the mineral richness of the sea.

> *(Tree, 1996)*

(b) Climate

Another primary factor is climate. Some holidaymakers travel primarily to escape the climate of their home region. Some like it hot, others seek snow and those who prefer it humid and warm search for tropical resorts. North Europeans are renowned for their search for the sun.

(c) Culture

The culture of a destination relates to both current ways of life and past times. It also includes the interpretation of historical events, the existence of buildings and monuments, many of which transcend any planned collection of visitor attractions. Culture also encompasses ways of life of the host population, in both negative and positive terms.

These three influences, above all else, are endowed on destinations; they are the very substance of the core offering.

17.2.2 Sustainable development

Human involvement obviously shapes the development process and in most destinations there has been a considerable impact base of natural resources in the area. Such development is the subject of controversy expressed in the literature. The guiding principles which can be distilled from this debate are that tourism marketers should aim to consider the following:

- adaptation of long term principles of sustainability in development;
- encouraging only development which does not radically alter the balance of the destination economy;
- seeking opinion from all quarters of the destination including local community groups as well as trade organizations;

- projecting the image of the destination to reflect all aspects of life at the destination, not only those associated with paradise;
- managing demand to avoid the excesses of tourism negativism;
- reviewing technical guidelines such as the physical and social carrying capacity of a destination on a regular basis.

17.3 CLASSIFICATION OF RESORTS

While some commentators argue that almost every city, resort or countryside region has an appeal to the visitor, it is only those which have sufficient primary attractors which become classical resorts, such as Hawaii or Prague. Other secondary destinations develop for a number of reasons. A classification could be made as follows:

17.3.1 Classic resorts

A destination where the natural, cultural or historical appeal encourages long stay holidays. The classic seaside resorts of San Sebastian and St Tropez have, for example, sustained a long heritage in attracting visitors, as have the pilgrimage sites of the world, such as the Taj Mahal in India, the Acropolis in Athens, Lourdes in France, or Niagara Falls in New York State.

17.3.2 Natural landscape or wildlife tourism resorts

These are the destinations which have high natural appeal and are the habitats of such rare species of flora, fauna or wildlife that they stimulate international appeal, places such as the Galapagos Islands in Ecuador, or the Serengeti wildlife reserve in East Africa.

17.3.3 Business tourism destinations

This is where an industrial or commercial centre rebuilds its historic quarter, and its retailing and entertainment sectors to encourage longer stays by business executives and partners. This is very often accompanied by a thriving corporate hospitality sector, and a strong desire on the part of the destination to heighten image through events marketing. Manchester, in the north west of England, has striven to build its tourism base in this way, as has Glasgow in Scotland.

17.3.4 Stopover destinations

Such places are situated half way between generating areas and holiday destinations. They are often characterized by having a wide ranging budget accommodation sector and a strong mix of restaurants and cafés. Classic examples are Calais or Boulogne in France.

17.3.5 Short break destinations

This type of destination has national appeal and very often international appeal if suitable attractions exist. The destination will range from small countryside towns to capital cities; places such as Pisa, Bruges and Amsterdam.

17.3.6 Day visitor destination

The most common of all destinations is the one which attracts primarily regional demand, the day visitor. They range from seaside resorts to major retailing centres in all parts of the world.

17.4 MARKETING METHODOLOGY

While the principles of marketing planning and tasks undertaken at a tactical level are similar to those deployed by enterprises, there are two fundamental differences which modify marketing methodology used by destinations. Seaton and Bennett (1996: 351) comment:

> Destination marketing is **always** an intentional or uninentional collaboration simply because all the tourism organizations marketing themselves in an area have some impact upon perceptions of the overall destination. Destination marketing at its best involves planned cooperation, coordination and linkages between tourism organizations in a country or region, not least in generating or obtaining funds through which the destination can be promoted coherently to its target markets.

Thus, any tourism office responsible for marketing a destination will usually take on a role of providing a core strategy document. This will outline the way in which private and public sector organizations can coordinate resources to develop and promote a destination. In some instances, a tourism authority will achieve some degree of success in planning tourism development, monitoring progress and communicating the principles and targets widely. In other instances the tourism authority does little more than disseminate promotional material produced by a tourism association or group of traders.

Tourism offices vary considerably as to levels of responsibility, resourcing and marketing planning undertaken. Unfortunately, most fit the promotional agency role, rather than coordinating all of the marketing functions.

17.4.1 Strategy formulation

In terms of strategy formulation, Cooper (1995) refers to the classic approaches, such as those of Porter (1980) and Jain (1985) used in strategic development. He argues that it is possible to use Jain's strategic thrust options to locate the positions taken by offshore islands of the UK, as shown in Figure 17.1, and postulates that the framework could well be useful to other destinations.

In terms of planning the future development of such island destinations, Cooper argues that that the traditional strategic planning approaches might be inappropriate:

> Indeed, the island case studies in this paper demonstrate the need for tailor-made approaches to the destination strategies; approaches which recognize the distinctive context of tourism destinations in general and islands in particular.
>
> *(Cooper, 1995, p. 207)*

17.4.2 The marketing planning steps

As part of the marketing planning process the tourism authority is likely to follow an approach as outlined by Laws (1995: 106), which sets out a diagnosis, prognosis and

Competitive position	Stages of Industry Maturity			
	Embryonic	*Growth*	*Mature*	*Aging*
Dominant	Fast grow Start-up	Fast growth Attain cost leadership Renew Defend position	Defend position Attain cost leadership Renew Fast grow	Defend position Focus Renew Grow with industry
Strong	Start-up Differentiate Fast grow	Fast grow Catch-up Attain cost leadership Differentiate	Attain cost leadership Renew, focus Differentiate Grow with industry	Find niche Hold niche Hang-in Grow with industry Harvest
Favourable	Start-up Differentiate Focus Fast Grow	Differentiate, focus Catch-up Grow with industry	Harvest hang-in Find niche, hold niche Renew, turnaround Differentiate, focus Grow with industry * JERSEY * GUERNSEY	Retrench Turnaround
Tenable	Start-up Grow with industry Focus	Harvest, catch-up Hold niche, hang-in Find niche Turnaround Focus Grow with industry	Harvest Turnaround Find niche Retrench * ISLE OF MAN * SMALLER CHANNEL ISLANDS	Divest Retrench
Weak	Find niche Catch-up Grow with industry	Turnaround Retrench	Withdraw Divest	Withdraw

Figure 17.1 Guide to strategic thrust options. *Source*: Cooper (1995) as adapted from the previous work of Jain (1985).

setting of objectives stage, which leads to implementation and monitoring. This approach is based on a systematic form of marketing planning, although in reality this is an idealized form which is amended to suit the vision, competency and resource base of a destination. A tourism office following this type of approach would undertake the series of steps outlined below.

(a) Market audit

This would include:

- an analysis of existing supply facilities, identifying gaps and oversupply;
- visitor surveys, which indicate flows of visitors, trends and profiles, including origin of the trip, length of stay, socioeconomic detail, level of spend and attitude towards the destination;
- statement of intent on the part of suppliers as to the direction of their businesses, levels of investment and the nature of their focused marketing activity.

(b) Marketing strategy

The audit would enable the tourism office to analyse the strengths of the resort in relation to market trends. It would also enable the authority to set down guidelines for development.

(c) Tactical marketing plans

Many tourism authorities are then able to prepare one-year rolling action plans in which tactical details and programmes of work are delineated.

(d) Monitoring and control

The audit itself will probably provide an annual review of activity and a collection of data. There will also be opportunities to introduce other monitoring exercises to review other projects.

17.5 TOURISM DESTINATION LIFE CYCLE

During the past 150 years tourism has witnessed an evolutionary pattern of resort development. This has been fuelled initially by transport innovation – in rail transport and to a lesser extent in cruise liners, then by the car and aeroplane in the latter decades of the twentieth century.

The nature of the marketing strategy adopted by a destination, it is argued, is often dictated by the tourism destination life cycle, otherwise known as the tourism area life cycle (TALC) (Butler, 1980: 5). Like the product life cycle, the tourism destination life cycle follows a pattern as outlined in Figure 17.2.

The assumption is that at each stage, the tourism marketer will plan the marketing effort to fit the next predicted phase of development, or possibly in the later stages, the resort's ultimate decline.

Furthermore, the theoretical perspective suggests that the destination will appeal to different markets as it matures. In this respect it fits with Plog's consumer typology framework (1974) which suggests that the adventurous outgoing visitor (allocentric) seeks the unfamiliar and unspoilt destination. Those who are more passive and like the familiar (psychocentrics) prefer the mature destination. Midcentrics (a mixture of the two extremes) head for resorts which are more developed, or heading for maturity.

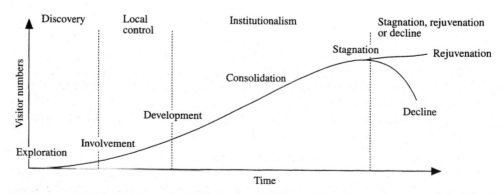

Figure 17.2 Hypothetical tourist area life cycle. *Source*: Butler (1980) adapted by Cooper *et al.* (1993).

17.5.1 Limitations of the concept

The concept is very appealing and has been the subject of both theoretical analysis and practical application during the past decade (Prosser, 1995: 318–28). Most authors have concluded that despite its limitations, the life cycle concept is useful, but has not been without its critics (Cooper, 1994: 28–39). The discussion highlights a number of limitations:

- As with the product life cycle, the TALC tends to be deterministic in approach, assuming that the resort will almost inevitably progress from one stage to another. This, in some cases, is borne out by empirical observation. Spanish coastal destinations, such as Benidorm, Malaga and Torremelinos, have progressed through the twentieth century from fishing villages to major resorts, having reached stages of stagnation or early rejuvenation. However, it is possible that resorts developing in other parts of the world, such as Turkey or Malaysia, might take less than 20 years to reach a similar stage of maturity.
- The second point relates to the problem of identifying when a particular stage in the cycle has been reached, especially between the exploration and exploitation stages (see Figure 17.2). The point of stagnation is more obvious. Hotels change use, little investment is ploughed into entertainment and refreshment facilities, and infrastructure shows obvious need of modernization or repair. Many north European seaside resorts exhibit these symptoms and have been the subject of a number of reports (Middleton, 1991). Classic economic theory would suggest that such resorts die, but political involvement means that rejuvenation is often the preferred option. Is there such a stage as terminal decline for destinations or will there always be a residual day visit or short break market?
- Defining and analysing destinations as a whole might be misleading. Certain parts of cities or destinations might suffer from stagnation while other parts flourish.
- As a conclusion, critics suggest that as a forecasting tool it is simplistic and there is often a lack of comparative data to enable tourism marketers to predict future demand with any degree of certainty as circumstances and locality are so different (Choy, 1992; Douglas, 1996: 1–22).

17.5.2 Destination image

Of all of the marketing management tasks, one of the most important for the tourism officer is to develop or maintain the destination image in line with the visitor groups being targeted. Image is therefore considered integral to the destination and is a well researched area in tourism (Gartner, 1993; Echtner and Ritchie, 1993).

The potential customer (rather than the repeat visitor) has little perception about the marketing of a destination. While the overall image might be imprecise, it does however provide a connected set of beliefs and attitudes based on word of mouth, pictorial reference, editorial copy and destination publicity. Within the context of urban tourism Bates (1995) comments:

> Each well known city in the world may be represented by a small series of iconic images or even one. These, as recognizable views of the city or some detail within it, are semiological signs which are also representations of others, the objects illustrated, objects of the 'Tourism Gaze'. Through repetition in the media these images are widely recognized and collectively understood.

A visitor, for example, might assess in a subconscious manner three or four potential destinations. Those which score high with favourable comments are likely to fare better than those with negatives, as the latter are considered much harder to change. Consider, for example, the following editorial comment on crime (*Sunday Times*, 1996):

Clampdown on conmen

Tourist boards have traditionally adopted a three-monkeys approach to crime against visitors. So it's good to see the Chinese authorities take a more honest stance on the current predicament at the Three Gorges. Holidaymakers are flocking to the area before it is flooded by the damming of the Yangtze River, and conmen are taking full advantage of the increase in business to offer bogus tours at vastly inflated prices. In response, officials have set up a telephone hotline on which sightseers can register complaints and future sightseers be forewarned. While the rest of the travel industry whistles, we highlight some of the best-known blackspots. Gypsies outside the Forum in Rome (who distract you with a newspaper and rob you); taxi-drivers in Prague (they'll do anything, including threatening to electrocute you); Nairobi (Nairobbery to its victims) for the old something-on-your-coat-trick; car-jacking in Johannesburg, and on the regular train journey from Cuzco to Machu Picchu, no matter what precautions you take, somebody will lighten your load.

Another aspect of negative image related to security is the visual imagery of unrest presented in the media. For example, the development of tourism in the Middle East hinges on the continuation of the peace process. Egypt's tourism arrivals mirror the media coverage of Iraq and Islamic fundamentalist campaigns. When scenes of violence or military intervention are exposed arrivals fall dramatically, as evidenced in the percentage changes of international arrivals recorded in Table 17.2.

Intermediaries

Most studies have concentrated on evaluating visitor perceptions of a destination either by using qualitative research, such as focus groups or in-depth interviews, or by quantitative studies, which assess values and attitudes using scaling techniques. One interesting area of work has been a study of tour operator executive attitudes towards the attributes, benefits and disadvantages of destinations in Latin America (Lumsdon and Swift, 1994). They are that the views of intermediaries warrant much more research than has been undertaken to date.

Table 17.2 Percentage changes of international arrivals recorded – Egypt

Year	Percentage change
1990	−12.4
1991	+34.9
1992	−22.2
1993	+2.8
1994	+21.9

Source: World Tourism Organization (1996).

17.5.3 Branding destinations

The dilemma for tourism authorities is how to respond to image perception, or more importantly, how to create an appropriate image which is both appealing yet truthful in content and style. This is currently an area which is difficult to assess.

Some destinations have chosen to use branding as a technique to communicate an image. Branding is defined in this context as the use of a combination of name, logo and design standards which make up a core identity for a product or service which differentiates it from competitor offerings.

The arguments for branding have been presented by a number of authors. The counter argument is that branding is problematic at destinations because of the composite amalgam of interests and companies represented. Many will have far stronger brand images than the location itself. Furthermore, controlling brand development or extension is also complicated, especially when attempting to communicate with a wide ranging group of market segments from different generating countries.

17.6 TOURISM DEVELOPMENT AT DESTINATIONS

The tourism marketer will also be involved in the process of developing a destination, either in terms of new building at established resorts or more likely in the rejuvenation of old ones. Part of the process involves estimating future demand, as in a feasibility study. Increasingly, however, emphasis is being placed on a multidisciplinary approach to evaluating the likely impacts of any development, both in a strategic sense and in more detail on a local basis. One of the major impacts is that of direct and indirect economic effects, as developed by tourism economists. Table 17.3 estimates direct benefits accruing to economies from tourism. More important is the need to develop techniques which monitor other impacts.

17.6.1 Management techniques

Strategic environmental assessment would analyse impacts relating to the changes of travel patterns, investment, employment and environmental factors resulting from a major project such as an airport extension. There would also be a need for an environmental impact study which would most probably focus on areas in close proximity to

Table 17.3 The multiplier effect for gross output (US dollars in billions)

Region	Direct	Indirect and induced	Total impact
Africa	38	95	133
North America	720	1 801	2 522
Latin America	107	268	376
Caribbean	42	104	145
Asia/Pacific	751	1 878	2 629
Western Europe	844	2 110	2 954
Eastern Europe	340	849	1 189
Middle East	59	147	205
World total	2 901	7 252	10 153

Source: WTTC (1993).

a proposed development. This is commonplace in many western countries where localized developments are planned in sensitive areas, such as a timeshare complex in or near to a national park.

The literature refers to four analytical frameworks:

(a) Environmental audit

As part of the sustainable development process of destinations it has been suggested that destinations review their policies and practices. Goodall and Stabler (1992) provide a framework for environmental evaluation which could be applied by a destination, as shown in Figure 17.3.

(b) Environmental impact analysis

Increasingly there is concern that major developments, such as integrated resorts, will lead to heavy impacts on the environment. For example, at Cancun in Mexico there are currently concerns that the large number of visitors will lead to problems of pollution and destruction of a coral reef. Environmental impact assessment attempts to set out the nature, magnitude and degree of importance of particular impacts which would occur as a result of a major piece of infrastructure being built, for example, a resort complex at a destination. In the UK there are guidelines for those planning projects: 'Preparation of Environmental Statements for Planning Projects that Require Environmental Assessment – A Good Practice Guide'. An environmental assessment would be expected to include:

- a comprehensive description of the development proposed including the site, designs envisaged, size or scale of development;
- sufficient data to allow the assessment of the main effects which the development is likely to have on the environment;
- a discussion of the likely significant effects relating to humans, flora and fauna, soil, water and air, climate and the landscape, material assets and cultural heritage;
- with regard to serious adverse effects, the statement should recommend possible alternatives, or remedial measures.

Increasingly, tourism marketers are becoming involved in such exercises with designers and developers. Not only are estimates of demand the key to understanding the possible impact level on any given community and landscape but they can also be used to plan future strategy.

(c) Carrying capacity

An associated concept is known as the carrying capacity. This concept relates to the relationship between level of demand and magnitude of impacts reflecting all aspects of community life from the ecological, economic and sociocultural norms (Canastrelli and Costa, 1991). Cooper et al. (1993: 94–107) define carrying capacity as 'that level of tourist presence which creates impacts on the host community, environment and economy that are acceptable to both tourists and hosts, and sustainable over future time periods'.

Cooper rightly refers to the 'tourist presence' because carrying capacity is not simply

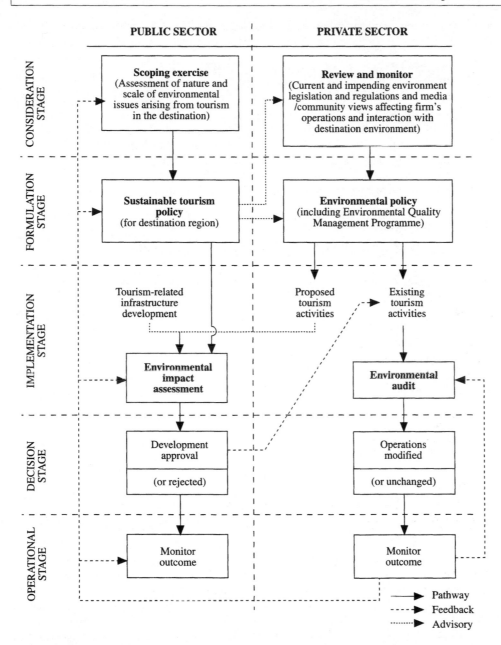

Figure 17.3 Framework for environmental evaluation of a tourism destination.
Source: Goodall and Stabler (1992).

a measure of tourist numbers but reflects length of stay, degree of concentration, seasonality and what visitors actually do when at a destination. Elliott (1990) defined a number of thresholds of capacity which are summarized as follows:

● the level above which the character of the place is damaged and the quality of the experience is threatened;
● the level above which physical damage occurs;

● the level above which irreversible damage takes place;
● the level above which the local community suffers unacceptable side effects.

Such measures might be quantified in terms of each specific destination. One measure is the trip index, a measurement of the proportion of a trip undertaken at a particular destination. The calculation involves dividing the length of stay at a destination by the length of the total trip, multiplied by 100.

While carrying capacity techniques offer opportunities for diagnosis, invariably the evaluation of a saturation point at a given stage in the destination's life cycle (Martin and Uysal, 1990: 327–33) is subject to managerial judgement. The lack of resources to control demand can bring major disbenefits. Shackley (1996: 5) makes the point well when discussing the growth of wildlife tourism in Africa:

> An area will not attract visitors if it is not adequately maintained or has inadequate infrastructure. Successful public-private sector partnerships have been formed (as in the case of the private game reserves within the Kruger National Park, South Africa) but tension is the more usual result. Take the case of Namibia which has a flourishing wildlife tourism industry. The extensive Namibian National Parks system comes under the control of the Ministry of Wildlife Conservation and Tourism which is systematically starved of capital funds. Visitor revenues received from (inadequate) entrance fees are not returned to park management which is therefore unable to maintain park accommodation to the high standard required by affluent western visitors. The result is that private companies are building high quality visitor accommodation outside major parks ...

This example highlights the need for strategic evaluation over an entire destination area rather than at specific locations in isolation.

(d) Community assessment techniques

The case for community participation in the development of destinations and the particular form that this might take is reasonably well documented in the literature (Getz, 1983: 239–63; Haywood, 1998: 154–67; Keogh, 1990: 449–65). This is particularly the case when the ratio of tourists to visitors is high. Table 17.4 illustrates the tourism intensity ratio in relation to Costa Rica in Central America. The ratio illustrates increasing pressure from visitors.

The result has been a number of models which now include the host community as an integral part of the tourism development process. This begs the question as to what is meant by the host community? The case for community involvement in tourism planning is beyond question but de Kadt (1992) is concerned that this is genuine participation by a wide range of groups in society and not those with a potential to gain commercially. Murphy (1985: 36–8) argues that there is a need to balance the pure business and development approach with a more community-oriented approach which 'views tourism as a local resource'. He adds, moreover, that 'the management of this resource for the common good and future generations should become the goal and criterion by which the industry is judged'.

Murphy outlines the main components for a community oriented tourism strategy as shown in Figure 17.4. The four main areas of consideration are:

● management issues, such as bringing all parties together;
● social and cultural considerations, such as local heritage;

Table 17.4 Tourism intensity ratio for Costa Rica, Central America

Year	Tourist arrivals (million)	Estimated population	TIR	
1990	435 037	3	14.50	
1991	504 649	3	16.82	
1992	610 591	3.1	20.35	
1993	684 005	3.2	21.36	
1994	761 448	3.3*	23.07	
1995	792 287	3.3*	24.00	(i.e. 2 visitors to 1 local resident)

* Estimate

$$\text{Tourist intensity ratio} = \frac{\text{International visitor arrivals}}{\text{Population}} \times 100$$

The table assumes a population growth averaging at between 1–2%
Other possible measures would be:

$$\text{Tourist density ratio} = \frac{\text{Av. length of stay} \times \text{No. of visitors}}{365 \times \text{Area in sq kms}} \times 100$$

This allows assessment of length of stay in relation to size of country.

● business and economic considerations;
● environmental and accessibility matters.

These all impact on the central focus, the community's tourist product, which is similar to the traditional tourism offering, but this model emphasizes what the community wants to present to the tourism market. There are a number of studies which focus on measuring the impact of tourism on changing attitudes of the host population (Lankford and Howard, 1993: 121–39). One study suggests that the nature of community involvement and resistance to tourism might be determined by the length of residency in any given area (McCool and Martin, 1994: 29–34).

It is precisely this type of tourism development framework which offers the promise of positive long term tourism benefit. It would be naive to present it as a panacea for all development processes, but quite clearly this approach fits into a framework of sustainability.

The tourism marketer needs to remain conversant with the models and techniques applied to the evaluation of environmental and social impact. It is reaffirmation of the fundamental principle indicated in the definition of tourism marketing (Chapter 2), which states that consumer satisfaction can only take place within the framework of environmental and societal responsibility. Those destinations which fail to grasp this will find it difficult to maintain a competitive edge. There will be many competitor destinations where environment and social integration are more accurately balanced.

17.7 SUMMARY The marketing of a destination brings together all sectors within the tourism business. The overall appeal of a destination depends on the degree of attractiveness of both the human and natural resource base as well as the built environment.

The marketing of a destination is a complex task involving the coordination of a range of public and private concerns as well as the host community in projecting an appealing image and commensurate tourism offering for the would be visitor. This is a challenging task given the lack of control over the components which make up a composite offering.

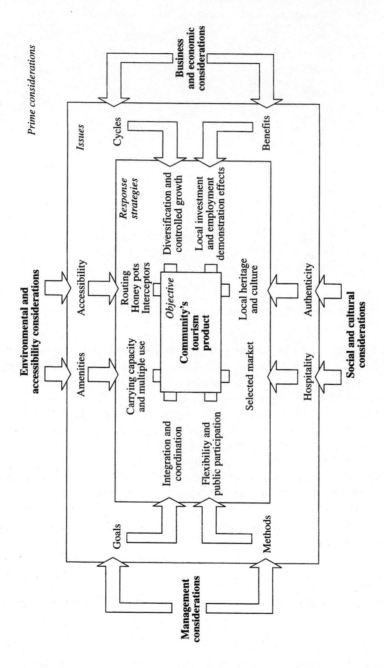

Figure 17.4 Major components for a community-oriented tourism strategy. *Source:* Murphy (1985).

REFERENCES

Bates, S. (1995) From Drawing Boards to Drawing Crowds: Constructing the Image of the City. A paper presented to The Urban Environment-Tourism International Conference, South Bank University, September 11–12.

Butler, R.W. (1980) The concept of a tourist area cycle of evolution: implications for management of resources. *Canadian Geographer,* **XXIV**(1), 5.

Canastrelli, E. and Costa, P. (1991) Tourist Carrying Capacity, A Fuzzy Approach. *Annals of Tourism Research,* **18**, 295–311.

Choy, D.J.L. (1992) Life Cycle Models of Pacific Island Destinations. *Journal of Travel Research,* **30**(3), 26–31.

Cooper, C. (1994) The destination image. In *Tourism: The State of the Art* (eds A.V. Seaton *et al.*), Wiley, Chichester.

Cooper, C. (1995) Strategic Planning for Sustainable Tourism: The Case of the Offshore Islands of the UK. *Journal of Sustainable Tourism,* **3**(4), 191–209.

Cooper, C., Fletcher, J., Gilbert, D. and Wanhill, S. (1993) *Tourism: Principles and Practice.* Pitman, London.

de Kadt, E. (1992) Making the Alternative Sustainable: Lessons from Development for Tourism. In *Tourism Alternatives: Potentials and Problems in the Development of Tourism* (eds V.L. Smith and W.R. Eadington), University of Pennsylvania Press and the International Academy of Tourism Study, Philadelphia.

Douglas, N. (1996) Applying The Life Cycle Model to Melanesia. *Annals of Tourism Research,* **24**(1), 1–22.

Echtner, C.M. and Ritchie, J.R.B. (1993) The measurement of destination image: an empirical assessment. *Journal of Tourism Studies,* **34**(4), 3–13.

Elliot, H. (1990) Task Force Ordered to Assess Tourism Impact. *The Times,* 2 August.

Garnham, H.L. (1995) *Maintaining the Spirit of the Place.* PDA Publishers, Arizona.

Gartner, W.C. (1993) Image Formation Process. *Journal of Travel and Tourism,* **2**, 191–216.

Getz, D. (1983) Capacity to Absorb Tourism: Concepts and Implications for Strategic Planning. *Annals of Tourism Research,* **10**, 239–63.

Goodall, B. and Stabler, M. (1992) Environmental Auditing in the Quest for Sustainable Tourism: The Destination Perspective. A paper presented to the Tourism in Europe, The 1992 Conference, Durham, 8–10 July.

Haywood, K.M. (1988) Responsible and Responsive Tourism Planning in the Community. *Tourism Management,* **9**(2), 105–18.

Jain, S.C. (1985) *Marketing, Planning and Strategy.* South Western Publishing Co., Cincinnati.

Keogh, B. (1990) Public Participation in Community Tourism Planning. *Annals of Tourism Research,* **17**, 449–65.

Lankford, S.V. and Howard, D.R. (1993) Developing a Tourism Impact Attitude Scale. *Annals of Tourism Research,* **21**, 121–39.

Laws, E. (1995) *Tourism Destination Management,* Routledge, London.

Lumsdon, L.M. and Swift, J.S. (1993) Latin American Cities – the Future of Tourism, a paper presented to the European Association of Development Research and Training Institutes (EADI) 7th General Conference, 'Transformation and Development: Eastern Europe and the South', Berlin, September.

Martin and Uysal (1990) An Examination of the Relationship Between Carrying Capacity and the Tourism Lifecycle: Management and Policy Implications. *Journal of Environmental Management.*

McCool, S.F. and Martin, S.R. (1994) Community Attachment and Attitudes toward Tourism Development. *Journal of Travel Research,* **32**(3), 29–34.

Meethan, K. (1996) Place, Image, and Power: Brighton as a Resort. In *The Tourist Image, Myths and Myth Making in Tourism* (ed. T. Selwyn), John Wiley, Chichester.

Middleton, V.T.C. (1991) *The Future of English Smaller Seaside Resorts,* English Tourist Board, London.

Murphy, P.E. (1985) *Tourism, A Community Approach,* Methuen, New York.

Porter, M.E. (1980) *Competitive Strategy: Techniques for analysing industries and competitors,* Collier and Macmillan, Free Press.

Prosser, G. (1995) Tourism Destination Life Cycles, Problems and Prospects. In *Proceedings of the National Tourism and Hospitality Conference* (ed. R.N. Shaw), Council for Australian University Tourism and Hospitality Education, Melbourne.

Seaton, A.V. and Bennett, M.M. (1996) *Marketing Tourism Products,* Thomson Business Press, London.

Shackley, M. (1996) *Wildlife Tourism,* Thomson Business Press, London.

Tree, I. (1996) Feel Good Factor. *Sunday Times, Travel,* 22 December.

WTTC (1993) Report – 1992 Complete Edition, World Travel and Tourism Council, London.

18 International tourism marketing

OBJECTIVES

This chapter explains:

- the principles of international and global marketing;
- the trends towards the globalization of tourism;
- the key issues in the development of international marketing strategies;
- the role of national tourism organizations in marketing countries on an international level.

18.1 INTRODUCTION

In Chapter 1 we concluded that tourism is primarily a business which services local and national markets rather than international markets. Nevertheless, examination of estimates provided by the World Tourism Organization or World Travel and Tourism Council indicates approximately 650 million international arrivals in the year 2000. Therefore, the international share of the market is both large and continues to maintain a sustained growth. Airlines and hotel groups have been at the forefront of the internationalization of tourism but increasingly several tour operators are now trading on an international basis. Furthermore, governments and regional tourism associations continue to build international marketing campaigns to attract foreign visitors. This chapter includes a review of the work of national tourism organizations.

18.2 THE PRINCIPLES OF INTERNATIONAL MARKETING

The principles of international marketing are based on the company or country's need to trade in a marketing environment which spans more than a domestic market (Paliwoda, 1986). This applies equally to the tourism market.

18.2.1 Growth and profitability

The primary driving force behind internationalization is growth and profitability which would not be available in a home market. This is more critical in tourism than many other business sectors, for while every country has a propensity to generate and attract visitors, some are primarily generators and others receivers. Those countries and companies which seek to stimulate tourism growth, by necessity, trade in the international environment. Those who specialize in outward bound tourism in any given country are inevitably driven into a wider web of destinations.

18.2.2 Free trade

The second principle is that of free trade which is projected by governments and world organizations such as that administering the General Agreement on Tariffs and Trade. This aims to reduce tariff and non-tariff barriers. Free trade theory assumes that there is a potential to gain differential advantage. In the same way that countries establish leadership in the production of commodities such as wheat and coffee, destinations specialize in different forms of tourism which can use a natural resource base to great effect. Kenya has nature and wildlife tourism, the Caribbean beautiful beaches and the Alps world beating ski slopes. Firms strive to widen these natural differential advantages by exploiting a destination's image in the marketplace.

18.2.3 Derived demand

The third principle of international tourism marketing is that much of it is derived demand stemming primarily from international business and is therefore concentrated in cities. There is a second area of demand, travel undertaken by friends and relatives; for example to weddings, family re-unions and social gatherings.

18.2.4 Economics of scale

The fourth principle is that suppliers seek economies of scale. These can be achieved through the penetration of existing markets and the prospecting of new markets. In this way the tour operator can allay risk of failure by being associated in one market only.

18.2.5 Trends towards globalization

It is necessary to distinguish between the terms international and global marketing as these are often used interchangeably. The process of globalization is described by Levitt (1983: 92):

> A powerful force drives the world toward a converging commonality, and that force is technology. It has proletarianized communication, transport, and travel. It has made isolated places and impoverished people eager for modernity's allurements. Almost everyone, everywhere wants all things they've heard about, seen, or experienced via the new technologies.

Global marketing refers to organizations which literally trade in all regions of the world following a global strategy which identifies only one market – the world. A global company is defined as:

> one that, by operating in more than one country, gains research and development, production, marketing and financial advantages in its costs reputation that are not available in purely domestic competitors.
>
> *(Kotler, Armstrong, Saunders and Wong, 1996: 170)*

There are numerous examples of globalization in other market sectors, such as computer technology, cosmetics and car manufacture. The classic examples in tourism are fast food giants such as McDonald's and Pepsico's Kentucky Fried Chicken. Others are hotel chains, such as those belonging to Groupe Accor or Hilton, which seek to build hotels in all major cities and resorts of the world wherever the market provides opportunity. An increasing number of companies are using acquisition strategies to move towards globalization, for instance British Airways and American Airlines. They are characterized by:

- standardization of operations;
- customer delivery and strategic reach across the world;
- no adherence to country boundaries as target market areas;
- looking for homogeneous markets on a regional scale.

The process also involves innovation, a fusion of creativity and practicality which leads to better ways of doing things on a global basis:

> ... a firm that operates in many countries has this unique opportunity to cross-fertilise ideas from a variety of cultures, styles, attitudes and patterns of human behaviour. To miss such an opportunity is certainly a regrettable failure to capitalise on one of the most important pay-offs of an international presence.
>
> *(Majaro, !993, pp. 256–7)*

International marketing is not the same. The concept underlines that companies and organizations choose to trade on an international scale but only in certain regions, possibly selected countries, certain resorts or cities. For example, a cruise line company such as the Greek shipping company, Festival Cruises, trades in Europe mainly. It offers cruises to the Mediterranean and Scandinavian coasts in summer, the Atlantic islands in the shoulder months and the Caribbean islands in winter. Passengers are drawn mainly from Italy, then north European countries for the most part but also from the American market for the Caribbean cruises (Wickers, 1996). The company trades internationally but is not looking to provide a standardized tourism offering across the world.

18.3 THE PROCESS OF INTERNATIONALIZATION

The development of strategy on an international level requires a detailed evaluation of markets and destinations (Taylor, 1991: 90–105). The process varies according to the type of development envisaged. Hotels are primarily concerned with locational analysis, to determine where to situate their hotels, in order to service an international marketplace. Tour operators, in contrast, devise strategies to source visitors from different generating countries, while at the same time undertaking an intensive screening of suppliers in receiving countries to service the requirements of their package in the host country or countries.

18.3.1 Strategic evaluation

In the case of either the hotel or the tour operator, the process includes the following:

(a) PEST analysis

The PEST analysis involves a detailed investigation of political, economic, social and technological factors. It is an audit of potential risks and opportunities, specifying how they might be managed.

A hotel group, for example, would evaluate not only a series of locations for a hotel within a resort or capital city but also the political, economic, social and technological (PEST) trends within the country. This includes, for example, the analysis of global demographics in relation to a country or region. When tour operators consider the potential of any given regional market, the population base is the first calculation. For example, the North American Free Trade Area (Canada, USA and Mexico) has a population of 370 million whereas Japan has 128 million.

(b) Analysis of market attractiveness

Most international tour operators undertake an analysis of the market attractiveness of competing packages, say from the USA to Central Africa, or Northern Europe to the Middle East. This would include an evaluation of the market size and trends in generating regions, the level of competition, the degree of span and control required to supply a package to this market. Finally, the tour operator would also profile competing destinations within and between world regions, assessing the potential for liaison with the regional or national government, airlines or transport carriers, and local tour operator interest.

(c) Company capability

The degree of market attractiveness would be matched with the company's capability at any given time, especially when one considers the level of capital required, the mix of local and external skills available, and the degree of competitive advantage to be gained by selecting one destination rather than another.

Yip (1992: 29–41) argues that as firms internationalize, they usually pass through three stages:

- Stage one – The organization begins to establish a core strategy which emphasizes international expansion. This is built firmly from a home base. The classic example is of the development of a strong brand at home such as Marriott or Club Mediterranée which is then rolled out internationally.
- Stage two – The second stage relates to the internationalization of core strategy. This might involve modifications to an existing approach to the market but essentially the core remains intact. Examples would include many of the international hotel groups which have a set approach to the market which is adjusted to meet local circumstances if necessary.
- Stage three – The third level of involvement is when the strategy is integrated across several countries such as the approach adopted by major airlines. For example, many airlines now offer standardized service levels across the globe. This stage is reached when a company integrates market, cost and environmental forces into a flexible strategic plan based on company capability.

18.3.2 Level of company commitment

During the process of internationalization the company then decides on the level of commitment at a strategic level. For example, marketing consortiums such as Best Western Hotels bring hundreds of independent hotels to an international marketplace. It is, however, no more than a marketing umbrella for independent hotel chains.

Strategic alliances or joint ventures, such as between airlines like North West and KLM, present a much firmer commitment especially where capital ties are involved. Similarly, franchise agreements are adopted by many of the hotel groups in North America and by some airlines such as British Airways. This approach allows expansion throughout the world without overburdening capital outlay. Of course, the alternative is generic growth through market penetration, which requires substantial capital to achieve territorial growth.

18.3.3 Standardization or customization

One major decision is whether or not to position the tourism offering on a global basis so that the customer can expect the same level of service and benefits throughout the world. The alternative is to modify the service offering to suit a variety of markets from different generating countries and local cultures. In reality, very few offerings are entirely standardized. Some hotel groups and airlines approach the idealized form, but most international tourism offerings are adapted to meet country or regional needs.

Invariably, the overall policy of standardization reflects whichever country or region dominates the market, both culturally and in terms of revenue potential. The rule of thumb appears to be to standardize as much as possible to effect economies of scale, but to adapt where the market dictates. Some international hotels do offer special features and facilities to attract specific markets, for example some offer Japanese food, but in terms of policy the approach is invariably one of standardization.

For tour operators, there are greater barriers to standardization. Factors such as cultural patterns and consumption of tourism vary so widely, markets are increasingly fragmented, language differences prevail, as do local regulations. These factors mean that there has to be a degree of customization of the tourism offering. Nevertheless, in many instances the core offering remains exactly the same. Take any resort beach hotel throughout the world and the only difference in terms of the package offering will be the tour representative and tour company handbook at reception. Hotel staff will speak English primarily to facilitate basic transactions but where a particular nationality prevails, such as German, staff will most probably be trained to speak the language accordingly. Thus, while there is some degree of customization this should not be overstated.

18.4 THE LEVELS OF INTERNATIONALIZATION

Strategic direction is important. Following analysis of the market and company capability, the organization will decide on the level of internationalization. Porter's work (1980) provides a useful guide to the various levels:

- **Competing globally:** The company decides to compete on a global basis to secure maximum use of resources, hence reduction of costs, market advantage and differentiation. The main fast food giants such as Kentucky Fried Chicken, Burger King and McDonald's fall into this category.

- **Global focus:** A key segment of the tourism sector is targeted. This means applying a degree of selectivity, so that while the company competes on a global basis, it is not entirely global in the distribution of outlets. The international hotel sector reflects this approach in that many groups wish to be represented throughout the globe but only in capital and major provincial cities.

- **Regional focus:** Here strategic focus is concentrated in one region as both a generating and destination area, such as in North America or Asia. Many airlines fall into this category. They might fly intercontinental routes but their business is firmly based in one region of the world. The sames applies to other transport operators. Eurolines, as its names suggests, concentrates on European intercity routes.

- **National focus:** This approach consolidates a strong leadership position in a given country in order to compete in a defensive way against international intruders into the market. Many airlines are national flagship carriers or have a powerful market share of a national market.

- **Protected niche:** This involves a selective approach to countries, or appealing to one or more narrow market segments which are capable of development and defence. This is common in speciality tour operation throughout the world.

While tourism is an international business, it is important to remember that many organizations which fall within the tourism sector trade primarily in a local or national market. Most tourism occurs within national boundaries and this in many respects leads to the preparation of a domestic market strategy only for many companies.

Considering the technological advances in the marketplace, especially in terms of the Internet, and global distribution and reservation systems, there are few barriers to entry for the small- to medium-sized company should they seek to develop an international marketing strategy.

18.5 THE INTERNATIONAL MARKETING MIX

The international marketing planning process involves an evaluation of alternative marketing strategies set against the company's capabilities and those of its suppliers. The process is summarized in Figure 18.1.

Organizations usually use the marketing mix framework to unfold strategies. The application of each element will vary according to each specific situation. Consider, for example, a main European based tour operator offering a range of packages for a north European market. The process of development would be as outlined below.

18.5.1 Creating a package

For most tour operators this reflects a major development cost.

(a) Negotiation

When a tour operator designs a package, it might necessitate liaison and negotiation with numerous local subcontractors, or providers, in a number of resorts, such as:

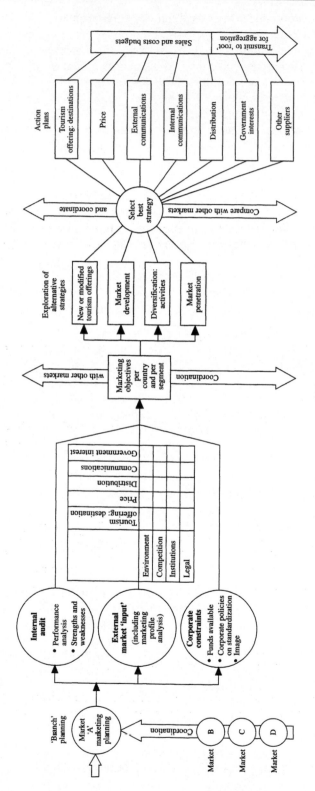

Figure 18.1 A descriptive framework for marketing planning. *Source*: adapted from Majaro (1993).

- owners of self catering accommodation;
- hotel groups – ensuring that the service levels and physical evidence are commensurate with the proposed package;
- transport operators at the airport and resort;
- local tourism officials;
- local tour guides;
- national carriers or other airlines;
- local financial services.

(b) Promotional material (physical evidence)

The imagery of a destination and constituent accommodation bases needs to be represented in promotional material for staff and clients. This will require detailed photographic work as well as the preparation of copy. Image projection has to match reality or otherwise a customer will be disappointed at the trial stage, perhaps to the point of creating negative word of mouth marketing.

(c) Distribution

The tour operator then has to prepare briefing notes about the inclusion of any new destinations in the portfolio for travel agencies, and other intermediaries, including possibly their own 'direct sell' section.

(d) Pricing

The tour operator will decide on price positioning in the market and possibly early booking incentives, or other price discounting techniques if demand is not sufficiently encouraging.

(e) Staff

Staff representatives will be recruited and trained prior to the season, briefings and contact made again with suppliers before destination information is issued, such as customer handbooks at hotel receptions and other elements to reaffirm brand identity. All of the processes will be checked by the management, from arrival at the airport, to booking in at the accommodation base.

(f) Processes

The tour operator needs to ensure that all suppliers are conversant with the processes necessary to book, confirm, and process a customer's stay at a destination. Each locality has its own nuances and customs which need to be assessed in the light of customer expectation. Technological support is vital to the successful management of a holiday, so that data can be easily transmitted between the tour operator and subcontractors.

18.6 NATIONAL TOURISM ORGANIZATIONS

There is another dimension to the marketing of tourism offerings on an international basis, and that is the role of national tourism organizations. The principal roles of such organizations are to identify market segments and promote generalized or specific campaigns to them. Other roles that have been afforded to them are:

- guardian of the image
- scene setter
- trail blazer
- marketing coordinator
- monitor of visitor satisfaction and target markets (Jefferson and Lickorish, 1991).

The interesting point is how such organizations customize campaigns to suit the cultural background of prospective generating countries. A review of the Netherlands Board of Tourism Marketing Plan (1992) is instructive. It outlined in their policy document for 1991–95 the use of seven criteria for the selection of markets, and therefore the level of marketing commitment in each particular market. The criteria were listed as follows:

- **Presence of existing (almost automatic) demand.** Some groups, such as families with young children, select the Netherlands for a second low cost seaside holiday.
- **Prospects.** The estimate of a market increasing from a sending destination.
- **Competition.** The degree of competition from other close destinations.
- **Phase of market development.** The stage of market development from new to saturation.
- **Costs of marketing.** The costs of marketing to generating countries differs, depending on market size and cost of promotion.
- **Level of industry interest.** Given the 50:50 financing system between NBT and the private sector, the level of interest of private parties has to be assessed.
- **Added value.** In some markets, the private sector already commits heavy resources to market penetration, therefore the NBT would be less able to add value to the campaign.

The NBT cross-referenced these criteria against four market zones – the Netherlands, neighbouring countries and other European and intercontinental destinations – in order to fine tune its marketing effort.

One example which illustrates how a plan is executed is the Wales Tourist Board Overseas Marketing Plans for 1995/6. The overall long term strategic objectives of the board at the time were to:

- improve Wales' market share of the overseas visitors that come to Britain;
- develop a clear and cohesive branding for Wales and to improve Wales' image in key markets.

The board had selected a number of markets within north America, Europe, Australasia and Japan. With regard to the latter it is interesting to note how the campaign was structured and budgets allocated. An analysis of the Japanese market by the BTA indicated that outbound travel to Europe had continued to grow in the 1990s, especially women travelling in groups. The reports also indicated that there had been a shift by the more experienced traveller from 'visual tours' to 'journeys of experience'.

Qualitative research indicated that Britain in general but Wales in particular was admired for its friendliness and local life and customs, but that there were several negatives:

Encouraging factors
- History
- Culture
- Language
- Natural beauty
- Sightseeing

Impediments
- Perception of food
- Sombre
- Masculine image
- Distance
- Not fashionable

Source: Wales Tourist Board (1995) based on BTA Tokyo information.

The key market segments were identified as in Table 18.1.
Objectives were set as follows:

- to increase visits to 22 500;
- to increase visitor spend by £3.5 million;
- to improve Wales' market share to 3 per cent.

The marketing tasks for 1995/97 were set out as follows:

- to extend positive image building by increasing core material to the travel trade in a number of planned steps;
- to explain the Celtic roots of European culture so as to appeal to the Japanese respect for 'unique cultural antiquity';
- to publicize aspects unique to Wales across the spectrum of tradition and folk custom;
- to enhance London and Tokyo based travel knowledge of Wales, reinforcing the perception of the 'elegant city Cardiff, capital of the country and people of Wales';
- to expand on existing London and Tokyo based media contacts and to enhance positive perceptions of Wales and its people;
- to enhance Wales' coverage in BTA themed publications;

Table 18.1 Key segments

Office ladies (a major segment)	Wales is well-placed to provide distinctive input to full and semi-packaged UK tours via Japanese HQs.
Semi-packaged London arrivals	Further development of dialogue with London offices is subject to considerable competition!
Honeymooners	Up-market country house hotels of distinction will grow in appeal.
Middle aged ladies (a growing segment)	Europe is preferred destination for 70% polled annually by JAL. Landscape, museums and galleries, and European cultural 'roots' of high potential.
Pre-graduation students and English language study	Cultural events, activity holidays in Snowdonia.
Europe-based 'exiles'	Country house product, cultural and sporting events, products linked to short break air and fly drive packages for German and French markets. Tactical mailings should have strong potential.
UK-based 'exiles'	Further develop editorial in specialist magazines for urban and rural high value products.

Source: Wales Tourist Board Overseas Marketing Plans 1995–6.

- to involve the Japanese community in Wales in marketing activity;
- to develop Wales' trade perception of the Japanese market;
- to familiarize BTA Tokyo information staff with Wales;
- to build links with the Japan Centre, London.

The action plan for 1995/96 is outlined in Figure 18.2. The revenue section is estimated on the basis of advertising support from companies interested in encouraging the Japanese market.

MARKETING/ACTION PLAN 1995/96

1. CONSUMER MARKETING

➤ Consumer brochure – *Wales for free Travellers*. Timing: May '95
BUDGET: £2K   *REVENUE: £17K*   *TOTAL BUDGET: £19K*

➤ National Orchestra – Tour of Japan – Support activity. Timing: December '95
BUDGET: £10K   *TOTAL BUDGET: £10K*

➤ Seminar – An educational for the trade in Wales. Timing: May '95
BUDGET: £1K   *TOTAL BUDGET: £1K*

2. TRADE MARKETING

➤ Elegant Britain Mission – The annual mission to Japan, for destination, attractions and transport products in Tokyo and Osaka with structured sales calls. Timing: May 21–28.
BUDGET: £7K   *TOTAL BUDGET: £7K*

➤ JATA Congress – Osaka – Major trade fair occurring every 2 years. Timing: November 30–December 3.
BUDGET: £7K   *TOTAL BUDGET: £7K*

➤ Miki Travel – Attendance at 2 workshops arranged by Miki in Tokyo and Osaka. Dates to be advised.
BUDGET: £8K   *TOTAL BUDGET: £8K*

➤ Destination Wales – Revision of current brochure in Japanese and English.
BUDGET: £7K   *REVENUE: £1K*   *TOTAL BUDGET: £8K*

➤ Activity – Trade educational for Kayokai and Japanese Trade and London Sales Calls. Timing: Spring and Autumn 1995.
BUDGET: £8K   *TOTAL BUDGET: £8K*

➤ Incentive to Operators – Lovespoon Gift and Harpist to play at events.
BUDGET: £6K   *TOTAL BUDGET: £6K*

➤ TABS – The continued attendance at TABS.
BUDGET: £2K   *TOTAL BUDGET: £2K*

3. PRESS/PR

➤ Any media activity not supported by B.T.A.
BUDGET: £2K   *TOTAL BUDGET: £2K*

REVENUE TARGET: £18K

TOTAL BUDGET: £78K

Figure 18.2
Marketing action plan 1995/96.
Source: Wales Tourist Board Overseas Marketing Plans 1995/96.

18.7 SUMMARY As Keegan (1995: 14–19) comments, global marketing has grown rapidly because the balance between driving forces (market needs and aspirations, technology, cost, quality) and restraining forces (government and commercial barriers to trade, management myopia) has been tipped in favour of the former. Those trading globally will seek to develop leverage in terms of economies of scale, transfer of experience and strategic development. These forces will continue to change the structure of the market and level of competition. The challenge will be for followers to keep up with a core of leaders who will increasingly shape future prospects.

National Tourism Organizations have an important rôle to play in the marketing of destinations previously on a global scale. The example of the Wales Tourist Board Campaign and the Japanese market illustrates the intricacy of detailed tactical planning.

REFERENCES

Jefferson, A. and Lickorish, L. (1991) *Marketing Tourism: A Practical Guide*, Longman, London.

Keegan, W.J. (1995) *Global Marketing Management*, 5th edition, Prentice Hall, Englewood Cliffs, New Jersey.

Kotler, P., Armstrong, G., Saunders, J. and Wong, J. (1996) *Principles of Marketing*, Prentice Hall, London.

Levitt, T. (1983) The Globalization of Markets. *Harvard Business Review,* May to June.

Majaro, S. (1993) *International Marketing, A Strategic Approach to World Markets,* 7th edition, Routledge, London.

Paliwoda, S.J. (1986) *International Marketing,* Heinemann, London.

Porter, M.E. (1980) *Competitive Strategy: Techniques for analyzing industries and competitors*, Collier and Macmillan, Free Press.

Taylor, W. (1991) The logic of global business. *Harvard Business Review,* March–April, 90–105.

Wales Tourist Board (1995) *Overseas Marketing Plans,* Wales Tourist Board, Cardiff.

Wickers, D. (1996) The Class System, *The Sunday Times Travel*, pp. 4–5, December 8.

Yip, G.S. (1992) *Total Global Strategy; Managing for Worldwide Competitive Advantage*, Prentice Hall, New Jersey.

19 Sustainable tourism

OBJECTIVES

This chapter explains:

- the principles of sustainable tourism;
- the distinctions and different terms used to define tourism development and sustainable tourism;
- the applications of sustainability in the tourism sector;
- how the concept of sustainability has been used in the field of marketing;
- a revised code of sustainability which could be adopted by tourism organizations.

19.1 INTRODUCTION

Development studies have not always embraced the tourism sector. Their main concern has been to explain the dynamism of development within an environment which is itself continually changing in a cultural, demographic, economic, social, political and technological context. Issues such as depletion and distribution of resources, competitiveness, globalization and human security have been key themes of discussion, but tourism has been peripheral to the main debate. Liu (1994: 20) argues that:

> The central task of development is to keep a dynamic fit between the development opportunities and industrial capabilities, both of which are determined by its external and internal environment respectively. Nowhere has the tourism industry's lack of control (and one might add, understanding) been more apparent than in the domain of trends and events in its external environment.

It is within the context of tourism development, especially in developing countries, that tourism specialists have begun to appraise the role of tourism within the development process. It is partly a response to the extensive reach of tourism, the rapid increase in demand for long haul tourism and above all else the real concern expressed by pressure groups about the impacts of tourism which have been badly managed (Gunn, 1994: 3; Smith, 1992: 306).

The wide range of perspectives, issues, policies and planning techniques discussed by Gunn and others cannot be restated here in full. Woodcock and France (1994: 111), however, provide a useful summary (Table 19.1) of three perspectives of development discussed by Harrison (1992: 18) in his discussion of tourism in developing countries. Some of the core ideas of tourism planning are, however, incorporated into the discussion.

Planning for sustainable development has now reached a critical point. Inskeep (1994: 7) comments:

> The underlying approach now applied to tourism planning, as well as to other types of development, is that of achieving sustainable development. The sustainable development approach implies that the natural, cultural, and other resources of tourism are conserved for continuous use in the future, while still bringing benefits to the present society.

The main issue of sustainability of tourism, however, has brought considerable criticism of the role of marketing within the process and requires careful consideration (Harris and Leiper, 1995: xxix).

19.1.1 Definitional issues

The fundamental issue of maintaining a balance between tourism and the environment has been the subject of debate since the 1970s. The dynamics of mass tourism were first subjected to critical analysis in the mid-1970s with the publication of influential titles including *The Golden Hordes* (Turner and Ash, 1975). During the 1980s authors such as Gunn (1988), Krippendorf (1987) and Murphy (1985) continued to diagnose the problems of tourism planning, and to offer alternative approaches.

However, much of the discussion in the 1990s has focused on the possibility of stimulating alternative tourism (or responsible tourism) as a solution to the problems of mass tourism, a notion that has been dismissed by a number of authors including Wheeller (1991: 91–5):

> Responsible tourism has grown as a reaction to mass tourism ... I would strongly question this latter assertion – it cannot, by its very nature, be the way forward everywhere and it is, in fact, dangerously misleading. We have, on the one hand, a problem of mass tourism growing globally, out of control, at an alarming rate. And what is our answer? Small-scale, slow, steady controlled development. They just do not add up.

The debate about development *per se* has also been stimulated by governments and world organizations (WTO, 1991). The UN World Commission on the Environment and Development, known as the Brundtland Commission (1987: 43) set clear guidelines for governments to pursue 'development which meets the needs of the present without compromising the ability of future generations to meet their own needs'.

The UN Conference on Environment and Development – the 'Earth Summit' – in Rio (1992) placed increasing pressure on governments to progress development which minimizes further damage to the environment. The participants committed themselves to an Earth Charter on the Environment and Development, as well as agreeing action on climatic change and maintenance of global biodiversity.

Furthermore, 182 governments agreed to Agenda 21 (i.e. for the twenty-first century), which is essentially a set of detailed action plans programming specific actions each country would undertake to meet the aims of sustainable development. In the UK as elsewhere, local governments have been given the key role in ensuring that

Table 19.1 Summary of major theories

Modernization theory	Underdevelopment theory	Sustainable approaches
1.1 Tourism is a mode of modernization enabling LDCs to develop along 'Western' lines.	1.2 Tourism is a new form of imperialism. It leads to the development of DCs at the expense of LDCs. Overdependence on tourism.	1.3 A useful economic activity that benefits hosts and guests. Tourism is not a panacea and should be part of a balanced economy.
2.1 Capital, expertise, technology and ideas originate outside LDCs where they are brought via MNCs. Tourism controlled by MNCs.	2.2 MNCs are main change agents of neocolonialism. MNC control of tourism is a concern.	2.3 Sensitive to needs and aspirations of host population. Local participation in decision-making. Local employment at all levels. Tourism controlled by host community.
3.1 Modernity and tradition seen as antithetical. Culture blocks development. If barriers are removed or minimized, growth can occur.	3.2 Disregard of culture and tradition is a loss to the host community.	3.3 Socially and environmentally considerate. It draws appeal from the total character of the host destination – scenery, history and culture.
4.1 Tourism is large scale, mass package form for foreigners. Market-led.	4.2 Tourists distinct from host population. Mass tourism. Competition among LDCs.	4.3 Scale and pace of tourism development respect character of the destination. Asset-led tourism. Balance between foreign and domestic tourism sought.
5.1 Minorities within destination country seen as change agents – as modernizing elite.	5.2 Existence of minority elites seen as a barrier to development for population as a whole.	5.3 Elitism is not favoured.
6.1 Tourism seen as a generator of employment, hence a benefit.	6.2 Tourism is seen as an exploiter of local labour.	6.3 Tourism seeks to bring varied, attractive and well-paid jobs.
		7.3 Recognition that physical and cultural environments have an intrinsic value that outweighs their value as a tourism asset: enjoyment by future generations should not be prejudiced by short term considerations.

Source: Woodcock and France (1994). Copyright John Wiley & Sons Limited. Reproduced with permission.

Agenda 21 commitments are progressed and this includes many key factors in tourism development, such as environmentally and socially acceptable development of land, sustainable transport, etc. With regard to Agenda 21, the World Travel and Tourism Council, the World Tourism Organization and the World Council and the Earth Council have published *Agenda 21 for the Travel and Tourism Industry: Towards Environmentally Sustainable Tourism,* which sets out the need to recognize the role of tourism in the process of appropriate development and offers a priority action plan for tourism organizations to translate the principles of sustainable tourism into practice.

Sustainable cities

In the literature on development it is recognized that the main issue of the twenty-first century is how to cope with a sustained trend of migration into cities in developing countries (Hall, 1994: 33–4). How cities might be made more sustainable within this context is a daunting task for any planner. Little has been discussed about the role of tourism in relation to other determinants of city growth limits. Lumsdon and Swift (1993) have outlined the implications for gateway cities in Latin America, concluding that visitors will merely bring increased congestion to failing systems. They argue that, in terms of sustainable tourism, gateway cities such as Buenos Aires, Bogota, Caracas and Lima can play a vital role in:

● dispersing visitors;
● offering an alternative holiday mix and hence easing pressure on more environmentally sensitive areas;
● reinforcing the cultural appeal of a particular area of a country;
● dispersing visitors from areas damaged by unmanaged demand;
● improving a country's image.

Their concern is that government and private sector financing will not be forthcoming to improve the core infrastructure of such cities and that tourism developers will move towards enclave tourism to retain their presence at destinations (Ortiz, 1990).

In Europe, there has been a number of studies which have investigated the major issues of tourism in urban areas, particularly a report by Brady, Shipman and Martin (1993) for the EU which recommended a series of pilot projects and further research. Another major EU study, *European Sustainable Cities* (EU, 1994), outlined a range of actionable ideas for developing sustainable cities, but there is little mention of tourism in this document.

A perceptible shift in the debate has also been brought about by the intervention of pressure groups such as the Eco-tourism Society, Tourism Concern and hundreds of localized groups. For example, the Surfrider Foundation campaigns for the protection of Australia's coastline. Ironically, the coast features heavily in the projection of Australia as a destination by the Australian Tourism Commission. Surfrider is seeking to hold back intrusive development of Australia's beaches following a survey undertaken in 1996 which found that 72 per cent of the beaches had development within 250 metres of the high tide mark already, and that 1 in 4 were affected by development proposals. One in 20 had lost their sand dunes and 80 per cent were strewn with litter (*Sunday Times*, 1996).

19.2 THE PRINCIPLES OF SUSTAINABILITY

Several authors have presented the principles of sustainability as they might appertain to tourism (Beaumont *et al.*, 1993: 19; Godfrey, 1995: 233–5). They draw attention to a need to conserve resources, minimize damage to the environment, reduce pollution and achieve social balance which allows host communities to achieve an acceptable equilibrium. From one of many sets of principles provided in the literature, the one presented in Table 19.2 is comprehensive.

19.2.1 Academic discussion

Academic literature on sustainable (also known as responsible, alternative or green) tourism continues to be nothing less than prolific (Cooper, 1995: 191–209; Hall and Butler, 1995: 99–105). Many writers have focused on one particular aspect of the discussion, ecotourism (Cater, 1993: 85–90; Moore and Carter, 1993: 123–30; Valentine, 1993: 107–15) which should not be confused with the broader principles underlying sustainability. Cater (1993), for example, points to the danger of 'viewing eco-tourism as the universal panacea, the eco-tourist as some magic breed, mitigating all tourism's ills'.

Table 19.2 Principles for sustainable tourism

1. USING RESOURCES SUSTAINABLY
    The conservation and sustainable use of resources – natural, social and cultural – is crucial and makes long-term business sense.

2. REDUCING OVER-CONSUMPTION AND WASTE
    Reduction of over-consumption and waste avoids the costs of restoring long-term environmental damage and contributes to the quality of tourism.

3. MAINTAINING DIVERSITY
    Maintaining and promoting natural, social and cultural diversity is essential for long-term sustainable tourism, and creates a resilient base for the industry.

4. INTEGRATING TOURISM INTO PLANNING
    Tourism development which is integrated into a national and local strategic planning framework and which undertakes environmental impact assessments, increases the long-term viability of tourism.

5. SUPPORTING LOCAL ECONOMIES
    Tourism that supports a wide range of local economic activities and which takes environmental costs and values into account, both protects those economies and avoids environmental damage.

6. INVOLVING LOCAL COMMUNITIES
    The full involvement of local communities in the tourism sector not only benefits them and the environment in general but also improves the quality of the tourism experience.

7. CONSULTING STAKEHOLDERS AND THE PUBLIC
    Consultation between the tourism industry and local communities, organisations and institutions is essential if they are to work alongside each other and resolve potential conflicts of interest.

8. TRAINING STAFF
    Staff training which integrates sustainable tourism into work practices, along with recruitment of local personnel at all levels, improves the quality of the tourism product.

9. MARKETING TOURISM RESPONSIBLY
    Marketing that provides tourists with full and responsible information increases respect for the natural, social and cultural environments of destination areas and enhances customer satisfaction.

10. UNDERTAKING RESEARCH
    On-going research and monitoring by the industry using effective data collection and analysis is essential to help solve problems and to bring benefits to destinations, the industry and consumers.

Source: Beyond the Green Horizon, 1992, editor Shirley Eber, published by WWF, UK.

In particular, there is increasing concern for the growing popularity of ecotourism at destinations, for example in Latin America, where the biodiversity of the Amazon, Belize, Costa Rica or the Galapagos is threatened by encroachment, or Antartica where even minute changes in the environment are long lasting:

> A footprint in the Antartic moss could last for decades, a plastic pen dropped on to an isolated beach could remain there for centuries and even a minor oil spill could upset an ecosystem and kill off rare species of plant or animal. The more ecotourists there are, the more likely it is that the environment being visited will be damaged.

> *(Masson, 1990: 56)*

The arguments are presented with conviction and are decidedly thought provoking, yet there is barely a mention of marketing in the literature. Such mentions that do exist are often limited; for example, Hunter and Green (1995: 93) comment:

> Many of the objectives behind the promotion of tourism developments will, potentially, conflict with environmental sustainability goals, as countries, regions, groups and individuals develop tourist activity with particular interests in mind.

19.3 MARKETING AND SUSTAINABILITY

Marketers have a responsibility to the environment and therefore have a contribution to make in terms of tourism development and management of the core resources in any given environment. This goes way beyond branding opportunities that green consumerism has offered. It requires a reconfiguration of the rapid growth model which often underpins conventional marketing practices, to a model which embraces other long term goals, for both companies and local communities.

There is also a need to reappraise the relationship between partners in tourism development, such as the tour operator and the destination, described by Pearce (1989: 10–11) as the 'agents of development'. One of the most useful contributions to the debate has been made by McKercher (1993: 6–16) in his discussion of what he describes as the fundamental truths about tourism (Table 19.3).

McKercher's first truth points to three related facets of tourism: it consumes

Table 19.3 Some fundamental truths about tourism

1. As an industrial activity, tourism consumes resources, creates waste and has specific infrastructure needs.
2. As a consumer of resources, it has the ability to over consume resources.
3. Tourism, as a resource dependent industry, must compete for scarce resources to ensure its survival.
4. Tourism is a private sector dominated industry, with investment decisions being based predominantly on profit maximization.
5. Tourism is a multifaceted industry and, as such, it is almost impossible to control.
6. Tourists are consumers, not anthropologists.
7. Tourism is entertainment.
8. Unlike other industrial activities, tourism generates income by importing clients rather than exporting its product.

Source: McKercher (1993).

resources, creates waste as a bi-product and requires specific infrastructure in order to take off. He suggests that rather than being an 'industry without smokestacks' there are strong similarities between heavy capitalized industries and industrialized mass tourism. They both require a high fixed cost infrastructure in order to develop. For example, airports and highways are required before hotels decide to invest. The management approaches are similar. Tourism, like other sectors, attempts to pursue economies of scale (the experience curve), reduction of costs in the value chain and technological gain. Furthermore, McKercher argues that profit maximization in a competitive market can only be realized through the reduction of costs. Therefore, it is misleading to suggest that tourism is any more benign than other forms of development. The processes are similar and the consequences can be as beneficial or as devastating depending on the degree of planning and management.

Whilst these management techniques are appropriate to companies, they are not necessarily acceptable to host communities or to the environment. As governments increasingly seek to regulate the environmental impact of heavy industries, so the marketer will have to accept that regulation of tourism sector businesses is likely and, most probably, desirable. There has been some progress in stimulating local policy makers to rethink tourism development. For example, at an international forum 'Parliaments and Local Authorities: Tourism Policy Makers' in Bali in 1996, the government of Indonesia launched the Bali Declaration on Tourism, which establishes four main guiding principles for tourism development:

1. Tourism development should be aimed at the well-being of local communities.
2. Tourism development should maintain a balance between the interests of local communities and those of tourists, based on the principle of equality.
3. Tourism development should be carried out on the basis of careful planning with the broad involvement of local communities, including women, young people and the private sector.
4. Tourism development should be implemented in a way that not only increases revenues at the state and local levels, but also improves the quality of life at the community level.

(World Tourism Organization, 1996: 2)

McKercher's fourth truth is also worthy of consideration. He considers that private sector tourism is driven primarily by profits, hence affording lower priority to environmental protection. He cites evidence from the Caribbean, Mediterranean and the Asia-Pacific region to illustrate how badly self-regulation (as suggested by the World Travel and Tourism Council) works, citing the work of Jeffreys (1988). Furthermore, he considers that evasion of environmental responsibility will be prevalent among many smaller companies who simply lack resources to invest.

Despite these reservations, there is now incremental evidence to suggest that business sectors are taking environmental issues more seriously within their strategic planning. The Tourism Industry Associations of Canada have established a code of ethics for tourists and tourism businesses. This was developed by consensus techniques in the early 1990s by a wide range of organizations (D'Amore, 1992). Another example is the development of the Green Globe, established in 1994 by the World Travel and Tourism Council as a worldwide environmental management and public awareness programme.

Critics, however, point to the continued exploitation of destinations and communities, and to the increased use of resources in the development of tourism. They argue that the projected changes in business practice are happening at a very slow pace, or are superficial (Tourism Concern and WWF, 1992). This therefore begs the question as to how useful codes of ethics and self-regulation are in addressing some of the major development problems facing the world.

Experience elsewhere indicates that governments and destinations are in the best position to regulate an industry and that many companies also consider that regulation is best in the hands of destinations and governments.

With regard to the fifth truth, the multifaceted nature of tourism, this is where political will is required: 'Controlling tourism is the most difficult challenge facing industry and government agencies. The development of strategic plans and control mechanisms are only as effective as the will to implement them' (McKercher, 1993: 11).

This might prove increasingly difficult, given that a tide of privatization is sweeping the world (Jenkins, 1994: 3–9). Jenkins concludes:

> There is no doubt that the role of government in tourism in developing countries is changing. Government is seen as being a control agent and as guiding development through selective interventions. More pressure is being exerted on governments, particularly by international agencies, to ensure that the private sector has a greater involvement in the development process, not just through the provision of services but also in contributing to the strategic development of the industry.

McKercher illustrates the point by referring to the use of resources. In this context it is difficult to agree with his statement that 'tourism represents an insidious form of consumptive activity', in that most commentators point to it being a conspicuous rather than insidious activity. It is, however, recognized that tourism relies on the consumption of 'public goods', such as the use of open spaces and local community facilities, as well as the more obvious pattern of shopping and sightseeing. What is perhaps less than acceptable is the parallel systems of consumption which have emerged in many developing countries. Local people, either through the lack of spending power or through cultural attrition, are not able to frequent the haunts of the visitor. The integrated resort complex, found increasingly in Latin America, has to be a prime example (Jesitus, 1993). In certain economies, such as Cuba, a parallel system of currency means that only those with US dollars (rather than the Cuban peso), can enter certain bars or shops in their own capital city.

McKercher also refers to waste created by tourism, such as sewage and car emissions. There is a case, as with other business sectors, that this cost has to be allocated accordingly, rather than remaining a hidden cost absorbed by a community. The environmental audit principle of making the polluter pay needs to be rigorously applied across the tourism field. This will have considerable implications for the pricing of tourism. The argument would be that the more energy consuming and waste producing a holiday is, the more the customer should pay for it. This partly addresses the point that McKercher makes about over consumption (Truth 2), and shared use of resources (Truth 3), which gives rise to traffic congestion, rising land prices and tensions between hosts and tourists.

Whilst pricing is in many respects a crude mechanism, coupled with other measures it can be effective in the maintenance of public goods, such as historic corners of towns, wildlife sanctuaries and even recreational spaces. There is a need to research ways of fine tuning pricing structures, or taxation of visitors, to secure the future of such facilities for both resident and visitor.

McKercher's other truths relate mainly to the mass tourism visitor, a person that to date has expressed little concern about impacts on the host community or on the environment. His or her primary concern is to seek escapism through a high level of entertainment and culture, however contrived. Marketers will obviously accept that one of the many prime motivational factors for many customers is to seek contrasts to everyday life, although in reality it might be the case that the visitor escapes a home based routine to adopt a leisure based one (Craik, 1991: 24). Either way, the entertainment level of a holiday is integral and renders the concept of responsible tourism somewhat misleading.

19.3.1 Consumer education

Nevertheless, there are examples of marketers attempting to inculcate in the pre-consumption stages a degree of education about host communities and how to respect them. For example, San Antoni in the Ballearics issues a leaflet to young people, advocating a preferred code of behaviour, and in a light hearted way. Furthermore if, as some authors assert, consumers are becoming more sophisticated, then promotional techniques will need to advance from the selective or impressionist format to a more informational (telling it how it is) approach. Perhaps there is also a case for supplier education.

19.4 REAPPRAISAL OF MARKETING

The authors mentioned above have established a useful framework for discussion. It is now for tourism marketers to explore ways in which their strategies and tactical plans can be adapted to meet the objectives of sustainability.

Classical theory suggests that the customer is the cornerstone of marketing and that the entire process is about satisfying customer wants. In reality, marketing is also about suppliers educating customers, thus it is a two way exchange process in every sense. Therefore, marketers should seek to determine how best to stimulate interest in the responsible as well as hedonistic aspects of holidaymaking. In this respect there is every reason why marketers should continue to embrace the concepts of sustainability, interweaving them into the mainstream of marketing activity; the principles are not mutually exclusive.

It would be inappropriate to suggest that the marketer can, in any significant way, alter the market. The customer is the ultimate judge of the tourism offering. Evidence suggests, however, that the seeds of change are beginning to grow (Poon, 1993). The agenda exists, it is simply a question of reordering priorities. There will be a balancing point where new tourism offerings are acceptable to consumer, supplier and community without being irreversibly detrimental to the environment in the long term.

This amounts to a tall order for the marketer, and most probably will require a rethinking of current core concepts. Surely this is the very essence of good marketing. A strategic reappraisal might lead to tourism offerings which will stand the test of time.

19.5 SUMMARY The principles of sustainability are well established in the literature. Furthermore, there are now an increasing number of studies which not only diagnose the impacts of tourism, but offer suggestions as to how the principles can be translated into actionable plans. The major stumbling block is implementation. There appears to be a major gap between academics and practitioners. However, the gap is narrowing and the consumer will be the final arbiter. Of course, the marketer that is closer the cutting edge will gain the advantage.

Haywood (1990) sets down a number of guidelines in his discussion of the marketing concept as applied to tourism. It is worth re-iterating his final remarks:

> In revising the marketing concept as a guiding philosophy, fundamental changes will have to be made in how we think and act about tourism. Laying down prescriptions for change is the cosy part. The challenge of achieving a more balanced community and customer orientation is more daunting – it requires a management revolution. If tourism is to become a truly successful community industry and be received enthusiastically by tourists and the citizenry, a revised marketing concept needs to be implemented now.

REFERENCES

d'Arcy, S. (1996) Australia's blighted beaches. *The Sunday Times, Travel,* 22 December.

Barke, M. and Newton, M. (1995) Promoting Tourism in an Urban Context: Recent Developments in Malaga City, Andalusia. *Journal of Sustainable Tourism*, **3**(3), 115–34.

Beaumont, J., Pederson, L. and Whitaker, B. (1993) *Managing the Environment,* Butterworth-Heinemann, Oxford.

Brady, Shipman, Martin (1993) *Urban Environment: The Problems of Tourism.* Final report to the European Union, Directorate General for Environment, DGXI, January.

Cater, E. (1993) Ecotourism in the Third World: problems for sustainable tourism development. *Tourism Management*, April, 85–90.

Cooper, C. (1995) Strategic Planning for Sustainable Tourism: The Case of the Offshore Islands of the UK. *Journal of Sustainable Tourism*, **3**(4), 191–209.

Craik, J. (1991) *Resorting to Tourism,* Allen and Unwin, North Sydney.

D'Amore, L.J. (1992) Promoting sustainable tourism – the Canadian approach. *Tourism Management,* September, 258–62.

European Union (1994) *European Sustainable Cities*, X1/822/94EN, October.

Godfrey, K. (1995) Tourism and Sustainable Development: Monitoring, Planning, Managing. *Annals of Tourism Research*, **22**(1), 235.

Gunn, C. (1994) *Tourism Planning,* 3rd edition, Taylor and Francis, London.

Hall, C.M. and Butler, R.W. (1995) Discussion: In Search of Common Ground: Reflections on Sustainability, Complexity and Process in the Tourism System. *Journal of Sustainable Tourism,* **3**(2), 99–105.

Hall, P. (1994) Can Cities Be Sustainable? In *The Human Face of the Urban Environment, Proceedings of the Second Annual World Bank Conference on Environmentally Sustainable Development* (eds I. Serageldin, M. Cohen and K.C. Sivaramakrishnan), World Bank, Washington, September.

Harris, R. and Leiper, N. (1995) *Sustainable Tourism, An Australian Perspective,* Butterworth-Heinemann, Chatswood.

Harrison, D. (1992) *Tourism and the Less Developed Countries,* Wiley, Chichester.

Haywood, K.M. (1990) Revising and Implementing the Marketing Concept as it Applies to Tourism. *Tourism Management,* September.

Hunter, C. and Green, H. (1995) *Tourism and the Environment: A Sustainable Relationship*, Routledge, London.

Inskeep, E. (1994) *National and Regional Tourism Planning, Methodologies and Case Studies*, Routledge, London.

Jeffreys, A. (1988) The environmental impact of tourism. In *Frontiers of Australian Tourism: The Search for New Perspectives in Policy Development and Research* (eds W. Faulkner and M. Fagence), Bureau of Tourism Research, Canberra.

Jenkins, C.L. (1994) Tourism in Developing Countries: The Privatisation Issue. In *Tourism, the State of the Art* (eds A.V. Seaton *et al.*), Wiley, Chichester.

Jesitus, J. (1993) Mega resort expected to boost Mexico's tourism. *Hotel and Motel Management*, 208 (2).

Krippendorf, J. (1987) *The Holidaymakers,* Heinemann, London.

Liu, Z.H. (1994) Tourism Development – A Systems Approach. In *Tourism, the State of the Art* (eds A.V. Seaton *et al.*), Wiley, Chichester.

Lumsdon, L.M. and Swift, J.S. (1993) The Development of Tourism in Latin American Gateway Cities. A paper presented to the VII General Conference of EADI, Berlin, 15–18 September.

Masson, D. (1990) Holidays to help the planet. *The Australian Magazine,* 3–4 March, p. 56.

McKercher, B. (1993) Some Fundamental Truths About Tourism: Understanding Tourism's Social and Environmental Impacts. *Journal of Sustainable Tourism,* 1(1), pp. 6–16.

Moore, S. and Carter, B. (1993) Ecotourism in the 21st century. *Tourism Management*, April, 123–30.

Muller, H.R. (1990) The Case for Developing Tourism in Harmony with Man and Nature. A paper presented to the Shades of Green Conference, April, York.

Murphy, P. (1985) *Tourism: A Community Approach*, Routledge, London.

Ortiz, M.F. (1990) A Global Perspective and Case Studies of Sustainable Development in Latin America. *RSA Journal,* Vol. CXXXXVIII, No 5405.

Pearce, D. (1989) *Tourism Development*, Longman.

Poon, A. (1993) *Tourism, Technology and Competitive Strategies*, CAB International, Wallingford.

Rodenberg, E.E. (1989) The effects of scale in economic development: Tourism in Bali. In *Towards Appropriate Tourism: The Case of Developing Countries* (eds T.V. Singh, H.L. Theuns and F.M. Go), Peter Lang, Frankfurt.

Smith, R.A. (1992) Beach Resort Evolution. *Annals of Tourism Research,* **19**, 304–22.

Tourism Concern and World Wide Fund for Nature (1992) *Beyond The Green Horizon: A Discussion Paper on Principles for Sustainable Tourism*, Tourism Concern and WWF, London.

Turner, L. and Ash, J. (1975) *The Golden Hordes: International Tourism and the Pleasure Periphery,* Constable, London.

Valentine, P.S. (1993) Ecotourism and nature conservation. *Tourism Management*, April, 107–15.

Wheeller, B. (1991) Tourism's troubled times. *Tourism Management,* 91–95, June.

Woodcock, K. and France, L. (1994) Development Theory Applied to Tourism in Jamaica. In *Tourism, the State of the Art* (eds A.V. Seaton *et al.*), John Wiley & Sons Ltd., Chichester.

World Commission on Environment and Development (1987) *Our Common Future,* Oxford University Press, Oxford (also known as the Brundtland Report).

World Tourism Organization (1991) The Manila Declaration, WTO, Madrid.

World Tourism Organization (1996) *World News,*No. 4 p. 2, WTO, Madrid.

The challenges of the twenty-first century

20

OBJECTIVES

This chapter explains:

- transformation in the marketplace;
- the challenges facing the tourism marketer.

20.1 INTRODUCTION

The cutting edge of tourism marketing is always exciting for it is where theories and forecasts are challenged and tested. The ground upon which you stand is not entirely certain but from analysis and discussion emerges a framework for development of new ideas and prospects for tourism.

This chapter is unlike the others in that it presents a summary of a number of the key issues documented by writers on tourism in the 1990s with regard to the question: 'Where is the tourism sector heading in the twenty-first century?' They could be noted as the challenges for the marketer.

20.2 A NEW AGE OF TOURISM?

Poon (1993: 9–24) in a stimulating discussion about tourism in transition argues that there is in emergence a new age of tourism. She chronicles the growth of mass tourism from the 1950s to the late 1970s then points to a change in the marketplace, not an abrupt change, but one which is gaining in significance. The life cycle of tourism is illustrated in Figure 20.1.

She also describes the differences between the old, which writers have traditionally referred to as mass tourism, and the new in terms of characteristics of consumers and their patterns of behaviour. The new tourist is, for example, interested in experiencing something different, understanding more about the history and culture of destinations and is more conscious of the impacts of his or her actions on the locality and in sensitive environments.

It is worth considering four key forces which are considered to be heralding this change:

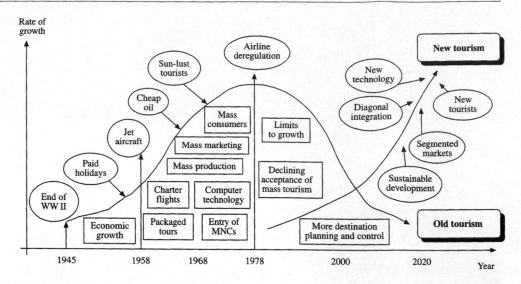

Figure 20.1 The tourism life cycle. *Source*: Poon (1993).

- **New consumers.** Poon argues that new consumers are more sophisticated, environmentally conscious, seeking experiences and quality of life rather than a break in the sun. In short, the market is far more fragmented than twenty years ago and therefore presents a dilemma to marketing strategists seeking standardization.
- **New technologies.** Several commentators have highlighted the advance of technology as applied to tourism. It has been rapid, perhaps moving faster than the change in the consumer market. This means that consumers can be segmented more accurately. The customer can choose destinations and services easily without the assistance of the tour operator and for little cost or risk. Furthermore, the technologies mean that suppliers can coordinate tourism offerings at a much reduced cost so that there is still a differential advantage gained without resorting to the traditional managerial response to economies of scale.
- **Limits to growth.** The third major force is the increasing number of constraints being placed on all business sectors regarding the environment. It has now been recognized that the provision of tourism services, which involve high energy use and heavy impact on the environment, is no longer acceptable. Increasingly, global organizations, governments and multinationals are having to come to terms with the negative effects of development and growth as envisaged by the strategists of previous decades.
- **New global practice.** Poon refers to a new paradigm where economies of scale and the experience curve will no longer apply to all aspects of tourism. She argues that the new order means flexibility in provision where there is variety and specialization, pliable systems, empowerment and training of staff at a local level and innovation. This type of schema fits the market which Fayos-Sola (1996: 406) describes aptly: 'The New Age of Tourism is characterized primarily by the super-segmentation of demand, the need for flexibility of supply and distribution, and achieving profitability through diagonal integration and subsequent system economies and integrated values instead of economies of scale.'

Cooper *et al.* (1993: 265–76), Middleton (1994: 359–75) and Seaton and Bennett (1996: 206–33) raise a number of other points which are salient to the discussion:

- limits to growth as markets mature;
- quality, refurbishment of destinations and differentiation;
- responsible or societal marketing;
- changing political structures;
- the changing distribution of tourism (a move in emphasis from North to South).

20.3 A NEW AGE OF TOURISM MARKETING?

The changing structure of the tourism market is not happening with the rapidity that some authors would suggest. Technological advances are important but is there sufficient evidence to suggest that market wants have altered significantly. The answer at this stage is that there are signals which point to changing patterns of demand in mature markets but these are not necessarily reflected in emergent markets.

The world of mass tourism will still dominate at the turn of the century and globalization will continue to stimulate organizations to seek standardization and economies of scale even though small scale tour operators and niche markets will flourish.

Consider, however, the indicators which might offer clues to a changing pattern of development in the twenty-first century. There are signs of a major structural shift in the marketplace evidenced by patterns of demand in the maturing markets of northern Europe and North America. The marketing environment is characterized by:

Market changes
- fragmentation of the market
- increasingly discerning visitors
- dissatisfaction with despoiled destinations
- more short break taking, which in the USA is occurring closer to home
- travel for pleasure becoming an integral part of life
- travel for business becoming a less attractive option than new technological access (such as video conferencing)
- rapidly emerging pocket markets in lesser developed countries.

Supply
- increased competition
- growth of new destinations
- rejuvenation of old destinations
- sharpening focus on quality and environment
- winners and losers in use of distribution systems.

Government
- developing a role as enabler in the face of continued privatization
- increasing regulation to meet the demands of local communities and pressure groups in favour of conservation
- renewed interest in regional agreements on tourism development and promotion to fit new trading alliances (such as Asean in Asia, Mercosur in Latin America).

20.4 THE CHALLENGES FOR THE MARKETER

The tourism marketer is therefore faced with a set of new challenges which need to be addressed in the short term rather than later. There is no particular order of presentation or priority, only to say that these challenges need to be placed within a strategic framework, for planning ahead is a prime assumption even in markets which are transforming, albeit in an incremental fashion.

The challenges are not meant to be universally applicable to the tourism sector. Some of them will be more important to the hotel marketer, others to the tourism officer at a destination. Many of the issues are not entirely new; in many respects it amounts to a refocusing of effort and techniques rather than a fundamental shift of emphasis. The overarching guiding principles of marketing remain. Tourism marketers should continue to work within a framework which accepts societal and sustainable values as well as meeting the needs of the customer.

The challenges are summarized as follows:

- **Better understanding of customer segments.** The marketer will need to segment markets more accurately than hitherto, especially in terms of benefit segmentation so that tourism offerings can be positioned with precision.
- **Accessibility to the market.** Technology allows one to one marketing without major cost penalties. Those who fail to make effective use of the new technologies will fall by the wayside. Destinations, in particular, will need to update and improve distribution systems as they lag behind other sectors.
- **Core offering.** Emphasis will increasingly be placed on the human resource element of tourism at the core offering, or the moments of service encounter. Staff will increasingly be recognized as ambassadors of the marketing effort and should be rewarded accordingly.
- **Competitive intensity.** Fayos-Sola draws attention to the increasing level of competitor intensity, represented in Figure 20.2. The degree of competitor activity will become far greater in all mature markets and strategy will be dominated by this factor.
- **Tourism development.** The scramble to develop resorts in unspoilt areas will be subject to critical appraisal by consumers and suppliers. A new pattern of tourism development based on long term sustainability will emerge but not in the short term and not before new sustainable policy frameworks are translated into practical actions by governments and tourism authorities. In this respect, monitoring will become a far more important aspect.
- **Destination marketing.** Mature destinations will seek to reshape their marketing strategies so that a succession of new tourism offerings are rolled out in a planned way rather than as a reaction to the market. The issue of visitor retention will become critical and the hitherto largely ignored local market will be nurtured. Many previously popular places, especially in northern Europe, will cascade from being holiday and short break destinations to locations which appeal to day visitors only.
- **Reformulated marketing mix.** Adherence to the framework of the traditional marketing mix will probably not suffice. Tourism marketers could well enhance the role of market planning, not only in terms of tourism development but also in the way in which tactical plans are structured. The emphasis will shift towards an interdisciplinary approach to staff recruitment, training and internal marketing.

There will also be a focus on tracking and retention of customers. Monitoring and control will become an essential ingredient at the heart of the process as fine tuning will become the essence of marketing to a segmented market.

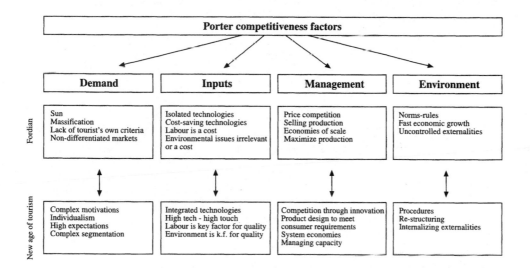

Figure 20.2 Porter's competitiveness factors applied to tourism. *Source*: Fayos-Sola (1994).

20.5 SUMMARY   Some companies and tourism organizations have already adopted a new marketing orientation, others still follow a pattern of internally driven values. The final challenge is for the tourism marketer to bring new ideas and techniques together to form the bedrock of strategy which exudes marketing orientation. Table 20.1 outlines the nature of the marketing orientation which is appropriate in a tourism organization which seeks to progress in the twenty-first century.

Table 20.1 Marketing orientation in tourism organizations

Market driven businesses	*Internally orientated businesses*
● Customer attraction and retention major concern	● Concern with internal processes, politics and power
● Segmentation by benefits	● Segment by product
● Precise understanding of consumer values and choice – marketing effort geared accordingly	● Assumed knowledge – traditional marketing mix
● Investment in customer information and tracking and environmental scanning	● Informal and imprecise systems from past
● Flexibility and innovation are hallmarks	● Status quo is fine
● Speedy reactions and proactive	● Rubbish competitor activity or follow the leader
● Understand and outflank competitors when appropriate	● Environmental scanning not important, societal values too vague
● Conversant with societal and sustainable principles and implement them	

The challenges facing the tourism marketer are fundamental. There are interesting times ahead for those who seek to address them.

REFERENCES

Cooper, C., Fletcher, J., Gilbert, D. and Wanhill, S. (1993) *Tourism Principles and Practice,* Pitman, London.

Fayos-Sola, E. (1996) Tourism Policy: a midsummer night's dream? *Tourism Management*, Elsevier Science, **17**(6), 405–12.

Middleton, V.T.C. (1994) *Marketing in Travel and Tourism,* Butterworth-Heinemann, Oxford.

Poon, A. (1993) *Tourism, Technology and Competitive Strategies,* CAB International, Oxford.

Seaton, A.V. and Bennett, M.M. (1996) *Marketing Tourism Products,* Thomson International Press, London.

Tourism: a select bibliography

General texts

Brent-Ritchie, J.R. and Goeldner, C.R. (1994) *Travel, Tourism, and Hospitality Research: A Handbook for Managers and Researchers,* John Wiley & Sons, New York.
Burns, P.M. and Holden, A. (1995) *Tourism: A New Perspective,* Prentice Hall, Hemel Hempstead.
Cooper, C., Fletcher, J., Gilbert, D. and Wanhill, S. (1993) *Tourism: Principles and Practice,* Pitman, London.
Mill, R.C. and Morrison, A.M. (1992) *The Tourism System – An Introductory Text,* 2nd edition, Prentice Hall International, London.
Pearce, D. (1995) *Tourism Today: A Geographical Analysis,* 2nd edition, Longman, Harlow.
Plog, S. (1991) *Leisure Travel: Making it a Growth Market Again,* John Wiley & Sons, New York.
Ryan, C. (1991) *Recreational Tourism: A Social Science Perspective,* Routledge, London.
Seaton, A.V. (ed.) (1994) *Tourism: The State of the Art,* John Wiley & Sons, Chichester.
Sinclair, M.T. and Stabler, M.J. (eds) (1991) *The Tourism Industry – An International Analysis,* CAB International, Wallingford.
Theobold, W. (ed.) (1994) *Global Tourism: The Next Decade,* Butterworth-Heinemann, Oxford.
Torkildsen, G. (1993) *Torkildsen's Guide to Leisure Management,* Longman, Harlow.
Urry, J. (1990) *The Tourist Gaze: Leisure and Travel in Contemporary Societies,* Sage, London.
Urry, J. (1995) *Consuming Places,* Routledge, London.
Witt, S.F. and Moutinho, L. (1995) *Tourism Marketing and Management Handbook,* Student Edition, Prentice-Hall, London.

Demand forecasting

Witt, S.F. and Witt, C. (1991) *Marketing and Forecasting Demand in Tourism,* Academic Press, London.

Destinations

Ashworth, G.J. and Goodall, B. (1990) *Marketing Tourism Places,* Routledge, London.
Ashworth, G.J. and Voogd, H. (1990) *Selling the City: Marketing Approaches in Public Sector Urban Planning,* Belhaven Press, London.
Gold, J.R. and Ward, S.V. (eds) (1994) *Place Promotion: The Use of Publicity and Marketing to Sell Towns and Regions,* John Wiley & Sons, Chichester.
Goodall, B. and Ashworth, G. (1988) *Marketing Tourism Places – The Promotion of Destination Regions,* Croom-Helm, London.
Law, C. (1993) *Urban Tourism: Attracting Visitors to Large Cities,* Mansell, London.
Laws, E.C. (1995) *Tourist Destination Management – Issues, Analysis and Policies,* Routledge, London.
Page, S. (1995) *Urban Tourism,* Routledge, London.

Events

Getz, D. (1991) *Festivals, Special Events, and Tourism,* Van Nostrand Reinhold, New York.
Hall, C.M. (1992) *Hallmark Tourist Events: Impacts, Management, and Planning,* Belhaven Press, London.

Hospitality

Buttle, F. (1994) *Hotel and Food Service Marketing: A Managerial Approach,* Cassell, London.
Olsen, M.D., Teare, R. and Gunnerson, E. (1995) *Service Quality in Hospitality Organisations,* Cassell, London.

Teare, R. and Olsen, M.D. (eds) (1995) *International Hospitality Management*, Pitman, London.
Wearne, N. and Morrison, A. (1996) *Hospitality Marketing*, Butterworth-Heinemann, Oxford.

Marketing

Dibb, S., Simkin, L., Pride, W.M. and Ferrell, O.C. (1994) *Marketing: Concepts and Strategies*, 2nd European edition, Houghton-Mifflin, London.
Holloway, J.C. and Robinson, C. (1995) *Marketing for Tourism*, 3rd edition, Longman, Harlow.
Horner, S. and Swarbrooke, J. (1996) *Marketing Tourism, Hospitality and Leisure in Europe*, Thomson, London.
Jefferson, A. and Lickorish, L. (1988) *Marketing Tourism*, Longman, Harlow.
Kotler, P. (1994) *Marketing Management: Analysis, Planning, Implementation, and Control*, 8th edition, Prentice-Hall, Englewood Cliffs, New Jersey.
Kotler, P., Bowen, J. and Makens, J. (1996) *Marketing for Hospitality and Tourism*, Prentice Hall, Upper Saddle River, New Jersey.
Middleton, V.T.C. (1994) *Marketing in Travel and Tourism*, 2nd edition, Butterworth-Heinemann, Oxford.
Morgan, M. (1996) *Marketing for Leisure and Tourism*, Prentice Hall, Hemel Hempstead.
Seaton A.V. and Bennett, M.M. (1996) *Marketing Tourism Products*, ITP, London.
Shaw, S. (1990) *Airline Marketing and Management*, 3rd edition, Pitman, London.

Quality and service

Boniface, P. (1995) *Managing Quality in Cultural Tourism*, Routledge, London.
Department of National Heritage (1996) *Tourism: Competing with the Best. Number 2: Benchmarking for Smaller Hotels.* Department of National Heritage, London.
Laws, E. (1991) *Tourism Marketing: Service and Quality Management Perspectives*, Stanley Thornes, Cheltenham.

Research issues/methodology

Pearce, W. and Butler, R.G. (1993) *Tourism Research – Critiques and Challenges*, Routledge, London.
Smith, S.J. (1995) *Tourism Analysis*, 2nd edition, Longman, Harlow.
Veal, A.J. (1992) *Research Methods for Leisure and Tourism: A Practical Guide*, Longman, Harlow.

Strategy

Hodgson, A. (ed.) (1987) *The Travel and Tourism Industry – Strategies for the Future*, Pergamon, Oxford.
Johnson, G. and Scholes, K. (1993) *Exploring Corporate Strategy*, 3rd edition, Prentice Hall, Hemel Hempstead.
McDonald, M.H.B. (1989) *Marketing Plans – How to Prepare Them: How to Use Them*, Heinemann, London.
Piercy, N. (1992) *Market-led Strategic Change*, Butterworth-Heinemann, Oxford.
Poon, A. (1993) *Tourism, Technology and Competitive Strategies*, CAB International, Wallingford.
Porter, M.E. (1986) *Competition in Global Industries*, Harvard Business Press, Boston, Massachusetts.
World Tourism Organization (1994) *National and Regional Tourism Planning – Methodologies and Case Studies*, Routledge, London.

Sustainable tourism

Hausler, N., Kamp, C., Muller-Rockstroh, P., Scholz, W. and Schulz, B.E. (eds) (1995) *Retracing the Track of Tourism – Studies on Travels, Tourists and Development*, ASA, Berlin.
Krippendorf, J. (1987) *The Holiday Makers: Understanding the Impact of Leisure and Travel*, Butterworth-Heinemann, Oxford.

Tourism development

Harrison, D. (ed.) (1995) *Tourism and the Less Developed Countries*, John Wiley & Sons, Chichester.
Pearce, D. (1989) *Tourist Development*, 2nd edition, Longman, Harlow.

Tourism economics

Bull, A. (1991) *The Economics of Travel and Tourism*, Longman, Melbourne.
Johnson, P. and Thomas, B. (eds) (1993) *Choice and Demand in Tourism*, Mansell, London.
Johnson, P. and Thomas, B. (eds) (1992) *Perspectives on Tourism Policy*, Mansell, London.
Lundberg, D.E., Krishnamoorthy, M. and Stavenga, M.H. (1995) *Tourism Economics*, John Wiley & Sons, Chichester.

REPORTS/INTELLIGENCE

Reports: examples

Economist Intelligence Unit (1995) EIU International Tourism Reports Nos 1, 2 and 3.
Euromonitor (annual) *European Travel and Tourism Marketing Directory*, Euromonitor, London.
Euromonitor (1994) *European Domestic Tourism and Leisure Trends*, Euromonitor, London.
European Marketing Pocket Book (1995, 1996) NTC Publications, Henley-on-Thames.
Key Note Report (1994) *A Market Sector Overview – Tourist Attractions*, Key Note Report, Key Note Ltd, London.
Mintel (1995) *Product Inclusive Tours*, London.
Organization for Economic Co-operation and Development (1995) *Tourism Policy and International Tourism in OECD Countries 1992–1993, Special Feature 'Tourism and Employment'*, Organization for Economic Co-operation and Development, France.

Tourist statistics

United Kingdom

The various Tourist Boards prepare reports such as:

British Tourist Authority (1995) *Visits to Tourist Attractions*, BTA, London.

Of particular use is *Insights*, the ETB Tourism Marketing Intelligence Service. It provides current data, comments and analysis.

The world

The primary source of data is from the World Tourism Organization, Madrid.

Index